PROFESSIONAL
IPHONE® AND IPAD™ DATABASE
APPLICATION PROGRAMMING

PROFESSIONAL

iPhone® and iPad™ Database Application Programming

PROFESSIONAL

iPhone® and iPad™ Database Application Programming

Patrick Alessi

Wiley Publishing, Inc.

Professional iPhone® and iPad™ Database Application Programming

Published by
Wiley Publishing, Inc.
10475 Crosspoint Boulevard
Indianapolis, IN 46256
www.wiley.com

Copyright © 2011 by Patrick Alessi

Published by Wiley Publishing, Inc., Indianapolis, Indiana

Published simultaneously in Canada

ISBN: 978-0-470-63617-6

ISBN: 978-1-118-00317-6 (ebk)

ISBN: 978-1-118-00299-5 (ebk)

ISBN: 978-1-118-00387-9 (ebk)

Manufactured in the United States of America

10 9 8 7 6 5 4 3 2 1

For general information on our other products and services please contact our Customer Care Department within the United States at (877) 762-2974, outside the United States at (317) 572-3993 or fax (317) 572-4002.

Wiley also publishes its books in a variety of electronic formats. Some content that appears in print may not be available in electronic books.

Library of Congress Control Number: 2010935566

For Cheryl—Without you, this would have never been possible.

CREDITS

ABOUT THE AUTHOR

PATRICK ALESSI has been fascinated with writing computer programs since he first saw his name flash across a terminal in 1980. Since then, he has written software using every language and hardware platform that he could get his hands on, including a brief and painful foray into Fortran on a VAX system during his engineering education. Patrick holds a B.S. degree in Civil Engineering from Rutgers University and an M.S. in Computer Science from Stevens Institute of Technology.

Professionally, Patrick has focused on data-centric applications for clients ranging from small business databases to large-scale systems for the United States Air Force. Currently, he is focused on the promise of mobility and developing connected applications for mobile devices such as the iPhone and iPad.

When he can back away from the computer, Patrick enjoys photography, traveling, and doing just about anything with his family. You can follow him on Twitter at pwalessi and read his blog at iphonedevsphere.blogspot.com.

ABOUT THE TECHNICAL EDITOR

MICHAEL GILBERT is a long-time systems programmer for various engineering firms. He got his start developing games for the Atari ST, and he was a frequent contributing editor for *STart* magazine. Over the years he has continued to develop gaming software on the PC and Mac for clients worldwide. He's also an expert Flash ActionScript programmer and has produced a popular Internet gaming environment called HigherGames. He now enjoys developing games for the iPhone and iPad, and currently has three games in the AppStore (Wordigo, Jumpin' Java, and Set Pro HD). In his spare time, he enjoys trying to defeat his wife Janeen in a friendly game of Scrabble.

ACKNOWLEDGMENTS

I WOULD LIKE TO TAKE THIS OPPORTUNITY to thank everyone who made this book possible. Carol Long, my executive editor, took a chance with a first-time author and shepherded my idea through the acquisitions process. My project editor, Brian MacDonald, was always there to answer every question that I had about writing and the publishing process. Mike Gilbert, my technical editor, gave up valuable app development time to review my work. I would also like to thank all of the other editorial and production staff that put many hours into this project to help get it to print. Finally, I would like to thank Jeff LaMarche for providing me with insight into writing a book from a software developer's perspective, which gave me the courage to move forward with the project.

I cannot thank my wife, Cheryl, and my stepdaughter, Morgan, enough for putting up with my fits, general crankiness, and lack of time for fun family activities as I worked my way through writing this book. Your patience with me is astounding. I want to thank my Mom for introducing me to computers at a very young age and teaching me the basics. And finally, I want to thank my Dad for pushing me to work hard and for showing me how to be a father.

CONTENTS

PART II: MANAGING YOUR DATA WITH CORE DATA

CHAPTER 5: INTRODUCING CORE DATA   123

CHAPTER 6: MODELING DATA IN XCODE   145

INTRODUCTION

WITH THE INTRODUCTION OF THE IPHONE, Apple revolutionized the mobile computing market. The iPhone transformed the mobile phone from a device that you could use to make calls, check e-mail, and look up movie times into a computer that could run almost any type of application that you can think of. Since the iPhone's release in 2007, developers have written over 200,000 applications for the device. These "apps" encompass many categories including games, utilities, social networking, reference, navigation, and business among many others.

The trend in the field of computing is moving toward mobility and mobile platforms like the iPhone and away from a desktop-based environment. Particularly in business and corporate environments, decision makers want convenient access to their data at all times. The iPhone is an ideal platform for mobile computing because of its small form factor and extensive set of libraries and APIs, and its general popularity as a mobile phone.

While there are many terrific books on iPhone software development on the market, I couldn't find one geared toward the enterprise developer that needs to mobilize corporate data or business applications. My original goal for this book was to present these developers with the information that they would need to be able to get enterprise data from a back office server, display and manipulate that data on a mobile device, and then get the appropriate information back into their corporate information system.

As I worked through writing the book, it became clear that the tools and techniques that I cover in the book are applicable to many classes of applications in addition to the business use case that I had in mind when I started. Developers of any type of application that needs to store data on the iPhone will certainly be interested in the extensive coverage of the Core Data API. Any developer attempting to send data to an external web service such as Facebook or Twitter can benefit from the section of the book dealing with XML and web services. Many applications need to display data using tables, which I also cover in detail. Even though my original goal was to write a book for enterprise developers, I believe that I have written one that is useful when developing applications of just about any type.

WHO THIS BOOK IS FOR

As I mentioned, I started out writing this book for enterprise developers tasked with mobilizing corporate data and producing applications that could present and manipulate this data on a mobile device. During the process of writing the book, I became convinced that the tools, APIs and development techniques that I was covering were valuable for many categories of application development outside of the business realm. Anyone writing an application that deals with data in just about any way should find this book useful.

This should not be your first book on iPhone application development. You will not find a "Hello World" iPhone application here. There are many very good books on learning to build basic iPhone applications. I have aimed this book at developers that already understand how to build an iPhone application and how to design and build a user interface using Interface Builder, and who have a firm foundation in Objective-C. That is not to say that beginners will find nothing of use here, only that I write from a position that the reader already understands the basic architecture of iPhone applications and knows his or her way around the Xcode tools.

WHAT THIS BOOK COVERS

This book covers the technologies that you will need to understand in order to build data-centric applications for the iPhone and iPad. You will find a chapter on SQLite, the database engine that is included on every iPhone and iPad. Here, you will learn how to import data into the database from different file formats and how to query that data on the device. I cover the UITableView control extensively, including different strategies for customizing the display of your data. You will also find extensive coverage of the Core Data API. You will find yourself using this terrific data persistence framework often, as you need to create and store data on the device. Finally, I cover handling and creating XML on the iPhone and integrating your applications with web services.

HOW THIS BOOK IS STRUCTURED

I've structured the book in three parts that loosely correspond to the flow of data in an enterprise application. The first part of the book covers getting data out of a large-scale database such as Oracle, MySQL, or SQLServer; getting it on the device; and displaying it. The second part of the book covers creating data on the device and the Core Data API. The final part covers getting data out of the device and communicating with web services. Although I have tried to present the material in a logical order from chapter to chapter, there is no need to read the book in order. If you are building a TableView-based application and need to know how to customize the look and feel of your table, jump right into Chapter 3. If you are building an app for the iPad, look at Chapter 4. If you need to implement Core Data, jump right into Part II. If you need to integrate with a web service, check out Chapters 10 and 11.

WHAT YOU NEED TO USE THIS BOOK

Because I geared this book toward intermediate to advanced iOS developers, you should already have all of the tools that you need to use this book. You will need an Apple computer with Mac OS X to build applications for iOS. Additionally, you need to install the Xcode development environment that Apple graciously includes free with every installation of Mac OS X. If you do not have Xcode installed, and do not have your installation disk, you can download the latest version of Xcode from Apple's developer web site at http://developer.apple.com.

The only other requirement is that if you intend to install your applications on a physical device, as opposed to simply running your code in the iPhone simulator, you will need to join the iOS developer program. At the time of this writing, joining the program costs $99 annually and entitles you to build and run programs on your device and to submit your finished applications to the Apple App Store for sale. If you are not currently part of the developer program, don't worry. There is very little in the book that requires you to run on an actual device. Nearly everything will work correctly in the simulator. Where there is a need to run on the device, I have noted that in the text.

CONVENTIONS

To help you get the most from the text and keep track of what's happening, I've used a number of conventions throughout the book.

Boxes with a warning icon like this one hold important, not-to-be forgotten information that is directly relevant to the surrounding text.

The pencil icon indicates notes, tips, hints, tricks, or asides to the current discussion.

As for styles in the text:

- ➤ We *highlight* new terms and important words when we introduce them.
- ➤ We show keyboard strokes like this: Ctrl+A.
- ➤ We show file names, URLs, and code within the text like so: `persistence.properties`.
- ➤ We present code in two different ways:

```
We use a monofont type with no highlighting for most code examples.
We use bold to emphasize code that's particularly important in the present
context.
```

SOURCE CODE

As you work through the examples in this book, you may choose either to type in all the code manually or to use the source code files that accompany the book. All of the source code used in this book is available for download at www.wrox.com. You will find the code snippets from the source code are accompanied by a download icon and note indicating the name of the program so you know it's available for download and you can easily locate it in the download file. Once at the site, simply locate the book's title (either by using the Search box or by using one of the title lists) and click the Download Code link on the book's detail page to obtain all the source code for the book.

Available for download on Wrox.com

Code snippets that are downloadable from wrox.com are easily identified with an icon; the file name of the code snippet follows in a code note that appears after the code, much like the one that follows this paragraph. If it is an entire code listing, the filename should appear in the listing title.

Code Filename

 Because many books have similar titles, you may find it easiest to search by ISBN; this book's ISBN is 978-0-470-63617-6.

Once you download the code, just decompress it with your favorite compression tool. Alternately, you can go to the main Wrox code download page at `www.wrox.com/dynamic/books/download.aspx` to see the code available for this book and all other Wrox books.

ERRATA

We make every effort to ensure that there are no errors in the text or in the code. However, no one is perfect, and mistakes do occur. If you find an error in one of our books, like a spelling mistake or faulty piece of code, we would be very grateful for your feedback. By sending in errata you may save another reader hours of frustration and at the same time you will be helping us provide even higher quality information.

To find the errata page for this book, go to `www.wrox.com` and locate the title using the Search box or one of the title lists. Then, on the book details page, click the Book Errata link. On this page, you can view all errata that has been submitted for this book and posted by Wrox editors. A complete book list including links to each book's errata is also available at `www.wrox.com/misc-pages/booklist.shtml`.

If you don't spot "your" error on the Book Errata page, go to `www.wrox.com/contact/techsupport.shtml` and complete the form there to send us the error you have found. We'll check the information and, if appropriate, post a message to the book's errata page and fix the problem in subsequent editions of the book.

P2P.WROX.COM

For author and peer discussion, join the P2P forums at p2p.wrox.com. The forums are a Web-based system for you to post messages relating to Wrox books and related technologies and interact with other readers and technology users. The forums offer a subscription feature to e-mail you topics of interest of your choosing when new posts are made to the forums. Wrox authors, editors, other industry experts, and your fellow readers are present on these forums.

At http://p2p.wrox.com you will find a number of different forums that will help you not only as you read this book, but also as you develop your own applications. To join the forums, just follow these steps:

1. Go to p2p.wrox.com and click the Register link.

2. Read the terms of use and click Agree.

3. Complete the required information to join as well as any optional information you wish to provide and click Submit.

4. You will receive an e-mail with information describing how to verify your account and complete the joining process.

 You can read messages in the forums without joining P2P, but in order to post your own messages, you must join.

Once you join, you can post new messages and respond to messages other users post. You can read messages at any time on the Web. If you would like to have new messages from a particular forum e-mailed to you, click the Subscribe to this Forum icon by the forum name in the forum listing.

For more information about how to use the Wrox P2P, be sure to read the P2P FAQs for answers to questions about how the forum software works as well as many common questions specific to P2P and Wrox books. To read the FAQs, click the FAQ link on any P2P page.

PROFESSIONAL

iPhone® and iPad™ Database Application Programming

PART I
Manipulating and Displaying Data on the iPhone and iPad

1

Introducing Data-Driven Applications

WHAT'S IN THIS CHAPTER?

➤ Creating a view-based application using Xcode

➤ Building a very simple data model

➤ Neatly displaying your data in a table using the UITableView control

Data is the backbone of most applications. This is not limited only to business applications. Games, graphics editors, and spreadsheets alike all use and manipulate data in one form or another. One of the most exciting things about the iPhone is that it enables you and your customers to take your data anywhere. The mobility of the device gives the developer an amazing platform for developing applications that work with that data. You can use the power of existing data to build applications that use that data in new ways. In this book, you will learn how to display data, create and manipulate data, and finally, to send data over the Internet.

In this chapter, you learn how to build a simple *data-driven* application. By the end of this chapter, you will be able to create a view-based application using Xcode that displays your data using the UITableView control. You will also gain an understanding of the Model-View-Controller architecture that underlies most iPhone applications.

BUILDING A SIMPLE DATA-DRIVEN APPLICATION

Many applications that you will build for the iPhone will need to handle data in one form or another. It is common to display this data in a table. In this section, you learn how to build an application that displays your data in a table in an iPhone application.

Creating the Project

In order to build applications for the iPhone, you need to use the Xcode development environment provided by Apple. Xcode is a powerful integrated development environment that has all of the features of a modern IDE. It integrates many powerful features including code editing, debugging, version control, and software profiling. If you do not have Xcode installed, you can install it either from your OS X installation DVD or by downloading it from the Apple developer web site at `http://developer.apple.com/technology/xcode.html`.

To get started, start up Xcode and select File ➪ New Project. A dialog box appears that displays templates for the various types of applications that you can create for the iPhone and Mac OS X, as shown in Figure 1-1.

FIGURE 1-1: New Project dialog

Each option presented provides you with the basic setup needed to start developing your application. When building data-centric applications, you will often use one of the following templates:

➤ **Navigation-based Application:** Use this template for applications where you want to use a Navigation Controller to display hierarchical data using a navigable list of items. The iPhone's native Contacts application is an example of a navigation-based application. The user selects from a list with the intention of drilling down deeper for more details. The Navigation Controller provides the capability to navigate up and down through a stack of controls.

➤ **Tab Bar Application:** This template is for applications where you want to provide navigation using a tab bar at the bottom of the screen. The iPod application is an example of a Tab Bar application in which the tab bar displays your various media types.

➤ **View-based Application:** This is a generic template used to start applications based on a single view. Calculator is a View-based application. There is no built-in navigation; the application is one screen with one very specific function.

For this sample application, you are going to use the straightforward View-based Application template.

Select View-based Application from the dialog box and click the Choose button. Set the name of your project to SampleTableProject, select a location to save your project, and click the Save button. Xcode will create your project and present the project window. You are now ready to get started!

Xcode now displays the project window, as in Figure 1-2. In the project window, you will see an organizer in the left-hand pane. You can use the organizer to navigate through the files in your project. Feel free to click on any of the folders, smart folders, or icons in the organizer to explore how Xcode organizes your project. You can add additional folders at any time to help keep your code and other project assets such as images, sound, and text files under control.

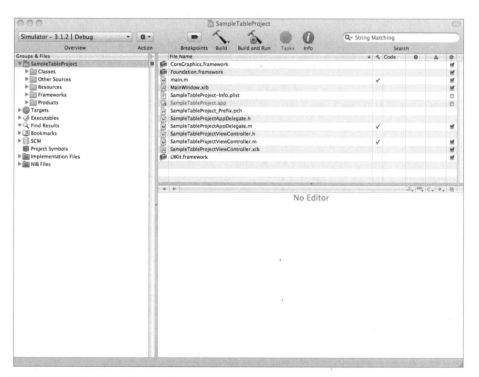

FIGURE 1-2: Xcode project window

The top-right pane is a file list. This pane contains a list of files in the container that you have selected in the organizer pane. If you select the Classes folder in the organizer pane, you will see a list of all of the classes in your project in the file list pane.

The bottom-right pane is the code window. Selecting a code file, one that ends with the .m extension for implementation files or .h for header files, causes the source code for that file to appear in the code pane. Double-clicking on a code file opens the code in a separate window. This can make your code easier to work with. You can dedicate more room to your code in the Xcode project window by selecting View ➪ Zoom Editor In or by pressing CMD-SHIFT-E. This command makes the file list disappear and fills the right side of Xcode with your source code.

Adding a UITableView

The most common control used to display data on the iPhone is the UITableView. As the name suggests, the UITableView is a view that you can use to display data in a table. You can see the UITableView in action in the iPhone's Contacts application. The application displays your list of contacts in a UITableView control. You learn much more about the UITableView control in Chapter 3.

Typically, when developing the interface for your iPhone applications, you will use Apple's Interface Builder. This tool is invaluable for interactively laying out, designing, and developing your user interface. However, the focus of this chapter is not on designing a beautiful interface; it is on getting data displayed on the iPhone. So instead of using Interface Builder to design the screen that will hold a TableView, you will just create and display it programmatically.

In order to create the TableView, you will be modifying the main View Controller for the sample project.

Model-View-Controller Architecture

Before I move on with the sample, it's important that you understand the basic architecture used to build most iPhone applications: Model-View-Controller. There are three parts to the architecture, shown in Figure 1-3. As you can probably guess, they are the model, the view, and the controller.

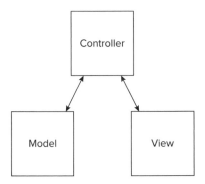

FIGURE 1-3: Model-View-Controller architecture

The *model* is the class or set of classes that represent your data. You should design your model classes to contain your data, the functions that operate on that data, and nothing more. Model classes should not need to know how to display the data that they contain. In fact, think of a model class as a class that doesn't know about anything else except its own data. When the state of the data in the model changes, the model can send out a notification to anyone interested, informing the listener of the state change. Alternatively, controller classes can observe the model and react to changes.

In general, model objects should encapsulate all of your data. Encapsulation is a very important object-oriented design principle. The idea of encapsulation is to prevent other objects from changing your object's data. To effectively encapsulate your data, you should implement interface methods or properties that expose the data of a model class. Classes should not make their data available through public variables.

A complete discussion of object-oriented programming is beyond the scope of this book, but there are many very good resources for learning all about OOP. I have included some sources in the "Further Exploration" section at the end of this chapter. Suffice it to say that encapsulating your data in model objects will lead to good, clean, object-oriented designs that can be easily extended and maintained.

The *view* portion of the MVC architecture is your user interface. The graphics, widgets, tables, and text boxes present the data encapsulated in your model to the user. The user interacts with your model through the view. View classes should contain only the code that is required to present the model data to the user. In many iPhone applications, you won't need to write any code for your view. Quite often, you will design and build it entirely within Interface Builder.

The *controller* is the glue that binds your model to your view. The controller is responsible for telling the view what to display. It is also responsible for telling your model how to change based on input from the user. The controller contains all of the logic for telling the view what to display. Almost all of the code in your iPhone applications will be contained in controller classes.

To quickly summarize, the model is your application data, the view is the user interface, and the controller is the business logic code that binds the view to the model.

In the sample application, you will be creating a class that acts as the model for the data. Xcode creates a default controller for the application as a part of the view-based code template, and you are going to add a `TableView` as the view so that you can see the data contained in the model. You will then code the controller to bind the view and model.

Adding the TableView Programmatically

Now that you have a basic understanding of the MVC architecture, you can move ahead and add the `TableView` to the application. Open up the Classes folder in the left-hand organizer pane by clicking on the disclosure triangle to the left of the folder. Select the `SampleTableProjectViewController.m` file to display its code in the code window, or double-click on it to bring it up in a larger editor.

Remove the `/*` and `*/` comment block tokens from around the `loadView` method. You are going to insert code into the `loadView` method so that when the View Controller tries to load the view, it will create an instance of the `UITableView` class and set its `view` property to the newly created view. Type the following code into the `loadView` method:

Available for download on Wrox.com

```
- (void)loadView {
    CGRect cgRct = CGRectMake(0, 20, 320, 460);
    UITableView * myTable = [[UITableView alloc] initWithFrame:cgRct];
    self.view = myTable;
}
```

SampleTableProjectViewController.m

The first line creates a CGRect, which is a Core Graphics structure used to specify the size and location for the TableView. You set it to have its origin at (0, 20), and be 320 pixels wide by 460 pixels high. The TableView will cover the entire screen, but start 20 pixels from the top, below the status bar.

The next line creates an instance of a UITableView and initializes it with the dimensions that you specified in the previous line.

Just creating the TableView instance is not enough to get it to display in the view. You have to inform the View Controller about it by setting the View Controller's view property to the TableView that you just created.

You can go ahead and click on the Build and Run icon in the toolbar at the top of the Xcode window to run the project. You will see that your application compiles successfully and starts in the simulator. You should also see a bunch of gray lines in the simulator, as shown in Figure 1-4. That is your TableView! Those gray lines divide your rows of data. Unfortunately, there is no data for your TableView to display yet, so the table is blank. You can, however, click in the simulator and drag the TableView. You should see the lines move as you drag up and down and then snap back into position as you let go of the mouse button.

FIGURE 1-4: Running an application with TableView

Retrieving Data

A table is useless without some data to display. To keep this first example simple, you are going to create a very simple data model. The data model will be a class that contains a list of names that you would like to display in the table. The model class will consist of an array to hold the list of data, a method that will return the name for any given index and a method that will return the total number of items in the model.

To create a new class in your project, begin by clicking on the Classes folder in the left pane in Xcode. Then, select File ➪ New File. You will see the New File dialog that shows all of the types of files that you can create in an Xcode project.

Select Cocoa Touch Class in the left pane of the dialog box and select Objective-C Class as the type of file that you want to create. Then select NSObject in the drop-down box next to "Subclass of." The template allows you to create Objective-C classes that are subclasses of NSObject, UITableViewCell, or UIView. In this case, you want to create a subclass of NSObject, so just leave NSObject selected. Click Next to create your class.

In the New NSObject subclass dialog, you can name your file. Name your new file **DataModel.m**. Ensure that the "Also create 'DataModel.h'" checkbox is selected. This will automatically create the header for your new class. The other options in this dialog allow you to specify the project to contain your new class and the build target to compile your file. Leave both of these options at their defaults and click Finish to have Xcode generate your new class file.

Implementing Your Data Model Class

In order for your class to serve data to the `TableView`, you'll need a method to return the requested data. So, let's create an interface method called `getNameAtIndex` that will return the name from the model that corresponds with the index that is passed in.

Bring up your `DataModel.h` header file by selecting it in the left-hand browser pane in Xcode. Below the right brace that closes the interface definition, add the following line of code to declare the `getNameAtIndex` interface method:

```
-(NSString*) getNameAtIndex:(int) index;
```

You'll also need an interface method that tells users of the class how many rows you'll be returning. So add another method to the interface called `getRowCount`. Below the declaration for `getNameAtIndex`, add the declaration for `getRowCount`:

```
-(int) getRowCount;
```

Your header file should look like this:

```
#import <Foundation/Foundation.h>

@interface DataModel : NSObject {

}

-(NSString*) getNameAtIndex:(int) index;
-(int) getRowCount;

@end
```

DataModel.h

Now, let's switch over to the data model implementation file `DataModel.m` and implement the new methods. You can quickly switch between a header and implementation file in Xcode by using the shortcut key combination CTRL-OPT-UP ARROW.

You will be well served to learn the keyboard shortcuts in Xcode. The small amount of time that you invest in learning them will more than pay off in time saved.

Below the `#import` statement in your implementation file, add a local variable to hold the data list. Typically, the data in your application will come from a database or some other datasource. To keep this example simple, you'll use an `NSArray` as the datasource. Add the following line to the `DataModel.m` file below the `#import` statement:

```
NSArray* myData;
```

Now, inside the `@implementation` block, you add the implementation of the `getNameAtIndex` method. Add the following code stub between the `@implementation` and `@end` tags in `DataModel.m`:

```
-(NSString*) getNameAtIndex:(int) index
{

}
```

Before you get to the lookup implementation, you need to initialize the data store, the `myData` array. For this example, you'll do that in the initializer of the class. Above the function stub `getNameAtIndex`, add the following code to initialize the class:

```
-(id)init
{
    if (self = [super init])
    {
        // Initialization code
        myData = [[NSArray alloc] initWithObjects:@"Albert", @"Bill", @"Chuck",
                    @"Dave", @"Ethan", @"Franny", @"George", @"Holly", @"Inez",
                    nil];
    }
    return self;
}
```

The first line calls the superclass's `init` function. You should always call `init` on the superclass in any subclass that you implement. You need to do this to ensure that attributes of the superclass are constructed before you begin doing anything in your subclass.

The next line allocates memory for the array and populates it with a list of names.

The final line returns an instance of the class.

Now that you have the data initialized, you can implement the function to get your data. This is quite simple in this example. You just return the string at the specified location in the array like so:

```
-(NSString*) getNameAtIndex:(int) index
{
    return (NSString*)[myData objectAtIndex:index];
}
```

This line of code simply looks up the object at the specified index in the array and casts it to an `NSString*`. You know that this is safe because you've populated the data by hand and are sure that the object at the given index is an `NSString`.

 To keep this example simple, I have omitted bounds checking that would be performed in a production application.

To implement `getRowCount`, you simply return the count of the local array like this:

```
-(int) getRowCount
{
```

```
    return [myData count];
}
```

At this point, if you build your project by clicking the build icon in the toolbar or pressing Command+B, your code should compile and link cleanly with no errors or warnings. If you have an error or warning, go back and take a look at the code provided and make sure that you have typed everything correctly.

I am a big proponent of compiling early and often. Typically, after every method that I write or any particularly tricky bit of code, I will attempt to build. This is a good habit to get into, as it is much easier to narrow down compile errors if the amount of new code that you've added since your last successful compile is small. This practice also limits the amount of errors or warnings that you receive. If you wait until you've written 2,000 lines before attempting to compile, you are likely to find the number of errors (or at least warnings) that you receive overwhelming. It is also sometimes difficult to track down the source of these errors because compiler and linker errors tend to be a little cryptic.

Your completed data model class should look like this:

```
#import "DataModel.h"

NSArray* myData;

@implementation DataModel

-(id)init
{
    if (self = [super init])
    {
        // Initialization code
        myData = [[NSArray alloc] initWithObjects:@"Albert", @"Bill", @"Chuck",
                    @"Dave", @"Ethan", @"Franny", @"George", @"Holly", @"Inez",
                    nil];
    }
    return self;
}

-(NSString*) getNameAtIndex:(int) index
{
    return (NSString*)[myData objectAtIndex:index];
}

-(int) getRowCount
{
    return [myData count];
}

-(void) dealloc
{
    [myData release];   // release the previously allocated NSArray
    [super dealloc];
}


@end
```

DataModel.m

Displaying the Data

Now that you have the view and model in place, you have to hook them up using the controller. In order for a `TableView` to display data, it needs to know what the data is and how to display it. To do this, a `UITableView` object must have a delegate and a datasource. The datasource coordinates the data from your model with the `TableView`. The delegate controls the appearance and behavior of the `TableView`. To guarantee that you have properly implemented the delegate, it must implement the `UITableViewDelegate` protocol. Likewise, the datasource must implement the `UITableViewDataSource` protocol.

Protocols

If you are familiar with Java or C++, protocols should also be familiar. Java interfaces and C++ pure virtual classes are the same as protocols. A protocol is just a formal contract between a caller and an implementer. The protocol definition states what methods a class that implements the protocol must implement. The protocol can also include optional methods.

Saying that a `TableView`'s delegate must implement the `UITableViewDelegate` protocol means you agree to a contract. That contract states that you will implement the required methods specified in the `UITableViewDelegate` protocol. Similarly, a class that will be set as the `datasource` for a `TableView` must implement the required methods specified in the `UITableViewDataSource` protocol. This may sound confusing but it will become clearer as you continue to work through the example.

To keep this example as simple as possible and to avoid introducing more classes, you'll make the `SampleTableProjectViewController` the delegate and datasource for the `TableView`. To do this, you will have to implement the `UITableViewDelegate` and `UITableViewDataSource` protocols in the `SampleTableProjectViewController`. You need to declare that the `SampleTableProjectViewController` class implements these protocols in the header file. Change the `@interface` line in the `SampleTableProjectViewController.h` header file to add the protocols that you plan on implementing in angle brackets after the interface name and inheritance hierarchy like so:

```
@interface SampleTableProjectViewController : UIViewController
    <UITableViewDataSource, UITableViewDelegate>
```

If you try to build your project now, you will get some warnings. Open the Build Results window by selecting Build Results from the Build menu (or by using the shortcut Command+Shift+B). You should see a dialog box that looks something like Figure 1-5.

You should see several warnings associated with the compilation of `SampleTableProjectViewController.m`; specifically, the warnings, "incomplete implementation of class 'SampleTableProjectViewController'" and "class 'SampleTableProjectViewController' does not fully implement the 'UITableViewDataSource' protocol."

These warnings are clear. You have not implemented the protocols that you claimed you would implement. In fact, the warnings are even more specific in that they specify the required methods that you failed to implement: "method definition for '-tableView:cellForRowAtIndexPath:' not found" and "method definition for '-tableView:numberOfRowsInSection:' not found." If you have any doubt about which methods are required to implement a protocol, a quick build will tell you with explicit warnings.

FIGURE 1-5: Build Results dialog

Implementing the UITableViewDataSource Protocol

Let's get rid of those warnings and move one step closer to a working application by implementing the UITableViewDataSource protocol.

Because you will be using the DataModel class in the SampleTableProjectViewController class, you have to import the DataModel.h header file. In the SampleTableProjectViewController.h header file, add the following #import statement just below the #import <UIKit/UIKit.h> statement:

```
#import "DataModel.h"
```

Now that you've imported the DataModel class, you'll have to create an instance variable of the DataModel type. In the SampleTableProjectViewController.m implementation, add the following declaration below the @implementation keyword:

```
DataModel* model;
```

To actually create the instance of the model class, add the following code to the beginning of the loadView method:

```
model = [[DataModel alloc] init];
```

Now that you have an initialized model ready to go, you can implement the required `UITableViewDataSource` protocol methods. You can see from the compiler warnings that the methods that you need to implement are `cellForRowAtIndexPath` and `numberOfRowsInSection`.

The `numberOfRowsInSection` method tells the `TableView` how many rows to display in the current section. You can divide a `TableView` into multiple sections. In the Contacts application, a letter of the alphabet precedes each section. In this example, you have only one section, but in Chapter 3, you see how to implement multiple sections.

To implement `numberOfRowsInSection`, get the number of rows that the datasource contains by calling the model's `getRowCount` method:

```
- (NSInteger)tableView:(UITableView *)tableView
    numberOfRowsInSection:(NSInteger)section{
    return [model getRowCount];
}
```

If you build your project now, you will see that the warning about not implementing `numberOfRowsInSection` is gone.

The `cellForRowAtIndexPath` method returns the actual `UITableViewCell` object that will display your data in the `TableView`. The `TableView` calls this method any time it needs to display a cell. The `NSIndexPath` parameter identifies the desired cell. So, what you need to do is write a method that returns the correct `UITableViewCell` based on the row that the `TableView` asks for. You do that like so:

```
- (UITableViewCell *)tableView:(UITableView *)tableView
        cellForRowAtIndexPath:(NSIndexPath *)indexPath
{
    static NSString *CellIdentifier = @"Cell";

    UITableViewCell *cell = [tableView
                            dequeueReusableCellWithIdentifier:CellIdentifier];
    if (cell == nil) {
        cell = [[[UITableViewCell alloc]
                initWithFrame:CGRectZero
                reuseIdentifier:CellIdentifier] autorelease];
    }

    NSUInteger row = [indexPath row];
    cell.textLabel.text = [model getNameAtIndex:row];
    return cell;
}
```

The first few lines of code return a valid `UITableViewCell` object. I won't go into the details of exactly what is happening here because I cover it in detail in Chapter 3, which is dedicated to the `UITableView`. For now, suffice it to say that for performance purposes you want to reuse `TableViewCells` whenever possible and this code does just that.

The last few lines of code find the row that the caller is interested in, look up the data for that row from the model, set the text of the cell to the name in the model, and return the UITableViewCell.

That's all there is to it. You should now be able to successfully build the project with no errors or warnings.

Delegates

In designing the iPhone SDK and the Cocoa libraries in general, Apple engineers frequently implemented common design patterns. You've already seen how to use the Model-View-Controller (MVC) pattern in an application design. Another pattern that you will see all across the Cocoa and Cocoa touch frameworks is *delegation*.

In the delegate pattern, an object appears to do some bit of work; however, it can delegate that work to another class. For example, if your boss asks you to do some work and you hand it off to someone else to do, your boss doesn't care that you or someone else did the work, as long as the work is completed.

While working with the iPhone SDK, you will encounter many instances of delegation, and the TableView is one such instance. A delegate for the TableView implements the UITableViewDelegate protocol. This protocol provides methods that manage selection of rows, control adding and deleting cells, and control configuration of section headings along with various other operations that control the display of your data.

Finishing Up

The only thing left to do with the sample is to set the UITableView's delegate and DataSource properties. Because you have implemented the delegate and datasource protocols, in the SampleTableProjectViewController, you set both of these properties to self.

In the loadView method of the SampleTableProjectViewController.m file, add the following code to configure the datasource and the delegate for the TableView:

```
[myTable setDelegate:self];
[myTable setDataSource:self];
```

The final code for the SampleTableProjectViewController.m should look something like Listing 1-1.

LISTING 1-1: SampleTableProjectViewController.m

```
#import "SampleTableProjectViewController.h"


@implementation SampleTableProjectViewController

DataModel* model;


// Implement loadView to create a view hierarchy programmatically, without
```

continues

LISTING 1-1 *(continued)*

```objc
// using a nib.
- (void)loadView {

    model = [[DataModel alloc] init];

    CGRect cgRct = CGRectMake(0, 20, 320, 460);
    UITableView * myTable = [[UITableView alloc] initWithFrame:cgRct];
    [myTable setDelegate:self];
    [myTable setDataSource:self];
    self.view = myTable;
}

- (void)didReceiveMemoryWarning {
    // Releases the view if it doesn't have a superview.
    [super didReceiveMemoryWarning];

}

- (void)viewDidUnload {
    // Release any retained subviews of the main view.
    // e.g. self.myOutlet = nil;
}


- (void)dealloc {
    [super dealloc];
}

//  UITableViewDataSource protocol methods
- (NSInteger)tableView:(UITableView *)tableView
    numberOfRowsInSection:(NSInteger)section
{

    return [model getRowCount];
}

- (UITableViewCell *)tableView:(UITableView *)tableView
        cellForRowAtIndexPath:(NSIndexPath *)indexPath
{
    static NSString *CellIdentifier = @"Cell";

    UITableViewCell *cell = [tableView
                            dequeueReusableCellWithIdentifier:CellIdentifier];
    if (cell == nil) {
        cell = [[[UITableViewCell alloc]
                initWithFrame:CGRectZero
                reuseIdentifier:CellIdentifier] autorelease];
    }

    // Set up the cell...
    NSUInteger row = [indexPath row];
    cell.textLabel.text = [model getNameAtIndex:row];
    return cell;
}

@end
```

You should now be able to build and run your application in the simulator. You should see the table populated with the names that are contained in your `DataModel` class, as in Figure 1-6.

Congratulations! You've successfully built your first data-driven application! Feel free to go back and modify the `DataModel` to use a different datasource, like a text file.

FURTHER EXPLORATION

In this chapter, you learned how to build an iPhone application that uses the `UITableView` control to display data. You also learned a little bit about design patterns, specifically the Model-View-Controller pattern that is prevalent in iPhone application development. In the next chapter, you learn how to use the SQLite database as your datasource. Then, in Chapter 3, you master the `UITableView` control. By the end of Chapter 3, you should be able to build a data-centric iPhone application on your own.

FIGURE 1-6: Running TableView with data

Design Patterns

If you are interested in writing maintainable, high-quality software, I highly recommend *Design Patterns: Elements of Reusable Object-Oriented Software* by Erich Gamma, Richard Helm, Ralph Johnson, and John Vlissides (Addison-Wesley, 1994). This is the bible of OO design patterns. The book illustrates each pattern with a UML model, very readable explanations of the patterns and their implementation, and code samples in both C++ and SmallTalk. If you don't already have this masterpiece of computer science, get it now — you won't regret it.

I would also recommend *Object-Oriented Design and Patterns* by Cay S. Horstmann (Wiley, 2005). Although the code in the book is in Java, you will find that the explanations of the patterns introduced in the design patterns book are outstanding and will help you to further understand the patterns and their importance in implementing high-quality software.

Even if you are not interested in either of these titles, do yourself a favor and search Google for "design patterns." There is a reason why there is a lot of literature on design patterns. It doesn't make any sense to try to re-invent the wheel. Others have already discovered the solutions to many of the problems that you will find in your software designs. These solutions have become design patterns. The point of these design patterns is to present well-tested designs to developers in a form that everyone can understand. The patterns are time proven and offer a common vocabulary that is useful when communicating your design to other developers.

Reading a Text File

If you are interested in making your simple table viewing application more interesting, it is easy to read data from a text file. The following code snippet shows you how:

```
NSError *error;

NSString *textFileContents = [NSString
    stringWithContentsOfFile:[[NSBundle mainBundle]
    pathForResource:@"myTextFile"
    ofType:@"txt"]
    encoding:NSUTF8StringEncoding
    error:&error];

// If there are no results, something went wrong
if (fileContents == nil) {
    // an error occurred
    NSLog(@"Error reading text file. %@", [error localizedFailureReason]);
}

NSArray *lines = [textFileContents componentsSeparatedByString:@"\n"];
NSLog(@"Number of lines in the file:%d", [lines count]  );
```

This code will read the contents of the file `myTextFile.txt`, which should be included in your code bundle. Simply create a text file with this name and add it to your Xcode project.

The first line declares an error object that will be returned to you should anything go wrong while trying to read your text file. The next line loads the entire contents of your file into a string.

The next line is an error handler. If you get `nil` back from the call to `stringWithContentesOfFile`, that means that something went wrong. The error will be output to the console using the `NSLog` function.

The next line breaks up the large string into an array separated by \n, which is the return character. You create an element in the `lines` array for each line in your file.

The final line outputs the number of lines read in from the file.

MOVING FORWARD

In this chapter, you have learned how to build a simple data-driven application using an `NSArray` as your datasource. You also explored the project options available when creating a project in Xcode. Then, you learned about the Model-View-Controller architecture and how the `TableView` fits in with that design. Finally, you looked at the important concepts of Protocols and Delegates.

In the next chapter, you will learn how to get data from a more robust datasource, the SQLite database. This is the embedded database that is included as part of the iPhone SDK. Learning to use this database will enable you to build rich, data-driven applications for the iPhone.

2

The iPhone and iPad Database: SQLite

WHAT'S IN THIS CHAPTER?

➤ Creating an SQLite database

➤ Connecting your application to a database and displaying its data

➤ Running SQL statements against an SQLite database to insert and select data

➤ Building a database and an iPhone application to view master-detail relationships

As an application developer, you have several options when it comes to storing the data used by your iPhone application. You could use plist files, XML, or plain text. While any of these solutions are acceptable in certain situations, they may not provide the best efficiency for your application. None of these formats allows you to query for specific data quickly, nor do they provide an efficient way to sort your data. If your application is designed to work with a large data set and you would like the ability to query and sort it, you should consider using SQLite.

In the last chapter, you learned how to display a small dataset that was stored in a simple array. As you move on to build more complicated applications, chances are that your data set will grow. Hard-coded arrays will probably not meet the demanding requirements of a more complicated application. You will find as you progress with your iPhone development that you need a data storage solution more robust than a simple array.

In this chapter, you will learn about the database engine that backs many iPhone applications, SQLite. By the end of this chapter, you will be able to build an application that uses SQLite as its backing data store.

To use SQLite, you will first learn to create a database using the command-line application provided with Mac OS X. This tool will enable you to create the schema of your database, populate it with data, and perform queries.

Next, you will learn how to deploy your database with an iPhone application, connect to it in code, and display the results or your SQL queries.

By the end of the chapter, you will know how to build a fully functional database application that can be used to view data that has a master-detail relationship: in this case, a product catalog.

WHAT IS SQLITE?

SQLite is an open source library, written in C, that implements a self-contained SQL relational database engine. You can use SQLite to store large amounts of relational data, and it is optimized for use on embedded devices like the iPhone.

While the Core Data API is also designed to store data on the iPhone, its primary purpose is to persist objects created by your application. SQLite excels when pre-loading your application with a large amount of data, whereas Core Data excels at managing data created on the device.

The SQLite Library

SQLite is an open source library, written in C, that implements a fully self-contained SQL database engine. All of the data required to implement the database is stored in a single, cross-platform disk file. Because SQLite is self-contained, it requires few external libraries and little support from the operating system. This is the prime reason that it is ideal for a mobile platform like the iPhone.

SQLite has been adopted for use on the iPhone for other reasons as well, including its very small footprint. Weighing in at less than 300K, the library is small enough to use effectively on mobile devices with limited memory. What's more, SQLite requires no configuration files, has no setup procedure, and needs no administration. You can just drop your database file on the iPhone, include the SQLite library in your iPhone project, and you are ready to roll.

Because SQLite implements most of the SQL92 standard, you will find working with an SQLite database intuitive if you already know SQL. You should keep in mind that there are some features of SQL92 that are not currently supported in SQLite. These include RIGHT and FULL OUTER JOIN, complete support for ALTER TABLE, FOR EACH STATEMENT triggers, writeable VIEWs, and GRANT and REVOKE permissions. For more detail on unsupported functionality, take a look at the SQLite web site http://www.sqlite.org/omitted.html.

Because the interface to SQLite is written in C, and Objective-C is a superset of C, you can easily incorporate SQLite into your Objective-C–based iPhone projects.

SQLite and Core Data

When starting a data-centric application for the iPhone, there is a significant architectural decision that you need to make. Should you use SQLite or Core Data for your data management needs?

Let's take a quick look at what Core Data is and isn't. First, Core Data is not a relational database like SQLite. Core Data is an object persistence framework. Its primary purpose is to provide the developer with a framework to persist objects created by the application. Core Data allows you to model your data as objects using a convenient graphical interface built into Xcode. You can then manipulate those objects in code with an extensive set of APIs. Designing and defining your data objects using the graphical interface can simplify the creation of the Model portion of the MVC architecture.

Core Data can use SQLite, among other storage types, as a backing store for its data. This causes some confusion for developers. It is a common misconception that because Core Data can use SQLite to store data, Core Data is a relational database. This is not correct. As mentioned, Core Data is not an implementation of a relational database. Although Core Data uses SQLite in the background to store your data, it does not store the data in a way that is directly accessible to the developer. In fact, you should never attempt to manually modify the backing database structure or its data. Only the Core Data framework should manipulate the structure of the database and the data itself. You can feel free to open the SQLite database and take a look at it if you are curious, but making any modifications to the data or database structure will likely invalidate it and cause problems when trying to access it using Core Data.

While Core Data is the preferred framework for dealing with data that is created on the iPhone, SQLite remains a useful tool for iPhone developers. If you need the functionality provided by a relational database, you should strongly consider using SQLite directly. However, if you only need to persist objects created during the use of your application, you should consider using Core Data. You explore the Core Data framework in detail in Part II of the book.

While Core Data is the recommended framework for creating data on the iPhone, you may want to forego Core Data and use the SQLite API directly for several reasons.

First, if you are targeting devices that could be running a version of the iPhone OS prior to 3.0, you cannot use Core Data. Core Data became available with the 3.0 release of the iPhone OS.

You might also choose to use the SQLite database directly if you need to preload a large amount of data on the device. Take, for example, a GPS navigation application. Navigation applications need a great deal of data, including points of interest and the maps themselves. A good option for the architectural design is to create an SQLite database that contains all of the POI and map data. You can then deploy that database with your application and use SQLite APIs to access the database.

It is easy to create an SQLite database using desktop tools. You can then use the same tools, scripts, or a desktop application to load your data into the database. Then, you can simply deploy the database to the device with your application.

In this chapter, you are going to build the database for a catalog application that could be used by a mobile sales force. The catalog will need to be preloaded with data, not populated on the iPhone itself, so SQLite will be used as the back-end data store.

BUILDING A SIMPLE DATABASE

In this section, you will build the back-end database for your sales catalog application. Before you start designing the database and the application, it is important to understand what the application will do. In the real world, you will (or should) get a detailed specification defining what the application should do and how it should look. Of course the implementation, or how it should work, is up to the designer and developer. So, let's lay out some simple requirements for the catalog application.

The purpose of the application is to display your company's catalog of widgets. Each widget will have a manufacturer, a product name, some details about the product, the price of the product, the quantity on hand, the country of origin, and a picture of the product.

The application should start up by showing a list of products. Tapping on a product should bring up a detail page showing detailed information about the product.

It is often helpful to mock up the user interface and design the database on paper as a first step in the design of an application. Often, the interface itself can help drive decisions about how to organize the data in the database. I like to use OmniGraffle by the Omni Group (http://www.omnigroup.com/applications/OmniGraffle/) to do my design work. It is an easy-to-use yet powerful vector graphics application for the Mac that allows me to quickly do my design work. Additionally, the output of the application is good enough to use in presentations to managers and other stakeholders who may not be technically inclined. It is far easier to explain an application design with pictures than words!

I suspect that the database gurus out there are pulling their hair out right now because it is common wisdom that the user interface and the data should be completely decoupled and that the data should be normalized independently. However, when developing applications that are designed to run on an embedded device like the iPhone, performance is a very important concern. Data that is fully normalized, with no duplicated data, can have a negative impact on performance. Sometimes the cost to execute a complicated query is higher than the cost of maintaining the same data in two tables. I'm not suggesting that you should not normalize your data at all, just keep in mind how the data will be displayed while working through the database design process.

Designing the Database

If you don't know, normalization is the process of breaking down your data in a way that makes it easy to query. Normalization helps to avoid common problems in database storage such as duplication of data. For example, when creating your database, a designer may want to store all of the data in a single table, as in Figure 2-1.

For those unfamiliar with the Entity-Relationship Diagram (ERD), the box represents an entity or table in the database. The ovals that are connected to the entity are the attributes of that entity or the fields of the table. So, this diagram shows one table with each attribute as a field in the table.

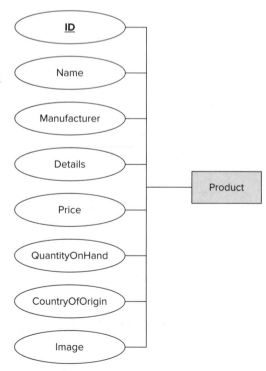

FIGURE 2-1: Storing the data in a single table

The problem with this database design is that it is not normalized. There will be duplication of data if there is more than one product in the catalog manufactured by the same manufacturer or if there is more than one product manufactured in a specific country. In that case, the data may look something like Figure 2-2.

ID	Name	Manufacturer	Details	Price	QuantityOnHand	CountryOfOrigin	Image
1	Widget A	Spirit Industries	...	...	...	USA	...
2	Widget B	Industrial Designs	...	...	...	Taiwan	...
3	Widget X	Spirit Industries	...	...	...	China	...
4	Widget Y	Industrial Designs	...	...	...	China	...
5	Widget Z	Design Intl.	...	...	...	Singapore	...
6	Widget R	Spirit Industries	...	...	...	USA	...

FIGURE 2-2: Data in a single table

You can see that the same manufacturer has more than one product in the database. Also, there is more than one product made in a specific country. This design is a maintenance problem. What happens if the data entry person populating the database types in "Spirit Industries" for item 1 and "Spit Industries" for item 3? It will appear in the application that two different companies make these products, when in reality they are both manufactured by "Spirit Industries." This is a data integrity problem that can be avoided by normalizing the data. You can remove the manufacturer and country of origin from the product table and create new tables for these fields. Then, in the product table, you can just reference the value in the related tables.

Additionally, this new design could allow you to add more detail about the manufacturer such as address, contact name, and so on. For the sake of simplicity, you won't be doing that, but proper normalization helps make this type of flexibility possible.

The new design should look something like Figure 2-3.

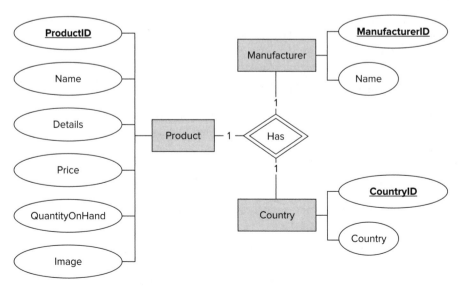

FIGURE 2-3: Normalized database tables

Figure 2-4 shows what the new normalized database will look like.

Product							
ID	Name	ManufacturerID	Details	Price	QuantityOnHand	CountryID	Image
1	Widget A	1	...	...	...	1	...
2	Widget B	2	...	...	...	2	...
3	Widget X	1	...	...	...	3	...
4	Widget Y	2	...	...	...	3	...
5	Widget Z	3	...	...	...	4	...
6	Widget R	1	...	...	...	1	...

Manufacturer	
ManufacturerID	Name
1	Spirit Industries
2	Industrial Designs
3	Design Intl.

Country	
CountryID	Country
1	USA
2	Taiwan
3	China
4	Singapore

FIGURE 2-4: Data in normalized tables

You can see that instead of specifying the manufacture and origin explicitly in the main Products table, you just reference the ID in the related tables. The fact that you can relate data in one table to data in another gives a relational database both its name and its power.

While normalization is important, it is possible to take it too far and over-normalize your data. For instance, you could create a separate table for price. In that case, all products that cost $1 would reference a row in a Price table that contains the value $1. While doing this would eliminate the duplication of data for all products that cost $1, it would be painful to write the code to maintain the relationship between the Product and Price tables. This would be considered over-normalized and should be avoided.

As important as normalization is, you should know that laying out the data in a way that optimizes its display is important as well. Optimizing the user experience on the iPhone is often a difficult and tedious process. Users expect a very fast and smooth user experience. If the data is over-normalized, it may be an optimal data storage strategy, but if accessing the data for display at runtime is too costly, the performance of the application will suffer. Remember that you are writing applications for a mobile platform with limited CPU capability. You will pay a penalty for using overly complex SQL to access your data. You are better off in some instances repeating data instead of using relationships. I am not advocating not normalizing your data at all; just keep in mind how the data will be used on the device as you design your database.

Creating the Database

You can use a couple of different methods to create, modify, and populate your SQLite database. Let's first look at is the command-line interface.

Using a command-line interface may not seem optimal in these days of graphical interfaces, but the command line does have its advantages. One feature that stands out is that you can create and populate a database using the command-line interface and scripts. For example, you could write a

PERL script that gets data out of an enterprise database such as Oracle or MySQL and then creates an SQLite database with a subset of the data. While scripting is beyond the scope of this book, I will show you how to create and populate a database using the command-line tool.

The command-line interface can also be used to import data from a file into a table, read in and execute a file that contains SQL, and output data from a database in a variety of formats including:

- ➤ Comma-separated values
- ➤ Left-aligned columns
- ➤ HTML <table> code
- ➤ SQL insert statements for TABLE
- ➤ One value per line
- ➤ Values delimited by .separator string
- ➤ Tab-separated values
- ➤ TCL list elements

To start the command-line tool, you'll need to bring up a terminal window. Next, change to the directory where you want to store your database file. For this example, you create the database in the root of your home directory and then copy it into the Xcode project that you will create later.

Start the command-line tool and create your new database by typing **sqlite3 catalog.db** at the command prompt. This command will start the command-line tool and attach the database catalog.db. The ATTACH DATABASE command will either attach an existing database to the SQLite tool or create a new database if the specified file doesn't already exist. You can attach multiple databases to a single instance of the command-line tool and reference data in each database using dot notation in the form database-name.table-name. This powerful feature can be used to migrate data from one database to another.

Aside from being able to execute SQL at the command line, the command-line interface tool has various metacommands that are used to control the tool itself. These can be displayed by typing **.help** from the command line. You can see what databases you have attached to the current instance of the tool by typing **.databases** at the command line. You can quit the command-line tool by typing **.exit** or **.quit**.

To create your main Product table, type the **CREATE TABLE** statement at the SQLite command prompt as follows:

```
CREATE  TABLE "main"."Product"
  ("ID" INTEGER PRIMARY KEY  AUTOINCREMENT  NOT NULL ,
   "Name" TEXT, "ManufacturerID" INTEGER, "Details" TEXT,
   "Price" DOUBLE, "QuantityOnHand" INTEGER,
   "CountryOfOriginID" INTEGER, "Image" TEXT );
```

A full discussion of the SQL language is beyond the scope of this book. You should pick up a copy of *SQL For Dummies* by Allen Taylor (Wiley, 2010) if you are interested in learning more about the SQL language.

The previous SQL statement creates a table called Product in the main database. It adds the fields that you designed in your ERD. Finally, it specifies that the ID field is the PRIMARY KEY and that it is an AUTOINCREMENT field. This means that you do not have to supply ID values; the database engine will generate them for you.

Now that you have created the Product table, let's move on to creating the Manufacturer and CountryOfOrigin tables. Type the following SQL commands at the command prompt:

```
CREATE  TABLE "main"."Manufacturer"
  ("ManufacturerID" INTEGER PRIMARY KEY  AUTOINCREMENT  NOT NULL ,
  "Name" TEXT NOT NULL );

CREATE  TABLE "main"."Country"
  ("CountryID" INTEGER PRIMARY KEY  AUTOINCREMENT  NOT NULL ,
  "Country" TEXT NOT NULL );
```

At the time of this writing, the SQLite engine provided with the Snow Leopard operating system is version 3.6.12. This version does not implement foreign key constraints. Foreign key constraints are planned for inclusion in SQLite version 3.6.19, but this is only a draft proposal. Thus, the developer is responsible for enforcing these constraints.

You have just successfully created your database. You should have a database file that contains three tables: Product, Manufacturer, and CountryOfOrigin. Now, let's get some data into the tables.

Populating the Database

Having a database is great, but the data is what really counts. You can populate your database one item at a time from the command line using INSERT SQL statements.

Creating Records with the INSERT Command

Figure 2-5 shows the syntax for the INSERT statement.

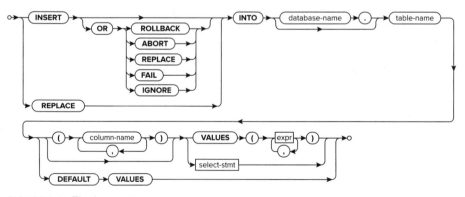

FIGURE 2-5: The Insert statement syntax

In case you aren't sure, I'll quickly go over how to read SQL syntax diagrams.

The open circles at the beginning and end are terminators. They show where the SQL statement starts and ends. The arrow that comes out of the terminator indicates the main branch of the statement.

Keywords are indicated in all caps. Keywords on the main branch are required. So, for the INSERT statement, INSERT, INTO, and VALUES are required for an INSERT statement to be valid SQL. Anything that is not on the main branch is optional. Choices for optional keywords are left-aligned. For example, the OR after INSERT is optional. If you do use OR, you must pick one and only one of the options ROLLBACK, ABORT, REPLACE, FAIL, or IGNORE.

Text that is not in all caps is data provided by the user. So, the INSERT SQL Figure 2-5 indicates that the user needs to specify the database name and table name into which the data will be inserted. Additionally, the user must specify the columns into which the data will be inserted and, finally, the values to be inserted.

You can insert a row into the Product table using the following INSERT statement:

```
INSERT INTO "main"."Product"
   ("Name","ManufacturerID","Details","Price","QuantityOnHand",
   "CountryOfOriginID","Image")
VALUES ('Widget A','1','Details of Widget A','1.29','5','1', 'Canvas_1')
```

While it is possible, inserting data one row at a time using SQL is not very efficient. I mentioned earlier that the command-line tool has the ability to import text files into the database. This can come in very handy when dumping data from another database, Microsoft Excel, or simply a text file. Instead of typing in each INSERT statement, you can create a text file for each of the database tables and then use the import functionality to get the data into the database.

Create a text file in your home directory called products.txt and include the following data. Note that tabs are used between each field as a delimiter. You can also download the file from this book's companion web site.

Available for download on Wrox.com

```
1    Widget A    1    Details of Widget A    1.29    5     1    Canvas_1
2    Widget B    1    Details of Widget B    4.29    15    2    Canvas_2
3    Widget X    1    Details of Widget X    0.29    25    3    Canvas_3
4    Widget Y    1    Details of Widget Y    1.79    5     3    Canvas_4
5    Widget Z    1    Details of Widget Z    6.26    15    4    Canvas_5
6    Widget R    1    Details of Widget R    2.29    45    1    Canvas_6
7    Widget S    1    Details of Widget S    3.29    55    1    Canvas_7
8    Widget T    1    Details of Widget T    4.29    15    2    Canvas_8
9    Widget L    1    Details of Widget L    5.29    50    3    Canvas_9
10   Widget N    1    Details of Widget N    6.29    50    3    Canvas_10
11   Widget E    1    Details of Widget E    17.29   25    4    Canvas_11
12   Part Alpha  2    Details of Part Alpha  1.49    25    1    Canvas_12
```

```
13   Part Beta   2   Details of Part Beta   1.89   35  1   Canvas_13
14   Part Gamma  2   Details of Part Gamma  3.46   45  2   Canvas_14
15   Device N    3   Details of Device N    9.29   15  3   Canvas_15
16   Device O    3   Details of Device O    21.29  15  3   Canvas_16
17   Device P    3   Details of Device P    51.29  15  4   Canvas_17
18   Tool A      4   Details of Tool A      14.99  5   1   Canvas_18
19   Tool B      4   Details of Tool B      44.79  5   1   Canvas_19
20   Tool C      4   Details of Tool C      6.59   5   1   Canvas_20
21   Tool D      4   Details of Tool D      8.29   5   1   Canvas_21
```

products.txt

Each column, separated by a tab in the text file, represents a field in the database. The fields must be in the order that they were created using the CREATE TABLE command. So the order of the fields is ID, Name, ManufacturerID, Details, Price, QuantityOnHand, CountryOfOriginID, and Image.

To import your data file into the database, open up the SQLite command prompt if you do not still have it open. Type the command **.separator "\t"** to specify that you are using the tab character \t as the field separator in the data file. Then, type **.import "products.txt" Product** to import the file products.txt into the Product table. Your data should have been successfully imported into the database.

Reading Your Rows with the SELECT Command

To verify that your data was successfully imported, you can display it using the SQL SELECT statement. The syntax for the SELECT statement appears in Figure 2-6:

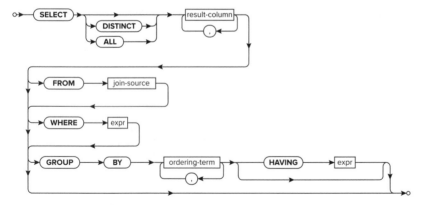

FIGURE 2-6: The Select statement syntax

Type **select * from Product;** to see all of the rows in your product table. The output should look like this:

```
1    Widget A    1    Details of Widget A    1.29     5    1    Canvas_1
2    Widget B    1    Details of Widget B    4.29    15    2    Canvas_2
3    Widget X    1    Details of Widget X    0.29    25    3    Canvas_3
4    Widget Y    1    Details of Widget Y    1.79     5    3    Canvas_4
5    Widget Z    1    Details of Widget Z    6.26    15    4    Canvas_5
6    Widget R    1    Details of Widget R    2.29    45    1    Canvas_6
7    Widget S    1    Details of Widget S    3.29    55    1    Canvas_7
8    Widget T    1    Details of Widget T    4.29    15    2    Canvas_8
9    Widget L    1    Details of Widget L    5.29    50    3    Canvas_9
10   Widget N    1    Details of Widget N    6.29    50    3    Canvas_10
11   Widget E    1    Details of Widget E   17.29    25    4    Canvas_11
12   Part Alpha 2    Details of Part Alpha 1.49    25    1    Canvas_12
13   Part Beta  2    Details of Part Beta  1.89    35    1    Canvas_13
14   Part Gamma 2    Details of Part Gamma 3.46    45    2    Canvas_14
15   Device N    3    Details of Device N    9.29    15    3    Canvas_15
16   Device O    3    Details of Device O   21.29    15    3    Canvas_16
17   Device P    3    Details of Device P   51.29    15    4    Canvas_17
18   Tool A      4    Details of Tool A     14.99     5    1    Canvas_18
19   Tool B      4    Details of Tool B     44.79     5    1    Canvas_19
20   Tool C      4    Details of Tool C      6.59     5    1    Canvas_20
21   Tool D      4    Details of Tool D      8.29     5    1    Canvas_21
```

This is identical to the input data file so you are ready to proceed.

Create another text file in your home directory called `manufacturers.txt` and include the following data:

```
1    Spirit Industries
2    Industrial Designs
3    Design Intl.
4    Tool Masters
```

Import the manufacturer data into the database by typing **`.import "manufacturers.txt"`
`Manufacturer`** to import the file `manufacturers.txt` into the Manufacturer table. You can again use the SQL SELECT statement to verify that your data has been imported correctly by typing **`select * from manufacturer;`**.

Finally, create another text file in your home directory called `countries.txt` and include the following data:

```
1    USA
2    Taiwan
3    China
4    Singapore
```

Import the country data into the database by typing **`.import "countries.txt" Country`** to import the file `countries.txt` into the Country table. You can again use the SQL SELECT statement to verify that your data has been imported correctly by typing **`select * from country;`**.

Now that you have your data in the database, feel free to experiment with all of the standard SQL that you already know! For example, if you want to see all of the products ordered by price, you can type **select name,price from product order by price;**. The result of that query is as follows:

```
Widget X     0.29
Widget A     1.29
Part Alpha   1.49
Widget Y     1.79
Part Beta    1.89
Widget R     2.29
Widget S     3.29
Part Gamma   3.46
Widget B     4.29
Widget T     4.29
Widget L     5.29
Widget Z     6.26
Widget N     6.29
Tool C       6.59
Tool D       8.29
Device N     9.29
Tool A       14.99
Widget E     17.29
Device O     21.29
Tool B       44.79
Device P     51.29
```

You can join your tables using standard SQL syntax. For example, you can show each product and the name of the country of origin using this SQL statement SELECT name,country FROM Product,country where product.countryoforiginid=country.countryid. The results are as follows:

```
Widget A     USA
Widget B     Taiwan
Widget X     China
Widget Y     China
Widget Z     Singapore
Widget R     USA
Widget S     USA
Widget T     Taiwan
Widget L     China
Widget N     China
Widget E     Singapore
Part Alpha   USA
Part Beta    USA
Part Gamma   Taiwan
Device N     China
Device O     China
Device P     Singapore
Tool A       USA
Tool B       USA
Tool C       USA
Tool D       USA
```

You can also filter your data using a WHERE clause. To find all products manufactured in China, you can use the following query:

```
SELECT name, country FROM Product, country where
product.countryoforiginid=country.countryid and country.country="China".
```

The result of this query is a list of all of the products made in China:

```
Widget X    China
Widget Y    China
Widget L    China
Widget N    China
Device N    China
Device O    China
```

Tools to Visualize the SQLite Database

As powerful as the command-line interface to SQLite is, sometimes it is easier to use a GUI interface to examine the database. Many applications provide this functionality. You can find a list of them on the SQLite web site at http://www.sqlite.org/cvstrac/wiki?p=ManagementTools.

Feel free to try out any or all of the applications listed on the SQLite site. These applications range in price from free to hundreds of dollars and offer a variety of capabilities including import/export from various tools and commercial databases, graphical ER modeling, SQL editors with syntax highlighting, and many other advanced features. If you are going to use SQLite for enterprise applications, it may very well be worth it to purchase one of these applications.

For developing simple iPhone applications that do not require intense database development, I prefer to use the SQLite Manager plug-in for the Firefox web browser. This free plug-in, available at the Google code web site (http://code.google.com/p/sqlite-manager/) provides you with the following features:

➤ Dialog interface for creation and deletion of tables, indexes, views, and triggers

➤ Ability to modify tables by adding and dropping columns

➤ Ability to create or open any existing SQLite databases

➤ Ability to execute arbitrary SQL or simply view all of the data in your tables

➤ Visual interface for database settings, eliminating the need to write pragma statements to view and change the SQLite library settings

➤ Ability to export tables/views, such as CSV, SQL, or XML files

➤ Ability to import tables from CSV, SQL, or XML files

➤ A tree view that shows all tables, indexes, views, and triggers

➤ Interface to browse data from any table/view

➤ Ability to edit and delete records while browsing data

The plug-in is very easy to install and use. You can use the plug-in to create new tables by simply clicking the Create Table icon. You are then presented with a dialog that contains all of the data that you need to create a new table, as shown in Figure 2-7. I have populated the dialog with the fields from the ERD diagram.

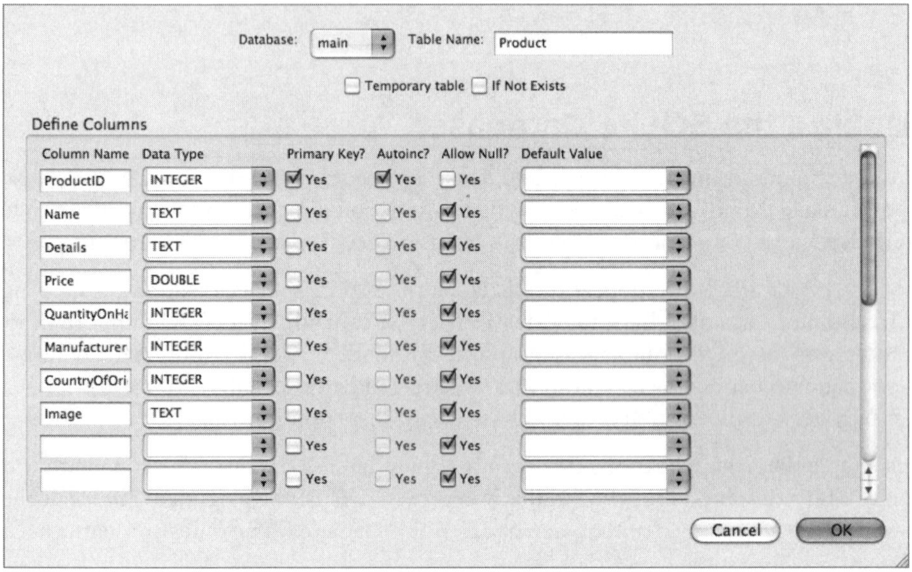

FIGURE 2-7: Creating a table with SQLite Manager

Click the disclosure triangle next to Tables in the left-hand pane of the interface to see a list of all of the tables in the database. Selecting a table, like Product in Figure 2-8, will reveal the details of the table. You can see the SQL that was originally used to create the table, the number of fields in the table, the number of records, and detailed information on all of the columns in the table. You can also add, alter, and drop columns from this view.

You can select the Browse & Search tab at the top of the right pane to view and edit the data in the selected table, as shown in Figure 2-8.

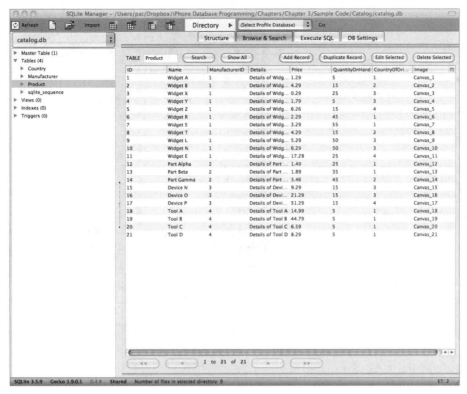

FIGURE 2-8: Browsing table data with SQLite Manager

Selecting the Execute SQL tab enables you to execute arbitrary SQL statements against the database. Finally, the DB Settings tab enables you to view and edit various database settings that are normally only available via pragma statements at the command prompt.

CONNECTING TO YOUR DATABASE

Now that you have a catalog database, let's get to writing the iPhone application that will be used to view the catalog. In order to do this, you'll need to create an application with a TableView to display the catalog. Clicking a cell in the TableView should navigate to a detail page that shows detailed information about the selected catalog entry. To build this interface, you will need to be able to connect to your database and run SQL statements against it. You'll also use a Navigation Controller to implement a master-child interface.

As I previously mentioned, it is often a good idea to mock up your application interface before you get started. It helps to get buy-in from your customer that the interface that you've designed meets their needs. It is far easier to move interface items around or redesign the look and feel of a mockup than it is to rework your actual application code. You want to find any problems with the design as early as possible to avoid costly and time-consuming changes to the software. A picture can go a long way in explaining to your customer what the application will look like. Figure 2-9 shows a mocked up interface in OmniGraffle.

The interface might not look pretty, but it will get the job done. You will spruce it up a bit in the next chapter. But, for now, it will do the job of demonstrating how to get data out of your SQLite database.

FIGURE 2-9: Application interface mockup

Starting the Project

For this project, you are going to implement a master-detail interface. As seen in the mockup, the main screen will show the entire product catalog and tapping on an item should display a screen with the details for that item. The UINavigationController is perfect for building this kind of interface. To get started, open up Xcode and create a new project using the Navigation-based application template.

This template creates a project that contains two Interface Builder xib files. The MainWindow .xib contains a NavigationController that manages the navigation of the application. The

FIGURE 2-10: MainWindow.xib

NavigationController, in turn, contains the RootViewController. You can see this by inspecting the MainWindow.xib file using Interface Builder (see Figure 2-10).

The UINavigationController

The Navigation Controller is used to display and manage a hierarchy of View Controllers. Any time that you need to display hierarchical data, consider using the UINavigationController. The Navigation Controller manages the state of the display using a "navigation stack." View controllers that you want to display are pushed on to the navigation stack when you are ready to display them. Pressing the Back button causes the current View Controller to be popped off the navigation stack. At the bottom of the stack is the Root View Controller.

You will implement navigation in the catalog application using the UINavigationController. The diagram in Figure 2-11 shows the application mockup along with the navigation stack.

FIGURE 2-11: Application screens and navigation stack state

The left side shows the product catalog displayed in the UITableView, which is included in the RootViewController. Selecting a row in the TableView causes a new View Controller that you will create called the ProductDetailViewController to be pushed onto the navigation stack. You see this in the image on the right. The status of the navigation stack appears at the bottom of the figure.

Tapping the catalog button in the navigation bar at the top of the screen will cause the ProductDetailViewController to be popped from the navigation stack, thus displaying the RootViewController again. The most important thing to remember is that the UINavigationController will always display the View Controller that is at the top of the navigation stack.

You can see what makes the Navigation Controller ideal for displaying hierarchical data. As a user navigates down a hierarchy, the application pushes View Controllers onto the stack. When the user presses the Back button, the View Controllers are popped back off of the stack, navigating back up the hierarchy.

The UITableViewController

If you take a look at the code header for the RootViewController, you will notice that the RootViewController is not a subclass of UIViewController as in the last chapter. Instead, it is a subclass of UITableViewController.

When implementing a View Controller that will control a `TableView`, you can subclass the `UITableViewController` class instead of `UIViewController`. `UITableViewController` is a great shortcut to use. When using a `UITableViewController`, you are freed from having to declare that you will be implementing the `UITableViewDataSource` and `UITableViewDelegate` protocols.

The `UITableViewController` also already has a `TableView` associated with it. You can get a reference to the `TableView` by using the `tableView` property. Because you are subclassing `UITableViewController`, you don't need to worry about creating the `TableView` as you did in the previous chapter. You simply need to implement the model and the controller. You are, however, still responsible for implementing the methods `numberOfSectionsInTableView`, `numberOfRowsInSection`, and `cellForRowAtIndexPath` as in the previous chapter.

The `#pragma mark Table view methods` section highlights which `TableView` methods must be implemented. You'll notice that they are all grouped together at the bottom of the implementation file for the `RootViewController` (`RootViewController.m`).

Because the `UITableView` is being loaded from the NIB file for the `RootViewController` (`RootViewController.xib`), the `dataSource` and `delegate` properties are read from the NIB. These properties both default to self, which is fine because the `RootViewController` will be the delegate and `dataSource` for your `UITableView`.

The Model Class

By simply creating a project based on the Navigation template, you get a lot of functionality for free. In fact, if you build and run the application, you should get something that looks like Figure 2-12.

You have added no code at all, yet you already have a navigation bar (the blue-gray area at the top) and a table view (the lines). Now, you need to fill the table view with data.

In keeping with the preferred application architecture on the iPhone, you'll design this application by following the Model-View-Controller design pattern. You already have your view and controller; you just need a model. You need to design a model class that represents your data. The model class should also have a method that returns the number of rows in the database and provides access to the data for a specific row.

For this application, your model will be based on the `Product` class. The `Product` class will mirror the fields in the `Products` table in the database. Your model will be a collection of `Product` objects.

To implement this model, create a new Objective-C class called `Product`. In the header, you will add a property for each database field. The following is the code for the header:

FIGURE 2-12: Running the Navigation template

```objc
#import <Foundation/Foundation.h>

@interface Product : NSObject {
    int ID;
    NSString* name;
```

```
        NSString* manufacturer;
        NSString* details;
        float price;
        int quantity;
        NSString* countryOfOrigin;
        NSString* image;
    }

    @property (nonatomic) int ID;
    @property (retain, nonatomic) NSString *name;
    @property (retain, nonatomic) NSString *manufacturer;
    @property (retain, nonatomic) NSString *details;
    @property (nonatomic) float price;
    @property (nonatomic) int quantity;
    @property (retain, nonatomic) NSString *countryOfOrigin;
    @property (retain, nonatomic) NSString *image;

    @end
```

Product.h

You can see that you simply declare a member variable for each database field and then create a property to access each field.

The implementation for this class is even easier:

Available for download on Wrox.com

```
#import "Product.h"

@implementation Product
@synthesize ID;
@synthesize name;
@synthesize manufacturer;
@synthesize details;
@synthesize price;
@synthesize quantity;
@synthesize countryOfOrigin;
@synthesize image;

@end
```

Product.m

Here, you just synthesize all of the properties declared in the header. At this point, it is a good idea to build and verify that there are no errors in your application.

The DBAccess Class

Now that you have your model object completed, you need to write the code to get the data out of the database and into your model class. It is a good idea to abstract out the database access. This gives you flexibility in the event that you want to move to a different database engine later. To do this, you'll create a database access class that talks to the database. This class will have methods to initialize the database, close the database, and most important, build and return an array of `Product` objects.

Before you get started on coding the database access class, you need to add the SQLite database to the Xcode project. Add the SQLite database to the project's Resources folder by right-clicking on the Resources folder and selecting Add ⇨ Existing Files. Navigate to your home directory or wherever you stored the catalog database and select it. Make sure that "Copy items into destination group's folder if needed" is selected, as in Figure 2-13.

To create the database access class, create a new Objective-C class called `DBAccess`. In the header, `DBAccess.h`, you will need to add an `import` statement for `sqlite3.h` as you intend to use functions from the `sqlite3` library in the data access class.

FIGURE 2-13: Adding an existing file

You'll also need to add three method signatures for the methods that you plan on implementing: `getAllProducts`, `closeDatabase`, and `initializeDatabase`. `closeDatabase` and `initializeDatabase` are self-explanatory. The `getAllProducts` method will return an array of all of the `Product` objects in the catalog. Because you will be referencing the `Product` object in this class, you need to add an `import` statement for `Product.h`.

The `DBAccess.h` header file should look like this:

```objc
#import <Foundation/Foundation.h>

// This includes the header for the SQLite library.
#import <sqlite3.h>
#import "Product.h"

@interface DBAccess : NSObject {


}

- (NSMutableArray*) getAllProducts;
- (void) closeDatabase;
- (void)initializeDatabase;

@end
```

DBAccess.h

In the implementation of the `DBAccess` class, add a class-level variable to hold a reference to the database:

```objc
// Reference to the SQLite database.
sqlite3* database;
```

You will populate this variable in the `initializeDatabase` function. Then, every other function in your class will have access to the database.

Now, you'll create the `init` function that is used by callers to initialize instances of this class. In `init`, you will make an internal call to initialize the database. The `init` function should look like this:

```
-(id) init
{
// Call super init to invoke superclass initiation code
  if ((self = [super init]))
    {
        // set the reference to the database
        [self initializeDatabase];
    }
    return self;
}
```

DBAccess.m

Your `initializeDatabase` function will do just that. It will go out and get the path to the database and attempt to open it. Here is the code for `initializeDatabase`:

```
// Open the database connection
- (void)initializeDatabase {

// Get the database from the application bundle.
  NSString *path = [[NSBundle mainBundle]
          pathForResource:@"catalog"
          ofType:@"db"];

    // Open the database.
    if (sqlite3_open([path UTF8String], &database) == SQLITE_OK)
    {
        NSLog(@"Opening Database");
    }
    else
    {
        // Call close to properly clean up
        sqlite3_close(database);
        NSAssert1(0, @"Failed to open database: '%s'.",
            sqlite3_errmsg(database));
    }
}
```

DBAccess.m

You can see that you need the path to the database file. Because you put the `catalog.db` file in the Resources folder, the database will get deployed to the device in the main bundle of the application. There is a handy class, `NSBundle`, for getting information about an application bundle. The `mainBundle` method returns a reference to the main application bundle and the `pathForResource:ofType:` method returns the path to the specified file in the bundle. Because you specified the resource as `catalog` and the type as `db`, the method will return the path to `catalog.db`.

Next, you use the C function `sqlite3_open` to open a connection to the database. You pass in the path to the database and the address to a variable of type `sqlite3*`. The second parameter will be populated with the handle to the database. The `sqlite3_open` function returns an `int`. It will return the constant `SQLITE_OK` if everything went fine. If not, it will return an error code. The most common errors that you will encounter are `SQLITE_ERROR`, indicating that the database cannot be found and `SQLITE_CANTOPEN`, indicating that there is some other reason that the database file cannot be opened. The full list of error codes can be found in the `sqlite3.h include` file.

You make sure that you got back `SQLITE_OK` and then log that you are opening the database. If you get an error, you close the database and then log the error message.

Next, you'll add a method to cleanly close the connection to the database. This is as simple as calling `sqlite3_close`, passing in a handle to the database like this:

Available for
download on
Wrox.com

```
-(void) closeDatabase
{
    // Close the database.
    if (sqlite3_close(database) != SQLITE_OK) {
        NSAssert1(0, @"Error: failed to close database: '%s'.",
            sqlite3_errmsg(database));
    }
}
```

DBAccess.m

The `sqlite3_close` will return a value just like `sqlite3_open`. If the call to `sqlite3_close` fails, you use the `sqlite3_errmsg` function to get a textual error message and print it to the console.

At this point, you should try to build the application. The build fails because the SQLite functions are not found. Although you included the proper header files, the compiler doesn't know where to find the binaries for the library. You need to add the `libsqlite` framework to your Xcode project. Right-click on the frameworks folder, select Add Existing Framework, and select `libsqlite3.0.dylib`. Now the compilation should succeed. You still receive a warning that tells you that the `getAllProducts` method is not implemented, but you can fix that by implementing the function.

Now comes the heart of the database access class, the `getAllProducts` method. You will implement the `getAllProducts` method to return an array of `Product` objects that represents the records in the product catalog database. The method will allocate an `NSMutableArray` to hold the list of products, construct your SQL statement, execute the statement, and loop through the results, constructing a `Product` object for each row returned from the query.

You'll start the method by declaring and initializing the array that will be used to hold the products. You'll use an `NSMutableArray` because you want to be able to add `Product` objects to the array one by one as you retrieve rows from the database. The regular `NSArray` class is immutable so you cannot add items to it on-the-fly.

Here is the beginning of your method:

```
- (NSMutableArray*) getAllProducts
{
    //  The array of products that we will create
    NSMutableArray *products = [[[NSMutableArray alloc] init] autorelease];
```

DBAccess.m

You will notice that the `products` array is sent the autorelease message. This ensures that the memory allocated by creating the `products` array will eventually be freed. It is an accepted convention in Objective-C that methods that do not contain the word "copy," or start with "new" or "alloc" return autoreleased objects.

It is important that callers of the `getAllProducts` method retain the returned array. If `retain` is not called, the object will be freed and the caller will be left with a pointer to a freed object. This will certainly cause the application to crash. You handle this by storing the array returned from `getAllProducts` in a property with the `retain` attribute set. This will cause `retain` to be called when the value of the property is set.

If the concepts of memory management in Objective-C are confusing, you should read Apple's Memory Management Programming Guide for Cocoa, which can be found at `http://developer` `.apple.com/iphone/library/documentation/Cocoa/Conceptual/MemoryMgmt/MemoryMgmt` `.html`. This is an outstanding document that is beneficial for even advanced Cocoa programmers. If you haven't already read it, take a break and read it now.

The next step in implementing `getAllProducts` is to declare a `char*` variable and populate it with your SQL statement:

```
//  The SQL statement that we plan on executing against the database
    const char *sql = "SELECT product.ID,product.Name, \
        Manufacturer.name,product.details,product.price,\
        product.quantityonhand, country.country, \
        product.image FROM Product,Manufacturer, \
        Country where manufacturer.manufacturerid=product.manufacturerid \
        and product.countryoforiginid=country.countryid";
```

The following is the SQL statement in a slightly more readable form:

```
SELECT product.ID,
    product.Name,
    Manufacturer.name,
    product.details,
    product.price,
    product.quantityonhand,
    country.country,
    product.image
FROM Product,Manufacturer, Country
WHERE manufacturer.manufacturerid=product.manufacturerid
    AND product.countryoforiginid=country.countryid
```

This book assumes that the reader already knows SQL, and thus doesn't provide full details. However, I will quickly note that this SQL statement gets data out of the three tables noted in the FROM clause: Product, Manufacturer, and Country.

You can see what fields are selected from each table in the SELECT portion of the query. The form for specifying fields to select is *table.field*. So, you are selecting the Name field from the Product table, then the Name field from the Manufacturer table.

Finally, you set up the joins in the WHERE clause. You only want data from the manufacturer table where the manufacturerID is the same as the manufacturerID in the product table. Likewise, you only want data from the country table where the countryID is the same as the countryoforiginID in the product table. This allows you to display the actual manufacturer name and country name in the query and in the application, instead of just displaying a meaningless ID number.

I recommend writing your queries in an application such as SQLite Manager or at the command line. It is much easier to develop your query when you can run it and instantly see the results, especially as you get into more complex queries. Figure 2-14 shows the query being run in SQLite Manager. You can see that you get the desired results when this query is executed.

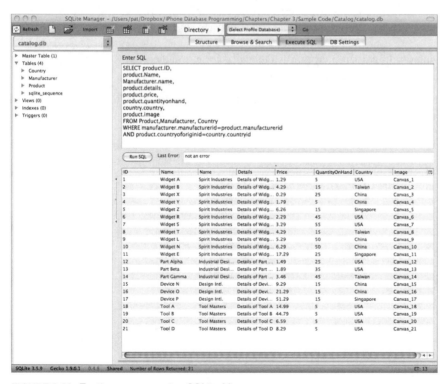

FIGURE 2-14: Testing a query using SQLite Manager

In order to run this SQL in your code, you need to create an SQLite statement object. This object will be used to execute your SQL against the database. You then prepare the SQL statement:

```
// The SQLite statement object that will hold our result set
sqlite3_stmt *statement;

// Prepare the statement to compile the SQL query into byte-code
 int sqlResult = sqlite3_prepare_v2(database, sql, -1, &statement, NULL);
```

DBAccess.m

The parameters for the `sqlite3_prepare_v2` function are a connection to the database, your SQL statement, the maximum length of your SQL or a –1 to read up to the first null terminator, the statement handle that will be used to iterate over the results, and a pointer to the first byte after the SQL statement, or NULL which you use here.

Like the other commands that you have run against SQLite in this chapter, `sqlite3_prepare_v2` returns an `int`, which will either be `SQLITE_OK` or an error code.

It should be noted that preparing the SQL statement does not actually execute the statement. The statement is not executed until you call the `sqlite3_step` function to begin retrieving rows.

If the result is `SQLITE_OK`, you step through the results one row at a time using the `sqlite3_step` function:

```
if ( sqlResult== SQLITE_OK) {
    // Step through the results - once for each row.
    while (sqlite3_step(statement) == SQLITE_ROW) {
```

For each row, allocate a `Product` object:

```
    // allocate a Product object to add to products array
    Product *product = [[Product alloc] init];
```

Now you have to retrieve the data from the row. A group of functions called the "result set" interface is used to get the field that you are interested in. The function that you use is based on the data type contained in the column that you are trying to retrieve. The following is a list of the available functions:

```
const void *sqlite3_column_blob(sqlite3_stmt*, int iCol);
int sqlite3_column_bytes(sqlite3_stmt*, int iCol);
int sqlite3_column_bytes16(sqlite3_stmt*, int iCol);
double sqlite3_column_double(sqlite3_stmt*, int iCol);
int sqlite3_column_int(sqlite3_stmt*, int iCol);
sqlite3_int64 sqlite3_column_int64(sqlite3_stmt*, int iCol);
const unsigned char *sqlite3_column_text(sqlite3_stmt*, int iCol);
const void *sqlite3_column_text16(sqlite3_stmt*, int iCol);
int sqlite3_column_type(sqlite3_stmt*, int iCol);
sqlite3_value *sqlite3_column_value(sqlite3_stmt*, int iCol);
```

The first parameter to each function is the prepared statement. The second parameter is the index in the SQL statement of the field that you are retrieving. The index is 0-based, so to get the first field in your SQL statement, the product ID, which is an int, you would use:

```
sqlite3_column_int(statement, 0);
```

To retrieve text or strings from the database, the `sqlite3_column_text` function is used. I like to create `char*` variables to hold the strings retrieved from the database. Then, I use the `?:` operator to either use the string if it is not null, or use an empty string if it is null. Here is the code to get all of the data from the database and populate your `product` object:

```
// The second parameter is the column index (0 based) in
// the result set.
char *name = (char *)sqlite3_column_text(statement, 1);
char *manufacturer = (char *)sqlite3_column_text(statement, 2);
char *details = (char *)sqlite3_column_text(statement, 3);
char *countryOfOrigin = (char *)sqlite3_column_text(statement, 6);
char *image = (char *)sqlite3_column_text(statement, 7);

//  Set all the attributes of the product
product.ID = sqlite3_column_int(statement, 0);
product.name = (name) ? [NSString stringWithUTF8String:name] : @"";
product.manufacturer = (manufacturer) ? [NSString
    stringWithUTF8String:manufacturer] : @"";
product.details = (details) ? [NSString stringWithUTF8String:details] : @"";
product.price = sqlite3_column_double(statement, 4);
product.quantity = sqlite3_column_int(statement, 5);
product.countryOfOrigin = (countryOfOrigin) ? [NSString
    stringWithUTF8String:countryOfOrigin] : @"";
product.image = (image) ? [NSString stringWithUTF8String:image] : @"";
```

Finally, you add the product to the products array, release the memory associated with the product object, and move on to the next row.

The product object must be released in order to avoid a memory leak. When an object is added to an `NSMutableArray`, it is sent the `retain` message. If you did not send it a release message here, the object would have a retain count of 2 and its memory would not be freed if it were removed from the array.

```
// Add the product to the products array
[products addObject:product];

// Release the local product object because the object is retained
// when we add it to the array
 [product release];
}
```

After you are finished looping through the result set, you call `sqlite3_finalize` to release the resources associated with the prepared statement. Then you log any errors and return your products array.

```
// finalize the statement to release its resources
       sqlite3_finalize(statement);
    }
    else {
        NSLog(@"Problem with the database:");
        NSLog(@"%d",sqlResult);
    }

    return products;

}
```

The whole database access class should look like Listing 2-1.

LISTING 2-1: DBAccess.m

```objc
//
//  DBAccess.m
//  Catalog
//
//  Created by Patrick Alessi on 12/31/09.
//  Copyright 2009 __MyCompanyName__. All rights reserved.
//

#import "DBAccess.h"


@implementation DBAccess

// Reference to the SQLite database.
sqlite3* database;


-(id) init
{
    // Call super init to invoke superclass initiation code
    if ((self = [super init]))
    {
        // set the reference to the database
        [self initializeDatabase];
    }
    return self;
}


// Open the database connection
```

continues

LISTING 2-1 *(continued)*

```
- (void)initializeDatabase {

    // Get the database from the application bundle.
    NSString *path = [[NSBundle mainBundle] pathForResource:@"catalog"
                                                    ofType:@"db"];

    // Open the database.
    if (sqlite3_open([path UTF8String], &database) == SQLITE_OK)
    {
        NSLog(@"Opening Database");
    }
    else
    {
        // Call close to properly clean up
        sqlite3_close(database);
        NSAssert1(0, @"Failed to open database: '%s'.",
                sqlite3_errmsg(database));
    }
}

-(void) closeDatabase
{
    // Close the database.
    if (sqlite3_close(database) != SQLITE_OK) {
        NSAssert1(0, @"Error: failed to close database: '%s'.",
                sqlite3_errmsg(database));
    }
}


- (NSMutableArray*) getAllProducts
{
    // The array of products that we will create
    NSMutableArray *products = [[[NSMutableArray alloc] init] autorelease];

    // The SQL statement that we plan on executing against the database
    const char *sql = "SELECT product.ID,product.Name, \
        Manufacturer.name,product.details,product.price,\
        product.quantityonhand, country.country, \
        product.image FROM Product,Manufacturer, \
        Country where manufacturer.manufacturerid=product.manufacturerid \
        and product.countryoforiginid=country.countryid";

    // The SQLite statement object that will hold our result set
    sqlite3_stmt *statement;

    // Prepare the statement to compile the SQL query into byte-code
    int sqlResult = sqlite3_prepare_v2(database, sql, -1, &statement, NULL);

    if ( sqlResult== SQLITE_OK) {
        // Step through the results - once for each row.
        while (sqlite3_step(statement) == SQLITE_ROW) {
```

```objc
    // allocate a Product object to add to products array
    Product  *product = [[Product alloc] init];

    // The second parameter is the column index (0 based) in
    // the result set.
    char *name = (char *)sqlite3_column_text(statement, 1);
    char *manufacturer = (char *)sqlite3_column_text(statement, 2);
    char *details = (char *)sqlite3_column_text(statement, 3);
    char *countryOfOrigin = (char *)sqlite3_column_text(statement, 6);
    char *image = (char *)sqlite3_column_text(statement, 7);


    // Set all the attributes of the product
    product.ID = sqlite3_column_int(statement, 0);
    product.name = (name) ? [NSString stringWithUTF8String:name] : @"";
    product.manufacturer =
        (manufacturer) ? [NSString
                            stringWithUTF8String:manufacturer] : @"";
    product.details = (details) ? [NSString
                                    stringWithUTF8String:details] : @"";
    product.price = sqlite3_column_double(statement, 4);
    product.quantity = sqlite3_column_int(statement, 5);
    product.countryOfOrigin =
    (countryOfOrigin) ? [NSString
                            stringWithUTF8String:countryOfOrigin] : @"";
    product.image = (image) ? [NSString
                                stringWithUTF8String:image] : @"";


    [products addObject:product];
    [product release];
    }

    // finalize the statement to release its resources
    sqlite3_finalize(statement);
}
else {
    NSLog(@"Problem with the database:");
    NSLog(@"%d",sqlResult);
}

return products;

}


@end
```

Parameterized Queries

Although I am not using them in this sample, it is possible and quite common to use parameterized queries.

For example, if you wanted to create a query that returned only products made in the USA, you could use the following SQL:

```
SELECT Product.name, country.country
FROM country,product
WHERE countryoforiginid=countryid and country='USA'
```

This query is perfectly fine if you always want a list of the products made in the USA. What if you wanted to decide at runtime which countries' products to display? You would need to use a parameterized query.

The first step in parameterizing this query is to replace the data that you want to parameterize with question marks (?). So your SQL will become:

```
SELECT Product.name, country.country
FROM country,product
WHERE countryoforiginid=countryid and country=?
```

After you prepare your statement with `sqlite3_prepare_v2` but before you start stepping through your results with `sqlite3_step`, you need to bind your parameters. Remember that preparing the statement does not actually execute it. The statement is not executed until you begin iterating over the result set using `sqlite3_step`.

A series of functions is used to bind parameters in a manner similar to the way that you retrieve data fields. Here are the bind functions:

```
int sqlite3_bind_blob(sqlite3_stmt*, int, const void*, int n, void(*)(void*));
int sqlite3_bind_double(sqlite3_stmt*, int, double);
int sqlite3_bind_int(sqlite3_stmt*, int, int);
int sqlite3_bind_int64(sqlite3_stmt*, int, sqlite3_int64);
int sqlite3_bind_null(sqlite3_stmt*, int);
int sqlite3_bind_text(sqlite3_stmt*, int, const char*, int n, void(*)(void*));
int sqlite3_bind_text16(sqlite3_stmt*, int, const void*, int, void(*)(void*));
int sqlite3_bind_value(sqlite3_stmt*, int, const sqlite3_value*);
int sqlite3_bind_zeroblob(sqlite3_stmt*, int, int n);
```

You need to use the bind function that corresponds with the data type that you are binding. The first parameter in each function is the prepared statement. The second is the index (1-based) of the parameter in your SQL statement. The rest of the parameters vary based on the type that you are trying to bind. Complete documentation of the bind functions is available on the SQLite web site.

In order to bind text at runtime, you use the `sqlite3_bind_text` function like this:

```
sqlite3_bind_text (statement,1,value,-1, SQLITE_TRANSIENT);
```

In the previous bind statement, `value` is the text that you would determine at runtime. In the example, that text would be "USA" but it could be changed dynamically at runtime. That is the advantage of using parameterized queries. Of course, you could just dynamically generate your SQL each time, but parameterized queries offer the performance advantage of preparing and compiling the statement once and the statement being cached for reuse.

Writing to the Database

If you modify the sample application, or create your own SQLite application that attempts to write to the database, you will have a problem. The version of the database that you are using in the sample code is located in the application bundle, but the application bundle is read-only, so attempting to write to this database will result in an error.

To be able to write to the database, you need to make an editable copy. On the iPhone, this editable copy should be placed in the documents directory. Each application on the iPhone is "sandboxed" and has access only to its own documents directory.

The following code snippet shows how to check to see if a writable database already exists, and if not, create an editable copy.

```
// Create a writable copy of the default database from the bundle
// in the application Documents directory.
- (void) createEditableDatabase {
    // Check to see if editable database already exists
    BOOL success;
    NSFileManager *fileManager = [NSFileManager defaultManager];
    NSError *error;
    NSArray *paths = NSSearchPathForDirectoriesInDomains
        (NSDocumentDirectory, NSUserDomainMask, YES);
    NSString *documentsDir = [paths objectAtIndex:0];
    NSString *writableDB = [documentsDir
        stringByAppendingPathComponent:@"ContactNotes.sqlite"];
    success = [fileManager fileExistsAtPath:writableDB];

    // The editable database already exists
    if (success) return;


    // The editable database does not exist
    // Copy the default DB to the application Documents directory.
    NSString *defaultPath = [[[NSBundle mainBundle] resourcePath]
        stringByAppendingPathComponent:@"Catalog.sqlite"];
    success = [fileManager copyItemAtPath:defaultPath
        toPath:writableDB error:&error];
    if (!success) {
        NSAssert1(0, @"Failed to create writable database file:'%@'.",
            [error localizedDescription]);
    }
}
```

You would then need to change your database access code to call this function and then refer to the editable copy of the database instead of the bundled copy.

Displaying the Catalog

Now that you have the DBAccess class done, you can get on with displaying the catalog. In the RootViewController, you will implement code to retrieve the products array from the DBAccess class and display it in the TableView.

In the header, RootViewController.h, add import statements for the Product and DBAccess classes:

```
#import "Product.h"
#import "DBAccess.h"
```

Add a property and its backing instance variable to hold your products array:

```
@interface RootViewController : UITableViewController {
    //  Instance variable to hold products array
    NSMutableArray *products;

}

@property (retain,nonatomic) NSMutableArray* products;
```

Notice that the products property is declared with the retain attribute. This means that the property setter method will call retain on the object that is passed in. You must specify the retain attribute to ensure that the products array is available for use when you need it. Recall that in the DBAccess class, you called autorelease on the array that is returned from the getAllProducts method. If you did not add the retain attribute, the products array would be released on the next pass through the application event loop. Trying to access the products property after the array is released would cause the application to crash. You avoid this by having the setter call retain on the array.

In the RootViewController.m implementation class, you need to synthesize the products property below the @implementation line:

```
@synthesize products;
```

Synthesizing a property causes the compiler to generate the setter and getter methods for the property. You can alternatively define the getter, setter, or both methods yourself. The compiler will fill in the blanks by defining either of these methods if you don't.

Continuing in the RootViewController.m implementation class, you'll add code to the viewDidLoad method to get your products array from the DBAccess class:

Available for
download on
Wrox.com

```
- (void)viewDidLoad {
    [super viewDidLoad];

    //  Get the DBAccess object;
    DBAccess *dbAccess = [[DBAccess alloc] init];

    //  Get the products array from the database
    self.products = [dbAccess getAllProducts];
```

```
    // Close the database because we are finished with it
    [dbAccess closeDatabase];

    // Release the dbAccess object to free its memory
    [dbAccess release];

}
```

RootViewController.m

Next, you have to implement your `TableView` methods. The first thing you have to do is tell the `TableView` how many rows there are by implementing the `numberOfRowsInSection` method as you did in the previous chapter. You will get the count of items to display in the `TableView` from your products array:

```
- (NSInteger)tableView:(UITableView *)tableView
    numberOfRowsInSection:(NSInteger)section {
    return [self.products count];
}
```

RootViewController.m

Finally, you have to implement `cellForRowAtIndexPath` to provide the `TableView` with the `TableViewCell` that corresponds with the row that the `TableView` is asking for. The code is similar to the example from the previous chapter. The difference is that now you get the text for the cell from the `Product` object. You look up the `Product` object using the row that the `TableView` is asking for as the index into the array. The following is the `cellForRowAtIndexPath` method:

```
// Customize the appearance of table view cells.
- (UITableViewCell *)tableView:(UITableView *)tableView
        cellForRowAtIndexPath:(NSIndexPath *)indexPath {

    static NSString *CellIdentifier = @"Cell";

    UITableViewCell *cell = [tableView
                        dequeueReusableCellWithIdentifier:CellIdentifier];
    if (cell == nil) {
        cell = [[[UITableViewCell alloc]
                initWithStyle:UITableViewCellStyleDefault
                reuseIdentifier:CellIdentifier] autorelease];
    }

    // Configure the cell.
    // Get the Product object
    Product* product = [self.products objectAtIndex:[indexPath row]];

    cell.textLabel.text = product.name;
    return cell;
}
```

RootViewController.m

To set the Catalog text at the top in the Navigation Controller, double-click `MainWindow.xib`. Then, click on the navigation item in Interface Builder and set the `Title` property to `Catalog`.

You should now be able to build and run the application. When you run it, you should see the product catalog as in Figure 2-15. When you touch items in the catalog, nothing happens, but the application should display the details of the product that is touched. To accomplish this, the `TableView` function `didSelectRowAtIndexPath` needs to be implemented. But before you do that, you need to build the view that you will display when a user taps a product in the table.

Viewing Product Details

When a user taps a product in the table, the application should navigate to a product detail screen. Because this screen will be used with the `NavigationController`, it needs to be implemented using a `UIViewController`. In Xcode, add a new `UIViewController` subclass to your project called `ProductDetailViewController`. Make sure that you select the option "With XIB for user interface." This creates your class along with a NIB file for designing the user interface for the class.

FIGURE 2-15: Running the Catalog application

In the `ProductDetailViewController.h` header, add Interface Builder outlets for the data that you want to display. You need to add an outlet for each label control like this:

```
IBOutlet UILabel* nameLabel;
IBOutlet UILabel* manufacturerLabel;
IBOutlet UILabel* detailsLabel;
IBOutlet UILabel* priceLabel;
IBOutlet UILabel* quantityLabel;
IBOutlet UILabel* countryLabel;
```

You will use the outlets in the code to link to the UI widgets created in Interface Builder. The use of Interface Builder is beyond the scope of this book. There are several good books on building user interfaces for the iPhone including *iPhone SDK Programming: Developing Mobile Applications for Apple iPhone and iPod Touch* by Maher Ali (Wiley, 2009).

You will transfer the data about the product that the user selected to the detail view by passing a `Product` object from the `RootViewController` to the `ProductDetailViewController`. Because you will be referencing the `Product` object in your code, you need to add an import statement for the `Product` class to the `ProductDetailViewController` header. You also need to add the method signature for the `setLabelsForProduct` method that will be used to receive the `Product` object from the `RootViewController` and set the text of the labels. The complete header should look like this:

```
#import <UIKit/UIKit.h>
#import "Product.h"

@interface ProductDetailViewController : UIViewController {

    IBOutlet UILabel* nameLabel;
    IBOutlet UILabel* manufacturerLabel;
    IBOutlet UILabel* detailsLabel;
    IBOutlet UILabel* priceLabel;
    IBOutlet UILabel* quantityLabel;
    IBOutlet UILabel* countryLabel;

}
-(void) setLabelsForProduct: (Product*) theProduct;

@end
```

ProductDetailViewController.h

Now, open up the `ProductDetailViewController.xib` file in Interface Builder. Here you will add a series of `UILabels` to the interface as you designed in the mockup. Your interface should look something like Figure 2-16.

Next, you'll need to hook up your labels in Interface Builder to the outlets that you created in the `ProductDetailViewController.h` header file. Make sure that you save the header file before you try to hook up the outlets or the outlets that you created in the header will not be available in Interface Builder.

To hook up the outlets, bring up the `ProductDetailViewController.xib` file in Interface Builder. Select File's Owner in the Document window. Press Cmd+2 to bring up the Connections Inspector. In this window, you can see all of the class's outlets and their connections. Click and drag from the open circle on the right side of the outlet name to the control to which that outlet should be connected in the user interface. You should see the name of the control displayed on the right side of the Connections Inspector as in Figure 2-17.

FIGURE 2-16: Product detail view

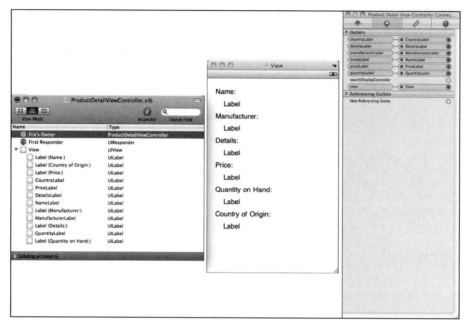

FIGURE 2-17: Building the detail view with Interface Builder

In `ProductDetailViewController.m,` implement `setLabelsForProduct` to set the text in the labels:

Available for
download on
Wrox.com

```
-(void) setLabelsForProduct: (Product*) theProduct
{
    //  Set the text of the labels to the values passed in the Product object
    [nameLabel setText:theProduct.name];
    [manufacturerLabel setText:theProduct.manufacturer];
    [detailsLabel setText:theProduct.details];
    [priceLabel setText:[NSString stringWithFormat:@"%.2f",theProduct.price]];
    [quantityLabel setText:[NSString stringWithFormat:@"%d",
                            theProduct.quantity]];
    [countryLabel setText:theProduct.countryOfOrigin];

}
```

ProductDetailViewController.m

This code accepts a `Product` object and uses its properties to set the text that is displayed in the interface labels.

In order to be able to navigate to your new screen, you need to add code to the `RootViewController` to display this screen when a user selects a product.

In the `RootViewController` header, you must add an import for `ProductDetailViewController` because you will create an instance of this class to push onto the navigation stack:

```
#import "ProductDetailViewController.h"
```

In the `RootViewController` implementation, add code to the `tableView:didSelectRowAtIndexPath:` method to instantiate a `ProductDetailViewController`, populate the data, and push it onto the navigation stack:

Available for
download on
Wrox.com

```
- (void)tableView:(UITableView *)tableView
    didSelectRowAtIndexPath:(NSIndexPath *)indexPath {

    // Get the product that corresponds with the touched cell
    Product* product = [self.products objectAtIndex:[indexPath row]];

    //   Initialize the detail view controller from the NIB
    ProductDetailViewController *productDetailViewController =
        [[ProductDetailViewController alloc]
            initWithNibName:@"ProductDetailViewController" bundle:nil];

    //   Set the title of the detail page
    [productDetailViewController setTitle:product.name];

    //   Push the detail controller on to the stack
    [self.navigationController
        pushViewController:productDetailViewController animated:YES];

    //   Populate the details
    [productDetailViewController setLabelsForProduct:product];

    //   release the view controller becuase it is retained by the
    //   Navigation Controller
    [productDetailViewController release];
}
```

ProductDetailViewController.m

That's all there is to it. Now you should be able to build and run your application. Try tapping on an item in the catalog. The application should take you to the detail page for that item. Tapping the Catalog button in the navigation bar should take you back to the catalog. Tapping another row in the TableView should take you to the data for that item.

You now have a fully functioning catalog application! I know that it doesn't look very nice, but you'll work on that in the next chapter where you dive into customizing the `UITableView`.

MOVING FORWARD

Now that you have a functioning application, feel free to play with it as much as you like! Spruce up the interface or add additional fields to the database tables and `Product` class.

There are a lot of good books on the SQL language, so if you were confused by any of the SQL used in this chapter, it may be a good idea to pick up a copy of *SQL For Dummies* by Allen Taylor.

Another resource that you should be aware of is the SQLite web site at `http://www.sqlite.org/`. There you will find extensive documentation of the database and the C language APIs that are used to access the database.

Although you've learned how to get your data out of SQLite and into an iPhone application, the catalog doesn't look that great. In the next chapter, you will learn how to display your data with more flair by customizing the TableView.

3

Displaying Your Data: The UITableView

WHAT'S IN THIS CHAPTER?

➤ Customizing the TableView by creating your own TableView cells

➤ Searching and filtering your result sets

➤ Adding important UI elements to your tables such as indexes and section headers

➤ Avoiding and troubleshooting performance issues with your TableViews

The focus of the book thus far has been on how to get your data on to the iPhone and how to access that data on the device. This chapter focuses on how you can enhance the display of your data by customizing the `TableViewCell`. It also examines how to make your data easier to use by adding an index, section headings, and search functionality to the `UITableView`. In the next several sections, you take a closer look at how to use the `TableView` to display your data in ways that make it more useful to your target audience.

CUSTOMIZING THE TABLEVIEW

You begin by taking a look at the default `TableView` styles that are available in the iPhone SDK. Then, you learn the technique of adding subviews to the content view of a `TableViewCell`. In the event that neither of these solutions meets your needs for customizing the display of your data, you will examine how to design your own `TableViewCell` from scratch using Interface Builder. If you had trouble with IB in the previous chapter, now is a good time to review Apple's documentation on using IB, which you can find at `http://developer.apple.com/`.

TableViewCell Styles

Several pre-canned styles are available to use for a `TableViewCell`:

➤ `UITableViewCellStyleDefault`: This style displays a cell with a black, left-aligned text label with an optional image view.

➤ `UITableViewCellStyleValue1`: This style displays a cell with a black, left-aligned text label on the left side of the cell and an additional blue text, right-aligned label on the right side.

➤ `UITableViewCellStyleValue2`: This style displays a cell with a blue text, right-aligned label on the left side of the cell and an additional black, left-aligned text label on the right side of the cell.

➤ `UITableViewCellStyleSubtitle`: This style displays a cell with a black, left-aligned text label across the top with a smaller, gray text label below.

In each style, the larger of the text labels is defined by the `textLabel` property and the smaller is defined by the `detailTextLabel` property.

Let's change the Catalog application from the last chapter to see what each of these styles looks like. You will change the application to use the name of the part manufacturer as the subtitle.

In the `RootViewController.m` implementation file, add a line to the `tableView:cellForRowAt IndexPath:` method that sets the cell's `detailTextLabel` text property to the product's manufacturer:

Available for
download on
Wrox.com

```
- (UITableViewCell *)tableView:(UITableView *)tableView
      cellForRowAtIndexPath:(NSIndexPath *)indexPath {

    static NSString *CellIdentifier = @"Cell";

    UITableViewCell *cell = [tableView
                        dequeueReusableCellWithIdentifier:CellIdentifier];
    if (cell == nil) {
        cell = [[[UITableViewCell alloc]
                initWithStyle:UITableViewCellStyleDefault
                reuseIdentifier:CellIdentifier] autorelease];
    }

    // Configure the cell.
    // Get the Product object
    Product* product = [self.products objectAtIndex:[indexPath row]];

    cell.textLabel.text = product.name;
    cell.detailTextLabel.text = product.manufacturer;
    return cell;
}
```

RootViewController.m

When you run the application, you will see something like Figure 3-1 (a). Nothing has changed. You may be wondering what happened to the subtitle. When you initialized the cell, the style was set to `UITableViewCellStyleDefault`. In this style, only the cell's `textLabel` is displayed, along with an optional image, which you will add in a moment.

(a) UITableViewCellStyleDefault

(b) UITableViewCellStyleValue1

(c) UITableViewCellStyleValue2

(d) UITableViewCellStyleSubtitle

FIGURE 3-1: TableView Cell Styles

On the line where you initialize the cell, change the code to use UITableViewCellStyleValue1:

```
cell = [[[UITableViewCell alloc] initWithStyle:UITableViewCellStyleValue1
                          reuseIdentifier:CellIdentifier] autorelease];
```

The table now displays the part name and the manufacturer as shown in Figure 3-1 (b).

Changing the default to UITableViewCellStyleValue2 results in a table that looks like Figure 3-1 (c).

Changing the default to UITableViewCellStyleSubtitle results in a table that looks like Figure 3-1 (d).

Now, you add some images to the catalog items. You can obtain the images used in the example from the book's web site. Add the images to your application by right-clicking on the Resources folder in the left-hand pane of Xcode and select Add Existing Files. Next, you should add code to the tableView:cellForRowAtIndexPath: method that will look for the image in the application bundle using the image name from the database.

```
NSString *filePath = [[NSBundle mainBundle] pathForResource:product.image
                                             ofType:@"png"];
UIImage *image = [UIImage imageWithContentsOfFile:filePath];
cell.imageView.image = image;
```

RootViewController.m

Finally, you can add an *accessory* to each cell. The accessory is the little arrow on the right side of a cell that tells the user that selecting the cell will take him or her to another screen. To add the accessory, you need to add a line of code to the tableView:cellForRowAtIndexPath: method to configure the cell's accessoryType:

```
cell.accessoryType = UITableViewCellAccessoryDisclosureIndicator;
```

There are a few different accessory types that you can use:

➤ UITableViewCellAccessoryDisclosureIndicator is the gray arrow that you have added. This control doesn't respond to touches and is used to indicate that selecting this cell will bring the user to a detail screen or the next screen in a navigation hierarchy.

➤ UITableViewCellAccessoryDetailDisclosureButton presents a blue button with an arrow in it. This control can respond to touches and is used to indicate that selecting it will lead to configurable properties.

➤ UITableViewCellAccessoryCheckmark displays a checkmark on the right side of the cell. This control doesn't respond to touches.

Figure 3-2 shows how a catalog looks after adding the images and a disclosure indicator accessory.

FIGURE 3-2: Catalog application with images

The final code for the `cellForRowAtIndexPath:` method should look like this:

```
- (UITableViewCell *)tableView:(UITableView *)tableView
    cellForRowAtIndexPath:(NSIndexPath *)indexPath {

    static NSString *CellIdentifier = @"Cell";

    UITableViewCell *cell = [tableView
                            dequeueReusableCellWithIdentifier:CellIdentifier];
    if (cell == nil) {
        cell = [[[UITableViewCell alloc]
                initWithStyle:UITableViewCellStyleSubtitle
                reuseIdentifier:CellIdentifier] autorelease];
    }

    // Configure the cell.
    // Get the Product object
    Product* product = [self.products objectAtIndex:[indexPath row]];

    cell.textLabel.text = product.name;
    cell.detailTextLabel.text = product.manufacturer;
    cell.accessoryType = UITableViewCellAccessoryDisclosureIndicator;

    NSString *filePath = [[NSBundle mainBundle] pathForResource:product.image
                                                ofType:@"png"];
    UIImage *image = [UIImage imageWithContentsOfFile:filePath];
    cell.imageView.image = image;

    return cell;
}
```

RootViewController.m

There are also other properties that you can use to provide additional customization for the `TableViewCell`. You can use the `backgroundView` property to assign another view as the background of a cell, set the `selectionStyle` to control how a cell looks when selected, and set the indentation of text with the `indentationLevel` property.

You can further customize a cell by modifying properties that are exposed in the `UIView` class because `UITableViewCell` is a subclass of `UIView`. For instance, you can set the background color of a cell by using the `backgroundColor` property of the `UIView`.

Adding Subviews to the contentView

If none of the existing `TableViewCell` styles work for your application, it is possible to customize the `TableViewCell` by adding subviews to the `contentView` of the `TableViewCell`. This approach is effective when the OS can perform the cell layout using autoresizing and the default behavior of the cell is appropriate for your application. If you need full control of how the cell is drawn or wish to change the behavior of the cell from the default, you will need to create a custom subclass of `UITableViewCell`. You will learn how to create this subclass in the next section.

Because `UITableViewCell` inherits from `UIView`, a cell has a content view, accessible through the `contentView` property. You can add your own subviews to this `contentView` and lay them out using the superview's coordinate system either programmatically or with IB. When implementing customization this way, you should make sure to avoid making your subviews transparent. Transparency causes compositing to occur, which is quite time-consuming. Compositing takes time and will result in degraded TableView scrolling speed. You look at this in more detail at the end of this chapter in the section on performance.

Suppose that your customer is not happy with the table in the current application. He wants to see all of the existing information plus an indication of where the product was made, and the price. You could use a flag icon to represent the country of origin on the right-hand side and add a label to display the price, as shown in the mockup in Figure 3-3. It's not a beautiful design, but it's what the customer wants.

It is impossible to achieve this layout using any of the default cell styles. To build this customized cell, you will hand-code the layout of the cell.

FIGURE 3-3: Catalog mockup with flags

Because you will be modifying the cell you display in the table, you will be working in the `RootViewController.m` file and modifying the `tableView: cellForRowAtIndexPath:` method.

First, you need variables for the two images and three labels that you plan to display. At the beginning of the method, add the declarations for these items:

```
UILabel *nameLabel, *manufacturerLabel, *priceLabel;
UIImageView *productImage, *flagImage;
```

Next, declare an `NSString` for the `CellIdentifier` and try to dequeue a cell using that identifier:

```
static NSString *CellIdentifier = @"Cell";

UITableViewCell *cell = [tableView
                    dequeueReusableCellWithIdentifier:CellIdentifier];
```

You have seen this code before in previous examples, but until now I haven't explained how it works. Creating `TableViewCells` is a relatively time-consuming process. In addition, memory is scarce on an embedded device such as the iPhone or iPad. It is inefficient to create all of the cells and have them hanging around using memory while off-screen and not viewable. Conversely, because it takes time to create cells, it would be a performance hit to create them dynamically each time they were needed.

In order to solve these problems, the engineers at Apple came up with a very good solution. They gave the `TableView` a queue of `TableViewCells` from which you can get a reference to an existing cell object. When you need a cell, you can try and pull one from the queue. If you get one, you can reuse it; if you don't, you have to create a new cell to use that will eventually be added to the queue. The framework handles the control logic by determining which cells are queued and available, and which are currently being used.

All you need to do as a developer is try to dequeue a cell and check the return. If the return is `nil`, you have to create the cell. If it is not, you have a valid cell that you can use. The type of cell that is dequeued is based on the cell identifer that you pass in when trying to dequeue. Remember that you set this identifier when you initialized a new cell with the `reuseIdentifier`.

The preceding code attempts to dequeue a cell using the `reuseIdentifier`, `Cell`. The following `if (cell==nil)` block either creates a new cell with the `Cell reuseIdentifier` or it goes on to work with the cell that was dequeued.

If the cell needs to be created, the following code is executed:

```
if (cell == nil) {
    // Create a new cell object since the dequeue failed
    cell = [[[UITableViewCell alloc] initWithStyle:UITableViewCellStyleSubtitle
                                    reuseIdentifier:CellIdentifier] autorelease];

    // Set the accessoryType to the grey disclosure arrow
    cell.accessoryType = UITableViewCellAccessoryDisclosureIndicator;

    // Configure the name label
    nameLabel = [[[UILabel alloc]
                    initWithFrame:CGRectMake(45.0, 0.0, 120.0, 25.0)]
                    autorelease];
    nameLabel.tag = NAMELABEL_TAG;

    // Add the label to the cell's content view
    [cell.contentView addSubview:nameLabel];

    // Configure the manufacturer label
    manufacturerLabel = [[[UILabel alloc]
                            initWithFrame:CGRectMake(45.0, 25.0, 120.0, 15.0)]
                            autorelease];
    manufacturerLabel.tag = MANUFACTURERLABEL_TAG;
    manufacturerLabel.font = [UIFont systemFontOfSize:12.0];
    manufacturerLabel.textColor = [UIColor darkGrayColor];

    // Add the label to the cell's content view
    [cell.contentView addSubview:manufacturerLabel];

    // Configure the price label
    priceLabel = [[[UILabel alloc]
                    initWithFrame:CGRectMake(200.0, 10.0, 60.0, 25.0)]
                    autorelease];
    priceLabel.tag = PRICELABEL_TAG;

    // Add the label to the cell's content view
    [cell.contentView addSubview:priceLabel];

    // Configure the product Image
    productImage = [[[UIImageView alloc]
                        initWithFrame:CGRectMake(0.0, 0.0, 40.0, 40.0)]
                        autorelease];
    productImage.tag = PRODUCTIMAGE_TAG;

    // Add the Image to the cell's content view
```

```
        [cell.contentView addSubview:productImage];

        // Configure the flag Image
        flagImage = [[[UIImageView alloc]
                    initWithFrame:CGRectMake(260.0, 10.0, 20.0, 20.0)]
                    autorelease];
        flagImage.tag = FLAGIMAGE_TAG;

        // Add the Image to the cell's content view
        [cell.contentView addSubview:flagImage];
    }
```

RootViewController.m

The first line allocates a new cell and initializes it with the `Cell reuseIdentifier`. You have to do this because `cell==nil` indicates that no existing cells are available for reuse.

Each block thereafter is similar. You first create the object to be added to the cell, either a `UILabel` or `UIImage`. Then, you configure it with the attributes that you want such as fonts and text colors. You assign a tag to the object that you can use to get the instance of the label or image if you are reusing an existing cell. Finally, you add the control to the `contentView` of the cell.

The tag values for each control must be integers and are commonly defined using `#define` statements. Put the following `#define` statements before the `tableView:cellForRowAtIndexPath:` method definition:

```
#define NAMELABEL_TAG 1
#define MANUFACTURERLABEL_TAG 2
#define PRICELABEL_TAG 3
#define PRODUCTIMAGE_TAG 4
#define FLAGIMAGE_TAG 5
```

RootViewController.m

The position of each UI element is set in the `initWithFrame` method call. The method takes a `CGRect` struct that you create using the `CGRectMake` function. This function returns a `CGRect` struct with the `x`, `y`, `width`, and `height` values set.

Next, code the `else` clause that gets called if you successfully dequeue a reusable cell:

```
    else {
        nameLabel = (UILabel *)[cell.contentView
                            viewWithTag:NAMELABEL_TAG];
        manufacturerLabel = (UILabel *)[cell.contentView
                                viewWithTag:MANUFACTURERLABEL_TAG];
        priceLabel = (UILabel *)[cell.contentView
                            viewWithTag:PRICELABEL_TAG];
        productImage = (UIImageView *)[cell.contentView
                                viewWithTag:PRODUCTIMAGE_TAG];
        flagImage = (UIImageView *)[cell.contentView
                                viewWithTag:FLAGIMAGE_TAG];
    }
```

RootViewController.m

You can now see how you use tags. The `viewWithTag` function of the `contentView` returns a pointer to the UI object that was defined with the specified tag. So, when you create a new cell, you define the UI objects with those tags. When you dequeue a reusable cell, the tags are used to get pointers back to those UI objects. You need these pointers to be able to set the text and images used in the UI objects in the final section of the method:

Available for download on Wrox.com

```
// Configure the cell.
// Get the Product object
Product* product = [self.products objectAtIndex:[indexPath row]];

nameLabel.text = product.name;
manufacturerLabel.text = product.manufacturer;
priceLabel.text = [[NSNumber numberWithFloat: product.price] stringValue];

NSString *filePath = [[NSBundle mainBundle] pathForResource:product.image
                                                     ofType:@"png"];
UIImage *image = [UIImage imageWithContentsOfFile:filePath];
productImage.image = image;

filePath = [[NSBundle mainBundle] pathForResource:product.countryOfOrigin
                                           ofType:@"png"];
image = [UIImage imageWithContentsOfFile:filePath];
flagImage.image = image;

return cell;
```

RootViewController.m

In this final section, you get an instance of the `Product` object for the row that you have been asked to display. Then, you use the `product` object to set the text in the labels and the images in the `UIImage` objects. To finish the method off, you return the cell object.

If you add the flag images to the project's resources folder, you should be able to build and run your application. The catalog should look like the mockup shown in Figure 3-3. You can see the running application in Figure 3-4.

Now that you know how to add subviews to the `contentView` for a `TableViewCell`, you have opened up a whole new world of customization of the `TableViewCell`. You can add any class that inherits from `UIView` to a cell. Now would be a good time to take some time to explore all of the widgets that are available to you and to think about how you could use them in `TableViews` to develop great new interfaces.

FIGURE 3-4: Running catalog application

Subclassing UITableViewCell

If you need full control of how the cell is drawn or wish to change the behavior of the cell from the default, you will want to create a custom subclass of `UITableViewCell`. It is also possible to eke out some additional performance, particularly when dealing with problems with table scrolling, by subclassing the `UITableViewCell`.

There are a couple of ways to implement the subclass. One is to implement it just as you did in the previous section by adding subviews to the contentView. This is a good solution when there are only three or four subviews. If you need to use more than four subviews, scrolling performance could be poor.

If you need to use more than four subviews to implement your cell, or if the scrolling performance of your TableView is poor, it is best to manually draw the contents of the cell. This is done in a subview of the contentView by creating a custom view class and implementing its drawRect: method.

There are a couple of issues with the approach of implementing drawRect. First, performance will suffer if you need to reorder controls due to the cell going into editing mode. Custom drawing during animation, which happens when transitioning into editing mode or reordering cells, is not recommended. Second, if you need the controls that are embedded in the cell to respond to user actions, you cannot use this method. You could not use this method if, for example, you had some buttons embedded in the cell and needed to take different action based on which button was pressed.

In the example, you will be drawing text and images in the view, so implementing drawRect is a viable option. The cell will look like it contains image and label controls, but will in fact contain only a single view with all of the UI controls drawn in. Therefore, the individual controls are not able to respond to touches.

Because the TableViewCell will have more than four controls, is not editable and doesn't have sub controls that need to respond to touches, you will implement the cell using drawRect. You will find that most, if not all, of the tables that you create to display data will fall into this category, making this a valuable technique to learn.

Getting Started

To work along with this example, download a copy of the original catalog project from the book's web site. You will use that as the starting point to build the custom subclass version of the application.

In the project, you will first add a new Objective-C class. In the Add class dialog, select subclass of UITableViewCell from the drop-down in the center of the dialog box. Call the new class CatalogTableViewCell. This will be your custom subclass of the TableViewCell.

In the header for CatalogTableViewCell, add an #import statement to import the Product.h header:

```
#import "Product.h"
```

The subclass will implement a method that sets the Product to be used to display the cell.

Add a setProduct method that users will call to set the Product to be used for the cell:

```
- (void)setProduct:(Product *)theProduct;
```

Create a new Objective-C class that is a subclass of UIView, called CatalogProductView. This will be the custom view that is used by your cell subclass to draw the text and images that you will display. This view will be the only subview added to the cell.

In the `CatalogProductView` header, add an `import` statement and instance variable for the `Product` object. Also, add a function `setProduct`. The cell uses this function to pass the product along to the view. The view will then use the product to get the data used to draw in the view. The `CatalogProductView` header should look like this:

```
#import <UIKit/UIKit.h>
#import "Product.h"

@interface CatalogProductView : UIView {
    Product* theProduct;
}

- (void)setProduct:(Product *)inputProduct;

@end
```

CatalogProductView.h

Switch back to the `CatalogTableViewCell` header and add a reference, instance variable, and property for your custom view. The `CatalogTableViewCell` header should look like this:

```
#import <UIKit/UIKit.h>
#import "Product.h"
#import "CatalogProductView.h"

@interface CatalogTableViewCell : UITableViewCell {
    CatalogProductView* catalogProductView;
}

@property (nonatomic,retain) CatalogProductView* catalogProductView;

- (void)setProduct:(Product *)theProduct;

@end
```

CatalogTableViewCell.h

In the `CatalogTableViewCell` implementation file, below the `@implementation` line, add a line to synthesize the `catalogProductView` property:

```
@synthesize catalogProductView;
```

Continuing in the `CatalogTableViewCell` implementation, you'll add code to `initWithStyle:reuseIdentifier:` to initialize the custom view to the size of the container and add the subview to the cell's content view:

```
- (id)initWithStyle:(UITableViewCellStyle)style
reuseIdentifier:(NSString *)reuseIdentifier {
    if (self = [super initWithStyle:style reuseIdentifier:reuseIdentifier]) {

        // Create a frame that matches the size of the custom cell
```

```
            CGRect viewFrame = CGRectMake(0.0, 0.0,
                                          self.contentView.bounds.size.width,
                                          self.contentView.bounds.size.height);

            // Allocate and initialize the custom view with the dimenstions
            // of the custom cell
            catalogProductView = [[CatalogProductView alloc]
                                 initWithFrame:viewFrame];

            // Add our custom view to the cell
            [self.contentView addSubview:catalogProductView];

        }
        return self;
    }
```

CatalogTableViewCell.m

You will now implement the `setProduct:` method. All it will do is call the view's `setProduct` method:

```
    - (void)setProduct:(Product *)theProduct
    {
        [catalogProductView setProduct:theProduct];
    }
```

CatalogTableViewCell.m

Now, let's get back to implementing the `CatalogProductView`. First, you need to implement the `initWithFrame:` method to initialize the view:

```
    - (id)initWithFrame:(CGRect)frame {
        if (self = [super initWithFrame:frame]) {
            // Initialization code
            self.opaque = YES;
            self.backgroundColor = [UIColor whiteColor];

        }
        return self;
    }
```

CatalogProductView.m

Here, you set the view to be opaque because there is a severe performance hit for using transparent views. If at all possible, always use opaque views when working with table cells. The next line sets the background color of the view to white.

Next, you implement the method `setProduct` that is called from the custom cell:

```
- (void)setProduct:(Product *)inputProduct
{
    // If a different product is passed in...
    if (theProduct != inputProduct)
    {
        // Clean up the old product
        [theProduct release];
        theProduct = inputProduct;

        // Hang on to the new product
        [theProduct retain];
    }

    // Mark the view to be redrawn
    [self setNeedsDisplay];
}
```

CatalogProductView.m

This method does a couple of things. First, it sets the product to be displayed, and then it marks the view to be redrawn. You should never directly call the `drawRect` method to redraw a view. The proper way to trigger a redraw is to tell the framework that a view needs to be redrawn. The framework will then call `drawRect` for you when it is time to redraw.

Implementing drawRect:

Now you get to the real meat of this example, drawing the view. This is done in the `drawRect` function and is relatively straightforward:

```
- (void)drawRect:(CGRect)rect {
    // Drawing code

    // Draw the product text
    [theProduct.name drawAtPoint:CGPointMake(45.0,0.0)
                        forWidth:120
                        withFont:[UIFont systemFontOfSize:18.0]
                     minFontSize:12.0
                   actualFontSize:NULL
                    lineBreakMode:UILineBreakModeTailTruncation
              baselineAdjustment:UIBaselineAdjustmentAlignBaselines];

    // Set to draw in dark gray
    [[UIColor darkGrayColor] set];

    // Draw the manufacturer label
    [theProduct.manufacturer drawAtPoint:CGPointMake(45.0,25.0)
                                forWidth:120
                                withFont:[UIFont systemFontOfSize:12.0]
                             minFontSize:12.0
                           actualFontSize:NULL
```

```
                    lineBreakMode:UILineBreakModeTailTruncation
           baselineAdjustment:UIBaselineAdjustmentAlignBaselines];

    // Set to draw in black
    [[UIColor blackColor] set];

    // Draw the price label
    [[[NSNumber numberWithFloat: theProduct.price] stringValue]
     drawAtPoint:CGPointMake(200.0,10.0)
     forWidth:60
     withFont:[UIFont systemFontOfSize:16.0]
     minFontSize:10.0
     actualFontSize:NULL
     lineBreakMode:UILineBreakModeTailTruncation
     baselineAdjustment:UIBaselineAdjustmentAlignBaselines];

    // Draw the images
    NSString *filePath = [[NSBundle mainBundle]
                      pathForResource:theProduct.image ofType:@"png"];
    UIImage *image = [UIImage imageWithContentsOfFile:filePath];
    [image drawInRect:CGRectMake(0.0, 0.0, 40.0, 40.0)];

    filePath = [[NSBundle mainBundle]
             pathForResource:theProduct.countryOfOrigin ofType:@"png"];
    image = [UIImage imageWithContentsOfFile:filePath];
    [image drawInRect:CGRectMake(260.0, 10.0, 20.0, 20.0)];
}
```

CatalogProductView.m

Basically, you render each string using the drawAtPoint:forWidth:withFont:minFontSize: actualFontSize:lineBreakMode:baselineAdjustment: method. Boy, that's a mouthful! This function accepts a series of parameters and renders the string to the current drawing context using those parameters.

So, for the product name, you draw it at the point (45,0) with a width of 120 pixels using the system font with a size of 18. You force a minimum font size of 12 because the renderer will shrink the text to fit within the width specified. You won't specify an actual font size because you specified that in the withFont parameter. The lineBreakMode sets how the lines will be broken for multiline text. Here, you just truncate the tail, meaning that the renderer will just show ". . ." if the text size is reduced to 12 and still cannot fit in the 120 pixels that you've allotted. Finally, the baselineAdjustment specifies how to vertically align the text.

Now that you've drawn the product name, you set the drawing color to dark gray to draw the manufacturer name. The next drawAtPoint: call does just that.

Next, you set the color back to black and draw the price string. Notice that you need to get a string representation of the floating-point price field. You do that by using the stringValue method of the NSNumber class.

Finally, you obtain the product image and the flag image just as you did in the previous example. Then you render the images using the `drawInRect:` method of the `UIImage` class.

Finishing Up

Now that you've got the new cell subclass and custom view implemented, it's time to put them to use. In the `RootViewController` header, add a `#include` for the custom cell:

```
#import "CatalogTableViewCell.h"
```

In the `RootViewController` implementation, change the `tableView:cellForRowAtIndexPath:` method to use the new cell control:

```
- (UITableViewCell *)tableView:(UITableView *)tableView
    cellForRowAtIndexPath:(NSIndexPath *)indexPath {

    static NSString *CellIdentifier = @"Cell";

    CatalogTableViewCell *cell = (CatalogTableViewCell *)
        [tableView dequeueReusableCellWithIdentifier:CellIdentifier];
    if (cell == nil) {
        cell = [[[CatalogTableViewCell alloc]
                initWithStyle:UITableViewCellStyleDefault
                reuseIdentifier:CellIdentifier] autorelease];
    }

    // Configure the cell.
    cell.accessoryType = UITableViewCellAccessoryDisclosureIndicator;

    // Get the Product object
    Product* product = [self.products objectAtIndex:[indexPath row]];

    // Set the product to be used to draw the cell
    [cell setProduct:product];

    return cell;
}
```

RootViewController.m

In this method, you replace the `UITableViewCell` with the new `CatalogTableViewCell`. When you try to dequeue the reusable cell, you must cast the return to a `CatalogTableViewCell*` because `dequeueReusableCellWithIdentifier:` returns a `UITableViewCell*`. If you are unsuccessful with the dequeue, you create a new `CatalogTableViewCell` just as you did with the `UITableViewCell`. Then, just as in the previous example, you set the accessory type and get the `Product` object that you want to display. Finally, you set the `product` in the custom cell object to be displayed and return the `cell` object.

Now all you have to do is add the flag images to the resources folder of your project, build, and run. You should get something that looks just like the previous example and Figure 3-4.

IMPLEMENTING SECTIONS AND AN INDEX

Now that you have the ability to create fantastic table cells, you need a better way to organize them. In this section, you learn to partition your data into sections, display them with section headers, and provide the user the ability to navigate them using an index.

If you have ever used the Contacts application on the iPhone, you should be familiar with section headers and the index. In Contacts, each letter of the alphabet is represented as a section header, the gray bar with the letter. Every contact whose name starts with that letter is grouped under the section header. The index on the right hand side of the screen can be used to quickly navigate to a section by tapping on the letter in the index that corresponds to the section.

You will be adding section headers and an index to the catalog application. When you are finished, your catalog application should look like Figure 3-5.

The data that you use to populate your indexed table needs to be organized such that you can easily build the sections. That is, the data should be an array of arrays where each inner array represents a section of the table. The scheme that you will use in the catalog application is shown in Figure 3-6.

These section arrays are then ordered in the outer array based on criteria that you provide. Typically, this ordering is alphabetical but you can customize it in any way that you wish.

You could take care of sorting and organizing the table data yourself, but there is a helper class in the iPhone SDK framework that has been specifically designed to help you with this task: `UILocalizedIndexedCollation`.

The `UILocalizedIndexedCollation` class is a helper class that assists with organizing, sorting, and localizing your table view data. The table view datasource can then use the collation object to obtain the section and index titles.

You will implement the indexed table using the `UILocalizedIndexedCollation` class. If you use this class, the data model object that you want to display in the table needs to have a method

FIGURE 3-5: Catalog application with sections and index

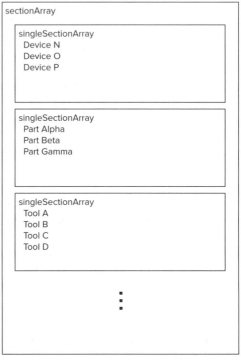

FIGURE 3-6: Data scheme for sectioned tables

or property that the `UILocalizedIndexedCollation` can call when creating its arrays. It is also helpful for your data model class to have a property that maintains the index of the object in the section array. Because the product model class already has a name property, you can use that to define the sections. You will need to add a property to hold the section number. Add the section instance variable and property to the `Product.h` header like this:

```objc
@interface Product : NSObject {
    int ID;
    NSString* name;
    NSString* manufacturer;
    NSString* details;
    float price;
    int quantity;
    NSString* countryOfOrigin;
    NSString* image;
    NSInteger section;
}
@property (nonatomic) int ID;
@property (retain, nonatomic) NSString *name;
@property (retain, nonatomic) NSString *manufacturer;
@property (retain, nonatomic) NSString *details;
@property (nonatomic) float price;
@property (nonatomic) int quantity;
@property (retain, nonatomic) NSString *countryOfOrigin;
@property (retain, nonatomic) NSString *image;
@property NSInteger section;
```

Product.h

Add the `synthesize` statement to the implementation:

```objc
@implementation Product
@synthesize ID;
@synthesize name;
@synthesize manufacturer;
@synthesize details;
@synthesize price;
@synthesize quantity;
@synthesize countryOfOrigin;
@synthesize image;
@synthesize section;
```

Product.m

The next thing that you need to do is load all of the data from your datasource into your model objects. In the case of the catalog application, you are already doing that in the `getAllProducts` method of the `DBAccess` class. If you recall, that method queries the SQLite database, creates a `Product` object for each row that is returned, and adds each `Product` object to an array.

You will use this array along with the `UILocalizedIndexedCollation` object to create the sections. To create the necessary data arrays, you will have to make some changes to the `viewDidLoad` method of the `RootViewController.m` implementation.

Here is the new implementation of `viewDidLoad`:

```objc
- (void)viewDidLoad {
    [super viewDidLoad];

    self.products = [NSMutableArray arrayWithCapacity:1];

    NSMutableArray *productsTemp;

    // Get the DBAccess object;
    DBAccess *dbAccess = [[DBAccess alloc] init];

    // Get the products array from the database
    productsTemp = [dbAccess getAllProducts];

    // Close the database because you are finished with it
    [dbAccess closeDatabase];

    // Release the dbAccess object to free its memory
    [dbAccess release];

    UILocalizedIndexedCollation *indexedCollation =
        [UILocalizedIndexedCollation currentCollation];

    // Iterate over the products, populating their section number
    for (Product *theProduct in productsTemp) {
        NSInteger section = [indexedCollation sectionForObject:theProduct
                                    collationStringSelector:@selector(name)];
        theProduct.section = section;
    }

    // Get the count of the number of sections
    NSInteger sectionCount = [[indexedCollation sectionTitles] count];

    // Create an array to hold the sub arrays
    NSMutableArray *sectionsArray = [NSMutableArray
                                    arrayWithCapacity:sectionCount];

    // Iterate over each section, creating each sub array
    for (int i=0; i<=sectionCount; i++) {
        NSMutableArray *singleSectionArray = [NSMutableArray
                                        arrayWithCapacity:1];
        [sectionsArray addObject:singleSectionArray];
    }

    // Iterate over the products putting each product into the correct sub-array
    for (Product *theProduct in productsTemp) {
        [(NSMutableArray *)[sectionsArray objectAtIndex:theProduct.section]
            addObject:theProduct];
    }

    // Iterate over each section array to sort the items in the section
    for (NSMutableArray *singleSectionArray in sectionsArray) {
        // Use the UILocalizedIndexedCollation sortedArrayFromArray: method to
        // sort each array
        NSArray *sortedSection = [indexedCollation
                            sortedArrayFromArray:singleSectionArray
```

```
                                   collationStringSelector:@selector(name)];
        [self.products addObject:sortedSection];
    }


}
```

The first part of the method is largely the same as the previous example, except that now you have added code to initialize the new `products` property. You then proceed to get the array of `Products` from the database access class, just as before.

After you release the `DBAccess` object, you move on to getting a reference to the `UILocalizedIndexedCollation` object:

```
UILocalizedIndexedCollation *indexedCollation = [UILocalizedIndexedCollation
                                    currentCollation];
```

Next, you iterate over all of the products to populate the section index property:

Available for
download on
Wrox.com

```
for (Product *theProduct in productsTemp) {
    NSInteger section = [indexedCollation sectionForObject:theProduct
                               collationStringSelector:@selector(name)];
    theProduct.section = section;
}
```

You determine the section index using the `UILocalizedIndexedCollation`'s `sectionForObject:collationStringSelector:` method. This method uses the property or method that is passed in as the `collationStringSelector` parameter to determine in which section the `sectionForObject` parameter belongs. So, in this case, the method uses the `name` property to determine the correct section for `theProduct`. You could use any method or property to organize your sections, as long as it returns a string.

The next section of code gets a count of all of the sections that you will need, creates the main array to hold all of the section sub-arrays, and creates each sub-array:

Available for
download on
Wrox.com

```
// Get the count of the number of sections
NSInteger sectionCount = [[indexedCollation sectionTitles] count];

// Create an array to hold the sub arrays
NSMutableArray *sectionsArray = [NSMutableArray
                                arrayWithCapacity:sectionCount];

// Iterate over each section, creating each sub array
for (int i=0; i<=sectionCount; i++) {
    NSMutableArray *singleSectionArray = [NSMutableArray arrayWithCapacity:1];
    [sectionsArray addObject:singleSectionArray];
}
```

Next, you loop through each product again, placing it into the correct sub-array. Remember that the index to the correct sub-array was determined before and stored in the new section property of the Product object:

```
// Iterate over the products putting each product into the correct sub-array
for (Product *theProduct in productsTemp) {
    [(NSMutableArray *)[sectionsArray objectAtIndex:theProduct.section]
        addObject:theProduct];
}
```

RootViewController.m

Finally, the last section of the code goes back over each sub-array, sorts the data within the array using the `UILocalizedIndexedCollation`'s `sortedArrayFromArray:collationStringSelector:` method, and then adds the array to the `products` array:

```
// Iterate over each section array to sort the items in the section
for (NSMutableArray *singleSectionArray in sectionsArray) {
    // Use the UILocalizedIndexedCollation sortedArrayFromArray:
    // method to sort each array
    NSArray *sortedSection = [indexedCollation
                                sortedArrayFromArray:singleSectionArray
                                collationStringSelector:@selector(name)];
    [self.products addObject:sortedSection];
}
```

RootViewController.m

Now you have the `products` array set up as you need it. It is now organized as an array of arrays, each of which contains a sorted list of Product objects, as shown in Figure 3-6.

The next thing that you need to do is configure the `TableView` to show the newly created sections. There are two `TableView` delegate methods that you need to implement: `numberOfSectionsInTableView:` and `numberOfRowsInSection:`.

The `numberOfSectionsInTableView:` method should return the number of sections that you will show in the `TableView`. You implement this by simply returning the count of objects in the `products` array:

```
- (NSInteger)numberOfSectionsInTableView:(UITableView *)tableView {
    return [self.products count];
}
```

The `tableView: numberOfRowsInSection:` method is used to return the number of rows in the requested section. To implement this, you just return the count of rows for the particular section that was requested:

```
- (NSInteger)tableView:(UITableView *)tableView
    numberOfRowsInSection:(NSInteger)section {
    return [[self.products objectAtIndex:section] count];
}
```

You also need to modify the `tableView:cellForRowAtIndexPath:` method to get the product from the products array by section and row. If you recall, when you had only the single array, you just indexed into it directly to get the `Product` that you wanted to display. Now, you need to get the `Product` object that corresponds with the section and row that you are being asked to display:

```
Product* product = [[self.products objectAtIndex:[indexPath section]]
                      objectAtIndex:[indexPath row]];
```

You can see that you get the section from the `indexPath` and use that to index into the outer array. Then, you use the row as the index to the sub-array to get the `Product`.

Another modification that you will need to make in `cellForRowAtIndexPath:` is to change the cell's `accessoryType` to `UITableViewCellAccessoryNone`. You need to remove the accessory view because the index will obscure the accessory and it will look bad:

```
cell.accessoryType = UITableViewCellAccessoryNone;
```

Now that you will be using headers in the table, you need to implement the method `tableView:titleForHeaderInSection:`. This method returns a string that will be used as the header text for the section. You obtain the title from the `UILocalizedIndexedCollation` by using the `sectionTitles` property:

```
- (NSString *)tableView:(UITableView *)tableView
    titleForHeaderInSection:(NSInteger)section {
    // Make sure that the section will contain some data
    if ([[self.products objectAtIndex:section] count] > 0) {

        // If it does, get the section title from the
        // UILocalizedIndexedCollation object
        return [[[UILocalizedIndexedCollation currentCollation] sectionTitles]
                objectAtIndex:section];
    }
    return nil;
}
```

RootViewController.m

Likewise, because you are implementing an index, you need to provide the text to use in the index. Again, the `UILocalizedIndexedCollation` helps out. The property `sectionIndexTitles` returns an array of the index titles:

```
- (NSArray *)sectionIndexTitlesForTableView:(UITableView *)tableView {
    // Set up the index titles from the UILocalizedIndexedCollation
    return [[UILocalizedIndexedCollation currentCollation] sectionIndexTitles];
}
```

RootViewController.m

Once you've set up the index, you have to link the index to the section titles by implementing the `tableView:sectionForSectionIndexTitle: atIndex:` method. Again, using the `UILocalizedIndexedCollation` greatly simplifies this implementation:

```
- (NSInteger)tableView:(UITableView *)tableView
    sectionForSectionIndexTitle:(NSString *)title atIndex:(NSInteger)index {
    // Link the sections to the labels in the index
    return [[UILocalizedIndexedCollation currentCollation]
            sectionForSectionIndexTitleAtIndex:index];
}
```

RootViewController.m

If you build and run the application, it should run and the table should be displayed with sections and an index. However, if you select a row, the application will not take you to the detail page. Because you modified how the data is stored, you need to go back and modify the `tableView:didSelectRowAtIndexPath:` method to use the new scheme. This is as simple as changing the line of code that obtains the product object to use in the detail view like this:

```
Product* product =  [[self.products objectAtIndex:[indexPath section]]
                         objectAtIndex:[indexPath row]];
```

Now, if you build and run again, all should be well. You should be able to navigate the application just as before, except that now you have a well-organized and indexed table for easy navigation.

IMPLEMENTING SEARCH

The sample application now has all of the items in the corporate catalog neatly organized into sections based on the product name, with an index for quick access to each section. The final piece of functionality that you will add is a search capability. Users should be able to search for particular products within the catalog, without having to scroll through the entire catalog.

You will implement functionality that is similar to the search capabilities of the built-in Contacts application. You will add a `UISearchBar` control at the top of the table and then filter the products list based on user input. The final interface will look like Figure 3-7.

When the user starts a search, you will remove the side index list and only show rows that meet the search criteria, as shown in Figure 3-8.

Implementing search requires two controls, the `UISearchBar` and the `UISearchDisplay Controller`, which was introduced in iPhone SDK 3.0. The `UISearchBar` is the UI widget that you will put at the top of the table to accept search text input. The `UISearchDisplayController` is used to filter the data provided by another View Controller based on the search text in the `UISearchBar`.

FIGURE 3-7: Catalog with search interface

FIGURE 3-8: Search in progress

The `UISearchDisplayController` is initialized with a search bar and the View Controller containing the content to be searched. When a search begins, the search display controller overlays the search interface above the original View Controller's view to display a subset of the original data. The results display is a table view that is created by the search display controller.

The first step is to create the `UISearchBar` and add it to the table. In the `RootViewController` header, add an instance variable and associated property for the search bar:

Available for download on Wrox.com

```objc
@interface RootViewController : UITableViewController {
    NSMutableArray *products;
    UISearchBar* searchBar;
}

@property (retain, nonatomic) NSMutableArray *products;
@property (retain, nonatomic) UISearchBar* searchBar;
```

RootViewController.h

In the `RootViewController` implementation file, synthesize the `searchBar`:

```objc
@synthesize searchBar;
```

You can now add the code to create the `SearchBar` and add it to the header of the `TableView` at the end of the `viewDidLoad` method:

Available for download on Wrox.com

```objc
// Create search bar
self.searchBar = [[[UISearchBar alloc] initWithFrame:
                    CGRectMake(0.0f, 0.0f, 320.0f, 44.0f)] autorelease];
self.tableView.tableHeaderView = self.searchBar;
```

RootViewController.m

Next, you will create and configure the `UISearchDisplayController`. This controller will be used to filter and display the data in the `RootViewController`'s TableView. In the header for `RootViewController`, add an instance variable and associated property for the SearchDisplayController:

```
@interface RootViewController : UITableViewController {
    NSMutableArray *products;

    UISearchBar* searchBar;
    UISearchDisplayController* searchController;
}

@property (retain, nonatomic) NSMutableArray *products;
@property (retain, nonatomic) UISearchBar* searchBar;
@property (retain, nonatomic) UISearchDisplayController* searchController;
```

RootViewController.h

Synthesize the property in the `RootViewController`'s implementation file:

```
@synthesize searchController;
```

Add the code to `viewDidLoad` to create and configure the display controller:

```
// Create and configure the search controller
self.searchController = [[[UISearchDisplayController alloc]
                          initWithSearchBar:self.searchBar
                          contentsController:self] autorelease];

self.searchController.searchResultsDataSource = self;
self.searchController.searchResultsDelegate = self;
```

RootViewController.m

Because you are going to be creating a new, filtered table, you need to create an array to hold the filtered product list. Add an instance variable and property to the `RootViewController` header:

```
@interface RootViewController : UITableViewController {
    NSMutableArray *products;
    NSArray *filteredProducts;

    UISearchBar* searchBar;
    UISearchDisplayController* searchController;
}

@property (retain, nonatomic) NSMutableArray *products;
@property (retain, nonatomic) NSArray *filteredProducts;
@property (retain, nonatomic) UISearchBar* searchBar;
@property (retain, nonatomic) UISearchDisplayController* searchController;
```

RootViewController.h

Synthesize the property in the `RootViewController`'s implementation file:

```
@synthesize filteredProducts;
```

You have now completed adding the additional controls and properties that you need to implement the search feature. The next step is to modify the `UITableView` methods that are used to populate the `UITableView`.

In each function you need to determine if you are working with the normal table or the filtered table. Then, you need to proceed accordingly. You can determine which `UITableView` you are dealing with by comparing the `UITableView` passed into the function to the View Controller's `tableView` property, which holds the normal `UITableView`.

The first method that you will modify is `numberOfSectionsInTableView`:

```
- (NSInteger)numberOfSectionsInTableView:(UITableView *)tableView {
    // Is the request for numberOfRowsInSection for the regular table?
    if (tableView == self.tableView)
    {
        // Just return the count of the products like before
        return [self.products count];

    }

    return 1;
}
```

RootViewController.m

The first thing that you do is compare the `tableView` that was passed into the method with the `RootViewController`'s `tableView`. If they are the same, you are dealing with the normal `TableView` and you will determine the number of sections just as you did in the previous example. If you are dealing with the filtered table, you return 1 because you do not want to use sections in the filtered table.

Next, you'll modify the `tableView:numberOfRowsInSection:` method to check to see which table you are working with and then return the appropriate row count. You will use `NSPredicate` to filter the data. Predicates will be covered in detail in Part II of this book on Core Data. For now, the only thing that you need to understand about predicates is that they are a mechanism for providing criteria used to filter data. Predicates work like the WHERE clause in a SQL statement. Before you can use the predicate, you need to flatten the array of arrays that contains the data. You flatten the array, and then use the `NSPredicate` to filter the array:

```
- (NSInteger)tableView:(UITableView *)tableView
    numberOfRowsInSection:(NSInteger)section {

    // Is the request for numberOfRowsInSection for the regular table?
    if (tableView == self.tableView)
    {
        // Just return the count of the products like before
        return [[self.products objectAtIndex:section] count];
```

```
    }

    // You need the count for the filtered table
    //  First, you have to flatten the array of arrays self.products
    NSMutableArray *flattenedArray = [[NSMutableArray alloc]
                                       initWithCapacity:1];
    for (NSMutableArray *theArray in self.products)
    {
        for (int i=0; i<[theArray count];i++)
        {
            [flattenedArray addObject:[theArray objectAtIndex:i]];
        }
    }

    // Set up an NSPredicate to filter the rows
    NSPredicate *predicate = [NSPredicate predicateWithFormat:
                              @"name beginswith[c] %@", self.searchBar.text];
    self.filteredProducts = [flattenedArray
                             filteredArrayUsingPredicate:predicate];

    //  Clean up flattenedArray
    [flattenedArray release];

    return self.filteredProducts.count;
}
```

RootViewController.m

This code uses the same methodology as the previous method for determining which TableView you are dealing with. If you are working with the normal TableView, you return the product count as in the previous example. If not, you need to determine the count of filtered products.

To accomplish this, you first flatten the products array of arrays into a single array. Remember that to implement sections, you should store your data as an array of arrays. Well, you need to flatten that structure down to a one-dimensional array in order to filter it with the NSPredicate. In order to flatten the products array, you simply loop over each array and put the contents of the sub-array into a new array called flattenedArray.

Next, you set up the NSPredicate object to filter out only rows that begin with the text that is input into the SearchBar. Then, you apply the predicate to the flattenedArray and put the result into the filteredProducts array. The filteredProducts array will be used from here on out when dealing with the filtered TableView. You then release the flattenedArray because you are finished with it and should free the memory. Finally, you return the count of items in the filteredProducts array.

Now that you have the correct row counts, you need to modify the tableView: cellForRowAtIndexPath: method to display the correct rows:

```
- (UITableViewCell *)tableView:(UITableView *)tableView
    cellForRowAtIndexPath:(NSIndexPath *)indexPath {

    static NSString *CellIdentifier = @"Cell";

    CatalogTableViewCell *cell = (CatalogTableViewCell *)
```

```
            [tableView dequeueReusableCellWithIdentifier:CellIdentifier];
    if (cell == nil) {
        cell = [[[CatalogTableViewCell alloc]
                initWithStyle:UITableViewCellStyleDefault
                reuseIdentifier:CellIdentifier] autorelease];
    }

    // Configure the cell.
    cell.accessoryType = UITableViewCellAccessoryNone;

    // Is the request for cellForRowAtIndexPath for the regular table?
    if (tableView == self.tableView)
    {

        // Get the Product object
        Product* product = [[self.products
                            objectAtIndex:[indexPath section]]
                            objectAtIndex:[indexPath row]];

        // Set the product to be used to draw the cell
        [cell setProduct:product];

        return cell;
    }

    // Get the Product object
    Product* product = [self.filteredProducts objectAtIndex:[indexPath row]];

    // Set the product to be used to draw the cell
    [cell setProduct:product];

    return cell;
}
```

RootViewController.m

In this method, you do the same type of thing as you have done in the previous two methods. You create the cell just as you did in the previous example. The difference here is that if you are dealing with the normal table, you get the Product object from the self.products array, but if you are dealing with the filtered table, you get the Product object from the self.filteredProducts array.

Now you will modify the didSelectRowAtIndexPath: method to use either the normal or filtered table:

```
- (void)tableView:(UITableView *)tableView
    didSelectRowAtIndexPath:(NSIndexPath *)indexPath {

    Product* product;

    if (tableView == self.tableView)
    {
        // Get the product that corresponds with the touched cell
        product =  [[self.products objectAtIndex:[indexPath section]]
                    objectAtIndex:[indexPath row]];
    }
```

```
        else {
            product = [self.filteredProducts objectAtIndex:[indexPath row]];

    }


        // Initialize the detail view controller from the NIB
        ProductDetailViewController *productDetailViewController =
            [[ProductDetailViewController alloc]
              initWithNibName:@"ProductDetailViewController" bundle:nil];

        // Set the title of the detail page
        [productDetailViewController setTitle:product.name];

        // Push the detail controller on to the stack
        [self.navigationController pushViewController:productDetailViewController
                                    animated:YES];

        // Populate the details
        [productDetailViewController setLabelsForProduct:product];

        // release the view controller becuase it is retained by the Navigation
        // Controller
        [productDetailViewController release];
    }
```

RootViewController.m

Again, in this method, you do the same thing that you did in the previous method. If you are dealing with the normal table, you get the `Product` object from the `self.products` array, but if you are dealing with the filtered table, you get the `Product` object from the `self.filteredProducts` array.

Finally, modify the `sectionIndexTitlesForTableView:` method to return the regular index for the normal table but `nil` for the filtered table because you don't want to show the index while displaying the filtered table:

```
- (NSArray *)sectionIndexTitlesForTableView:(UITableView *)tableView {
    if (tableView == self.tableView)
    {
        // Set up the index titles from the UILocalizedIndexedCollation
        return [[UILocalizedIndexedCollation currentCollation]
                sectionIndexTitles];
    }

    return nil;
}
```

RootViewController.m

You should now be able to build and run the code and have full searching capabilities. In a nutshell, you implement search by adding a `SearchBar` and a `SearchDisplayController` to your

`ViewController` and then modify your `TableView` methods to handle dealing with either the normal or filtered data.

OPTIMIZING TABLEVIEW PERFORMANCE

In this chapter, you have explored how to use the `TableView` in detail. You have learned how to customize the `TableView` to look exactly as you want by using styles, adding subviews to the `contentView`, and creating your own cells by subclassing the `UITableViewCell` class. You have also learned how to organize your table and make it easy to use by adding sections, an index, and search capability. The final aspect of the `TableView` that you will look at is how to optimize performance.

The iPhone and iPad are amazing devices, and users expect an amazing experience from their apps. Apple has set the standard with the pre-installed applications. You should strive to get your applications to function as fluidly and elegantly as the default applications.

The primary problem that you will encounter when building an application with a `TableView` is poor scrolling performance. This can be caused by several factors, as you will see in the following sections.

Reusing Existing Cells

Creating objects at runtime can be an expensive operation in terms of how much processor time is used to create the object. Additionally, objects that contain a hierarchy of views, such as the `TableViewCell`, can consume a significant amount of memory.

On embedded devices like the iPhone and iPad, the processors are generally not as fast as those on desktop and laptop computers so you must try to do whatever you can to optimize your code for execution on these slower machines. Also, on devices such as the iPhone and iPad, memory is at a premium. If you use too much memory, the OS on the device will notify you to release some memory. If you fail to release enough memory, the OS will terminate your application. Random termination of your application does not lead to happy customers.

One step that you can take to optimize the code of your `TableViews` is to reuse existing cells when appropriate. The first step in debugging scrolling problems with the `TableView` is to look at object allocations. If objects are being allocated as you scroll, there is a problem.

The designers at Apple have provided us with a private queue that can be used to store `TableViewCells` for reuse. In the `cellForRowAtIndexPath:` method, you can access this queue to get an existing cell from the queue instead of creating a new one. In fact, you have done this in the code examples in this chapter.

If you want to see the difference that this optimization makes in your sample code, change the following line in `cellForRowAtIndexPath:`

```
UITableViewCell *cell = [tableView
                    dequeueReusableCellWithIdentifier:CellIdentifier];
```

to this:

```
UITableViewCell *cell = nil;
```

Now the code will not try to use a cell from the queue; it will create a new cell each time the `TableView` asks for a cell. The performance difference may not be too noticeable with a table with only a few rows, but imagine creating all of these cells if your data consisted of thousands of rows. Additionally, the final project is using subclassing and custom-drawn cells. Try going back and making this change to the code where you added subviews to the `contentView`. You should notice a significant slowdown in scrolling speed.

A common point of confusion with cell reuse is the cell identifier. The string that you provide in `dequeueReusableCellWithIdentifier:` is the identifier. This identifier does not define the cell's contents, only its style. When you plan on re-using the style of a cell, assign a string to the reuse identifier, and then pass that string into `dequeueReusableCellWithIdentifier:`. This allows you to create cells with different styles, store them with different identifiers, and queue them up for quick access.

When you call `dequeueReusableCellWithIdentifier:` the method returns either a cell that you can use, or `nil`. If the return is `nil`, you need to create a new cell to use in your table.

A final note about the `cellForRowAtIndexPath:` method. Do not do anything in `cellForRowAtIndexPath` that takes a long time. I recently saw an example of a developer downloading an image from the Web each time `cellForRowAtIndexPath` was called. This is a very bad idea! You need to make sure that `cellForRowAtIndexPath` returns very quickly as it is called each time the `TableView` needs to show a cell in your table. In the case where it will take a long time to create the content for a cell, consider pre-fetching the content and caching it.

Opaque Subviews

When you are using the technique of programmatically adding subviews to a cell's content view, you should ensure that all of the subviews that you add are opaque. Transparent subviews detract from scrolling performance because the compositing of transparent layers is an expensive operation. The `UITableViewCell` inherits the `opaque` property from `UIView`. This property defaults to `YES`. Do not change it unless you absolutely must have a transparent view.

Additionally, you should ensure that the subviews that you add to the `UITableViewCell` have the same background color as the cell. Not doing this detracts from the performance of the `TableView`.

It is possible to view layers that are being composited by using the Instruments application, which Apple provides for free as a part of Xcode. The tool is very useful in debugging applications and can be used to do a lot of helpful things including tracking memory leaks and logging all memory allocations. The Core Animation tool in Instruments can be used to show layers that are being composited. The Core Animation tool can only be used when running your application on a device.

In order to see where compositing is occurring in your application, start the Instruments tool. Instruments can be found in `/Developer/Applications`. When the tool, starts, it will ask you to choose a template for the trace document. In the left-hand pane, choose iPhone/All.

In this dialog, select Core Animation. This will open the Instruments interface with a Core Animation instrument. Click on the third icon from the left at the bottom of the screen to expand the detail view. In the debug options, select Color Blended Layers, as shown in Figure 3-9.

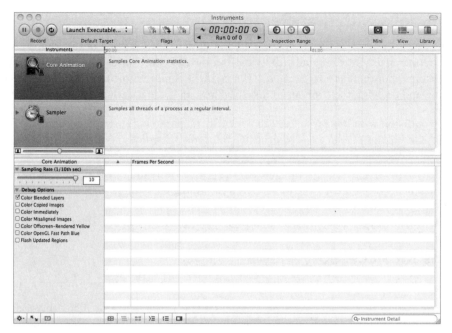

FIGURE 3-9: Instruments tool

Now, when you run your application on the device, layers that are not composited are overlaid with green, while composited layers are red.

To see the difference, you can make a change to the `RootViewController`. In the `cellForRowAtIndexPath:` method, add a line to set `productImage.alpha = 0.9` under the line `productImage.tag = PRODUCTIMAGE_TAG`. The snippet of code should look like this:

Available for download on Wrox.com

```
// Configure the product Image
productImage = [[[UIImageView alloc]
                initWithFrame:CGRectMake(0.0, 0.0, 40.0, 40.0)] autorelease];
productImage.tag = PRODUCTIMAGE_TAG;
productImage.alpha = 0.9;
// Add the Image to the cell's content view
[cell.contentView addSubview:productImage];
```

RootViewController.m

Now run the application. You should see all of the product images overlaid with red. This means that these images are being composited, and that is not good. Remember that compositing takes a long time and should be avoided if possible.

There is an issue that you should be aware of with PNG images. If you are using PNG files, as in the sample, they should be created without an Alpha layer. Including the Alpha layer causes compositing to occur regardless of how the opaque property is set on the `UIImageView`.

You examine how to use Instruments in more detail in Appendix A.

Custom Drawn Cells with drawRect

You have examined this technique in the "Subclassing UITableViewCell" section of this chapter. The fastest way to render a cell is by manually drawing it in the `drawRect` method. It may take more work from the developer, but there is a large payoff. If a cell will contain more than three subviews, consider subclassing and drawing the contents manually. This can dramatically increase scrolling performance.

The technique basically boils down to collapsing multi-view `TableCells` down to one view that knows how to draw itself.

A subclass of `UITableViewCell` may reset attributes of the cell by overriding `prepareForReuse`. This method is called just before the `TableView` returns a cell to the datasource in `dequeueReusable CellWithIdentifier:`. If you do override this method to reset the cell's attributes, you should only reset attributes that are not related to content such as alpha, editing, and selection state.

UI Conventions for Accessory Views

You should abide by the following conventions when adding accessory views to cells in your table:

The `UITableViewCellAccessoryDisclosureIndicator` is a disclosure indicator. The control does not respond to touches and is used to indicate that touching the row will bring the user to a detail screen based on the selected row.

The `UITableViewCellAccessoryDetailDisclosureButton` does respond to touches and is used to indicate that configuration options for the selected row will be presented.

The `UITableViewCellAccessoryCheckmark` is used to display a checkmark indicating that the row is selected. The checkmark does not respond to touches.

For more information, you should read the iPhone Human Interface Guidelines located at: http://developer.apple.com

MOVING FORWARD

In this chapter, you have learned how to use the `UITableView` to display data in your application. Then, you learned how to customize the display of your data by building custom `UITableViewCells`. Next, you learned how to allow your user to manipulate the display of his data by searching and filtering the results. Finally, you learned how to avoid and troubleshoot performance problems with the `UITableView`.

In the next chapter, you will learn how to display and navigate your data using some of the unique UI elements that are available for use on the iPad. Then, in Part II of the book, you will move on to learn how to create and query data using the Core Data framework.

iPad Interface Elements

WHAT'S IN THIS CHAPTER?

➤ Building a master-detail view using the UISplitViewController

➤ Displaying informational messages using the UIPopoverController

➤ Recognizing and reacting to various user gestures using the UIGestureRecognizer

➤ Sharing files between the iPad and desktop machines with file-sharing support

In the previous chapter, you learned how to display your application data using the UITableView control. Then, you took that knowledge a step further by building custom cells, adding search and filter capabilities, and implementing indexes and section headers.

In this chapter, you learn about the interface elements and other features that are unique to the iPad. You will then apply this knowledge to build better data-driven applications.

You will explore the UISplitViewController and UIPopoverController, which you can use when building iPad applications. You will also learn how to use the new UIGestureRecognizer class and its subclasses to interpret user gestures. Finally, you will learn how to share files between the iPad and desktop computers using file-sharing support.

DISPLAYING MASTER/DETAIL DATA WITH THE UISPLITVIEWCONTROLLER

Quite often, when you're building a data centric application, you will want to show data in a master/detail format. For instance, in an address book application, the master view typically consists of a simple list of contact names. Selecting a contact from the list then presents the details for that contact such as address, phone number, and company.

On the iPhone, you generally build master/detail displays using the Navigation Controller. You would typically use a `UITableView` to show the master records. Tapping on a master record advances the user to a second screen that displays the details for the record that the user selected. Because there is very limited space on the iPhone screen, two separate screens are necessary to display the master and detail data. The catalog application that you built in the previous chapter uses this model, as shown in Figure 4-1.

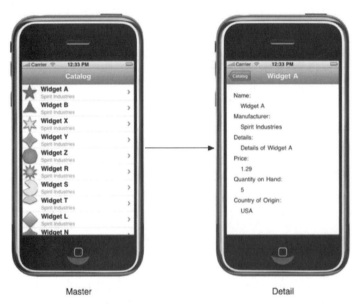

Master   Detail

FIGURE 4-1: Master-Detail view on the iPhone

Introducing the UISplitViewController

With the extended amount of screen space available to you on the iPad, you have a better option. Instead of displaying the master data and detail data separately on two different screens, you can combine the two so that all of this information is visible at the same time. The release of the iPhone SDK 3.2 included new functionality specifically designed for the iPad. In this release, Apple introduced a new control called the `UISplitViewController`. You can use this new user interface element to display two distinct View Controllers side by side in landscape mode, as you can see in Figure 4-2. This enables you to take advantage of the extra screen space afforded by the iPad's large screen.

FIGURE 4-2: UISplitViewController in Landscape Mode

In portrait mode, the controller allows the user to view the detail data onscreen while popping up the master data on demand by tapping a button in the interface. Figure 4-3 shows the same View Controller as Figure 4-2, but in this case, I have rotated the iPad into portrait mode. The UISplitViewController automatically changes the display of its child View Controllers based on the orientation of the device.

The UISplitViewController does not do anything to support communication between its child View Controllers. That code is your responsibility. In the template code when you start a new Split View–based Application project, the RootViewController maintains a reference to the DetailViewController, which is set in the MainWindow.xib file. However, you are free to delete this implementation and build the communication between the two views in any way that you choose.

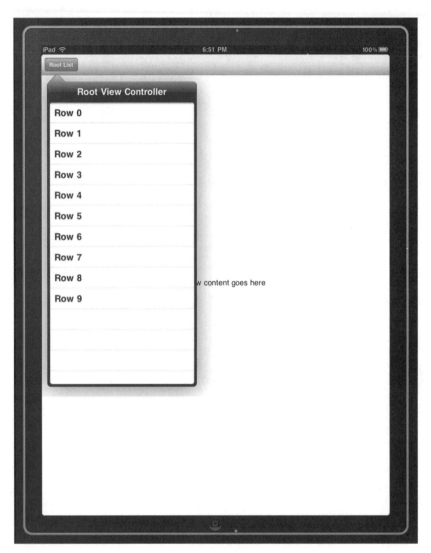

FIGURE 4-3: UISplitViewController in portrait mode

The UISplitViewControllerDelegate Protocol

When the orientation of the device changes, the `UISplitViewController` calls its delegate methods. The `UISplitViewControllerDelegate` protocol defines these methods.

The Split View Controller calls the `splitViewController:popoverController: willPresentViewController:` method when the popover containing the Root View Controller should appear. This happens when the user taps the button in the toolbar while the device is in the portrait orientation. If you are using any other popover controls in your application, you should make sure that you dismiss them in this delegate method. It is a violation of the Apple Human

Interface Guidelines to display more than one Popover Controller at a time. If you do, Apple will reject your application during the review process.

The Split View Controller calls the `splitViewController:willHideViewController:` `withBarButtonItem:forPopoverController:` method when the View Controller passed into the method is hidden. This occurs when the user rotates the device from landscape to portrait orientation. In this method, you need to add the button that will call the Popover Controller to the toolbar. The application template code implements this method for you.

The Split View Controller calls the `splitViewController:willShowViewController:` `invalidatingBarButtonItem:` method when the user rotates the device from portrait orientation back to landscape orientation. This indicates that the left View Controller will be displayed again. The code in this method should remove the toolbar button from the toolbar that the interface uses in portrait mode to display the popover. Again, this is implemented already if you start your project by using the Split View–based Application template.

Starting the Split View Sample Application

In this chapter, you build a sample application that implements some very basic survey features. Survey takers that are out in the field collecting data could use an application like this. The application will use a `UISplitViewController` to display the names of the people that the user has surveyed on the left side as the master data. The right side will display the actual survey data that the user entered as the child data. Figure 4-4 shows the completed application in landscape mode.

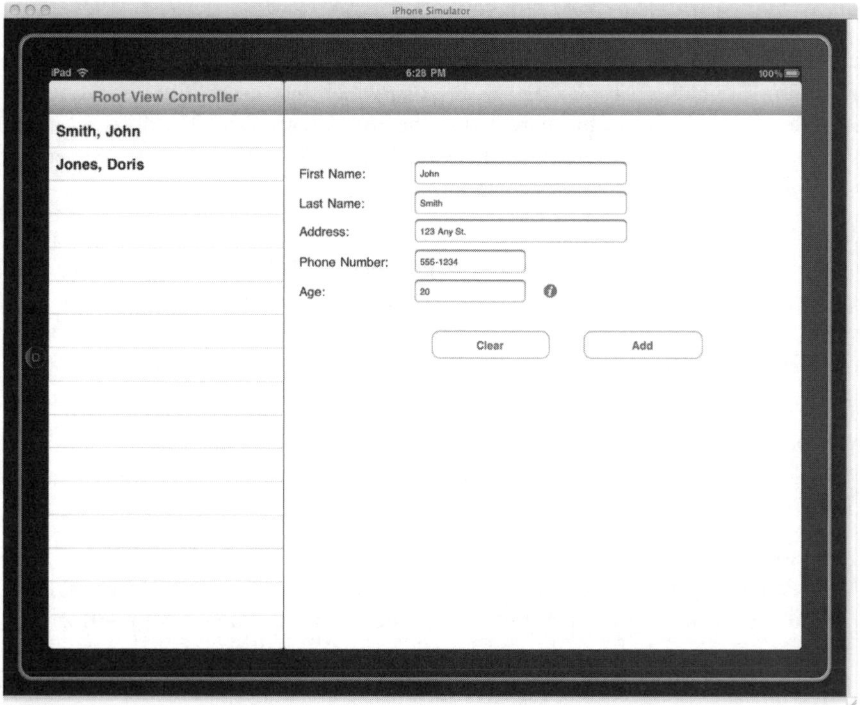

FIGURE 4-4: Completed survey application

The application will allow the user to add new survey responses to the data set and view existing responses. To keep the application focused on demonstrating the user interface features that are unique to the iPad, you will not be implementing every feature that would be required for a complete application. For instance, I won't cover adding the code to modify existing surveys, or to delete surveys.

 You need at least the iPhone SDK 3.2 to develop applications for the iPad.

To begin the Survey application, open Xcode and create a new project. Choose to use the Split View–based Application template for the new project. Make sure that you leave the "Use Core Data for storage" checkbox unchecked. You will learn about Core Data in the next section of the book. Call your new application Survey.

Just to see the basic functionality that you get from the template code, build and run the application. When the iPad simulator starts, you will see the simulated iPad in portrait mode. Notice how the detail view takes up the whole screen. Click on the Root List button and you will see a View Controller with some data in a popover control as you saw in Figure 4-3.

Press Command+Left Arrow to rotate the iPad in the simulator. You will see the split view change to show the detail in the right pane and the root list in the left pane, as shown in Figure 4-2.

Now, you will take a brief look at the code and XIB that the template provides. First, double-click the `MainWindow.xib` file located in the project's Resources folder. This will open the file in Interface Builder so that you can look at the structure of the interface.

In the Interface Builder window, click the disclosure triangle next to the Split View Controller item. Next, open the Navigation Controller by clicking the disclosure icon next to it. You should now see the Root View Controller. The thing to notice here is that the Split View Controller does not actually do anything on its own. It is simply a container for the Root View Controller, which implements the left-hand pane, and the Detail View Controller, which implements the right-hand pane.

Next, select the Detail View Controller and press Command+2 to bring up the connections pane for the Detail View Controller. Click the disclosure triangle next to Multiple to see the referencing outlets for the `detailViewController`. You will see that the App Delegate and Root View Controller reference the `detailViewController`. This reference is the communication mechanism that allows the Root View Controller to set the data that the Detail View Controller will display.

Next, select the Survey App Delegate. If you look at the outlets for the Survey App Delegate, you will see that the App Delegate has references to both the Root View Controller and the Detail View Controller. You will take advantage of this in your application when you need to communicate back from the Detail View Controller to the Root View Controller.

Now let's take a brief look at the template code for the `RootViewController`. The `RootViewController` defaults to a `UITableViewController`, which the template places in the left pane in landscape mode and the popover in portrait mode. The template code is a straightforward implementation of a table just like you learned in the last chapter. You will find the typical TableView delegate methods `numberOfSectionsInTableView:`, `tableView:numberOfRowsInSection:`, and `tableView:cellForRowAtIndexPath:` implemented in this class.

The `DetailViewController` is a `UIViewController` subclass. The template creates an associated XIB file called `DetailView.xib`. This XIB contains the user interface elements that you will display in the detail view. By default, the XIB contains a label only. In the sample, you will add other controls to allow the user to enter and view survey data.

When the user selects an item in the `RootViewController`, the Table View calls the `tableView:didSelectRowAtIndexPath:` method. The default implementation of this method sets the `detailItem` property of the `detailViewController`, which, by default, is of type `id`.

Instead of synthesizing the `detailItem` property of the `DetailViewController`, there is code that implements the setter. This is a departure from most of the properties that we have seen so far. The setter is coded because you need to do some additional processing aside from simply setting the associated instance variable. The method sets the `detailItem` instance variable and then calls the `configureView` method. The `configureView` method updates the display to show the new `detailItem` data. Then, the setter dismisses the popover, if it is visible.

Building the Detail Interface

Now you are ready to start working on the detail view interface. First, however, there are a couple of changes that you need to make to the `DetailViewController` header file in preparation for the changes that you will make to the view in Interface Builder.

In the `DetailViewController` header, change the type of the `detailItem` instance variable to `NSDictionary*`:

```
NSDictionary* detailItem;
```

Also, change the type in the property declaration for the `detailItem` property:

```
@property (nonatomic, retain) NSDictionary*  detailItem;
```

Next, you will add instance variables and outlet properties for the `UITextField`s that you will use in Interface Builder to collect the survey data. In the `@interface` section, add the following instance variables:

Available for download on Wrox.com

```
UITextField* firstNameTextField;
UITextField* lastNameTextField;
UITextField* addressTextField;
UITextField* phoneTextField;
UITextField* ageTextField;
```

DetailViewController.h

Then, add the associated properties:

Available for download on Wrox.com

```
@property (nonatomic, retain) IBOutlet UITextField* firstNameTextField;
@property (nonatomic, retain) IBOutlet UITextField* lastNameTextField;
@property (nonatomic, retain) IBOutlet UITextField* addressTextField;
```

```
@property (nonatomic, retain) IBOutlet UITextField* phoneTextField;
@property (nonatomic, retain) IBOutlet UITextField* ageTextField;
```

DetailViewController.h

Next, add the `clearSurvey` and `addSurvey` `IBAction` methods that will execute when the user taps on the Clear or Add buttons in the interface:

```
-(IBAction)clearSurvey:(id)sender;
-(IBAction)addSurvey:(id)sender;
```

Because you will not use the `detailDescriptionLabel`, delete the `detailDescriptionLabel` instance variable and outlet property.

Now, switch over to the `DetailViewController` implementation file. Implement the `viewDidUnload` method to set the properties that hold the user interface controls to `nil`:

```
- (void)viewDidUnload {
    // Release any retained subviews of the main view.
    // e.g. self.myOutlet = nil;
    self.popoverController = nil;

    self.firstNameTextField = nil;
    self.lastNameTextField = nil;
    self.addressTextField = nil;
    self.phoneTextField = nil;
    self.ageTextField = nil;
}
```

DetailViewController.m

Finally, implement the `dealloc` method to free the memory that your interface controls use:

```
- (void)dealloc {
    [popoverController release];
    [toolbar release];

    [detailItem release];
    [firstNameTextField release];
    [lastNameTextField release];
    [addressTextField release];
    [phoneTextField release];
    [ageTextField release];

    [super dealloc];
}
```

DetailViewController.m

Now you are ready to move on to building the user interface in Interface Builder. Double-click on the DetailView.xib file to open the file in Interface Builder. Delete the UILabel that is in the view by default.

You will be building an interface like the one in Figure 4-5. Add a UILabel for each field in the interface. Change the text to match the text in Figure 4-5. Next, add a UITextField next to each of the labels that you just created. Finally, add two UIButtons at the bottom of the form and change their text to read Clear and Add.

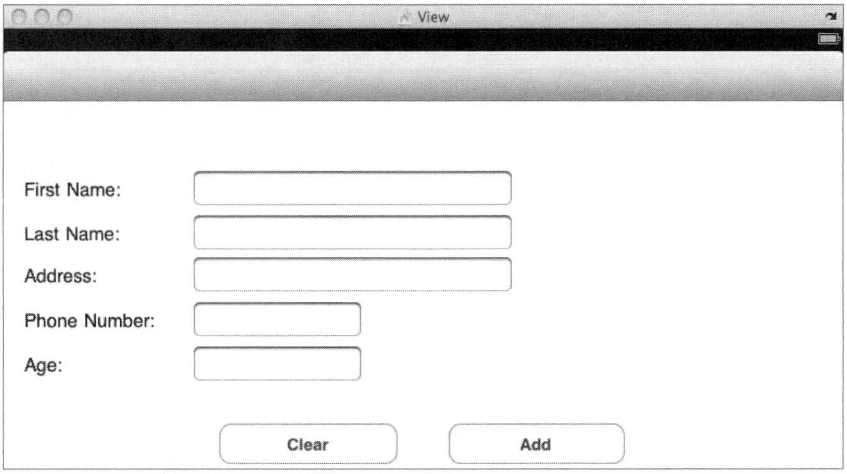

FIGURE 4-5: DetailViewController interface

Now you need to connect each UITextField in Interface Builder to the appropriate outlet in File's Owner. This will enable you to retrieve the data from these controls or populate the controls with data. Finally, connect the Touch Up Inside event of the Clear button to the clearSurvey: method in File's Owner. Likewise, connect the Touch Up Inside event of the Add button to the addSurvey: method in File's Owner.

Implementing Save and Master/Detail View

In this section, you implement the basic functionality of the application that demonstrates using the split view to show master/detail view relationships.

Setting Up the DetailViewController

First, you will implement stubs for the clearSurvey: and addSurvey: methods in the DetailViewController. These methods will create a log entry in the console when they execute. This will allow you to verify that you have correctly linked the buttons in the user interface to the source code.

The `clearSurvey:` method should log that the user has invoked the method. Then, it should clear all of the user interface elements. Here is the implementation of the `clearSurvey:` method:

```
-(IBAction)clearSurvey:(id)sender
{
    NSLog (@"clearSurvey");
    // Update the user interface for the detail item.
    self.firstNameTextField.text = @"";
    self.lastNameTextField.text = @"";
    self.addressTextField.text = @"";
    self.phoneTextField.text = @"";
    self.ageTextField.text = @"";
}
```

DetailViewController.m

You will eventually code the `addSurvey:` method to save the survey data. Because you are not quite ready to do that yet, simply implement the method to log that the user has invoked it by tapping the Add button. Here is the implementation:

```
-(IBAction)addSurvey:(id)sender
{
    NSLog (@"addSurvey");
}
```

Build and run your application. When the application starts in the iPad simulator, click each button and verify that you see the correct log statement in the console. This will prove that you have properly connected the buttons to the code.

Now you are ready to modify the `configureView` method in the `DetailViewController` to take the data from the `detailItem` model object and populate the `UITextFields` that display the data in the user interface. Here is the new implementation of the `configureView` method:

```
- (void)configureView {
    // Update the user interface for the detail item.
    self.firstNameTextField.text = [detailItem objectForKey:@"firstName"];
    self.lastNameTextField.text = [detailItem objectForKey:@"lastName"];
    self.addressTextField.text = [detailItem objectForKey:@"address"];
    self.phoneTextField.text = [detailItem objectForKey:@"phone"];
    self.ageTextField.text = [[detailItem objectForKey:@"age"] stringValue];
}
```

DetailViewController.m

Each survey is stored in an `NSDictionary`. If you are not familiar with this class, you can use an `NSDictonary` to store a set of key-value pairs, as long as each key is unique. This method simply calls the `objectForKey` method on the `detailItem` dictionary to obtain the value that you will display in the text field. The only wrinkle is that the age field is stored as an `NSNumber`, so you need to convert the number to a string by calling the `stringValue` method.

Changes to the RootViewController

Now you need to move on to the `RootViewController`. Here, you will add an `NSMutableArray*` to hold the collection of surveys. You cannot simply use an `NSArray` because you will need to be able to add surveys to the collection on-the-fly. Remember, `NSArray` is immutable, meaning that once you have created it, you cannot modify it.

In the `RootViewController` header file, add an instance variable called `surveyDataArray` of type `NSMutableArray*`:

```
NSMutableArray* surveyDataArray;
```

Add a property for your new `surveyDataArray`:

```
@property (nonatomic, retain) NSMutableArray* surveyDataArray;
```

Switch over to the `RootViewController` implementation file and modify the `@synthesize` statement to synthesize your new `surveyDataArray` property:

```
@synthesize detailViewController, surveyDataArray;
```

Modify the `viewDidUnload` and `dealloc` methods to clean up your new property:

```
- (void)viewDidUnload {
    // Relinquish ownership of anything that can be recreated in viewDidLoad or
    // on demand.
    // For example: self.myOutlet = nil;
    self.surveyDataArray = nil;
}


- (void)dealloc {
    [detailViewController release];
    [surveyDataArray release];
    [super dealloc];
}
```

RootViewController.m

Finally, modify the `viewDidLoad` method to create and initialize the `NSMutableArray`:

```
- (void)viewDidLoad {
    [super viewDidLoad];
    self.clearsSelectionOnViewWillAppear = NO;
    self.contentSizeForViewInPopover = CGSizeMake(320.0, 600.0);

    NSMutableArray* array = [[NSMutableArray alloc] init];
    self.surveyDataArray = array;
    [array release];
}
```

RootViewController.m

Modify the TableView Methods

The next step is to modify the Table View datasource methods to use the `surveyData` array as the `UITableView`'s datasource. First, you will need to update the `tableView:numberOfRowsInSection:` method to return the number of items in the array, like this:

```
- (NSInteger)tableView:(UITableView *)aTableView
    numberOfRowsInSection:(NSInteger)section {
    // Return the number of rows in the section.
    return [self.surveyDataArray count];
}
```

RootViewController.m

Now, you should change the `tableView:cellForRowAtIndexPath:` method to get data from the `surveyDataArray` to use as the text in the table cells:

```
- (UITableViewCell *)tableView:(UITableView *)tableView
        cellForRowAtIndexPath:(NSIndexPath *)indexPath {

    static NSString *CellIdentifier = @"CellIdentifier";

    // Dequeue or create a cell of the appropriate type.
    UITableViewCell *cell =
        [tableView dequeueReusableCellWithIdentifier:CellIdentifier];
    if (cell == nil) {
        cell = [[[UITableViewCell alloc]
                initWithStyle:UITableViewCellStyleDefault
                reuseIdentifier:CellIdentifier] autorelease];
        cell.accessoryType = UITableViewCellAccessoryNone;
    }

    // Configure the cell.
    NSDictionary* sd = [self.surveyDataArray objectAtIndex:indexPath.row];

    cell.textLabel.text = [NSString stringWithFormat:@"%@, %@",
                        [sd objectForKey:@"lastName"],
                        [sd objectForKey:@"firstName"]];
    return cell;
}
```

RootViewController.m

In this method, you get an `NSDictionary` object from the `surveyDataArray` with an index based on the row that the table has requested. Then, you get the `lastName` and `firstName` strings from the dictionary and display them in the cell's `textLabel`.

The last thing that you need to do in the Table View methods is to update the `tableView:didSelectRowAtIndexPath:` method. In this method, you need to set the `detailItem` in the `detailViewController` to the `NSDictionary` that you retrieve from the `surveyDataArray`. This passes the data that you want to display, the survey that the user has chosen, to the `DetailViewController`. Remember that the setter for the `detailItem` property contains code;

it is not just a synthesized property. This code calls the `configureView` method that updates the view to display the record that the user has chosen. Here is the code for the `tableView: didSelectRowAtIndexPath:` method:

```objectivec
- (void)tableView:(UITableView *)aTableView
    didSelectRowAtIndexPath:(NSIndexPath *)indexPath {

    /*
    When a row is selected, set the detail View Controller's detail item to the
    item associated with the selected row.
    */
    [aTableView deselectRowAtIndexPath:indexPath animated:NO];

    NSDictionary* sd = [self.surveyDataArray objectAtIndex:indexPath.row];
    detailViewController.detailItem = sd;
}
```

RootViewController.m

Adding Surveys

To complete this example, you will add code to the project to enable the user to add surveys to the application. In the `RootViewController` header, you will need to declare a method to add a survey. You should call this method `addSurveyToDataArray` and the signature should look like this:

```objectivec
-(void) addSurveyToDataArray: (NSDictionary*) sd;
```

Recall that you are using an `NSDictionary` to hold the data for each survey. Therefore, the `addSurveyToDataArray` method accepts an `NSDictionary*` that holds the survey data that you want to add to the array of completed surveys.

Next, switch over to the `RootViewController` implementation. You should implement the `addSurveyToDataArray` function as follows:

```objectivec
-(void) addSurveyToDataArray: (NSDictionary*) sd
{
    NSLog (@"addSurveyToDataArray");

    // Add the survey to the results array
    [self.surveyDataArray addObject:sd];

    // Refresh the tableview
    [self.tableView reloadData];
}
```

RootViewController.m

This method simply adds the dictionary object that it receives to the `surveyDataArray`. Then, because the user has modified the data for the Table View, you need to tell the Table View to reload its data in order to refresh the display and show the new survey.

Now, you need to move over to the `DetailViewController` to implement the `addSurvey` method. This method runs when the user taps the Add button in the user interface. First, however, you will need to add `#import` statements to the `DetailViewController` header to import the `RootViewController` and `SurveyAppDelegate` headers:

```
#import "RootViewController.h"
#import "SurveyAppDelegate.h"
```

DetailViewController.h

Now you can move into the `DetailViewController` implementation to implement the `addSurvey` method:

```objc
-(IBAction)addSurvey:(id)sender
{
    NSLog (@"addSurvey");

    // Create a new NSDictionary object to add to the results array of the root
    // View Controller

    // Set the values for the fields in the new object from the text fields of
    // the form

    NSArray *keys = [NSArray arrayWithObjects:@"firstName", @"lastName",
                        @"address", @"phone", @"age", nil];
    NSArray *objects = [NSArray arrayWithObjects:self.firstNameTextField.text,
                        self.lastNameTextField.text,
                        self.addressTextField.text,
                        self.phoneTextField.text,
                        [NSNumber
                            numberWithInteger:[ self.ageTextField.text intValue]],
                        nil];

    NSDictionary* sData = [[NSDictionary alloc]
                            initWithObjects:objects forKeys:keys];


    // Get a reference to the app delegate so we can get a reference to the
    // Root View Controller
    SurveyAppDelegate* appDelegate =
        [[UIApplication sharedApplication] delegate];
    RootViewController* rvc = appDelegate.rootViewController;

    // Call the addSurveyToDataArray method on the rootViewController to
    // add the survey data to the list
    [rvc addSurveyToDataArray:sData];

    // Clean up
    [sData release];

}
```

DetailViewController.m

In this method, you need to build an `NSDictionary` that you will pass to the `RootViewController` to add to the `surveyDataArray`. To create the dictionary, you first create two `NSArrays`, one for the keys of the dictionary and one for the related objects. The keys can be any arbitrary `NSStrings`. You obtain the objects for the dictionary from the `UITextField` objects that you added in Interface Builder. Once you have built your arrays, you create an `NSDictionary` by passing in the `objects` array and the `keys` array.

Next, you need to call the `addSurveyToDataArray` method on the `RootViewController`. If you remember, the `RootViewController` holds a reference to the `DetailViewController`. However, the `DetailViewController` does not hold a reference to the `RootViewController`. There are a couple of ways that you can remedy this. For this example, I have chosen to simply get a reference to the `RootViewController` from the `SurveyAppDelegate`.

You can get a reference to the app delegate at any time by calling the `delegate` method on the application's `UIApplication` object. `UIApplication` is the core object at the root of all iPhone and iPad applications. `UIApplication` is a singleton class to which you can obtain a reference by calling the `sharedApplication` method. Once you obtain a reference to the application, you can call its `delegate` method to get a reference to your application delegate. In this case, the delegate holds references to both the `RootViewController` and the `DetailViewController`. The code then goes on to get a reference to the `RootViewController` from the application delegate. Finally, you call the `addSurveyToDataArray` method on the `RootViewController` to add the newly created survey dictionary to the array.

You are now ready to build and run the application. You should be able to add new surveys and see them appear in the left hand pane in portrait mode. Select an item in the list and you will see the display in the right-hand pane change to the item you selected. Rotate the device to see how the `UISplitViewController` behaves in both landscape and portrait modes.

DISPLAYING DATA IN A POPOVER

Another user interface element that is new and unique to the iPad is the `UIPopoverController`. You can use this controller to display information on top of the current view. This allows you to provide context-sensitive information on top of the main application data without swapping views as would be required in an iPhone application. The `UISplitViewController` uses a `UIPopoverController` to display the master data list when the device is in portrait orientation and the user taps the button to disclose the master list. For example, when your Survey application is in portrait orientation and the user taps the Root List button, the `RootViewController` is displayed in a `UIPopoverController`.

Another interesting feature of the popover is that the user can dismiss it by simply tapping outside its bounds. Therefore, you can use this controller to display information that might not necessarily require any user action. In other words, the user does not have to implicitly accept or cancel any action to dismiss the popover.

The `UIPopoverController` displays a `UIViewController` as its content. You can build the content view in any way that you wish. You should, however, consider the size of the popover as you are building the view that it will contain. You should also consider the position in which you want to show the popover. You should display a popover next to the user interface element that displayed it. When presenting a popover, you can either attach it to a toolbar button or provide a CGRect structure to give the popover a reference location. Finally, you can specify the acceptable directions for the arrow that points from the popover to the reference location. You should generally permit UIKit to control the location of the popover by specifying UIPopoverArrowDirectionAny as the permitted direction for the arrow.

In this section, you will create a UIPopoverController and display it in the Survey application. The popover will simply display a new UIViewController that will show some helpful information on performing surveys, as you can see in Figure 4-6.

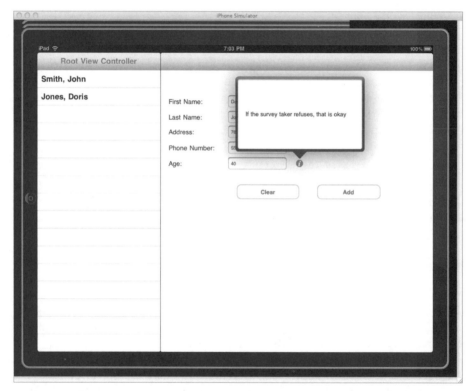

FIGURE 4-6: The Survey Application Informational Popover

Building the InfoViewController

The UIPopoverController is a container that you can use to display another View Controller anywhere on the screen on top of another view. Therefore, the first thing that you need to do when you want to display content in the popover is build the View Controller that you would like to display. For the Survey application, you will create a new class called `InfoViewController`. Then, you will display this class in a `UIPopoverController` when the user taps an informational button.

The first step is to create your new class. Add a new `UIViewController` subclass called `InfoViewController` to your project. As you add the class, make sure that the "Targeted for iPad" and "With XIB for user interface" checkboxes in the New File dialog box are selected.

Open your new `InfoViewController` header file. Add a `UILabel*` instance variable called `infoLabel`. Then, add an `IBOutlet` property that you can use to set and get your new instance variable. Finally, add a method signature for a new method called `setText`. You will use the `setText` method to set the text that you want to display in the popover. The header file for the `InfoViewController` should look like this:

```objc
#import <UIKit/UIKit.h>


@interface InfoViewController : UIViewController {
    UILabel* infoLabel;
}

@property (nonatomic, retain) IBOutlet UILabel* infoLabel;
-(void) setText: (NSString*) text;

@end
```

InfoViewController.h

Next, you will open the `InfoViewController` XIB file with Interface Builder to build the user interface for the new View Controller. Double-click on the `InfoViewController` XIB file to open it in Interface Builder. For this application, the user interface will be extremely simple, just a lone `UILabel`. However, you can build views that are as complex as you want with Interface Builder and use the methodology outlined here to display those interfaces using popovers.

Once you have the XIB file opened in Interface Builder, open the Attributes inspector for the View by pressing Command+1 or selecting Tools ➪ Attributes Inspector from the menu bar. Make sure that you have the View selected. In the Attributes Inspector, set the Status Bar attribute to Unspecified because you do not want the view to have a status bar. Then, using the Size Inspector, which you can open by pressing Command+3 or selecting Tools ➪ Size Inspector from the menu bar, resize the view to a width of 320 pixels and a height of 175 pixels.

Now that you have the view configured correctly, add a `UILabel` control and resize it to fill most of the view. The exact size and position are not particularly important for this example.

Finally, connect the new `UILabel` to the `infoLabel` property of File's Owner. This connects your code to the interface that you built in Interface Builder. You can now save your `InfoViewController` XIB file and close Interface Builder.

Now, you will need to add some logic to the InfoViewController implementation file. First, you should add code to the viewDidUnload and dealloc methods to clean up the instance variable and property of the class:

```
- (void)viewDidUnload {
    [super viewDidUnload];

    self.infoLabel = nil;

    // Release any retained subviews of the main view.
    // e.g. self.myOutlet = nil;
}


- (void)dealloc {
    [infoLabel release];

    [super dealloc];
}
```

InfoViewController.m

Next, add a line to synthesize the infoLabel property:

```
@synthesize infoLabel;
```

The next step is to implement the viewDidLoad method. In this method, you will set the size of the View Controller to display in the popover. Here is the code:

```
- (void)viewDidLoad {
    [super viewDidLoad];

    CGSize size;
    size.width=320;
    size.height = 175;
    self.contentSizeForViewInPopover = size;
}
```

InfoViewController.m

The original size of the popover comes from the View Controller's contentSizeForViewInPopover property. The default size for a UIPopoverController is 320 pixels by 1100 pixels. There are two ways that you can change the size of the popover. First, you can set the size in the View Controller that the popover will hold by setting the View Controller's size using the contentSizeForViewInPopover property. Alternatively, you can set the size of the popoverContentSize property of the Popover Controller. Keep in mind that if you use this method and change the View Controller that you are displaying in the popover, the popover will automatically resize to the size of the new View Controller. The custom size that you set in the popoverContentSize property is lost.

In this example, you created a `CGSize` struct to define the size of the popover in the View Controller. You set the size to 320 pixels wide by 175 pixels high. Then, you set the `contentSizeForViewInPopover` property on the View Controller.

Finally, you need to implement the `setText` method that clients who want to display the `InfoViewController` will use to set the text to display. This method does nothing more than set the text in the `UILabel`:

```
-(void) setText: (NSString*) text
{
    self.infoLabel.text = text;
}
```

InfoViewController.m

Displaying the UIPopoverController

Now that you have a View Controller, you need to display it in a popover. You will display the popover when the user taps a button in the `DetailViewController`. Therefore, you will need to make some changes to the `DetailViewController` header file. First, add a `#import` statement for the new `InfoViewController.h` header file:

```
#import "InfoViewController.h"
```

Next, you will add a new action method called `showInfo`. The user will invoke this method when he taps on the information button in the user interface. Here is the declaration:

```
-(IBAction)showInfo:(id)sender;
```

The next step is to add a new outlet and instance variable for the `UIButton*` called `infoButton`. Inside of the interface declaration, add the instance variable for the `UIButton*`:

```
UIButton* infoButton;
```

Outside of the interface declaration, declare the `infoButton` property:

```
@property (nonatomic, retain) IBOutlet UIButton* infoButton;
```

Now add an instance variable for the `UIPopoverController`. Call it `infoPopover`:

```
UIPopoverController *infoPopover;
```

Add a property for the `infoPopover`:

```
@property (nonatomic, retain) UIPopoverController *infoPopover;
```

Now you need to move over to the `DetailViewController` implementation file.

In the implementation, synthesize the new `infoButton` and `infoPopover` properties:

```
@synthesize infoButton,infoPopover;
```

Next, you will implement the `showInfo` method to show the `InfoViewController` in the `infoPopover`:

```
-(IBAction)showInfo:(id)sender
{
    NSLog (@"showInfo");

    // Instatiate Info View Controller
    InfoViewController *ivc = [[InfoViewController alloc] init];

    UIPopoverController *popover =
        [[UIPopoverController alloc] initWithContentViewController:ivc];

    [ivc setText:@"If the survey taker refuses, that is okay"];

    [ivc release];

    // Set the infoPopover property
    self.infoPopover = popover;

    // Clean up the local popover
    [popover release];

    [self.infoPopover presentPopoverFromRect:self.infoButton.frame
                           inView:self.view
             permittedArrowDirections:UIPopoverArrowDirectionAny
                           animated:YES];

}
```

DetailViewController.m

The first thing that you do in this method, after logging the method name, is create an instance of the `InfoViewController`.

Next, you allocate a `UIPopoverController` and initialize it by calling the `initWithContentViewController` method. You pass the View Controller that you want to display in the popover as a parameter to this method. Next, you set the text that you want to display in the popover and release the `InfoViewController`. You must send the `InfoViewController` the release message or you will leak memory. When you pass the View Controller in to the popover in the `initWithContentViewController` method, the popover will retain the View Controller.

The next step is to set the `infoPopover` property to the new popover that you created in this method. Then, you can release the local popover.

Finally, you call the `presentPopoverFromRect:inView:permittedArrowDirections:animated:` method to present the popover. The first parameter to this method specifies the `CGRect` structure from which the popover should emanate. In this example, you use the frame of the info button that you will add to the user interface. Then, you specify the view that will hold the popover. The `permittedArrowDirections` parameter allows you to specify from which direction the popover will appear with respect to the frame that you specified in the first parameter. Generally, you should specify any direction as permitted and leave the layout and positioning of the popover to the UIKit framework. The permitted directions are specified using members from the `UIPopoverArrowDirection` enumeration. Valid direction values are:

➤   `UIPopoverArrowDirectionUp`

➤   `UIPopoverArrowDirectionDown`

➤   `UIPopoverArrowDirectionLeft`

➤   `UIPopoverArrowDirectionRight`

➤   `UIPopoverArrowDirectionAny`

➤   `UIPopoverArrowDirectionUnknown`

Finally, the last parameter specifies whether the framework should animate the display of the popover.

The last step is to clean up the `infoButton` and `infoPopover` properties in the `dealloc` and `viewDidUnload` methods:

Available for download on Wrox.com

```objc
- (void)viewDidUnload {
    // Release any retained subviews of the main view.
    // e.g. self.myOutlet = nil;
    self.popoverController = nil;

    self.firstNameTextField = nil;
    self.lastNameTextField = nil;
    self.addressTextField = nil;
    self.phoneTextField = nil;
    self.ageTextField = nil;

    self.infoButton = nil;
    self.infoPopover = nil;
}

- (void)dealloc {
    [popoverController release];
    [toolbar release];

    [detailItem release];
    [firstNameTextField release];
    [lastNameTextField release];
    [addressTextField release];
    [phoneTextField release];
    [ageTextField release];
    [infoButton release];
    [infoPopover release];
    [super dealloc];
}
```

DetailViewController.m

Now, you need to add the info button to the user interface in Interface Builder. Open the `DetailView.xib` file in Interface Builder. Add a new `UIButton` next to the age `UITextField`. In the attributes inspector for the button, change the type of the button to Info Dark. This will change the button from a rounded rectangle to a gray circle with a white letter i inside.

Next, wire the File's Owner `infoButton` property to the new button. Then, wire the `infoButton`'s `touchUpInside` event to the File's Owner `showInfo` method.

You are finished with the interface so you can save the XIB file and close Interface Builder.

Build and run the application. When the interface appears, tap the new info button. You should see the message appear in a popover next to the info button.

GESTURE RECOGNIZERS

The basic UIKit controls such as the `UIButton` can detect simple user interactions such as pressing down on the button and lifting a finger up. You can see these events in Interface Builder by selecting a `UIButton` and opening the Connections inspector.

Before iPhone OS 3.2, if your application required a more complex behavior such as recognizing swipe or pinch gestures, you had to implement these features yourself. This would involve writing your own code to examine the stream of user touches and the implementation of heuristics algorithms to determine if the user was performing the gestures. To assist developers, Apple introduced the concept of Gesture Recognizers in iPhone OS 3.2. You can use gesture recognizers on both the iPhone and the iPad as long as the device that you are targeting is running at least iOS 3.2.

The UIGestureRecognizer Class

The `UIGestureRecognizer` class is an abstract base class that defines what gesture recognizer classes must do and how they should operate. Apple has provided the concrete subclasses `UIPinchGestureRecognizer`, `UIPanGestureRecognizer`, and `UISwipeGestureRecogsnizer` that you can use in your applications to recognize pinch, pan, and swipe gestures respectively. This saves you from having to write the significant amount of code required to interpret a series of touches as one of these common gestures. However, if your application requires gestures that the framework does not support, you can implement your own custom gesture recognizer as a `UIGestureRecognizer` subclass to define any gesture that your application may need.

To use a gesture recognizer, you must attach the gesture recognizer to a view. When you attach a gesture recognizer to a view, the framework routes touches in the application to the gesture recognizer before sending them to the view. This gives the gesture recognizer the chance to evaluate the touches to see if they qualify as a gesture. If the touches meet the requirements of a gesture, the framework cancels the touch messages and instead of sending the touches to the view, the framework sends a gesture message instead. If the touches do not qualify as a gesture, the framework sends the touches to the view.

There are two different types of gestures, *discrete* and *continuous*. A discrete gesture, such as a tap, causes the gesture recognizer to simply send one action message when the action is complete. A continuous gesture, like a pinch, results in the gesture recognizer calling the action message multiple times until the continuous action is completed.

You implement a gesture recognizer in your code by instantiating a gesture recognizer concrete class. This can be one of the Apple provided classes mentioned above, or your own custom subclass of UIGestureRecognizer. Then, you assign a target and an action to the recognizer. The target is the class that will receive the action and the action is the method that the gesture recognizer will call when a gesture is recognized. Finally, you attach the gesture recognizer to the view in which you want gestures recognized.

In this section, you will add gesture recognizers to your Survey application. You will use a UISwipeGestureRecognizer to determine if the user has swiped across the DetailViewController screen. If he has, you will navigate either forward or backward in the survey list, depending on the direction of the swipe, and display the appropriate record.

Using Gesture Recognizers

The first step in using a gesture recognizer is to create an instance of the recognizer that you want to use and attach it to a view. You will do this in the viewDidLoad method of the DetailViewController like this:

Available for download on Wrox.com

```
- (void)viewDidLoad {
    [super viewDidLoad];

    // Create the right swipe gesture recognizer
    UISwipeGestureRecognizer *swipeRight = [[UISwipeGestureRecognizer alloc]
        initWithTarget:self action:@selector(handleSwipeRight:)];

    swipeRight.direction=UISwipeGestureRecognizerDirectionRight;

    // Attach it to the view
    [self.view addGestureRecognizer:swipeRight];


    // Create the left swipe gesture recognizer
    UISwipeGestureRecognizer *swipeLeft = [[UISwipeGestureRecognizer alloc]
        initWithTarget:self action:@selector(handleSwipeLeft:)];

    swipeLeft.direction=UISwipeGestureRecognizerDirectionLeft;

    // Attach it to the view
    [self.view addGestureRecognizer:swipeLeft];


    // Clean up
    [swipeRight release];
    [swipeLeft release];
}
```

DetailViewController.m

First, you call the superclass viewDidLoad method to ensure that the class is set up correctly.

Next, you create an instance of the UISwipeGestureRecognizer. In creating this instance, you need to specify the target class that will receive the action method call when the gesture recognizer detects a swipe. The action parameter specifies the method that the gesture recognizer should call when it detects the gesture. In this case, the target is `self` and the method the gesture recognizer will call is `handleSwipeRight`, which you will implement in a moment.

After you create an instance of the `UISwipeGestureRecognizer`, you need to specify which swipe direction you want to detect. Here, you have specified that you would like to detect swipes to the right.

Finally, you add the gesture recognizer to the view by calling the view's `addGestureRecognizer` method, passing in the gesture recognizer.

The code then goes on to perform the same procedure to attach another swipe gesture recognizer to the view. This time, you configure the recognizer to detect swipes to the left. You have also set this gesture recognizer to call the `handleSwipeLeft` method as its action.

Lastly, you release both of the gesture recognizers that you created in this method.

In the `DetailViewController` header, add action methods for the gesture recognizers `handleSwipeRight` and `handleSwipeLeft`:

```
-(void)handleSwipeRight:(UIGestureRecognizer*) sender;
-(void)handleSwipeLeft:(UIGestureRecognizer*) sender;
```

DetailViewController.h

In order to be able to implement the functionality to navigate forward and backward in the survey array using gestures, you have to add a variable and a couple of methods to the `RootViewController`. In the `RootViewController` header file, add an instance variable of type `int` called `currentIndex`. You will use this variable to maintain the index of the record that you are displaying in the `DetailViewController`. Here is the declaration:

```
int currentIndex;
```

You also need to add declarations for two new methods, `moveNext` and `movePrevious`. The gesture recognizer action methods will call these methods on the `RootViewController` to tell the `RootViewController` to navigate to the next or previous record. Here are the declarations for the `moveNext` and `movePrevious` methods:

```
-(void) moveNext;
-(void) movePrevious;
```

DetailViewController.h

In the `RootViewController` implementation, you will need to add code to the `viewDidLoad` method to initialize the `currentIndex` instance variable:

```
- (void)viewDidLoad {
    [super viewDidLoad];
    self.clearsSelectionOnViewWillAppear = NO;
    self.contentSizeForViewInPopover = CGSizeMake(320.0, 600.0);
```

```
        // Set up surveyDataArray
        NSMutableArray* array = [[NSMutableArray alloc] init];
        self.surveyDataArray = array;

        // Initialize the current index
        currentIndex = 0;
    }
```

RootViewController.m

Next, you need to modify the `tableView:didSelectRowAtIndexPath:` method to set the `currentIndex` instance variable to the row that the user has selected in the table:

```
- (void)tableView:(UITableView *)aTableView
    didSelectRowAtIndexPath:(NSIndexPath *)indexPath {

    /*
    When a row is selected, set the detail View Controller's detail item to the
    item associated with the selected row.
    */
    [aTableView deselectRowAtIndexPath:indexPath animated:NO];

    NSDictionary* sd = [self.surveyDataArray objectAtIndex:indexPath.row];
    detailViewController.detailItem = sd;

    // Set the currentIndex
    currentIndex = indexPath.row;

}
```

RootViewController.m

Finally, you will implement the `moveNext` and `movePrevious` methods:

```
-(void) moveNext
{
    NSLog (@"moveNext");
    // Check to make sure that there is a next item to move to
    if (currentIndex < (int)[self.surveyDataArray count] -1)
    {
        NSDictionary* sd = [self.surveyDataArray objectAtIndex:++currentIndex];
        detailViewController.detailItem = sd;
    }
}

-(void) movePrevious
{
    NSLog (@"movePrevious");
    // Check to make sure that there is a previous item to move to
    if (currentIndex > 0)
    {
```

```
            NSDictionary* sd = [self.surveyDataArray objectAtIndex:--currentIndex];
            detailViewController.detailItem = sd;
        }


    }
```

RootViewController.m

In the moveNext method, you first check to make sure that the next record exists. If it does, you increment the currentIndex, get the object at the new index from the surveyDataArray, and set the detailItem of the DetailViewController to the corresponding NSDictionary.

The movePrevious method is the same with one minor exception. You need to test to make sure that the user is not trying to navigate backward if the current index is already 0.

Back in the DetailViewController implementation, you are ready to implement the handleSwipeRight and handleSwipeLeft methods:

```
-(void)handleSwipeRight:(UIGestureRecognizer*) sender
{
    NSLog (@"handleSwipeRight");
    // Get a reference to the app delegate so we can get a reference to the
    // Root View Controller
    SurveyAppDelegate* appDelegate =
        [[UIApplication sharedApplication] delegate];
    RootViewController* rvc = appDelegate.rootViewController;

    // Call the movePrevious method on the rootViewController to move to the
    // previous survey in the list
    [rvc movePrevious];
}

-(void)handleSwipeLeft:(UIGestureRecognizer*) sender
{
    NSLog (@"handleSwipeLeft");
    // Get a reference to the app delegate so we can get a reference to the
    // Root View Controller
    SurveyAppDelegate* appDelegate =
        [[UIApplication sharedApplication] delegate];
    RootViewController* rvc = appDelegate.rootViewController;

    // Call the moveNext method on the rootViewController to move to the
    // next survey in the list
    [rvc moveNext];
}
```

DetailViewController.m

In the handleSwipeRight and handleSwipeLeft methods, you do almost the same thing. First, you get a reference to the app delegate so that you can get a reference to the RootViewController. Then, you call the appropriate method, either moveNext or movePrevious, on the RootViewController.

Build and run the application. You should be able to add new surveys to the application. Then, select a row, or just start with the first row. Swipe right in the `DetailViewController` and the application should display the data in the `DetailViewController` for the next entry in the completed survey list. Swiping to the left should display the detail information for the previous entry in the list.

FILE SHARING SUPPORT

Sometimes, when building applications, you will create data on the device that you want to share with the desktop or vice versa. In iPhone SDK 3.2, Apple introduced the capability of sharing files between the desktop and the device through iTunes. If you have purchased the Pages, Numbers, or Keynote application for the iPad, you have seen that you can create documents on your computer and make them available on the iPad. Conversely, you can create new documents on the iPad and they are available in iTunes to move onto the computer.

Using the file sharing support with the 3.2 iPhone SDK, developers can make the contents of the application's `/Documents` directory available to the user on the computer. Keep in mind that file-sharing support does not enable sharing of documents between applications on the device.

Enabling file sharing is simple. You need only make a change to the `Info.plist` file that you deploy with your application. In this section, you will add code to the Survey application that will store the completed surveys as an XML file. Then, using file sharing, you will see that you can access this file on the computer after syncing through iTunes.

Enable File Sharing in the Sample Application

First, you need to add a new key, `UIFileSharingEnabled,` to the `Survey-Info.plist` file. This file is located in the Resources folder of your Xcode project. You can add this key inside of Xcode by first selecting the `Survey-Info.plist` file in the browser pane. You should see the plist file displayed in the right hand pane. Click in the right hand margin next to any of the plist entries and you will see a plus sign appear. Click the plus sign to add a new entry to the plist. In the dropdown list that appears, select "Application supports iTunes file sharing." To the right of the key, you will then see a box with a checkmark in it. Leave the box checked to enable file sharing.

That is all that you need to do to enable file sharing.

Serializing the Survey Data Array

Next, you will add code to serialize the `surveyDataArray` and store the serialized file in the `/Documents` folder for the application.

When the user installs an application on an iPhone or iPad, the installation process creates a home directory for that application. Each application has its own home directory. You should write your application data files to the `/Documents` directory. Additionally, iTunes backs up this directory when the user syncs the device with a computer.

Now that you understand where to save the application data, you will add code to the `applicationWillTerminate` method in the `SureveyAppDelegate` to serialize the array and save it to a file. *Serialization* simply takes a data structure that is stored in memory, in this case an array, and converts it to a format that can be saved to a file or sent over a network. Here is the implementation:

```
- (void)applicationWillTerminate:(UIApplication *)application {
    // Serialize the rootViewController's surveyDataArray
    NSData *serializedData;
    NSString *error;

    serializedData = [NSPropertyListSerialization
                        dataFromPropertyList:rootViewController.surveyDataArray
                        format:NSPropertyListXMLFormat_v1_0
                        errorDescription:&error];

    if (serializedData)
    {
        // Serialization was successful, write the data to the file system
        // Get an array of paths.
        // (This function is carried over from the desktop)
        NSArray *documentDirectoryPath =
            NSSearchPathForDirectoriesInDomains(NSDocumentDirectory,
                                                NSUserDomainMask, YES);
        NSString *docDir = [NSString stringWithFormat:@"%@/serialized.xml",
                            [documentDirectoryPath objectAtIndex:0]];

        [serializedData writeToFile:docDir atomically:YES];
    }
    else
    {
        // An error has occurred, log it
        NSLog(@"Error: %@",error);
    }
}
```

SurveyAppDelegate.m

First, you serialize the data in the surveyData array by using the NSPropertyListSerialization class. This class provides methods that covert the types of objects that you can use in a property list (NSData, NSString, NSArray, NSDictionary, NSDate, and NSNumber) into different serialized forms. In this case, you will convert an NSArray into XML format. I chose XML for this example so that you could open the file on your computer after syncing with iTunes and verify that the data in the file is the same as the data that is contained in the application. For production applications, it is generally more efficient to use the binary format.

After serializing the array to XML, the code obtains the path to the /Documents directory for the application. Here, you use the NSSearchPathForDirectoriesInDomains function to obtain the path to the /Documents directory by passing in the NSDocumentDirectory constant as the directory parameter. The NSSearchPathDirectory enumeration provides several predefined constants that you can use to help you to navigate to specific directories.

Next, you use the path to the /Documents directory to build a string that represents the file that you want to save. Finally, you call the writeToFile method of the serializedData object to write the XML to a file.

Deserializing and Loading the Survey Data Array

Now that you have written code to save the survey data array to disk, you need to add code to load the array from disk when the application starts. The process of taking the data from its on-disk format and turning it back into an object is called *deserialization*. You will do that in the RootViewController's viewDidLoad method. Modify the viewDidLoad method to use the data from the plist, if it exists, like this:

```
- (void)viewDidLoad {
    [super viewDidLoad];
    self.clearsSelectionOnViewWillAppear = NO;
    self.contentSizeForViewInPopover = CGSizeMake(320.0, 600.0);

    // Set up surveyDataArray
    // Get an array of paths. (This function is carried over from the desktop)
    NSArray *documentDirectoryPath =
    NSSearchPathForDirectoriesInDomains(NSDocumentDirectory,
                                        NSUserDomainMask, YES);
    NSString *docDir = [NSString stringWithFormat:@"%@/serialized.xml",
                        [documentDirectoryPath objectAtIndex:0]];
    NSData* serializedData = [NSData dataWithContentsOfFile:docDir];

    // If serializedData is nil, the file doesn't exist yet
    if (serializedData == nil)
    {
        NSMutableArray* array = [[NSMutableArray alloc] init];
        self.surveyDataArray = array;
        [array release];
    }
    else
    {
        // Read data from the file
        NSString *error;

        self.surveyDataArray =
        (NSMutableArray *)[NSPropertyListSerialization
                            propertyListFromData:serializedData
                            mutabilityOption:kCFPropertyListMutableContainers
                            format:NULL errorDescription:&error];
    }

    // Initialize the current index
    currentIndex = 0;
}
```

RootViewController.m

This code is the opposite of the code that you wrote in the previous section. First, you create the file name the same way that you did before using the NSSearchPathForDirectoriesInDomains function. Then, you create an NSData object from the serialized file by calling the dataWithContentsOfFile method.

Next, you need to check if the serialized data exists. If there is no data, you need to create a new `NSMutableArray*` to hold the completed surveys. If there was data, you populate the `surveyDataArray` from the `NSData` object by calling the `propertyListFromData:mutabilityOption:format:errorDescription:` method of the `NSPropertyListSerialization` class.

Sharing the Data

Now you are ready to build and run the application on an iPad device. Add some survey data and then quit the application.

To retrieve the data from the iPad, hook your iPad up to your computer and sync it with iTunes. Click on the iPad under Devices in iTunes and select the Apps tab. If you scroll to the bottom, you should see Survey listed as one of the applications in the Apps box, as in Figure 4-7. Click on Survey and you should see `serialized.xml` in the Survey Documents window. Click on `serialized.xml` and click the Save to button. Save the file to your desktop or some other convenient location.

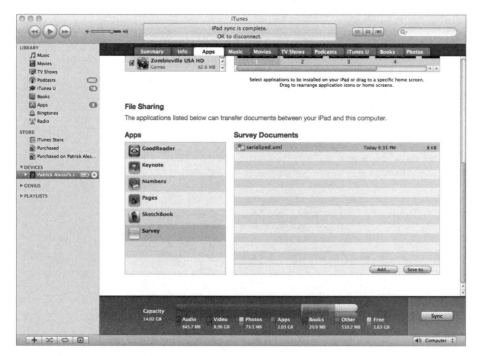

FIGURE 4-7: Survey application and data in iTunes

You should be able to navigate to that XML file using the Finder. If you open the XML file, you should see an XML representation of your data. The XML for the sample data looks like this:

```xml
<?xml version="1.0" encoding="UTF-8"?>
<!DOCTYPE plist PUBLIC "-//Apple//DTD PLIST 1.0//EN" "http://www.apple.com/DTDs/
    PropertyList-1.0.dtd">
<plist version="1.0">
<array>
    <dict>
        <key>address</key>
        <string>123 Any St.</string>
        <key>age</key>
        <integer>20</integer>
        <key>firstName</key>
        <string>John</string>
        <key>lastName</key>
        <string>Smith</string>
        <key>phone</key>
        <string>555-1234</string>
    </dict>
    <dict>
        <key>address</key>
        <string>789 Town St.</string>
        <key>age</key>
        <integer>40</integer>
        <key>firstName</key>
        <string>Doris</string>
        <key>lastName</key>
        <string>Jones</string>
        <key>phone</key>
        <string>555-1234</string>
    </dict>
</array>
</plist>
```

MOVING FORWARD

In this chapter, you learned how to use some of the features of the iPhone SDK that are specific to the iPad. First, you explored using the UISplitViewController to build master/detail displays. Then, you learned how to display informational messages on top of another view using the UIPopoverController. Next, you discovered how to use gesture recognizers to handle complex user interactions. Finally, you found out how you can share data between the device and the computer by using file-sharing support.

This concludes Part I, where you learned how to build a simple data-based application, how to get data onto the device and store it using SQLite, and how to display data and customize the display of data using the UITableView.

In Part II, you will learn about the Core Data framework. Core Data is a powerful library that you can use to create and manage data on the iPhone. Core Data comes with a powerful modeling tool that you will use to help you define the data model for your applications.

PART II
Managing Your Data with Core Data

5

Introducing Core Data

WHAT'S IN THIS CHAPTER?

➤ Describing what the Core Data API can do for you

➤ Understanding the various objects that make up the Core Data API

➤ Understanding how the template code works to configure your application to use Core Data

➤ Creating a simple application that uses Core Data to maintain application state

Now that you have completed the first part of the book, you should be comfortable using an SQLite database and implementing views into your data with the UITableView control. You have learned to build data-driven applications for the iPhone that can efficiently access large amounts of data stored in an SQLite database and display that data with your own, highly customized, tables.

Up until this point, you have not looked at how to store the data that users create on the device. For instance, if you wanted to create a task manager, you would need to be able to save the user-created tasks. You could use SQLite to INSERT the data, now that you know how to execute arbitrary SQL statements against the database. However, there is an API designed specifically for storing the objects in your application model: Core Data.

In this chapter, you learn about the architecture of the Core Data API and the classes that you use to build a Core Data application. You will walk through a Core Data template application to learn how to implement the architecture in code. Then you will learn how to build a simple application that uses Core Data for storage.

This chapter prepares you for the next few chapters where you dive deeply into the Core Data tools and API.

THE BASICS OF CORE DATA

Core Data is a set of APIs designed to simplify the persistence of data objects. Sometimes you will hear people refer to Core Data as an object persistence framework or an object graph manager. Core Data provides a framework for saving your model objects and retrieving them later. Core Data also manages changes to your object model, provides undo support, and ensures the consistency of relationships between your model objects. All of these features help to free you from having to write the code to implement this functionality. In essence, Core Data simplifies the creation of the Model part of the Model-View-Controller architecture.

The foundation of the Core Data tool set is a code-based API used to manipulate your data objects in code. However, the tool set also includes a graphical data modeler that you can use to define your model objects. The modeler allows you to define your data objects, their attributes, and their relationships with the other objects in your application. You can even specify constraints and simple validation rules inside the graphical tool. You explore the data modeling tool and all of its uses in the next chapter.

The graphical modeler simplifies creation of the model in the same way that Interface Builder simplifies the creation of the view. Using Core Data and Interface Builder, you can quickly build the Model and View components of the MVC architecture, leaving only the controller business logic left to code. This can significantly reduce the development time of your projects.

In addition to its ease of use, Core Data provides some important performance enhancements as well. Core Data can use SQLite as its backing data store. This provides a Core Data with high performance query engine. When compared to searching and sorting through flat data files or plists, Core Data is the clear choice for speed. Additionally, the API is able to conserve memory by retrieving only the data that you need at any specific time. For example, if you have two related entities, Core Data will not retrieve the child entities until you ask for them. This conserves memory, which is a scarce resource on mobile devices. You learn more about this functionality, called *faulting*, in the chapters to come.

Core Data provides many of the functions that you would expect to find when dealing with data objects. Specifically, you can filter your data using predicates with the `NSPredicate` class, and sort your data using the `NSSortDescriptor` class. I touch on these classes here and get into much finer detail in Chapter 6.

THE CORE DATA ARCHITECTURE

To understand how to use Core Data, it helps to have an understanding of the underlying architecture. While you will not be accessing most of the objects contained in the API directly, you will be much more proficient if you understand how Core Data works.

The Core Data Stack

The design of Core Data is a stack structure, as shown in Figure 5-1. The key components are the data store, the Persistent Store Coordinator, the Managed Object Model, and the Managed Object Context. While I feel that it is important to understand what is going on behind the scenes, try not to get confused by the terminology introduced in this section. It may seem overwhelming now, but as you work through the template and the sample in this chapter, the details of how you use Core Data should become clear.

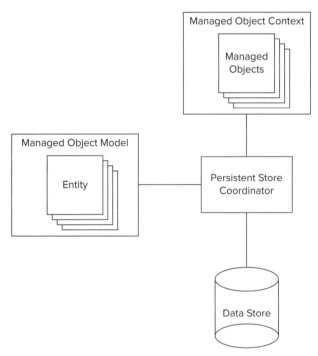

FIGURE 5-1: The Core Data stack

The Data Store

The data store is the file or group of files that hold your data. This is the actual file written to the disk when the save message is sent to Core Data. Typically, in a mobile application, only one data store file is used. However, it is possible to use a group of files as the data store.

The data store can be a binary data file, an SQLite database, or an in-memory data file, depending on the parameters used when creating the data store. You will see how to specify the storage type for your data in the example at the end of the chapter.

As the developer, you will never directly access the data store. The Persistent Store Coordinator abstracts away access to the data file. In addition, you do not need to concern yourself with the data store implementation. Simply consider it a file that holds all of your data.

The Persistent Store Coordinator

This Persistent Store Coordinator acts as a mediator between the managed object context and the data store. The coordinator takes requests for data from the context and forwards them to the appropriate data store. The coordinator also allows the context to access one or more data stores as if they were one. Finally, the coordinator associates a data store with a Managed Object Model. The Persistent Store Coordinator is an instance of the NSPersistentStoreCoordinator class.

 You need to be aware that the NSPersistentStoreCoordinator *class is not thread safe. Therefore, if you plan to access a data store simultaneously across multiple threads, you have to either create a coordinator for each thread or lock and unlock the single coordinator manually.*

The Managed Object Model

The Managed Object Model represents the data model schema. In code, the Managed Object Model is an instance of the NSManagedObjectModel class.

The model consists of a set of entities that define the data objects in your application. When designing your model, you specify the data entities that your application will deal with. You can specify attributes for these entities and define the relationships between them.

You typically create the model graphically using the Xcode data-modeling tool although it is possible to define the model in code. You can think of the managed object model like the Entity-Relationship diagram that you would create when designing a database.

The data model should define each data object used in your application. The Persistent Store Coordinator uses the model to create Managed Objects according to conventions from the entities defined in the model. The coordinator also maps the entities in the model into the physical data store file that Core Data writes to disk.

You will rarely access the object model through your code. If the need arises, you can use the NSManagedObjectModel class. You access the Managed Objects created from the model entities using the Managed Object Context.

The Managed Object Context

The Managed Object Context, also referred to as the *context*, provides the main interface that you will use to access your managed data objects. The managed object context is an instance of the NSManagedObjectContext class.

You use the context to hold all of your managed data objects. Your managed data objects are either instances or subclasses of the NSManagedObject class. The name Managed Object makes sense as the Managed Object Context manages all of these objects.

You can think of the context as the sandbox that holds all of your application data. You can add objects to the context, delete them, and modify them in memory. Then, when you are ready, you can tell the context to commit its current state to disk. Behind the scenes, the context uses the Persistent Store Coordinator to write your data out to the data store on disk. The context uses the object model to ensure that your data is in a consistent state with respect to your defined relationships, constraints, and validation rules before committing it to disk.

You make fetch requests against the context to fetch data from the data store back into the context. You fetch data into Managed Objects that you use to manipulate and display your data. Fetch requests are similar to SQL SELECT statements. When creating a fetch request, you can provide a predicate to filter your data such as the SQL WHERE clause. You also provide a sort array that functions like the SQL ORDER BY clause.

SQLite and Core Data

In Chapter 2, you learned how to use SQLite as the database engine for your application. Now that you have learned about Core Data, you may be wondering how the two are related.

SQLite is a library that provides a relational database implementation used on the iPhone. Core Data can use SQLite as the on-disk data store to persist your data. Core Data can also use a proprietary binary data file for the data store. However, I would not generally recommend this because the binary format requires that your entire object graph be loaded into memory as opposed to using the SQLite format, which allows parts of the object graph to be loaded as needed.

While you learned how to view and modify the schema and data in an SQLite database, you should never attempt to manually modify the schema or data in a Core Data SQLite data store. Core Data requires that the data in the database be stored in a specific way in order to function. You should feel free to browse the schema and data if you care to, but you should never attempt to modify either.

USING CORE DATA: A SIMPLE TASK MANAGER

Now that you are familiar with the terminology and the Core Data API architecture, I am going to walk through a simple example application so that you can get your feet wet with using Core Data. You will first take a look at everything that you get "for free" when you start a new application and tell Xcode that you want to use Core Data as the backing data store. Then, you will customize the template-generated code to create an application to keep track of a very simple task list.

You may feel overwhelmed by all of the information that you learned in the previous section. You should take two things away from the previous section. First is that most, if not all, of your interaction with Core Data in your code will be through the Managed Object Context and Managed Objects. The other is that you will define your data model graphically using the tool provided in Xcode.

Creating the Project

The application that you are going to create is a simple task manager. It will allow you to enter new tasks and remove completed tasks. When you create a task, it will be time-stamped. The application will sort the tasks based on the timestamp with the newest tasks at the top of the list. Figure 5-2 shows the application in action.

FIGURE 5-2: The completed Tasks application

To start the project, open Xcode and create a new Navigation-based Application from the new project template. Make sure that you select the option to "Use Core Data for storage" in the new project window. Call the new project "Tasks."

After you have created the project, build and run it. You will see that you get quite a bit of functionality from the template without adding any code at all.

If you click on the plus button in the upper-right corner, time-stamp entries get added to your TableView. You can swipe across an entry and click the Delete button to delete individual timestamps. You can also click the Edit button to go into editing mode where you can delete entries by clicking the icon to the left of a timestamp and then clicking the Delete button.

If you click the Home button in the iPhone simulator and then click the icon on the home screen for your Tasks application, you will see that any timestamps that you did not delete are still there. Your application already includes the code required to persist your data.

Examining the Template Code

Before you get into modifying the code to create and display tasks, let's take a walk through the template code. This should provide you with some insight into how the application works along with showing you how to implement the Core Data architecture in code. Keep in mind that all of this code is auto-generated when you select the Navigation-based Application template and opt to use Core Data for storage.

Two classes are created by the template: RootViewController and AppDelegate. You create these same classes in any typical Navigation-based application. Additionally, if you open the Resources folder of your project, you will see a data model file that was also auto-generated called Tasks .xcdatamodel. Let's look at each of these files.

TasksAppDelegate

While you won't be modifying any of the code in the app delegate, it is instructive to look at the code. The code in the app delegate sets up the Core Data stack. Therefore, as you might imagine, there is code to create a Persistent Store Coordinator, Managed Object Model, and Managed Object Context.

The persistentStoreCoordinator getter method returns the Persistent Store Coordinator for the application. Here is the code:

```
- (NSPersistentStoreCoordinator *)persistentStoreCoordinator {

    if (persistentStoreCoordinator != nil) {
        return persistentStoreCoordinator;
    }

    NSURL *storeUrl = [NSURL fileURLWithPath:
                        [[self applicationDocumentsDirectory]
                         stringByAppendingPathComponent: @"Tasks.sqlite"]];

    NSError *error = nil;
    persistentStoreCoordinator = [[NSPersistentStoreCoordinator alloc]
```

```
                initWithManagedObjectModel:[self managedObjectModel]];
    if (![persistentStoreCoordinator
        addPersistentStoreWithType:NSSQLiteStoreType
        configuration:nil URL:storeUrl
        options:nil
        error:&error]) {
    /*
    Replace this implementation with code to handle the error
    appropriately.

    abort() causes the application to generate a crash log and terminate.
    You should not use this function in a shipping application, although
    it may be useful during development. If it is not possible to recover
    from the error, display an alert panel that instructs the user to quit
    the application by pressing the Home button.

    Typical reasons for an error here include:
    * The persistent store is not accessible
    * The schema for the persistent store is incompatible with current
      managed object model
    Check the error message to determine what the actual problem was.
    */
    NSLog(@"Unresolved error %@, %@", error, [error userInfo]);
    abort();
    }

    return persistentStoreCoordinator;
}
```

TasksAppDelegate.m

The code first determines if the Persistent Store Coordinator already exists. If it exists, the method returns it to you.

If the coordinator does not exist, the code must create it. In order to create the coordinator, you need to pass in a URL that points to the data store. The template uses the `fileURLWithPath:` method on the `NSURL` class to create the URL. You can see that the store name will be `Tasks.sqlite`.

Next, the code allocates an `NSError` object to hold the error data that the Persistent Store Coordinator generates if there is a problem configuring the coordinator.

The next line allocates and initializes the coordinator using the Managed Object Model. You will look at the `managedObjectModel` getter method in a moment. Remember that you use the Persistent Store Coordinator to mediate between the Managed Object Context, the Managed Object Model, and the data store. Therefore, it makes sense that the coordinator would need to have a reference to the model.

Now that the coordinator knows about the model, the code goes on to tell it about the data store. The next line of code adds the data store to the coordinator. You will notice that the type of the data store is `NSSQLiteStoreType`. This indicates that the template uses the SQLite backing data store. If you wanted to use the binary store, you would change this enumeration value to `NSBinaryStoreType`, and if you wanted to use the in-memory store, you would set the value to `NSInMemoryStoreType`. Remember that most often you will be using the SQLite backing store.

The rest of the code logs an error if there was a problem adding the SQLite store to the coordinator. If there was no error, the method returns the coordinator.

The getter function to return the Managed Object Model is very straightforward:

```
- (NSManagedObjectModel *)managedObjectModel {

    if (managedObjectModel != nil) {
        return managedObjectModel;
    }
    managedObjectModel = [[NSManagedObjectModel
                            mergedModelFromBundles:nil] retain];
    return managedObjectModel;
}
```

TasksAppDelegate.m

If the model already exists, the getter method returns it. If not, the code creates a new Managed Object Model by merging all of the model files contained in the application bundle. The Tasks.xcdatamodel file in the Resources folder contains the object model. This file is included with the application bundle, so this method takes that file and uses it to create the NSManagedObjectModel object.

The last bit of interesting code in the App Delegate is the managedObjectContext getter method:

```
- (NSManagedObjectContext *) managedObjectContext {

    if (managedObjectContext != nil) {
        return managedObjectContext;
    }

    NSPersistentStoreCoordinator *coordinator =
        [self persistentStoreCoordinator];
    if (coordinator != nil) {
        managedObjectContext = [[NSManagedObjectContext alloc] init];
        [managedObjectContext setPersistentStoreCoordinator: coordinator];
    }
    return managedObjectContext;
}
```

TasksAppDelegate.m

This method works similarly to the previous two. The first thing it does is check to see if the context already exists. If the context exists, the method returns it.

Next, the code gets a reference to the persistentStoreCoordinator. If you refer back to Figure 5-1, you will see that the Managed Object Context needs only a reference to the Persistent Store Coordinator.

If the code successfully gets a reference to the coordinator, it goes on to create the context. Then, the code sets the coordinator for the context and returns the context.

I hope that the way in which all of the objects in the Core Data stack fit together is becoming a bit clearer. Remember that you did not have to write any code to create the data store, the Persistent Store Coordinator, the Managed Object Model, or the Managed Object Context. The template code takes care of all of this for you automatically. You will see that the only interface that you need to deal with is that of the Managed Object Context.

The Data Model

Before you examine the `RootViewController` and how to use it to create your `TableView` using Core Data, let's look at the template Managed Object Model. If you open the Resources folder in Xcode and double-click on `Tasks.xcdatamodel`, you should see something similar to Figure 5-3.

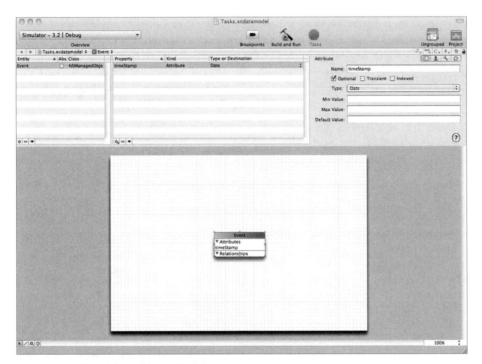

FIGURE 5-3: The default Object Model

The code template creates a default entity called "Event." The blue highlighting and resize handles indicate that the Event entity is selected. Click anywhere else in the diagram to de-select the Event entity and it will turn pink to indicate that it is no longer selected. Click on the Event entity again to select it.

There are three panes in the top of the data-modeling tool. From left to right they are the Entities pane, the Properties pane, and the Detail pane. The Entities pane provides a list of all of the entities in your model. The Properties pane lists the properties of the currently selected entity, and the Detail pane shows details related to whatever is currently selected, either an entity or property. The bottom portion of the tool displays a graphical representation of your model called the Diagram View. The next chapter provides more detail on using the data-modeling tool.

You can see in Figure 5-3 that the Event entity has an attribute called `timeStamp`. If you select the Event entity and then select the `timeStamp` property in the Properties pane, you will see the details of the `timeStamp` attribute in the Detail pane. You should see that the `timeStamp` attribute is optional and that it is a Date type.

Your managed object context will manage the objects defined by the Event entity. Remember that when you created the Persistent Store Coordinator, you initialized it with all of the managed object models in the bundle. Then, when you created the context, it used the Persistent Store Coordinator. Next, you will see how you use the Event entity to create and manage Core Data Managed Objects in code.

RootViewController

The `RootViewController` is a subclass of `UITableViewController` and contains the `TableView` that you will use to display your data. This class has a property that holds the context, which the Application Delegate sets when it creates the `RootViewController` instance. The `RootViewController` also has a property that holds an `NSFetchedResultsController`.

The `NSFetchedResultsController` class is the glue that binds the results of a fetch request against your datasource to a `TableView`. You will look at the `NSFetchedResultsController` class in more detail in Chapter 6.

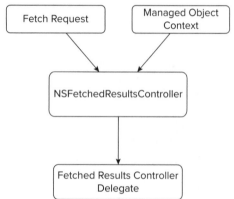

Figure 5-4 shows a high-level view of how the `NSFetchedResultsController` class works. The class takes a fetch request and a context as its inputs and calls delegate methods when the data in the fetch request changes. The controller implements methods that you use when implementing the `TableView` delegate methods that you are familiar with from Chapter 3.

FIGURE 5-4: NSFetchedResultsController usage

The first thing to notice is that the `RootViewController` implements the `NSFetchedResultsControllerDelegate` protocol. You can see this in the `RootViewController.h` header file. Remember that declaring that you implement a protocol is a contract that commits you to implementing certain methods. Classes that do not implement this protocol cannot be delegates for an `NSFetchedResultsController`.

The following is the code for the getter method for the `fetchedResultsController` property:

```
- (NSFetchedResultsController *)fetchedResultsController {

    if (fetchedResultsController != nil) {
        return fetchedResultsController;
    }

    /*
```

```
     Set up the fetched results controller.
     */
    // Create the fetch request for the entity.
    NSFetchRequest *fetchRequest = [[NSFetchRequest alloc] init];
    // Edit the entity name as appropriate.
    NSEntityDescription *entity =
        [NSEntityDescription entityForName:@"Event"
                        inManagedObjectContext:managedObjectContext];
    [fetchRequest setEntity:entity];

    // Set the batch size to a suitable number.
    [fetchRequest setFetchBatchSize:20];

    // Edit the sort key as appropriate.
    NSSortDescriptor *sortDescriptor =
        [[NSSortDescriptor alloc] initWithKey:@"timeStamp"
                                    ascending:NO];
    NSArray *sortDescriptors =
        [[NSArray alloc] initWithObjects:sortDescriptor, nil];

    [fetchRequest setSortDescriptors:sortDescriptors];

    // Edit the section name key path and cache name if appropriate.
    // nil for section name key path means "no sections".
    NSFetchedResultsController *aFetchedResultsController =
        [[NSFetchedResultsController alloc]
            initWithFetchRequest:fetchRequest
            managedObjectContext:managedObjectContext
            sectionNameKeyPath:nil cacheName:@"Root"];

    aFetchedResultsController.delegate = self;
    self.fetchedResultsController = aFetchedResultsController;

    [aFetchedResultsController release];
    [fetchRequest release];
    [sortDescriptor release];
    [sortDescriptors release];

    return fetchedResultsController;
}
```

RootViewController.m

The first part of the code should be familiar. It checks to see if you have already created the fetchedResultsController. If it already exists, the method returns the controller. If not, the code goes on to create it.

The next section of code creates and configures the objects needed by the fetchedResultsController. As you can see from Figure 5-4, you need a fetch request and a context to be able to use the fetchedResultsController. Because you already have a context, in the managedObjectContext property, the code only needs to create a fetch request.

You can think of a fetch request as a SQL SELECT statement. The code creates a FetchRequest object, creates an entity based on the "Event" entity in the context, and then sets the entity used by the `fetchRequest`. Next, the code sets the batch size of the `fetchRequest` to a reasonable number of records to receive at a time.

The next bit of code creates an `NSSortDescriptor`. You use the `NSSortDescriptor` to sort the results in the `fetchRequest`. You can think of the `NSSortDescriptor` as a SQL ORDER BY clause. Here, you order the result set based on the `timeStamp` field in descending order. The `NSSortDescriptor` then sets the sort descriptor used by the fetch request.

Finally, calling the `initWithFetchRequest:managedObjectContext:sectionNameKeyPath:cacheName:` method creates and initializes `fetchedResultsController`. The template then sets the delegate to `self`, assigns the `fetchedResultsController` property, and then the template releases the local objects.

The only delegate method from the `NSFetchedResultsControllerDelegate` protocol implemented by the template is `controllerDidChangeContent:`. The `fetchedResultsController` calls this method when all changes to the objects managed by the controller are complete. In this case, you tell the table to reload its data.

```
- (void)controllerDidChangeContent:(NSFetchedResultsController *)controller {
    // In the simplest, most efficient, case, reload the table view.
    [self.tableView reloadData];
}
```

RootViewController.m

Now that you have seen how you create and configure the `fetchedResultsController`, let's look at how you configure the `RootViewController` at startup. You do this in the `viewDidLoad` method:

```
- (void)viewDidLoad {
    [super viewDidLoad];

    // Set up the edit and add buttons.
    self.navigationItem.leftBarButtonItem = self.editButtonItem;

    UIBarButtonItem *addButton = [[UIBarButtonItem alloc]
        initWithBarButtonSystemItem:UIBarButtonSystemItemAdd
                             target:self
                             action:@selector(insertNewObject)];

    self.navigationItem.rightBarButtonItem = addButton;
    [addButton release];

    NSError *error = nil;
    if (![[self fetchedResultsController] performFetch:&error]) {
        // Log the error
        NSLog(@"Unresolved error %@, %@", error, [error userInfo]);

        // Quit
        abort();
    }
}
```

RootViewController.m

The method first calls the superclass version of `viewDidLoad` to ensure that you perform any initialization required by the superclass.

Next, the code configures the Edit button, creates the Add button and adds the buttons to the navigation at the top of the screen. You can see in the initialization of the `addButton` that the `insertNewObject` method will be called when someone taps the Add button.

Finally, you call the `performFetch:` method on the `fetchedResultsController` to execute the fetch request and retrieve the desired data.

Now, you will look at how you use the `TableView` delegate methods to display your data. These should be familiar to you from Chapter 3.

The first method is `numberOfSectionsInTableView:`.

Available for download on Wrox.com

```
- (NSInteger)numberOfSectionsInTableView:(UITableView *)tableView {
    return [[fetchedResultsController sections] count];
}
```

RootViewController.m

As you may recall, the `TableView` calls this method when it needs to know how many sections to display. Here, the code simply asks the `fetchedResultsController` for the number of sections.

The next `TableView` delegate method is `numberOfRowsInSection:`.

Available for download on Wrox.com

```
- (NSInteger)tableView:(UITableView *)tableView
    numberOfRowsInSection:(NSInteger)section {

    id <NSFetchedResultsSectionInfo> sectionInfo =
        [[fetchedResultsController sections] objectAtIndex:section];
    return [sectionInfo numberOfObjects];
}
```

RootViewController.m

Again, you call upon the `fetchedResultsController` to return the number of rows to display.

Finally, you configure the cell in the `cellForRowAtIndexPath:` method.

Available for download on Wrox.com

```
- (UITableViewCell *)tableView:(UITableView *)tableView
        cellForRowAtIndexPath:(NSIndexPath *)indexPath {

    static NSString *CellIdentifier = @"Cell";

    UITableViewCell *cell = [tableView
                        dequeueReusableCellWithIdentifier:CellIdentifier];
    if (cell == nil) {
        cell = [[[UITableViewCell alloc]
                initWithStyle:UITableViewCellStyleDefault
                reuseIdentifier:CellIdentifier] autorelease];
    }
```

```
        // Configure the cell.
        NSManagedObject *managedObject = [fetchedResultsController
                                    objectAtIndexPath:indexPath];
        cell.textLabel.text =
            [[managedObject valueForKey:@"timeStamp"] description];

        return cell;
    }
```

RootViewController.m

This code should be familiar down to the point where it retrieves the managed object. Again, the code asks `fetchedResultsController` for the object pointed to by the index path. Once it obtains this object, the code uses key-value coding to get the value for the `timeStamp` property. You learn more about key-value coding in Chapter 6.

The `commitEditingStyle:forRowAtIndexPath:` method contains the code to handle editing rows in the `TableView`. The `TableView` calls this method when editing of the `TableView` will cause a change to the underlying data. In this case, deleting an object in the `TableView` should delete the object from the context.

```
    - (void)tableView:(UITableView *)tableView
        commitEditingStyle:(UITableViewCellEditingStyle)editingStyle
        forRowAtIndexPath:(NSIndexPath *)indexPath {

        if (editingStyle == UITableViewCellEditingStyleDelete) {
            // Delete the managed object for the given index path
            NSManagedObjectContext *context =
                [fetchedResultsController managedObjectContext];

            [context deleteObject:
                [fetchedResultsController objectAtIndexPath:indexPath]];

            // Save the context.
            NSError *error = nil;
            if (![context save:&error]) {
                NSLog(@"Unresolved error %@, %@", error, [error userInfo]);
                abort();
            }
        }
    }
```

RootViewController.m

The code first determines if the user has deleted a cell. Then, it gets a reference to the context and tells the context to delete the object that was deleted from the `TableView`. Last, the context changes are committed to disk by calling the `save:` method.

The last interesting bit of code in the `RootViewController` is the `insertNewObject` method. Recall that this is the method that will be called when a user taps the Add button at the top of the screen.

```
- (void)insertNewObject {

    // Create a new instance of the entity managed by the fetched results
    // controller.
    NSManagedObjectContext *context =
        [fetchedResultsController managedObjectContext];
    NSEntityDescription *entity =
        [[fetchedResultsController fetchRequest] entity];
    NSManagedObject *newManagedObject =
        [NSEntityDescription insertNewObjectForEntityForName:[entity name]
                                     inManagedObjectContext:context];

    // If appropriate, configure the new managed object.
    [newManagedObject setValue:[NSDate date] forKey:@"timeStamp"];

    // Save the context.
    NSError *error = nil;
    if (![context save:&error]) {
        NSLog(@"Unresolved error %@, %@", error, [error userInfo]);
        abort();
    }
}
```

RootViewController.m

Like the `commitEditingStyle:forRowAtIndexPath:` method, this code first gets a reference to the context. Next, the code creates a new entity based on the entity that the `fetchedResultsController` uses. The code then creates a new managed object based on that entity and inserts it into the context. Next, the code configures the managed object with the appropriate data; in this case, a timestamp. Finally, the context is committed to disk with the `save:` method.

Modifying the Template Code

Now that you are familiar with how the template code works, you will modify it to create tasks instead of timestamps. To build the task application, you will modify the data model by creating a Task entity, create a new `ViewController` that you will use to create tasks, and update the `RootViewController` to use the new Task entity.

The first thing that you will do is to modify the data model by changing the existing Event entity to make it a Task entity. If you make a change to the data model and attempt to run your application, you will get an error that looks something like this:

```
2010-03-31 12:50:34.595 Tasks[2424:207] Unresolved error Error
    Domain=NSCocoaErrorDomain Code=134100 UserInfo=0x3d12140
"Operation could not be completed. (Cocoa error 134100.)", {
    metadata =       {
        NSPersistenceFrameworkVersion = 248;
        NSStoreModelVersionHashes =          {
            Location = <fa099c17 c3432901 bbaf6eb3 1dddc734 a9ac14d2 36b913ed
                97ebad53 3e2e5363>;
            Task = <40414517 78c0bd9f 84e09e2a 91478c44 d85394f8 e9bb7e5a
                abb9be27 96761c30>;
        };
```

```
            NSStoreModelVersionHashesVersion = 3;
            NSStoreModelVersionIdentifiers =              (
            );
            NSStoreType = SQLite;
            NSStoreUUID = "762ED962-367C-476C-B4BD-076A6D1C33A9";
            "_NSAutoVacuumLevel" = 2;
        };
        reason = "The model used to open the store is incompatible with the one
            used to create the store";
    }
```

RootViewController.m

This error says that "The model used to open the store is incompatible with the one used to create the store." This means exactly what it sounds like: The data store on the device is not compatible with your revised data model, so Core Data cannot open it. When you encounter this situation, you will need to use Core Data migration to move your data from one data model to another. Core Data migration is covered in detail in Chapter 9. For now, simply delete the existing application from the simulator or device before trying to run it again. This will force Core Data to build a new data store that is compatible with the data model.

Open the `Tasks.xcdatamodel` file, and then select the Event entity. Change the name of the entity to "Task" in the Detail pane. Add a new property to the Task entity by clicking the plus icon below the Properties pane and selecting Add Attribute. Call the attribute `taskText` and set its type to `String` in the Properties pane. You will use the new attribute to store the text for your tasks. Your data model should look like Figure 5-5.

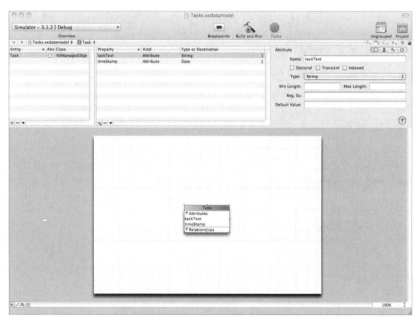

FIGURE 5-5: Revised Tasks data model

Next, you need to build a new screen for entering the Task text. In a production application, you would probably want to use Interface Builder to build a nice user interface for this screen. However, to keep this example simple, you will just build a very simple interface in code.

Add a new `UIViewController` subclass to your project. Make sure you clear the checkboxes for "UITableViewController subclass" and "With XIB for user interface." Call your new class `TaskEntryViewController`.

Modify the `TaskEntryViewController.h` header to include instance variables for a `UITextField` and the Managed Object Context. When the `RootViewController` calls up the `TaskEntryViewController`, it will set the reference to the context. Declare the properties for the `UITextField` and the managed object context. Finally, modify the interface definition to indicate that you will be implementing the `UITextFieldDelegate` protocol. You use this protocol to receive messages from the `UITextField`. Specifically, you will be implementing the `textFieldShouldReturn:` method that runs when the Return button is pressed in a `TextField`.

The code for the `TaskEntryViewController.h` header should look like this:

```objc
#import <UIKit/UIKit.h>

@interface TaskEntryViewController : UIViewController <UITextFieldDelegate>{
    UITextField *tf;

    NSManagedObjectContext *managedObjectContext;

}

@property (retain, nonatomic) UITextField *tf;
@property (retain, nonatomic) NSManagedObjectContext *managedObjectContext;

@end
```

TaskEntryViewController.h

Now you will implement the `TaskEntryViewController`. First, synthesize the `TextField` and the context properties:

```objc
@synthesize tf, managedObjectContext;
```

Next, you need to add code to `TaskEntryViewController.m` to programmatically create the UI in the `loadView` method:

```objc
- (void)loadView {
    [super loadView];

    self.tf = [[UITextField alloc] initWithFrame:CGRectMake(65, 20, 200, 20)];
    [self.tf setBackgroundColor:[UIColor lightGrayColor]];
    [self.tf setDelegate:self];
    [self.view addSubview:self.tf];

    UILabel *lbl = [[UILabel alloc] initWithFrame:CGRectMake(5, 20, 60, 20)];
```

```
    [lbl setText:@"Task:"];

    [self.view addSubview:lbl];
    [lbl release];

}
```

TaskEntryViewController.m

The code creates a `TextField` object with the specified screen coordinates. Then, it sets the background color so it is easy to see. The delegate is then set and the code adds the control to the main view. The code also creates a `UILabel` so that users will know what the text field represents. Remember that when you are creating a production application, you will not need this code. You will most likely use Interface Builder to build a nicer interface than a plain text label and a gray text entry field.

The next step is to add the `textFieldShouldReturn:` method to `TaskEntryViewController.m`. The framework calls this `UITextFieldDelegate` method when Return is pressed. The code inserts a new `Task` object into the context:

```
- (BOOL)textFieldShouldReturn:(UITextField *)textField
{
    // Create a new instance of the entity managed by the fetched results
    // controller.
    NSManagedObjectContext *context = self.managedObjectContext;

    NSEntityDescription *entity = [NSEntityDescription
                            entityForName:@"Task"
                            inManagedObjectContext:context];

    NSManagedObject *newManagedObject =
    [NSEntityDescription insertNewObjectForEntityForName:[entity name]
                            inManagedObjectContext:context];

    // If appropriate, configure the new managed object.
    [newManagedObject setValue:[NSDate date] forKey:@"timeStamp"];
    [newManagedObject setValue:[self.tf text] forKey:@"taskText"];

    // Save the context.
    NSError *error = nil;
    if (![context save:&error]) {
        /*
         Replace this implementation with code to handle the error
         appropriately.

         */
        NSLog(@"Unresolved error %@, %@", error, [error userInfo]);
        abort();
    }

    [self dismissModalViewControllerAnimated:YES];
    return YES;
}
```

TaskEntryViewController.m

First, this code gets a pointer to the context. Then, you define a new
Task entity from the context. Next, it inserts a managed object into the
context. Then, the code configures the managed object using a timestamp
and the text entered in the `TextField`. The context is then committed to
disk and you dismiss the modal view controller. The interface will look
like Figure 5-6.

The last thing to do is modify the `RootViewController` to use the new
`Task` entity and to call up the Text Entry interface when a user clicks the
plus button to enter a new task.

Because you will be referencing the `TaskEntryViewController`, you
will need to add an `import` statement to `RootViewController.m`
for `TaskEntryViewController.h`:

```
#import "TaskEntryViewController.h"
```

Next, you need to modify the `fetchedResultsController` getter
method to use the `Task` entity instead of the `Event` entity. I have
presented the modified code in bold.

FIGURE 5-6: Text entry
interface

```
- (NSFetchedResultsController *)fetchedResultsController {

    if (fetchedResultsController != nil) {
        return fetchedResultsController;
    }

    /*
     Set up the fetched results controller.
    */
    // Create the fetch request for the entity.
    NSFetchRequest *fetchRequest = [[NSFetchRequest alloc] init];
    // Edit the entity name as appropriate.
    NSEntityDescription *entity = [NSEntityDescription entityForName:@"Task"
        inManagedObjectContext:managedObjectContext];
    [fetchRequest setEntity:entity];

    ...
```

RootViewController.m

Now, delete the old `insertNewObject` method. You will need to recode this method to present the
`TaskEntryViewController` like this:

```
- (void)insertNewObject {

    //  Ask for text from TaskEntryViewController
    TaskEntryViewController *tevc = [[TaskEntryViewController alloc] init];
```

```
            tevc.managedObjectContext = self.managedObjectContext;

    [self presentModalViewController:tevc
                           animated:YES];

        [tevc release];


    }
```

This code simply creates a `TaskEntryViewController`, sets the context, and presents it as a modal controller.

The final step is to modify the `tableView: (UITableView *)tableView cellForRowAtIndexPath:` method to use the `taskText` attribute for the main text and the `timeStamp` attribute for the detail text:

```
- (UITableViewCell *)tableView:(UITableView *)tableView
        cellForRowAtIndexPath:(NSIndexPath *)indexPath {

    static NSString *CellIdentifier = @"Cell";

    UITableViewCell *cell =
        [tableView dequeueReusableCellWithIdentifier:CellIdentifier];
    if (cell == nil) {
        cell = [[[UITableViewCell alloc]
                initWithStyle:UITableViewCellStyleSubtitle
                reuseIdentifier:CellIdentifier] autorelease];
    }

    // Configure the cell.
    NSManagedObject *managedObject = [fetchedResultsController
                                objectAtIndexPath:indexPath];

    cell.textLabel.text =
        [[managedObject valueForKey:@"taskText"] description];
    cell.detailTextLabel.text =
        [[managedObject valueForKey:@"timeStamp"] description];
    return cell;
}
```

First, this method tries to dequeue a cell. If it fails, it creates a new cell using the `UITableViewCellStyleSubtitle` cell style so that you can display both the task text and the timestamp. Next, the code retrieves that managed object for the cell using the `fetchedResultsController`. Then, the code sets the cell's `textLabel.text` property to the string contained in the `taskText` attribute of the managed object and sets the `detailTextLabel.text` property to the `timeStamp` attribute.

You should now be able to build and run the application. Try clicking on the plus icon to add new tasks. After typing in the text and hitting Return, you should see your task listed in the `TableView`. Try adding a few more tasks and then swiping across a task in the `TableView`. You should see a Delete button, which will allow you to delete the task. Tap the Edit button and notice that you go into edit mode. If you tap a red circle icon in Edit mode, you see a Delete button, which allows you to delete the row. The completed application should look like Figure 5-2.

MOVING FORWARD

In this chapter, you have learned about the basics of Core Data. You examined the Core Data architecture and you learned the basic terminology necessary to understand the Core Data API stack. Then, you explored the template code to understand how to implement the Core Data architecture. Finally, you modified the template application to produce a functional task manager application.

In the next few chapters, your knowledge of Core Data will go from cursory to detailed. In the next chapter, you learn to use the Xcode data modeler to develop a model that incorporates many of the features of Core Data. Then, in Chapter 7 you learn how to bring that model to life through code.

Modeling Data in Xcode

WHAT'S IN THIS CHAPTER?

➤ Defining entities and their attributes

➤ Expressing the relationships between entities

➤ Creating fetched properties and fetch requests using the predicate builder

➤ Generating custom subclasses of NSManagedObject from your model

In the previous chapter, you learned the fundamentals of working with Core Data. In this chapter, you explore the Xcode Data Modeling tool and learn how to create data models graphically.

In this chapter, you learn how to use the Xcode Data Modeling tool to graphically create your Core Data model. The tool is easy to use and can dramatically speed the development time of your next data-driven application. Think of the Data Modeling tool as Interface Builder for your data.

You can use the tool to model the entities and attributes that you will use in your application. You can also use the tool to define relationships between entities, create fetched properties, and even build fetch requests.

MODELING YOUR DATA

In Chapter 2, you learned about the importance of modeling your data before you begin work on your application. I showed you how I use Omni Graffle to create my Entity-Relationship Diagrams. Then, you explored how to turn those diagrams into an SQLite database. In this chapter, you learn how to use the Xcode Modeling tool to model your data and turn the model into Core Data objects.

The Xcode Modeling tool uses a multi-pane interface, as shown in Figure 6-1. There are three panes at the top of the tool. They are (from left to right) the Entities pane, the Properties pane, and the Detail pane. The Entities pane provides a list of all of the entities in your model. The Properties pane lists the properties of the currently selected entity, and the Detail pane shows details related to whatever is currently selected, either an entity or a property. The bottom pane, called the Diagram view, displays a graphical representation of your model. As you walk through the creation of the various aspects of a data model, you will learn how each pane is used.

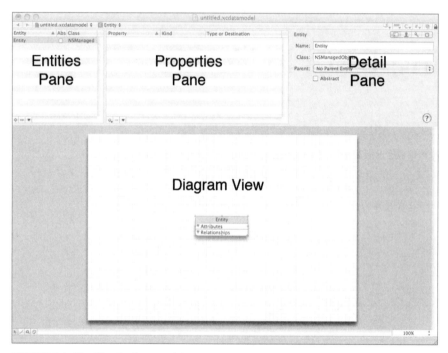

FIGURE 6-1: The Xcode data modeler

Defining Entities and Their Attributes

In order to show all of the features of the data modeler, I will walk you through the creation of a data model for a catalog application like the one you created in Chapters 1 through 3. Then, at the end of the chapter, you will create an extended version of the Task data model from Chapter 5, which you will use in the example code in Chapter 7.

Figure 6-2 shows the Entity-Relationship Diagram that you developed in Chapter 2. If you recall, this diagram represents the data that you needed to build a catalog application. The application presented a company's product catalog and contained information about the products, manufacturers, and countries of origin of the products. This chapter presents the creation of the catalog data model as a tutorial, but you do not necessarily need to follow along — you will not be using it in code. I am just walking you through the process to demonstrate all of the capabilities of the data-modeling tool. At the end of this chapter, you will create another data model for a task application that you will use going forward into Chapter 7.

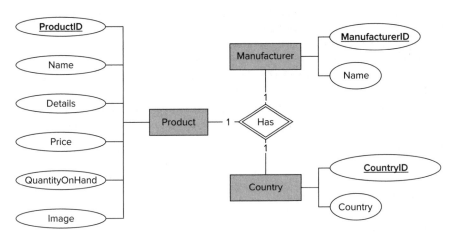

FIGURE 6-2: Catalog database Entity-Relationship Diagram

The main entity in the catalog application is the Product. So, let's create a Product entity in the tool. There are a couple of ways to create entities. You can right-click in the Diagram view and select Add Entity from the contextual menu. You can also create an entity from the menu bar by selecting Design ➪ Data Model ➪ Add Entity. Finally, you can create a new entity by clicking the plus icon at the bottom-left of the Entity pane. Choose one of these methods and create a new entity.

After you create a new entity, the Diagram view shows the entity as selected: A selected entity is blue and has resize handles. Because you have selected the entity, you can see its details in the Detail pane.

Entity Details

The Detail pane has four tabs — General, User Info, Configurations, and Synchronization — as you can see in Figure 6-3.

The General tab contains general information about the selected entity. In the Name field, you can change the name of your entity. Change the name of this entity from Entity to Product.

The class field displays the name of the class that represents the entity in code. The tool sets the class field to `NSManagedObject` by default. Later in the

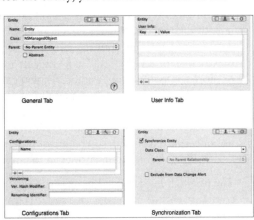

FIGURE 6-3: Entity detail tabs

chapter, when you create custom subclasses of NSManagedObject, you will see the name change to the name of the custom subclass.

Using the parent field, you can implement an inheritance hierarchy in your model between entities like those that you would implement between classes in code. Suppose that all of your products shared common attributes such as Name, Price, and Quantity, but each category of product had different sub-attributes. You could design your model such that different data entities would represent different categories. For example, if your company was selling screws, a screw entity might have attributes such as head type, thread pitch, and length. An entity to model hammers would not need the attributes of screws, but might need attributes such as weight and claw length. You could define the hammer and screw as entities in your model with a parent type of Product. That way, the hammer and screw classes would both inherit all of the attributes and relationships of the parent class, Product, while still being able to define their own unique relationships and attributes.

Create two new entities in the model and call them Hammer and Screw. For each of these new entities, set the Parent in the Detail pane to Product. You will see an inheritance arrow drawn from the subclasses to the superclass, as in Figure 6-4. You can tell Core Data that an entity is abstract by selecting the abstract checkbox. You cannot instantiate abstract classes and can use them only as base classes.

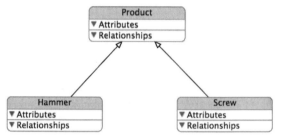

FIGURE 6-4: Subclassed entities

The next tab in the Detail pane is the User Info tab. The NSManagedObject class that you create to represent your Core Data entity in code has a property called entity that returns an NSEntityDescription. The NSEntityDescription has a userInfo property that returns an NSDictionary containing user-defined key-value pairs. The User Info tab allows you to create key-value pairs and associate them with the current entity. At runtime, you can access these values using the userInfo property of the NSEntityDescription. Use the plus at the bottom of the window to add a new key-value pair to the entity and use the minus to remove the selected pair.

The third tab is the Configurations tab. Configurations enable you to name various groups of entities in your data model. You create a configuration using the plus button at the bottom of the tab and delete configurations with the minus button. Once you create a configuration, that configuration is available for all entities. Then you can go through each entity individually and assign it to one or more configurations. At runtime, you can retrieve the entities in a configuration using the entitiesForConfiguration method on the NSManagedObjectModel class. This method will return an NSArray of entities in the chosen configuration. You use Configurations to split the entities in a model across multiple data stores. When developing applications for the iPhone, you will generally use only one data store, so you may not have much use for configurations. However, it is useful to know that you can group entities in the modeler and retrieve your groups at runtime.

The final tab in the Detail pane is the Synchronization tab. You use the Synchronization tab to configure entities for use with Sync Services. You can use Sync Services to synchronize data between a mobile application and a desktop application. Developing a desktop application and using Sync

Services is beyond the scope of this book, but if you want more information on using Sync Services, refer to the Apple Sync Services Programming Guide available at http://developer.apple.com/mac/library/documentation/cocoa/Conceptual/SyncServices/SyncServices.pdf.

Adding Attributes

Now that you have created the Product entity, you need to add the attributes of the entity. The Product should have the attributes defined in the Entity-Relationship Diagram, as shown previously in Figure 6-2.

Select the Product entity in the data model. With the entity selected, click the plus icon at the bottom of the Properties pane. A pop-up menu opens, allowing you to add various properties to the Product entity. Select Add Attribute from this pop-up menu to add a new attribute to the entity. The Detail pane tabs that are available when you select an attribute are slightly different from those available when you select an entity, as you can see in Figure 6-5.

The General tab in the Detail pane allows you to define the name and type of your attribute. Change the name of the attribute that you just added to name. You will store the name of the product in this attribute. Change the type of the name attribute to String.

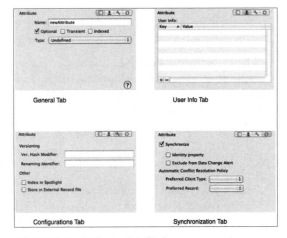

FIGURE 6-5: Attribute detail tabs

Depending on the data type that you select for your attribute, the dialog will display different fields that allow you to set additional options for the attribute.

For the numeric types, Integer 16, Integer 32, Integer 64, Decimal, Double, Float, and Date, the pane allows you to enter minimum and maximum values to use for validation. If the user attempts to save an entity with a value that is outside of the specified range, Core Data will raise an error to notify you that a validation rule has been broken. You can also enter a default value for any of the numeric types.

For a String, the pane presents you with Minimum and Maximum length constraints. Again, if the user attempts to save an entity with a string that violates either the minimum or maximum length, Core Data will raise an error to notify you that a validation rule has been broken. There is also a field for entering a default string value.

There is also a field that allows you to build a regular expression that the framework will use to validate the String. Regular expressions are special strings that define a set of rules. For example, you can write a regular expression that constrains the String to be all capital letters, or to allow only certain characters. The framework compares the String that the user enters for the attribute at runtime with the regular expression. If the String fails the comparison, meaning that it does not conform to the rules defined by the regular expression, Core Data will raise an error indicating that a validation rule has failed. A detailed look at regular expressions is beyond the scope of this book.

For Boolean attributes, the only option that you will see in the pane is for the default value. Your options here are YES, NO, or None.

The `Binary` data type does not have any options. Use this type if you plan to store binary data such as an image in the attribute.

The final data type is `Transformable`. Transformable attributes enable you to store non-standard data types such as your own custom classes or C structs. Behind the scenes, Core Data converts the attribute into an `NSData` object using the `NSValueTransformer` class. This binary data is then stored in the persistent store.

There are three checkboxes below the Name of your attribute. The Optional checkbox allows you to indicate if the attribute is optional or required. If the attribute is not optional, you should provide a default value. If you attempt to save an entity with a non-optional field that is blank, Core Data will raise an error indicating that a validation rule has failed.

You use the Transient checkbox to indicate that you do not want the attribute saved in the persistent store. You use this to retain data in memory that will not be necessary to restore later or data that you compute dynamically at runtime.

The Indexed checkbox sets whether or not the attribute should be indexed in the persistent store. This is particularly important when your backing store is the SQLite database. Selecting this box will cause Core Data to create a database index on the attribute. Proper use of indexes can greatly speed up queries that filter or sort on the indexed attribute. You need to be aware, however, that creating too many indices can reduce performance. You should carefully consider which fields you need indexed. Generally, if you are searching or sorting based on an attribute, you should index on the attribute.

Now that you know how to create attributes, go ahead and create the remaining attributes for the Product entity.

Adding Relationships Between Entities

Now that you have modeled the Product entity, it is time to add the related entities. Create two new entities named Manufacturer and Country. Feel free to add any attributes that make sense for the two new entities. I have added attributes for the `name`, `address`, and `preferred provider status` for the Manufacturer. I have also added attributes for `name` and `region` to the Country entity.

If you examine the Entity-Relationship Diagram in Figure 6-2, you will notice that the Product entity and Manufacturer entity are related. Each Product has a Manufacturer. A Manufacturer can have many products. You need to express this relationship in your Core Data model. Including this information in the model will allow Core Data to enforce the relationship and will provide additional functionality when you go to build an application that uses the model. It is important to include as much information as you can when building your model. Core Data will use all of this information at runtime to ensure that the data in your application is consistent with the design expressed in the model.

Select the Product entity. In the Properties pane, click the plus icon and select Add Relationship. This will add a new relationship property to the Product entity. The General tab of the Detail pane now displays options related to a relationship, as you can see in Figure 6-6. In the Name field, change the name of the relationship to "manufacturer."

FIGURE 6-6: General tab for relationship details

The Optional and Transient checkboxes have the same functionality as for attributes.

The Destination drop-down allows you to select the entity on the receiving end of the relationship. In this case, the manufacturer relationship should point to the Manufacturer entity. So in the destination drop-down, select Manufacturer. Once you set the Destination, you will notice that the tool draws a line between the Product and Manufacturer entities in the Diagram view. The arrowhead on the line points to the destination entity.

You use the Inverse drop-down to set an inverse relationship. In your case, you want to create an inverse relationship between manufacturers and products. To specify this relationship, you must first define a relationship for the Manufacturer entity. In the Manufacturer entity, add a new relationship called products. Make the Destination for this new relationship Product. You will see that there is now a line in the Diagram view pointing from Manufacturer to Product. Select the Product entity and change the Inverse dropdown from "No Inverse Relationship" to "products." The two lines that were in the diagram change to one line with arrowheads on each end. If you select the products relationship in the Manufacturer entity, you can see that the tool has automatically set its inverse to manufacturer. You have established a two-way relationship between these entities.

Selecting the next checkbox defines the relationship as a To-Many Relationship. Let's assume that only one manufacturer makes a specific product, but a manufacturer can make many different products. In the Product entity, you should leave the To-Many checkbox unchecked for the manufacturer relationship because there is only a single manufacturer for a given product. However, you should check the checkbox for the products relationship in the Manufacturer entity because one manufacturer can build many products. Select the Manufacturer entity and then the products relationship. Then, select the To-Many Relationship checkbox. You will see that the arrow that points to the Product entity now has two arrowheads indicating that the Product entity is the destination of a To-Many relationship. Your diagram should now look like Figure 6-7.

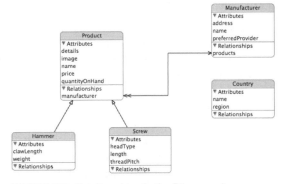

FIGURE 6-7: Relationships in the Diagram view

The next fields in the Detail pane, the Min Count and Max Count, allow you to optionally set the minimum and maximum number of entities contained in the relationship. For the manufacturer relationship, these fields are both set to 1 because the relationship of manufacturers to products is 1 to 1. You cannot change these fields unless you have declared a To-Many relationship. If you select the products relationship in the Manufacturer entity, you will see that these fields default to none. This means the number of products that can be associated with a manufacturer is unlimited.

The final field is the Delete Rule drop-down. You use this to specify what happens when you try to delete the source object in a relationship. The options are No Action, Nullify, Cascade, and Deny.

No Action means that the framework does nothing to the destination object in the relationship. Using No Action is discouraged because this option leaves maintenance of the integrity of the model up to you. Part of the power of Core Data is its ability to manage the integrity of the data model. In the example in this chapter, imagine that you set the manufacturer relationship in the Product entity to No Action. Now, if you deleted a Product entity, its related Manufacturer object will still appear related to the now non-existent product. It would be up to you to remove the now defunct product from the Manufacturer entity. This functionality is automatic when you choose one of the other Delete Rule options.

The Nullify option is the default. This option nulls out the inverse relationship for you automatically. This only works for relationships where the inverse relationship is optional. Consider the previous example with the Delete Rule changed from No Action to Nullify. In this case, if you delete a Product, that product will no longer appear in the Manufacturer's products relationship.

The Cascade option cascades deletes from the source to the destination of the relationship. In this case, let's examine the products relationship of the Manufacturer object. If this relationship had its Delete Rule set to Cascade, deleting a manufacturer would delete all of the products made by that manufacturer.

Finally, the Deny option prevents the deletion of source objects if there are objects at the destination. In the case of the products relationship of the Manufacturer object, if you attempted to delete a manufacturer that still had products, Core Data would raise a validation error. In this case, you would have to manually delete all products associated with a manufacturer before you could delete the manufacturer.

The last aspect of relationships that you will look at is the many-to-many relationship. Imagine that many different countries produce a product and that a country could make many different products. Create a countries relationship in the Product entity and point it to the Country entity. Mark this new relationship as a To-Many relationship. Now, create a products relationship in the Country entity, mark it as a To-Many relationship, and point it to the Product entity. Now, set the inverse relation to products. This may cause you some concern if you are an experienced database developer because in an SQL database, you would have to create a join table to implement this design. Core Data automatically creates the join table behind the scenes in the SQLite database so that you don't need to worry about creating it in your model. You can simply create a many-to-many relationship and let Core Data handle the implementation details for you.

You can also express reflexive relationships in Core Data. A *reflexive relationship* is a relationship where the source and destination entities are the same. For instance, suppose that you want to keep track of all of the other Product entities related to a specific Product entity. You could create a relatedProducts relationship in the Product entity that has a destination of Product since both the source and destination entities in the relationship are Product entities. For example, suppose that you have a Screw entity and wanted to create a relationship that maps a particular Screw to all other screws of the same type. You could create a relatedScrews relationship that has a Screw entity as both its source and destination. You will see the arrow coming out of the Product entity and then circle around and point right back to itself.

Creating Fetched Properties and Fetch Request Templates

In the previous section, you learned how to create relationships between your entities. *Fetched properties* work similarly to relationships. An important difference is that you can apply predicates to filter the entities returned by a Fetched Property. For instance, the Product entity has a manufacturer relationship. You must add a Manufacturer to a Product for the relationship to have any meaning. The framework can calculate a Fetched Property without your having to specify which entities meet the criteria. You can use Fetch Request Templates to prepare a fetch request in your model and include variables for resolution at runtime. You can think of Fetch Request Templates like stored queries.

Fetched Properties

Suppose that you wanted to always be able to find a list of cheap products, say products that sold for under $1. You can use a Fetched Property to add a property called `cheapProducts` to the Products entity. You then specify a predicate that the framework applies to filter your search results. Add a Fetched Property to the Product entity, and call it `cheapProducts`. Set the destination entity to Product because the Fetched Property should query all of the Product entities. Click the Edit Predicate button to bring up the predicate builder, which you can use to specify your search criteria. Modify the predicate to indicate that you want to retrieve items whose price is less than $1, as shown in Figure 6-8.

FIGURE 6-8: Predicate Builder

In your code, when you have a Product and retrieve the cheapProducts property, you will get back an `NSArray` of products that cost less than $1.

This predicate works fine for a constant value such as $1. However, suppose that you wanted to be able to get back a list of products that are cheaper than the current product. You can accomplish this by using a variable in your predicate. Change the name of the Fetched Property that you just created to `cheaperProducts`. Next, click the Edit Predicate button to edit the predicate. You are still going to be comparing against the price field, so leave the left-hand operand alone. If you Control-click (or right-click) in the row, you will get a pop-up menu that displays more options for defining the right-hand operand in your predicate. In this case, you are interested in the top three options: Constant, Variable, and Key.

The field is currently set at a constant of 1.00. However, you do not want to compare to a constant; you want to compare the prices of two different entities. To do this, you might think that you would want to use a Key type of price and compare price versus price. This is incorrect. The Key type always refers to the values contained in the current object under test for inclusion. So, the predicate price<price will never be true. In this situation, you need to use a variable.

Core Data has a special variable called $FETCH_SOURCE, which is a reference to the object executing the Fetched Property. Your predicate should compare the price of the object under consideration to the price of the object executing the property. So, change the field type to Variable and in the Variable text box, type **FETCH_SOURCE.price**. Be sure to leave off the $ in the beginning of the variable name, as the tool will add it for you. Your Fetched Property should now look like Figure 6-9.

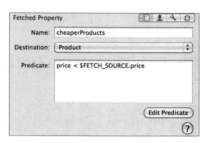

FIGURE 6-9: Fetched property with a variable

The predicate builder is not limited to building only simple, one-line filters. You can use Boolean operators such as AND and OR to combine criteria and generate complex predicates. You can add Boolean operators to your predicate by clicking on the plus sign to the right of a line in the predicate builder. It doesn't make much sense, but suppose that you wanted mid-priced products made in China by Manufacturer A or Manufacturer B. You would construct this predicate as in Figure 6-10. The text representation of this predicate is:

```
((price < 5 OR price > 1) AND ANY countries.name == "China") AND
(manufacturer.name ==
"Manufacturer A" OR manufacturer.name == "Manufacturer B").
```

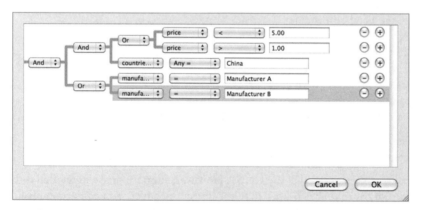

FIGURE 6-10: Complex predicate

You can also use predefined expressions in your predicate. For instance, you can use the @avg expression to determine the average of a series of numbers or @sum to calculate the sum. You use the expression in the key path of the object that you want to use for your calculation. So, a Fetched Property to return products with below-average prices would use the predicate price < $FETCH_SOURCE.@avg.price.

Fetch Request Templates

If you plan to execute the same fetch repeatedly, only changing the value of a variable, you can predefine a Fetch Request template in the data model. You can think of a Fetch Request template as a stored query or view. You can pass variable values into the template at runtime that the framework applies in the predicate.

To create a Fetch Request Template, click the plus icon in the Properties pane and select Fetch Request. The Properties pane will change its filter and show you only fetch requests so you will be able to see the new fetch request that you created.

In the Detail pane, you will see the name of your new fetch request along with the predicate used to define the fetch. Clicking the Edit Predicate button will bring up the Predicate Editor that you explored in the last section.

Suppose that you needed a screen in your application that allowed the user to specify a certain weight and then you wanted to display all hammers of that weight. You could build this screen by fetching all of the hammers and then filter the ones that don't meet your criteria as you create your table cells. However, this would waste memory, as you would be bringing objects into memory that you aren't going to use. Another option would be to define your predicate in code and apply that to the fetch request. That is a perfectly viable option; in fact, that is what a stored fetch request does. Using a stored fetch request can simplify your code because you can define the fetch request in the model instead of having to do it in code.

To add a Fetch Request Template to your Hammer entity, select the Hammer entity and then click the plus icon at the bottom of the Properties pane. Select Add Fetch Request to create the new fetch request. In the Detail pane, change the name of the fetch request to `getHammersByWeight`. Next, click the Edit Predicate button to create the criteria for the fetch request. In the first drop-down, select the `weight` property. Select the equal sign as your operator. Right-click next to the last field and change it to a Variable type. You want to define the field as a variable because you will pass the value into the fetch request at runtime. Make the variable name `WEIGHT`. Click OK to close the dialog. Your predicate will look like this: `weight == $WEIGHT`.

In your code, you will retrieve the fetch request using the `fetchRequestFromTemplateWithName: substitutionVariables:` method of the `NSManagedObjectModel` object. This method accepts the name of your Fetch Request Template and an `NSDictionary` of key-value pairs used to substitute for the variables in your template.

CREATING CUSTOM NSMANAGEDOBJECT SUBCLASSES

In the previous chapter, you learned how to get data out of an entity retrieved by Core Data using the `NSManagedObject` class. All instances of entities returned by a fetch request are instances of `NSManagedObject`. If you remember, you accessed the data inside of your managed object by using key-value coding. Therefore, to access the name field in a Product entity, you would use the `valueForKey:` method on the `NSManagedObject` instance that you got back from your fetch request. This method is perfectly fine, but a problem occurs, however, if you incorrectly type the name of the key. At runtime, Core Data would not be able to find the key that you specified and an error would occur. It would be nice if you could have a compile-time check of your field names. This is possible by subclassing `NSManagedObject`.

There are several advantages to creating custom subclasses of `NSManagedObject` to represent your data objects. The first is that the subclass provides access to your data fields using properties. If you use the properties to access your data instead of key-value coding, the compiler can verify that the properties exist at compile time. Xcode will also provide code completion help by displaying a list of the properties for an object after you type the period key.

Another advantage to creating a subclass is that you can extend the functionality of your data object beyond simply providing access to your data. Your data objects can implement complex validation rules for single or multiple fields. You could also implement intelligent default values that you cannot express by specifying a default string or number in the data modeler. You can also define calculated fields that are not stored in the data store. You would then write code to calculate the values for these fields at runtime in your custom subclass.

Creating a custom subclass of `NSManagedObject` for an entity in your model is simple. In your object model, select the entity for which you want to generate a custom subclass. Next, from the Xcode pull-down menu, choose File ⇨ New File, just as you would when creating a new class file. You should notice that there is a new option in the New File dialog called Managed Object Class. Select this option and click the Next button. The next dialog asks where you want to save your new class, the project to add it to, and the build target that should include the file. Accept the default values and click next. The final dialog asks which entities you want to generate classes for, as shown in Figure 6-11. Select the Product class and click the Finish button to generate your custom class.

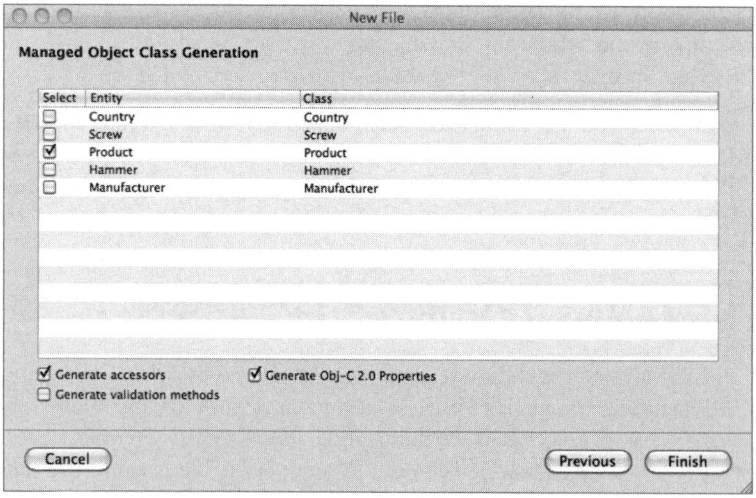

FIGURE 6-11: Managed Object Class Generation dialog

If you look in the Xcode browser, you will see two new files in your project, Product.h and Product.m. The managed object class generation tool generated these classes for the Product entity based on your data model.

The following is the header code for the Product entity class. Note that the order of the properties in you header may differ from what's shown here.

```objectivec
#import <CoreData/CoreData.h>


@interface Product : NSManagedObject
{
}

@property (nonatomic, retain) NSNumber * quantityOnHand;
@property (nonatomic, retain) NSString * details;
@property (nonatomic, retain) NSString * name;
@property (nonatomic, retain) NSString * image;
@property (nonatomic, retain) NSDecimalNumber * price;
@property (nonatomic, retain) NSManagedObject * manufacturer;
@property (nonatomic, retain) NSSet* relatedProducts;
@property (nonatomic, retain) NSSet* countries;

@end


@interface Product (CoreDataGeneratedAccessors)
- (void)addRelatedProductsObject:(Product *)value;
- (void)removeRelatedProductsObject:(Product *)value;
- (void)addRelatedProducts:(NSSet *)value;
- (void)removeRelatedProducts:(NSSet *)value;

- (void)addCountriesObject:(NSManagedObject *)value;
- (void)removeCountriesObject:(NSManagedObject *)value;
- (void)addCountries:(NSSet *)value;
- (void)removeCountries:(NSSet *)value;

@end
```

Product.h

You can see from the header that the tool defines properties to implement all of the attributes in your model entity. Notice that the relationships return instances of NSSet, so the entities returned from a relationship are unordered. You can also see that the tool generated interface methods to allow you to add and remove entities from the relatedProducts and countries relationships.

The following is the code for the Product implementation:

```objectivec
#import "Product.h"


@implementation Product

@dynamic quantityOnHand;
```

```
@dynamic details;
@dynamic name;
@dynamic image;
@dynamic price;
@dynamic manufacturer;
@dynamic relatedProducts;
@dynamic countries;

@end
```

Product.m

The tool uses the `@dynamic` keyword instead of `@synthesize` to define properties. `@synthesize` instructs the compiler to create the getter and setter methods for you, whereas `@dynamic` tells the compiler that you will create the getter and setters. You don't use `@synthesize` here because you don't want the compiler to generate these methods for you at compile time; Core Data takes care of generating the getters and setters for you at runtime.

Implementing Validation Rules

Aside from exposing your entity's attributes as properties, another benefit to creating subclasses of `NSManagedObject` is the ability to add complex custom validation rules. Earlier in the chapter, I covered how to add a simple validation range to an attribute using the modeler. Most data types allow you to set simple validation rules on the general tab of the Properties pane. These rules are limited to min/max values for number and date types, and min/max length or a regular expression for a string type. These options are okay for general use, but they do not give you much flexibility when trying to express complex business logic.

Suppose that your application allowed you to create new products on the device. You might want to be able to prevent the user from entering certain words as part of the name of the product, to avoid embarrassment when showing the catalog off to a client. You could implement a custom validation function that checks the input against a list of inappropriate words before insertion into the database.

The implementation of validation rules for a single field is very straightforward. Core Data will automatically call a method `validateNnnn:error:`, where *Nnnn* is the name of your attribute, for every attribute in your class. If the method does not exist, it is not a problem. You are free to implement as many or few of these methods as you want. The method should return a `BOOL` with a value of `YES` if the validation is successful and `NO` if it fails. If the validation fails, it is common practice to return an `NSError` object to provide further information about why the validation failed.

In the case described, you would implement the function `-(BOOL)validateName:(id *)ioValue error:(NSError **)outError`. You should notice a couple of things in this method. First, it accepts the input parameter as an `id` pointer. Because you are receiving a pointer to the input, you could conceivably change the value that you received. You should avoid this, as it is bad design and introduces a side effect to validating a piece of data. Additionally, changing the value within the validation method will cause Core Data to try to validate the value again, possibly causing an infinite loop.

The NSError object that you return is a pointer to a pointer. This is a consequence of the fact that Objective-C passes all objects by value. If you passed the NSError pointer as a regular pointer, you would only be able to modify the NSError that you passed into the method. Accepting a pointer to a pointer allows you to pass back a completely different NSError object than the one that you passed into the method. Therefore, instead of changing the values in the object that you passed in, you can create a new NSError with your own values to return.

Implementing validate*Nnnn*:error: methods work when you are trying to validate the value for one field. Suppose, however, that you need to validate multiple fields simultaneously because they depend on each other's value. Imagine that you wanted to make the details attribute required only when the price of a product was greater than $1.

The framework calls two methods after all of the single field validation methods are completed. These are validateForInsert: for inserting new objects and validateForUpdate: for updates. As in the single field validation, these functions return a BOOL indicating whether validation is successful. You could write a function to check the price field and return NO if the price is greater than $1 and the details field is empty. Then, you could put a call to this function in the validateForInsert: and validateForUpdate: methods so that the rule runs any time a new object is inserted into Core Data or when an existing object is modified.

Implementing Default Values

As you have seen with custom validation rules, it is possible to code rules that are more complex than what you can create in the modeling tool. You can apply the same principle to implementing default values for the attributes of your entity.

Most of the data types allow you to hard-code in a default value in the modeling tool. However, suppose that you want to dynamically determine the default value at runtime. You could also use this technique for setting the default value for Transformable objects because the tool does not allow you to specify a default transformable object.

To implement custom default values, you override the awakeFromInsert method. The framework calls this method after code inserts the object into the context but before the object becomes available for use. You could use this method to set the current date as the default in date fields or for any other purpose where you need to determine your default value at runtime.

CREATING THE TASKS MODEL

Now that you are familiar with Core Data and using the modeler to create a data model, you will build the model for the application that you will code in the next chapter. The application will be a task manager like the one that you built in the previous chapter, but it will have more features to demonstrate some of the functionality of Core Data that you learned about in this chapter.

The Tasks application will implement a feature where you will be able to assign locations to your tasks so that you know what you have to do when you are in a specific location. Tasks will also have due dates that will be used to indicate if a task is overdue. You will also give the task a priority attribute so that you can mark and filter tasks based on priority.

To begin, start a new Xcode Navigation–based project called Tasks. Ensure that you select the "Use Core Data for storage" checkbox. This will generate your template application and the associated data model.

Open up the `Tasks.xcdatamodel` file to begin editing the data model. Delete the Event entity because you won't be using it in this example. You will be creating your entities from scratch.

Click the plus icon at the bottom of the Entities pane to create a new entity. Rename the new entity "Task."

Next, you will add the attributes for your Task entity. Create a `dueDate` attribute using the `Date` data type. You can leave the `dueDate` marked as optional. To go along with the `dueDate`, create a Boolean `isOverdue` attribute. Mark this attribute as Transient as you will dynamically compute its value at runtime and it won't be stored in the data store.

Now, add a required `priority` attribute of type `Integer 16`. You will use this to store the priority of the task. Set the minimum value to 0, which you will use to indicate that there is no priority set, and the maximum to 3, indicating high priority. Set the default value to 0.

Last, add a `String` attribute called `text` that will be used to store the text of your task. Clear the Optional checkbox and set the Default Value to "Text." Remember that it is wise to specify a default value when defining required attributes.

The next item that you will add to the Task entity is a `highPriTasks` Fetched Property. You will use this property in the application to get a list of all tasks that are marked as high priority. So, add a new Fetched Property to the Task entity called `highPriTasks`. Set the destination entity to `Task`. Edit the predicate so that your filter criteria is `priority == 3`.

You now need to add a new entity to store the locations where you will perform the task. Add a new entity called Location. Add a string attribute to the Location entity called name. Clear the Optional checkbox because a location without a name would be useless in the application.

Now, you will add a relationship to the Task entity to store the location where the user will perform a task. Select the Task entity, click the plus button below the Properties pane, and select Add Relationship. Set the relationship name to "location." Set the Destination to Location.

Next, you will create an inverse relationship in the Location entity to hold a list of tasks for a particular location. Select the Location entity and add a new relationship called tasks. Set the Destination for this relationship to Task and set the Inverse relationship to location. Also, check the To-Many Relationship checkbox as one location could have many tasks assigned to it.

The last thing that you will do is to add a Fetch Request template to the Task entity to retrieve the list of tasks due sooner than the selected task. Select the Task entity and create a new fetch request using the plus icon at the bottom of the Properties pane. Call the fetch request `tasksDueSooner`. Click the Edit Predicate button to define the predicate to use in the fetch request. Select the dueDate field from the first drop-down list. Change the equal sign in the middle drop-down to less than (<) because you want to return items with a due date less than the one passed into the fetch request.

Before you set the value in the right-hand pane that you want to test for, you need to change its type from a constant to a variable. Remember that the Predicate Editor defaults the right-hand side to a constant. In this case, however, you will not be testing against a constant. You want to be able to pass in the due date at runtime and return the tasks that occur before that date. To change the type, right- (or Control-) click to the right of the text box to bring up the context menu for the type. Select variable from the pop-up menu. You should see a text label that says Variable next to the text box after you change the type to Variable. In the variable text box, type **DUE_DATE**. This is the name that you will use in code to replace the variable in the model with an actual location name. Press OK to accept your changes and close the Predicate Editor. Your predicate should be `dueDate < $DUE_DATE`.

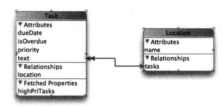

You are finished editing the model. The model should look like Figure 6-12. You can now save the model and quit out of Xcode.

FIGURE 6-12: Tasks data model

MOVING FORWARD

In this chapter, you learned how to express your application's data model graphically using the Xcode data modeling tool. You have also laid the framework for building a complete task management application.

By creating custom subclasses of `NSManagedObject` from your model, you now have the ability to access the data in your object model as properties of an Objective-C class. You also now know how to use the predicate builder to easily generate complex queries on the data in your model.

You are now ready to combine the knowledge that you learned from the previous chapter on the Core Data architecture with what you learned in this chapter about defining your data model to build a fully featured Core Data application. You will write the code to implement your Task model in the next chapter.

7

Building a Core Data Application

WHAT'S IN THIS CHAPTER?

➤ Fetching data using the NSFetchedResultsController

➤ Filtering and sorting your data using NSPredicate and NSSortOrdering

➤ Displaying related data using the UITableView

➤ Implementing complex validation and default values using custom subclasses of NSManagedObject

In the last chapter, you explored the Xcode Data Modeling tool and learned how to graphically create a data model. In this chapter, you learn how to build a complete data-driven application using Core Data. You will learn how to fetch, filter, and sort your data and display it in a UITableView using the NSFetchedResultsController. You also learn how to modify and delete existing data and take advantage of the relationships that you have defined between your data entities. Finally, you learn how to implement complex validation rules and default values using custom subclasses of NSManagedObject.

I have introduced these topics in the previous chapter. In this chapter, you build a fully functional task manager application while learning how to put the concepts that you learned in the last chapter into action.

THE TASKS APPLICATION ARCHITECTURE

Before you sit down to start coding a new application, it is good to have an idea of what the application will do and how the application will do it. The client on the project typically determines what the application must do. The client should communicate the desired functionality in the form of user requirements or specifications. Usually, you, as the developer, determine how the software will fulfill these requirements.

The application that you build in this chapter will be a task manager like the one that you built in Chapter 4. We will add more functionality to help demonstrate some of the features of Core Data that you learned about in Chapter 5. In this more advanced tasks application, the user should be able to:

➤   Create, edit, and delete tasks

➤   View overdue tasks in red, sort tasks alphabetically in ascending and descending order, and filter the data to view only high-priority tasks

➤   Create task locations, assign a location to a task, and view tasks grouped by their location

➤   Display a list of tasks due sooner than a particular task

The Data Model

The first piece of the application is the data model. You need to design a data model that has the entities and attributes needed to implement the functions that I laid out in the previous section. Fortunately, you already did that in Chapter 6. Figure 7-1 shows the data model that you built.

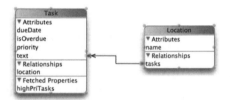

FIGURE 7-1: Tasks application data model

The main entity in this application is the task. Tasks have attributes for due date, priority, and text. There is a transient property that you will calculate at runtime that indicates if a task is overdue. You have also included a fetched property that will list all high-priority tasks. Additionally, you created a relationship to relate a location to a task. Finally, you added a fetch request to determine tasks that are due sooner than the selected task.

The other entity is the location. A task can be marked with a location. Locations have only a `name` attribute and the task's inverse relationship.

The Class Model

Now that you have a data model, you need to think about how you will design the architecture for the application. The Tasks application that you will build in this chapter consists of a series of table View Controllers and regular View Controllers that a user will use to view, create, and edit tasks. There will also be custom `NSManagedObject` subclasses that you will use to implement defaulting and data validation.

In Figure 7-2, you can see the class model for the completed Tasks application. This model was generated with Xcode by using Design ➪ Class Model ➪ Quick Model. The diagram shows that most of the screens for editing individual pieces of data inherit from `UITableViewController`. The only exception is the `EditDateController`. The reason for this is that I wanted the `UIDatePicker` to be at the bottom of the screen and not be part of a table. Every other edit screen consists of a table that is used to display the data to be edited or a list of values that can be chosen for fields such as `location` and `priority`. Editing data in the form of a table should be familiar to you if you have used the Contacts application that comes with the iPhone.

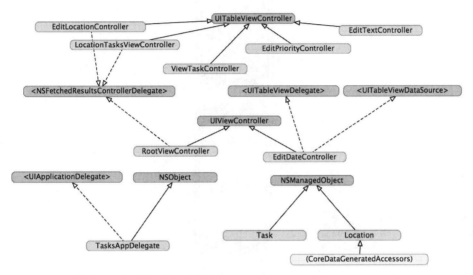

FIGURE 7-2: Tasks application class Model

You may have noticed that the `RootViewController` is not a `UITableViewController`. It is a subclass of `UIViewController`. I did this so that I could embed a `UIToolbar` at the bottom of the screen for filtering and sorting the data in the table. In summary, any screens that consist solely of a table are subclasses of `UITableViewController` and screens that contain other controls in addition to the table are subclasses of `UIViewController`.

Finally, the `Location` and `Task` objects are subclasses of `NSManagedObject`. You will generate these classes from the data model that you built in the last chapter. Then, you will implement custom functionality in the `Task` class to create default due dates at runtime and to perform single field and multiple field validation.

The User Interface

Now that you have seen the data model and class model for the Tasks application, it is time to look at the user interface. Keep in mind that I designed the interface to provide an example of using Core Data. It is not a model of the most beautiful iPhone application ever built, but it will serve to demonstrate most of the features of Core Data that you will likely use in your own applications.

Figure 7-3 show the UI and the process flow of the application. The `RootViewController` is the main Tasks screen. This screen displays all of the user's tasks. It also provides a toolbar to perform sorting and filtering of high-priority tasks. There is also a button that will bring the user to the `LocationTasksViewController`, which displays a list of tasks grouped by location.

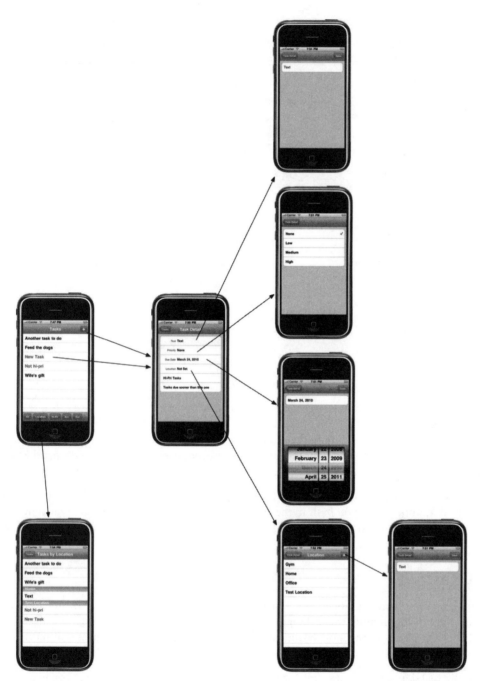

FIGURE 7-3: Tasks application user interface

Tapping the plus button on the top of the `RootViewController` adds a new task and takes the user to the `ViewTaskController`. Likewise, tapping on an existing task will also take the user to the `ViewTaskController`. This screen shows the details of the chosen task or the new task. There are also options on this screen to see all high-priority tasks and to see a list of tasks that are due sooner than the currently selected task.

Tapping a row on the `ViewTaskController` will take the user to the appropriate editing screen. Aside from allowing the user to select a location for a task, the location selection screen also has the capability to create new locations or delete existing locations. You will see each of these screens in full detail as you build the application.

CODING THE APPLICATION

Now that you are familiar with the basic concepts behind the application, it is time to start writing some code.

In order to complete this application, you will need to do the following:

1. Build the `RootViewController` and its interface using Interface Builder.

2. Generate the `NSManagedObject` subclasses for use with Core Data.

3. Implement the `ViewTaskController` to allow users to create and edit tasks.

4. Build the sub-screens used to edit the individual task fields.

5. Implement the filtering and sorting buttons on the toolbar of the `RootViewController` and the `LocationTasksViewController` used to view tasks grouped by location.

6. Implement the advanced features of custom `NSManagedObjects` in the `Task` object.

When you are finished, you should have a detailed understanding of how to implement many of the most important features of Core Data. Additionally, you will have a fully featured Core Data–based task management application that you can use to continue experimenting with the features of Core Data. So, let's get started.

ROOTVIEWCONTROLLER AND THE BASIC UI

The first step in creating the Tasks application is to build the `RootViewController` screen, as shown in Figure 7-4. This is the first screen that the user sees and should contain a list of all of the current tasks. There will be a plus button in the navigation bar used to create new tasks. Additionally, you need a toolbar at the bottom of the screen to allow the user to filter and sort the tasks along with a button to allow the user to bring up the group by location view.

FIGURE 7-4: RootView Controller screen

Open up the Tasks project that you created in the previous chapter. Next, double-click on the `RootViewController.xib` file to open it with Interface Builder.

 This book assumes that you already know how to use Interface Builder to create and edit user interfaces for your iPhone applications. If you need a refresher on using Interface Builder, I would recommend that you take a look at James Bucanek's book Professional Xcode 3 *(Wrox, 2010), which provides thorough coverage of all of the tools in the Xcode suite, including Interface Builder.*

Now, add a `UIView` object at the root level and move the `UITableview` that is currently at the root level into the View as a sub-node.

You will need to add a toolbar and its buttons to the interface. Add a `UIToolbar` control to the view. Next, add four `UIBarButtonItem` objects to the toolbar so that the toolbar contains five buttons. Open the view in IB. Move the toolbar to the bottom of the view and expand the TableView to fill the rest of the view. Set the title of each `UIBarButtonItem` to All, Location, Hi-Pri, Asc, or Dsc.

The look of the interface is now complete. The next thing that you need to do is add appropriate outlets and action methods to the `RootViewController.h` header file. Open `RootViewController.h` in Xcode. Change the superclass for `RootViewController` from `UITableViewController` to `UIViewController`. This screen will have controls besides the `TableView`, so it is not appropriate to subclass `UITableViewController`. The interface declaration should look like this:

```
@interface RootViewController :
    UIViewController <NSFetchedResultsControllerDelegate>
```

Add a `UITableView` instance variable for the `taskTableView` inside the braces of the interface declaration:

```
UITableView* taskTableView;
```

Outside of the interface declaration, add an outlet for the `UITableView`:

```
@property (nonatomic, retain) IBOutlet UITableView* taskTableView;
```

When a user clicks one of the buttons in the toolbar, you need to invoke a method in your code. Therefore, the next step is to add the action methods called when the user clicks on the toolbar buttons:

```
-(IBAction)toolbarSortOrderChanged:(id)sender;
-(IBAction)toolbarFilterHiPri:(id)sender;
-(IBAction)toolbarFilterAll:(id)sender;
-(IBAction)locationButtonPressed:(id)sender;
```

The RootViewController header file should look like Listing 7-1.

LISTING 7-1: RootViewController.h

```
@interface RootViewController :
    UIViewController <NSFetchedResultsControllerDelegate> {
    NSFetchedResultsController *fetchedResultsController;
    NSManagedObjectContext *managedObjectContext;
    UITableView* taskTableView;
}

-(IBAction)toolbarSortOrderChanged:(id)sender;
-(IBAction)toolbarFilterHiPri:(id)sender;
-(IBAction)toolbarFilterAll:(id)sender;
-(IBAction)locationButtonPressed:(id)sender;

@property (nonatomic, retain)
    NSFetchedResultsController *fetchedResultsController;
@property (nonatomic, retain) NSManagedObjectContext *managedObjectContext;
@property (nonatomic, retain) IBOutlet UITableView* taskTableView;

@end
```

Now that the interface and header are ready, you need to get in and modify the
RootViewController.m implementation file. First, you'll need to synthesize the new
taskTableView property. You can just add the taskTableView to the existing synthesize
statement:

```
@synthesize fetchedResultsController, managedObjectContext,taskTableView;
```

In the controllerDidChangeContent method, change the reference from self.tableview
to self.taskTableView. If you recall, this class used to inherit from UITableViewController.
In UITableViewController, there is a property called tableview. Because you are no longer
inheriting from UITableViewController, you had to create your own taskTableView property.
You are changing the code to reflect this change. The controllerDidChangeContent method
should now look like this:

```
- (void)controllerDidChangeContent:(NSFetchedResultsController *)controller {
    [self.taskTableView reloadData];
}
```

Next, although you are not ready to implement the full functionality, you should add stub
implementations of the action methods that you declared in the header file. The stubs use the
NSLog function to log a message when the user presses a button. This is helpful in debugging
issues with Interface Builder because it proves that you have linked the buttons to the methods in
Interface Builder. On more than one occasion, I have found myself searching for an elusive bug
only to realize that I did not hook up the control to the action method in Interface Builder. Using

this easy method, you can see a message in the console any time a button is pressed. The stub code should look like this:

```
-(IBAction)toolbarSortOrderChanged:(id)sender;
{
    NSLog(@"toolbarSortOrderChanged");
}

-(IBAction)toolbarFilterHiPri:(id)sender{
    NSLog(@"toolbarFilterHiPri");
}

-(IBAction)toolbarFilterAll:(id)sender
{
    NSLog(@"toolbarFilterAll");
}

-(IBAction)locationButtonPressed:(id)sender
{
    NSLog(@"locationButtonPressed");
}
```

The `RootViewController` will be displaying data from the `Task` entity. Therefore, you need to modify the `fetchedResultsController` accessor method to use the `Task` entity instead of the default `Event` entity:

```
NSEntityDescription *entity =
    [NSEntityDescription entityForName:@"Task"
        inManagedObjectContext:managedObjectContext];
```

RootViewController.m

You will also need to change the sort descriptor to use the `Task` entity's `text` attribute instead of `timestamp`:

```
NSSortDescriptor *sortDescriptor =
        [[NSSortDescriptor alloc] initWithKey:@"text" ascending:YES];
```

RootViewController.m

The last thing that you will need to do in the implementation file is implement the cleanup methods `dealloc` and `viewDidUnload`. It is important to set your properties to `nil` in `viewDidUnload` to avoid the possibility of sending messages to objects that you have released. Sending messages to `nil` is not an error in Objective-C, so setting released pointers to `nil` is a good thing to do to ensure that your application doesn't crash from sending a message to an invalid pointer.

Because Objective-C on the iPhone is not a garbage-collected language, you are responsible for managing memory yourself. You should release the memory for any properties that you are retaining in the `dealloc` method. Here is the implementation for the `viewDidUnload` and `dealloc` methods:

```
- (void)viewDidUnload {
    self.managedObjectContext=nil;
    self.fetchedResultsController = nil;
    self.taskTableView=nil;
    [super viewDidUnload];
}

- (void)dealloc {
    [fetchedResultsController release];
    [managedObjectContext release];
    [taskTableView release];
    [super dealloc];
}
```

RootViewController.m

You are finished with the `RootViewController` for now. The final step is to go back into Interface Builder and hook up the actions and outlets that you created in the `RootViewController` header to the appropriate interface items.

Open the `RootViewController.xib` and select File's Owner in the Document window. Using the Connections Inspector window, link the `view` outlet in File's Owner to the View in the xib. Next, link the `taskTableView` outlet in File's Owner to the Table View nested under the View. Last, go through each button bar nested under the toolbar and link the selectors in the button bar items to the correct methods in File's Owner. The All button selector should point to the `toolbarFilterAll` action method, Location should point to `locationButtonPressed`, Hi-Pri should point to `toolbarFilterHiPri`, and the Asc and Dsc buttons should point to `toolbarSortOrderChanged`.

You should now be able to build and run the application. Verify that you receive no errors or warnings during the build process. Once the application comes up in the simulator, click all of the toolbar buttons. Because you added those stub action methods with the `NSLog` statement, you should be able to quickly verify that you have hooked up the buttons properly in IB by examining the Xcode console. Each time you press a button, the appropriate log message should print.

GENERATING THE MANAGED OBJECT SUBCLASSES

Now that you have built the `RootViewController`, the next task is to generate your custom `NSManagedObject` subclasses from the data model. Open the `Tasks.xcdatamodel` file.

From the File menu, select New File. In the New File dialog box, you should see an option that is not usually there to create a Managed Object Class. Xcode shows this option only when you open this dialog while using the data modeler. After selecting Managed Object Class, click Next. You will see a screen that lets you pick the data model entities for which you want to generate code. Select the Location entity. Make sure that you have selected the "Generate accessors" and "Generate Obj-C 2.0 Properties" checkboxes and click Finish.

Repeat the process to create the Task object. You would think that you could just check both the Task and Location entities the first time through to generate classes for both entities. Generally, you would be correct. However, because there is a dependency between the Task and Location objects, if you generate both classes at the same time and Xcode generates the Task class first, the tool will not create the correct reference in the Task header for the type (Location*) of the location property. This appears to be a bug in the tool.

When you have finished generating the classes, go back into Xcode. In the left pane, create a new group under Classes called Managed Objects. Groups are like folders and can help you to keep your project organized. Move the Task.m, Task.h, Location.m, and Location.h files into the new Managed Objects group.

Open the header for the Task class, Task.h. Add a property for the highPriTasks fetched property and the isOverdue dynamic property:

```
@property (nonatomic,retain) NSArray* highPriTasks;
@property (nonatomic, retain) NSNumber * isOverdue;
```

Task.h

Finally, in Task.m, add an @dynamic statement for the highPriTasks fetched property and isOverdue property to tell the compiler that the framework will dynamically generate these properties at runtime:

```
@dynamic highPriTasks;
@dynamic isOverdue;
```

Task.m

Add a method stub for the isOverdue getter function to return NO. You will implement the actual function later on in the chapter:

```
- (NSNumber*) isOverdue
{
    BOOL isTaskOverdue = NO;

    return [NSNumber numberWithBool:isTaskOverdue];
}
```

ADDING AND VIEWING TASKS

Now that you have built the main screen where a user can add and select tasks, you need to build a way for your users to view and edit tasks. You will implement this functionality with the ViewTaskController. You can see the interface for the ViewTaskController in Figure 7-5.

FIGURE 7-5: The ViewTaskController

Building the ViewTaskController

In Xcode, create a new `UIViewController` subclass called `ViewTaskController`. Make sure that the `UITableViewController` subclass option is selected and that "With XIB for user interface" is not selected.

In the `ViewTaskController.h` header file, add imports for the `Task.h` and `Location.h` headers:

```
#import "Task.h"
#import "Location.h"
```

ViewTaskController.h

In the interface section, add a member variable to hold an instance of the managed object context. Add another member to hold a `Task` object:

```
NSManagedObjectContext *managedObjectContext;
    Task* managedTaskObject;
```

ViewTaskController.h

Add properties for both of the member variables that you added previously:

```
@property (nonatomic, retain) NSManagedObjectContext *managedObjectContext;
@property (nonatomic, retain) Task* managedTaskObject;
```

ViewTaskController.h

The completed header should look like Listing 7-2.

LISTING 7-2: ViewTaskController.h

```
#import <UIKit/UIKit.h>
#import "Task.h"
#import "Location.h"

@interface ViewTaskController : UITableViewController {
    NSManagedObjectContext *managedObjectContext;
    Task* managedTaskObject;
}

@property (nonatomic, retain) NSManagedObjectContext *managedObjectContext;
@property (nonatomic, retain) Task* managedTaskObject;

@end
```

You will add code to the `RootViewController` to create an instance of the `ViewTaskController` when a user selects a row in the table or when a user clicks the plus sign to add a new task. You will then populate the `ViewTaskController` properties with a pointer to the managed object context and a pointer to the `Task` object that the `ViewTaskController` will display.

This design prevents the `ViewTaskController` from having to know anything about the class that is calling it. The `ViewTaskController` doesn't need to know how to find the `Task` object that it will display. This prevents the `ViewTaskController` from needing a reference to the context. In general, it is a good practice to pass in all of the data that an object needs to function. This loosely couples the class to other classes in the application.

Sure, the `ViewTaskController` could have obtained a pointer to the managed object context from the app delegate, but that would tightly couple it to this application. A more generic and reusable design is to build the controller such that it has all of the information that it needs to operate without having to look outside of the class.

Now that you have the `ViewTaskController` header coded, it's time to move on to the implementation. Open the `ViewTaskController.m` implementation file. Synthesize the properties that you declared in the header file:

```
@synthesize managedObjectContext, managedTaskObject;
```

Next, uncomment the `viewDidLoad` method and add a line of code to set the title of the screen. The Nav Bar control displays this title at the top of the screen as well as in the Back button on subsequent screens. The `viewDidLoad` method should look like this:

```
- (void)viewDidLoad {
    [super viewDidLoad];

    // Uncomment the following line to display an Edit button in the navigation
    // bar for this view controller.
    self.navigationItem.title = @"Task Detail";
}
```

ViewTaskController.m

Now, uncomment the `viewWillAppear` method and add a line of code to reload the data in the `tableView`. The `viewWillAppear` method should look like this:

```
- (void)viewWillAppear:(BOOL)animated {
    [super viewWillAppear:animated];

    // Reload the data for the table to refresh from the context
    [self.tableView reloadData];

}
```

ViewTaskController.m

You need to add code to clean up the memory used by the instance variables and properties defined in the `ViewTaskController` just as you did in `RootViewController`. Implement `viewDidUnload` and `dealloc` to free the memory and set the properties used by the class to `nil`:

```
-  (void)viewDidUnload {
    self.managedObjectContext=nil;
    self.managedTaskObject = nil;
    [super viewDidUnload];
}
-  (void)dealloc {
    [managedObjectContext release];
    [managedTaskObject release];
    [super dealloc];
}
```

ViewTaskController.m

Because you implemented the ViewTaskController as a UITableViewController, you need to implement the TableView methods as you learned in the previous chapters on using the UITableView control.

You can leave the numberOfSectionsInTableView method alone because the table will display only one section.

You will need to modify the tableView:numberOfRowsInSection: method to return six rows. You will populate each of these six rows with data in the tableView:cellForRowAtIndexPath: method. The tableView:numberOfRowsInSection: method should look like this:

```
// Customize the number of rows in the table view.
-  (NSInteger)tableView:(UITableView *)tableView
    numberOfRowsInSection:(NSInteger)section {
    return 6;
}
```

ViewTaskController.m

Next, you will implement the tableView:cellForRowAtIndexPath: method to display the appropriate content for each row in the table. Building this table will be a little different from what you have seen before, as you are not building each row dynamically based on its content as you have done in the past. Each row will have a static label based on the row number and will have some dynamic content taken from the Task object that corresponds with that row.

Here is the code for the TableView:cellForRowAtIndexPath: method:

```
// Customize the appearance of table view cells.
-  (UITableViewCell *)tableView:(UITableView *)tableView
        cellForRowAtIndexPath:(NSIndexPath *)indexPath {

    static NSString *CellIdentifier = @"Cell";

    UITableViewCell *cell =
        [tableView dequeueReusableCellWithIdentifier:CellIdentifier];
    if (cell == nil) {
        cell = [[[UITableViewCell alloc]
                initWithStyle:UITableViewCellStyleValue2
```

```objc
                    reuseIdentifier:CellIdentifier] autorelease];
}

// Set up the cell...
switch (indexPath.row) {
    case 0:
        cell.textLabel.text = @"Text";
        cell.detailTextLabel.text = managedTaskObject.text;
        break;
    case 1:
        cell.textLabel.text = @"Priority";

        // Get the priority number and convert it to a string
        NSString* priorityString=nil;

        switch ([managedTaskObject.priority intValue]) {
            case 0:
                priorityString = @"None";
                break;
            case 1:
                priorityString = @"Low";
                break;
            case 2:
                priorityString = @"Medium";
                break;
            case 3:
                priorityString = @"High";
                break;
            default:
                break;
        }

        cell.detailTextLabel.text = priorityString;
        [priorityString release];

        break;
    case 2:
        cell.textLabel.text = @"Due Date";

        // Create a date formatter to format the date from the picker
        NSDateFormatter* df = [[NSDateFormatter alloc] init];
        [df setDateStyle:NSDateFormatterLongStyle];
        cell.detailTextLabel.text =
            [df stringFromDate:managedTaskObject.dueDate ];
        [df release];

        break;
    case 3:
        cell.textLabel.text = @"Location";
        Location* locationObject = managedTaskObject.location;
        if (locationObject!=nil)
        {
            cell.detailTextLabel.text = locationObject.name;
        }
```

```
            else {
                cell.detailTextLabel.text = @"Not Set";

            }

            break;
        case 4:
            // Show hi-pri tasks alert
            cell.detailTextLabel.text = @"Hi-Pri Tasks";
            break;
        case 5:
            // Show sooner tasks alert
            cell.detailTextLabel.text = @"Tasks due sooner than this one";
            break;

        default:
            break;
    }

    return cell;
}
```

ViewTaskController.m

The first portion of this code should be familiar. It tries to dequeue a cell, and if it cannot, it creates a new cell.

The rest of the code executes a `switch` statement to determine the content of the row based on which row the `TableView` requests.

The first row of the table will display a label that says "Text" and the text attribute from the `Task` object.

Row two displays the label "Priority" and then converts the integer priority from the `Task` object into a `priority` string that the `TableView` displays in the cell.

The next row displays the "Due Date" label and uses an `NSDateFormatter` to convert the `NSDate` object stored in the managed object into a string. You can use one of the pre-defined formats or you can define your own. For more information on using `NSDateFormatter`, look at the Xcode SDK documentation or browse to `http://developer.apple.com/iphone/library/documentation/Cocoa/Reference/Foundation/Classes/NSDateFormatter_Class/Reference/Reference.html`.

The fourth row displays the Location label. Then, the code tries to get a `Location` object from the `Task`'s `location` property. The code displays the `name` property of the `Location` object, if it exists. If not, the code displays "Not Set."

The final two cases display labels to inform the user that tapping these cells will bring up a list of high-priority tasks or a list of tasks that are due sooner than the currently displayed task. You will implement `didSelectRowAtIndexPath` to do something when the user taps these rows later in the chapter.

Leave the default implementation of the `tableView:commitEditingStyle:forRowAtIndexPath:` and `tableView:canMoveRowAtIndexPath:` methods.

Changes to the RootViewController

Now that you have built the `ViewTaskController`, you need to make some changes to the `RootViewController` to access the new screen.

First, you will configure the `RootViewController` navigation bar. In the `viewDidLoad` method of the `RootViewController.m` implementation file, remove the line:

```
self.navigationItem.leftBarButtonItem = self.editButtonItem;
```

This screen will not be using the Edit button.

At the end of `viewDidLoad`, add the following line of code to set the title of the screen in the navigation bar:

```
self.title = @"Tasks";
```

You will also need to add `import` statements to import the headers for the `Location` and `Task` objects as well as the `ViewTaskController`. Add the following imports to the top of the `RootViewController` implementation file:

```
#import "ViewTaskController.h"
#import "Location.h"
#import "Task.h"
```

RootViewController.m

Next, you need to implement the `insertNewObject` method. This method creates a new `Task` object and then passes control off to the `ViewTaskController` to edit the new task. Tapping the plus button in the navigation bar calls the `insertNewObject` method. Here is the `insertNewObject` method:

```
- (void)insertNewObject {

    NSManagedObjectContext *context = self.managedObjectContext;

    Task *newTask =
    [NSEntityDescription insertNewObjectForEntityForName:@"Task"
                                   inManagedObjectContext:context];

    ViewTaskController* taskController =
        [[ViewTaskController alloc] initWithStyle:UITableViewStyleGrouped];
    taskController.managedTaskObject=newTask;
    taskController.managedObjectContext = self.managedObjectContext;

    [self.navigationController pushViewController:taskController animated:YES];

    [taskController release];
```

RootViewController.m

This method is straightforward. First, you use the context to create a new `Task` object. Then, you create an instance of the `ViewTaskController` and populate its `managedTaskObject` and managedObjectContext properties. Last, you push the new ViewTaskController onto the navigation stack and then release it.

The last change in the RootViewController is to implement the TableView methods. You can leave the default numberOfSectionsInTableView:, tableView:numberOfRowsInSection:, tableView: commitEditingStyle:forRowAtIndexPath: and tableView:canMoveRowAtIndexPath: methods.

You do need to implement the tableView:cellForRowAtIndexPath: to display the text property of the Task object for the row. You will also add some code to check the isOverdue transient property and display overdue tasks in red. Here is the code for tableView:cellForRowAtIndexPath:

```objc
- (UITableViewCell *)tableView:(UITableView *)tableView
        cellForRowAtIndexPath:(NSIndexPath *)indexPath {

    static NSString *CellIdentifier = @"Cell";

    UITableViewCell *cell =
        [tableView dequeueReusableCellWithIdentifier:CellIdentifier];
    if (cell == nil) {
        cell = [[[UITableViewCell alloc]
                initWithStyle:UITableViewCellStyleDefault
                reuseIdentifier:CellIdentifier] autorelease];
    }

    // Configure the cell.
    Task *managedTaskObject =
        [fetchedResultsController objectAtIndexPath:indexPath];
    cell.textLabel.text = managedTaskObject.text;

    // Change the text color if the task is overdue
    if (managedTaskObject.isOverdue==[NSNumber numberWithBool: YES])
    {
        cell.textLabel.textColor = [UIColor redColor];
    }
    else {
        cell.textLabel.textColor = [UIColor blackColor];
    }

    return cell;
}
```

RootViewController.m

You should be familiar with how this code works. The beginning of the method tries to dequeue a cell and if it cannot, it creates a new one. Next, the code gets the Task object from the fetchedResultsController that corresponds to the requested cell. Then, the cell's textLabel is set with the text from the Task object. Finally, use the value of the Task's isOverdue property to determine the color of the text.

Build and run the application. You should not get any errors or warnings. The application should now allow you to create new default tasks and then navigate to the ViewTaskController screen. You should also be able to select tasks in the Tasks screen and view them in the ViewTaskController screen.

BUILDING THE EDITING CONTROLLERS

Your Tasks application now has the capability to create new tasks, and view existing tasks. Although there is some decent functionality there, the application is useless without being able to edit the contents of your tasks. In this section, you will implement the screens shown in Figure 7-6. These screens will allow the user to edit each individual piece of data in a task. Create a new group under Classes called Sub Controllers to hold all of your edit controller code.

(a) Text Editing
Screen - EditTextController

(b) Priority Selection
Screen - EditPriorityController

(c) Location Selection
Screen - EditLocationController

(d) Date Editing
Screen - EditDateController

FIGURE 7-6: Task data editing screens

Editing Text with the EditTextController

The `EditTextController` screen, as you can see in Figure 7-7, will allow the user to edit the text used in the `Task` and `Location` objects. The screen consists of a `UITableView` with one cell. Embedded in that cell is a `UITextField`. This design is consistent with the behavior of the text editing screens in the stock iPhone applications such as Contacts.

In the new Sub Controllers group, create a new `UITableviewController` without NIB called `EditTextController`. Open the `EditTextController.h` header file and add instance variables for an `NSManagedObject` and the `NSManagedObjectContext`:

```
NSManagedObject* managedObject;
NSManagedObjectContext *managedObjectContext;
```

EditTextController.h

The parent screen will set the managed object and the context before it pushes the `EditTextController` on to the navigation stack.

You also need to add an instance variable to hold an `NSString*` called `keyString`. Because this screen supports editing both the `text` property of the `Task` object and the `name` property of the `Location` object, you will use key-value coding (KVC) to take the text entered on the screen and update the managed object. This is also the reason that the screen accepts an `NSManagedObject` instead of one of your custom subclasses. That way, the screen is generic enough to edit text fields on any Managed Objects and is not limited to editing only `Task` or `Location` objects. Add the `keyString` member variable to the following header:

```
NSString* keyString;
```

Finally, add a member variable to hold the `UITextField` that you will embed in the `TableView`:

```
UITextField* textField;
```

FIGURE 7-7: EditText Controller Screen

The last thing that you need to do is add property declarations for your instance variables. Your finished header file should look like Listing 7-3.

LISTING 7-3: EditTextController.h

```
#import <UIKit/UIKit.h>

@interface EditTextController : UITableViewController {
    NSManagedObject* managedObject;
```

continues

LISTING 7-3 *(continued)*

```
        NSManagedObjectContext *managedObjectContext;
        NSString* keyString;

        UITextField* textField;
}

@property (nonatomic, retain) NSManagedObject* managedObject;
@property (nonatomic, retain) NSManagedObjectContext *managedObjectContext;
@property (nonatomic, retain) NSString* keyString;

@end
```

Now, you have to work on the implementation file, EditTextController.m. The first thing that you will need to do is synthesize the properties that you declared in the header:

```
@synthesize managedObject,keyString,managedObjectContext;
```

Next, uncomment and implement the viewDidLoad method:

```
- (void)viewDidLoad {
    [super viewDidLoad];

    // Create the textfield
    textField = [[UITextField alloc] initWithFrame:CGRectMake(10, 10, 200, 20)];

    // Notice how you use KVC here because you might get a Task or a Location in
    // this generic text editor
    textField.text = [managedObject valueForKey:keyString];
    textField.clearsOnBeginEditing=YES;

    // Add the save button
    UIBarButtonItem* saveButton =[[UIBarButtonItem alloc]
        initWithBarButtonSystemItem:UIBarButtonSystemItemSave
                            target:self
                            action:@selector (saveButtonPressed:)];

    self.navigationItem.rightBarButtonItem = saveButton;
    [saveButton release];
}
```

EditTextController.m

The first thing that you need to do in viewDidLoad is call super viewDidLoad. In general, you want to call the superclass version of a method before you do anything in your method to ensure that everything in the superclass is set up properly before you begin your work. Conversely, you may have noticed that in `viewDidUnload` and `dealloc`, you do your work first and then call the superclass version of those methods at the end.

Next, you move on to create and configure the `textfield` instance variable. The code sets the text of the `textfield` using key-value coding, not the specific `text` or `name` property of the `Task` or `Location` object. Remember that you are building this screen generically to be able to handle the text input for any field in any managed object.

Last, the code creates the Save button and sets it as the `rightBarButtonItem` in the nav bar.

The next task is to implement the `saveButtonPressed` method. Pressing the Save button in the nav bar calls the `saveButtonPressed` method. In this method, you will get the text from the text field and use KVC to set the appropriate key in the managed object. Remember that the previous screen set the `keyString` before displaying the `EditTextController`. Then, you save the context and pop the View Controller off the navigation stack. Here is the code:

```
-(void) saveButtonPressed: (id) sender
{

    // Configure the managed object
    // Notice how you use KVC here because you might get a Task or a Location
    // in this generic text editor
    [managedObject setValue:textField.text forKey:keyString];

    // Save the context.
    NSError *error = nil;
    if (![self.managedObjectContext save:&error]) {
        NSLog(@"Unresolved error %@, %@", error, [error userInfo]);
        abort();
    }

    // pop the view
    [self.navigationController popViewControllerAnimated:YES];

}
```

EditTextController.m

In the `viewDidUnload` method, set the properties of the class to `nil`:

```
- (void)viewDidUnload {
    self.managedObjectContext=nil;
    self.managedObject = nil;
    self.keyString=nil;
    [super viewDidUnload];
}
```

EditTextController.m

Leave the `numberOfSectionsInTableView` method with the default implementation. The table will have only one section. Change the `tableView:numberOfRowsInSection:` method to return one row:

```objc
- (NSInteger)numberOfSectionsInTableView:(UITableView *)tableView {
    return 1;
}

// Customize the number of rows in the table view.
- (NSInteger)tableView:(UITableView *)tableView
    numberOfRowsInSection:(NSInteger)section {
    return 1;
}
```

EditTextController.m

Next, you should implement the `tableView:cellForRowAtIndexPath:` method to show the `textField` in the `tableView` cell:

```objc
// Customize the appearance of table view cells.
- (UITableViewCell *)tableView:(UITableView *)tableView
        cellForRowAtIndexPath:(NSIndexPath *)indexPath {

    static NSString *CellIdentifier = @"Cell";

    UITableViewCell *cell =
        [tableView dequeueReusableCellWithIdentifier:CellIdentifier];

    if (cell == nil) {
        cell = [[[UITableViewCell alloc]
                initWithStyle:UITableViewCellStyleDefault
                reuseIdentifier:CellIdentifier] autorelease];
    }

    // Set up the cell...
    if (indexPath.row == 0)
    {
        UIView* cv =  cell.contentView;

        [cv addSubview:textField];

    }

    return cell;
}
```

EditTextController.m

Implement `tableView:didSelectRowAtIndexPath:` to deselect the selected cell. You don't necessarily have to do this to complete the functionality of your application, but the Apple Human Interface Guidelines suggest that you deselect a tableview cell after its selection. Therefore, I'm including the following code:

```
- (void)tableView:(UITableView *)tableView
   didSelectRowAtIndexPath:(NSIndexPath *)indexPath {
   //  Deselect the currently selected row according to the HIG
   [tableView deselectRowAtIndexPath:indexPath animated:NO];
}
```

EditTextController.m

Last, but not least, you need to implement the `dealloc` method to clean up any memory that your class has allocated:

```
- (void)dealloc {
   [managedObject release];
   [managedObjectContext release];
   [keyString release];
   [super dealloc];
}
```

EditTextController.m

Setting Priorities with the EditPriorityController

FIGURE 7-8: EditPriority Controller Screen

The `EditPriorityController` screen, which you can see in Figure 7-8, allows the user to choose the priority for a task. Again, you will implement the screen as a `TableView`. This time, there will be a row for each priority level. In the Sub Controllers group, create a new `UITableviewController` without a NIB called `EditPriorityController`.

In the header file, you will need to add instance variables and properties for a `Task` object and the context. You will also need to add a `#import` directive for the `Task.h` header file. Your header should look like Listing 7-4.

LISTING 7-4: EditPriorityController.h

```
#import <UIKit/UIKit.h>
#import "Task.h"


@interface EditPriorityController : UITableViewController {
```

continues

LISTING 7-4 *(continued)*

```
      Task* managedTaskObject;
      NSManagedObjectContext *managedObjectContext;

}

@property (nonatomic, retain) Task* managedTaskObject;
@property (nonatomic, retain) NSManagedObjectContext *managedObjectContext;


@end
```

In the implementation file, you first need to synthesize the properties that you declared in the header:

```
@synthesize managedTaskObject,managedObjectContext;
```

As in the `EditTextController`, you should implement the `viewDidUnload` method to set the properties defined in the class to `nil`:

Available for
download on
Wrox.com

```
- (void)viewDidUnload {
    self.managedObjectContext=nil;
    self.managedTaskObject = nil;
    [super viewDidUnload];
}
```

EditPriorityController.m

Leave the `numberOfSectionsInTableView` method with the default implementation because the table will have only one section. Change `tableView:numberOfRowsInSection:` to return four rows, one for each priority level.

Next, implement the `tableView:cellForRowAtIndexPath:` method to show the priority options in the appropriate cell:

Available for
download on
Wrox.com

```
// Customize the appearance of table view cells.
- (UITableViewCell *)tableView:(UITableView *)tableView
        cellForRowAtIndexPath:(NSIndexPath *)indexPath {

    static NSString *CellIdentifier = @"Cell";

    UITableViewCell *cell =
        [tableView dequeueReusableCellWithIdentifier:CellIdentifier];

    if (cell == nil) {
        cell = [[[UITableViewCell alloc]
                initWithStyle:UITableViewCellStyleDefault
                reuseIdentifier:CellIdentifier] autorelease];
    }
```

```
         // Set up the cell...
         switch (indexPath.row) {
             case 0:
                 cell.textLabel.text = @"None";
                 break;
             case 1:
                 cell.textLabel.text = @"Low";
                 break;
             case 2:
                 cell.textLabel.text = @"Medium";
                 break;
             case 3:
                 cell.textLabel.text = @"High";
                 break;
             default:
                 break;
         }

         // place the checkmark next to the existing priority
         if (indexPath.row == [managedTaskObject.priority intValue] )
         {
             cell.accessoryType=UITableViewCellAccessoryCheckmark;
         }

         return cell;
     }
```

EditPriorityController.m

This method should be familiar to you. The first few lines try to dequeue a cell as usual. Then, the code determines the text of the cell based on which cell you are providing. The last bit of code displays a checkmark next to the currently chosen priority for the task.

When a user taps a row, you need to save that selection in the Task object. You will do that in the `tableView:didSelectRowAtIndexPath:` method:

```
 - (void)tableView:(UITableView *)tableView
     didSelectRowAtIndexPath:(NSIndexPath *)indexPath {
     //  Deselect the currently selected row according to the HIG
     [tableView deselectRowAtIndexPath:indexPath animated:NO];

     // Configure the managed object
     managedTaskObject.priority=[NSNumber numberWithInt:indexPath.row];

     // Save the context.
     NSError *error = nil;
     if (![self.managedObjectContext save:&error]) {
         // There was an error validating the date
```

```
        // Display error information

            NSLog(@"Unresolved error %@, %@", error, [error userInfo]);

        UIAlertView* alert = [[UIAlertView alloc]
            initWithTitle:@"Invalid Due Date"
            message:[[error userInfo] valueForKey:@"ErrorString"]
            delegate:nil cancelButtonTitle:@"OK" otherButtonTitles:nil ];
        [alert show];
        [alert release];

        // Roll back the context to
        // revert back to the old priority
        [self.managedObjectContext rollback];


    }
    else {
        // pop the view
        [self.navigationController popViewControllerAnimated:YES];

    }
}
```

EditPriorityController.m

The first thing that this method does is deselect the selected row as I explained in the last section.

The next line sets the `Task` object's `priority` field to the priority level selected on the screen. Then, the code saves the context. Because you are going to add a validation rule that includes the priority, there is a possibility that the new priority could fail the validation. If the validation fails, the `save` method will fail, so you need to roll the context back to its state before the failed save. If the save method fails, you revert the `priority` back to its original state using the `rollback` method of the context. The `rollback` method undoes all changes to the context that have not yet been committed with a successful `save` call. If an error occurs, such as a validation failure, you show the user an alert to inform him that a problem has occurred. If there is no problem, the code pops the View Controller from the stack.

Finally, implement the `dealloc` method to release the member variables that you allocated in the class:

```
- (void)dealloc {
    [managedTaskObject release];
    [managedObjectContext release];
    [super dealloc];
}
```

EditPriorityController.m

Adding and Editing Locations with the EditLocationController

The user navigates to the `EditLocationController` by tapping the location cell on the `ViewTaskController`. The `EditLocationController`, as shown in Figure 7-9, allows the user to select a location, add new locations, and delete existing locations. To create the `EditLocationController`, create a new `UITableviewController` without a NIB called `EditLocationController`.

Modify your new header file to create instance variables and properties to hold the context and `Task` objects that the parent screen will configure. You will also need to add a member variable and property for the `NSFetchedResultsController` that you will use to display your location list. Additionally, you will need to add `#import` directives for the `Task` and `Location` header files. The completed header file should look like Listing 7-5.

FIGURE 7-9: EditLocation Controller Screen

LISTING 7-5: EditLocationController.h

```objc
#import <UIKit/UIKit.h>
#import "Task.h"
#import "Location.h"

@interface EditLocationController :
    UITableViewController <NSFetchedResultsControllerDelegate> {

    NSFetchedResultsController *fetchedResultsController;
    NSManagedObjectContext *managedObjectContext;
    Task* managedTaskObject;
}

@property (nonatomic, retain) NSFetchedResultsController
                                *fetchedResultsController;
@property (nonatomic, retain) NSManagedObjectContext *managedObjectContext;
@property (nonatomic, retain) Task* managedTaskObject;

@end
```

Let's move on to the implementation file. Add an `import` statement for `EditTextController.h`:

```objc
#import "EditTextController.h"
```

You will use the `EditTextController` to add the text for newly added locations. Next, synthesize the properties that you declared in the header file:

```objc
@synthesize fetchedResultsController, managedObjectContext, managedTaskObject;
```

Uncomment and implement the `viewDidLoad` method:

```
- (void)viewDidLoad {
    [super viewDidLoad];

    // Set up the add button
    UIBarButtonItem *addButton = [[UIBarButtonItem alloc]
        initWithBarButtonSystemItem:UIBarButtonSystemItemAdd
        target:self action:@selector(insertNewLocation)];

    self.navigationItem.rightBarButtonItem = addButton;
    [addButton release];

    NSError* error;

    if (![[self fetchedResultsController] performFetch:&error]) {
        NSLog(@"Unresolved error %@, %@", error, [error userInfo]);
        abort();
    }

    // set the title to display in the nav bar
    self.title = @"Location";

}
```

EditLocationController.m

This code creates the `addButton` and sets it to call the `insertNewLocation` method. It then adds the `addButton` to the nav bar. Next, you tell the fetched results controller to fetch its data. Finally, you set the title of the screen to Location.

Next, you need to set the class properties in the `viewDidUnload` method to `nil`:

```
- (void)viewDidUnload {
    self.fetchedResultsController=nil;
    self.managedTaskObject=nil;
    self.managedObjectContext=nil;
    [super viewDidUnload];
}
```

EditLocationController.m

Now, add the `insertNewLocation` method that runs when the user taps the Add button that you created in `viewDidLoad`. This method adds a new `Location` to the context and pushes the text controller on to the navigation stack to allow the user to edit the location name. Here is the `insertNewLocation` method:

```
- (void)insertNewLocation {

    NSManagedObjectContext *context = self.managedObjectContext;

    Location *newLocation =
```

```
    [NSEntityDescription insertNewObjectForEntityForName:@"Location"
                              inManagedObjectContext:context];

    EditTextController* textController =
        [[EditTextController alloc] initWithStyle:UITableViewStyleGrouped];
    textController.managedObject=newLocation;
    textController.managedObjectContext = self.managedObjectContext;
    textController.keyString=@"name";

    [self.navigationController pushViewController:textController animated:YES];

    [textController release];
}
```

EditLocationController.m

Next, implement the fetched results controller accessor method to fetch the Location entities and sort them in ascending order by name:

```
- (NSFetchedResultsController *)fetchedResultsController {

    if (fetchedResultsController != nil) {
        return fetchedResultsController;
    }

    // Set up the fetched results controller.
    // Create the fetch request for the entity.
    NSFetchRequest *fetchRequest = [[NSFetchRequest alloc] init];
    // Edit the entity name as appropriate.
    NSEntityDescription *entity =
        [NSEntityDescription
            entityForName:@"Location"
            inManagedObjectContext:managedObjectContext];
    [fetchRequest setEntity:entity];

    // Edit the sort key as appropriate.
    NSSortDescriptor *sortDescriptor =
        [[NSSortDescriptor alloc]
            initWithKey:@"name"
            ascending:YES];
    NSArray *sortDescriptors = [[NSArray alloc]
                                initWithObjects:sortDescriptor, nil];

    [fetchRequest setSortDescriptors:sortDescriptors];

    // Edit the section name key path and cache name if appropriate.
    // nil for section name key path means "no sections".
    NSFetchedResultsController *aFetchedResultsController =
        [[NSFetchedResultsController alloc]
            initWithFetchRequest:fetchRequest
            managedObjectContext:managedObjectContext
            sectionNameKeyPath:nil cacheName:nil];
```

```
        aFetchedResultsController.delegate = self;
        self.fetchedResultsController = aFetchedResultsController;

        [aFetchedResultsController release];
        [fetchRequest release];
        [sortDescriptor release];
        [sortDescriptors release];

        return fetchedResultsController;
    }
```

EditLocationController.m

Implement the `controllerDidChangeContent` delegate method to reload the table data:

Available for
download on
Wrox.com

```
    // NSFetchedResultsControllerDelegate method to notify the delegate
    // that all section and object changes have been processed.
    - (void)controllerDidChangeContent:(NSFetchedResultsController *)controller {

        [self.tableView reloadData];
    }
```

EditLocationController.m

Change the `numberOfSectionsInTableView` and `tableView:numberOfRowsInSection:` methods
to use the `fetchedResultsController`:

Available for
download on
Wrox.com

```
    - (NSInteger)numberOfSectionsInTableView:(UITableView *)tableView {
        return [[fetchedResultsController sections] count];
    }

    // Customize the number of rows in the table view.
    - (NSInteger)tableView:(UITableView *)tableView
        numberOfRowsInSection:(NSInteger)section {

        id <NSFetchedResultsSectionInfo> sectionInfo =
            [[fetchedResultsController sections] objectAtIndex:section];
        return [sectionInfo numberOfObjects];
    }
```

EditLocationController.m

Now, implement the `tableView:cellForRowAtIndexPath:` method to show the locations from the
fetched results controller:

Available for
download on
Wrox.com

```
    // Customize the appearance of table view cells.
    - (UITableViewCell *)tableView:(UITableView *)tableView
            cellForRowAtIndexPath:(NSIndexPath *)indexPath {

        static NSString *CellIdentifier = @"Cell";
```

```
        UITableViewCell *cell =
            [tableView dequeueReusableCellWithIdentifier:CellIdentifier];
        if (cell == nil) {
            cell = [[[UITableViewCell alloc]
                    initWithStyle:UITableViewCellStyleDefault
                    reuseIdentifier:CellIdentifier] autorelease];
        }

        Location *managedLocationObject =
            [fetchedResultsController objectAtIndexPath:indexPath];

        // If the location in the task object is the same as the location object
        // draw the checkmark
        if (managedTaskObject.location == managedLocationObject)
        {
            cell.accessoryType=UITableViewCellAccessoryCheckmark;

        }

        cell.textLabel.text = managedLocationObject.name;

        return cell;
    }
```

EditLocationController.m

You can see that the code does the usual cell setup and dequeuing. Then, it obtains a `Location` object for the cell from the `fetchedResultsController`. The code then checks to see if the location that it will use is also the location in the `Task`. If it is, the code displays the checkmark accessory for the cell. Last, you use the `name` property of the `Location` object as the cell text.

Next, you need to implement `tableView:didSelectRowAtIndexPath:` to save the selected location:

```
tableView:didSelectRowAtIndexPath: to save off the selected location
- (void)tableView:(UITableView *)tableView
        didSelectRowAtIndexPath:(NSIndexPath *)indexPath {

    // Deselect the currently selected row according to the HIG
    [tableView deselectRowAtIndexPath:indexPath animated:NO];

    // set the Task's location to the chosen location
    Location *newLocationObject =
        [fetchedResultsController objectAtIndexPath:indexPath];

    managedTaskObject.location=newLocationObject;

    // Save the context.
    NSError *error = nil;

    if (![self.managedObjectContext save:&error]) {
        NSLog(@"Unresolved error %@, %@", error, [error userInfo]);
        abort();
    }
```

```
        else {

            // pop the view
            [self.navigationController popViewControllerAnimated:YES];
        }
    }
```

This code gets the selected `Location` object from the `fetchedResultsController`, sets the `location` in the `Task` object, saves the context, and pops the view from the navigation stack.

In order to allow the user to delete locations, uncomment and implement the `tableView:commitEditingStyle:` method:

```
// Override to support editing the table view.
- (void)tableView:(UITableView *)tableView
    commitEditingStyle:(UITableViewCellEditingStyle)editingStyle
    forRowAtIndexPath:(NSIndexPath *)indexPath {

    if (editingStyle == UITableViewCellEditingStyleDelete) {
        // Delete the managed object for the given index path
        NSManagedObjectContext *context =
            [fetchedResultsController managedObjectContext];

        [context deleteObject:[fetchedResultsController
                                  objectAtIndexPath:indexPath]];

        // Save the context.
        NSError *error = nil;
        if (![context save:&error]) {
            NSLog(@"Unresolved error %@, %@", error, [error userInfo]);
            abort();
        }
    }
}
```

This code enables the delete editing style that displays the Delete button when a user swipes across a row. The code then gets the context, deletes the `Location` that the user selected, and saves the context.

Finally, implement `dealloc` to release your properties:

```
- (void)dealloc {
    [fetchedResultsController release];
    [managedObjectContext release];
    [managedTaskObject release];
    [super dealloc];
}
```

Modifying Dates with the EditDateController

The last edit controller that you will implement is the EditDateController, which you can see in Figure 7-10. Like the RootViewController, you will need to create the interface for this controller using Interface Builder and a NIB because the screen will need to hold a UIDatePicker control in addition to the TableView that will display the selected date.

Create a new UIViewController with NIB called EditDateController. Make sure that you have unchecked "UITableViewController subclass" and that you have checked "With XIB for user interface." I like to keep my projects organized, so I moved the XIB file into the Resources folder.

In the EditDateController.h header file, add an import statement for your Task object:

```
#import "Task.h"
```

FIGURE 7-10: Edit DateController Screen

Add references to the UITableViewDelegate and UITableViewDataSource protocols in the interface definition to indicate that you plan to implement these protocols:

```
@interface EditDateController :
    UIViewController <UITableViewDelegate, UITableViewDataSource>
```

Add member variables and properties for a Task object, the context, a UITableView, and a UIDatePicker. Finally, add an action method, dateChanged, that will run when the user changes the date in the UIDatePicker. The finished header should look like Listing 7-6.

Available for download on Wrox.com

LISTING 7-6: EditDateController.h

```
#import <UIKit/UIKit.h>
#import "Task.h"

@interface EditDateController :
    UIViewController <UITableViewDelegate, UITableViewDataSource>
{
    Task* managedTaskObject;
    NSManagedObjectContext *managedObjectContext;
    UIDatePicker* datePicker;
    UITableView* tv;
}

@property (nonatomic, retain) Task* managedTaskObject;
@property (nonatomic, retain) NSManagedObjectContext *managedObjectContext;
@property (nonatomic, retain) IBOutlet UIDatePicker* datePicker;
@property (nonatomic, retain) IBOutlet UITableView* tv;

-(IBAction)dateChanged:(id)sender;

@end
```

Make sure that you save your completed header. You need to save because Interface Builder will only read the last saved version of the header, and you need IB to see your `DatePicker`, `TableView`, and `dateChanged` methods.

Now it's time to move into Interface Builder and work on the UI. Double-click on the `EditDateController.xib` file to open it using IB. Drag a `UIDatePicker` control into the view widow and place it at the bottom of the view. In the attributes inspector for the `DatePicker`, set the Mode to Date. There are various date and time display modes, but you only need to allow the user to select a date.

Drag a `UITableView` into the view window and position it at the top of the view. Stretch the `TableView` to fill the whole screen. Then send it to the back using Layout ➪ Send to Back. In the attributes inspector for the `TableView`, set the Style to Grouped.

Next, you need to connect the interface to the code class. Hook up the `TableView`'s `dataSource` and `delegate` to File's Owner. Hook up the File's Owner `tv` variable to the `TableView` and `datePicker` variable to the `UIDatePicker`. Finally, hook up the `UIDatePicker`'s Value Changed action to the File's Owner `dateChanged:` method.

You can now move on to the `EditDateController.m` implementation file. First, you need to synthesize the properties that you defined in the header:

```
@synthesize managedTaskObject,managedObjectContext,datePicker,tv;
```

Uncomment and implement the `viewDidLoad` method:

Available for download on Wrox.com

```
- (void)viewDidLoad {
    [super viewDidLoad];

    // Add the save button
    UIBarButtonItem* saveButton =
        [[UIBarButtonItem alloc]
          initWithBarButtonSystemItem:UIBarButtonSystemItemSave
          target:self
          action:@selector (saveButtonPressed:)];
    self.navigationItem.rightBarButtonItem = saveButton;
    [saveButton release];

    // Set the date to the one in the managed object, if it is set
    // else, set it to today
    NSDate* objectDate = managedTaskObject.dueDate;
    if (objectDate!=nil)
    {
        datePicker.date = objectDate;
    }
    else {
        datePicker.date = [NSDate date];
    }
}
```

EditDateController.m

This method creates the Save button and adds it to the nav bar. It also sets the `date` in the date picker control to the `date` in the `Task` object, if it exists, or to the current date.

Implement the `viewDidUnload` method to set the class's properties to `nil`:

```
- (void)viewDidUnload {
    self.managedObjectContext=nil;
    self.managedTaskObject = nil;
    self.datePicker = nil;
    self.tv=nil;
    [super viewDidUnload];
}
```

EditDateController.m

The user invokes the `saveButtonPressed` method when she clicks the Save button created in `viewDidLoad`. You need to implement `saveButtonPressed` to save the currently selected date to the `Task` object. Here is the code:

```
-(void) saveButtonPressed: (id) sender
{

    // Configure the managed object
    managedTaskObject.dueDate=[datePicker date];

    // Save the context.
    NSError *error = nil;
    if (![self.managedObjectContext save:&error]) {
        // There was an error validating the date
        // Display error information
        UIAlertView* alert =
            [[UIAlertView alloc]
            initWithTitle:@"Invalid Due Date"
            message:[[error userInfo] valueForKey:@"ErrorString"]
            delegate:nil cancelButtonTitle:@"OK" otherButtonTitles:nil ];
        [alert show];
        [alert release];

        // Roll back the context to
        // revert back to the original date
        [self.managedObjectContext rollback];

    }
    else{
        // pop the view
        [self.navigationController popViewControllerAnimated:YES];
    }
}
```

EditDateController.m

Because you are going to add a validation rule that includes the date, there is a possibility that the new date can fail the validation. If the validation fails, the save method will fail, so you need to roll the context back to its old state before the failed save. If the save method fails, you revert the dueDate back to the originally selected date by calling the rollback method of the context. Then, you show an alert to the user. If the save is successful, you simply pop the controller from the navigation stack.

Next, implement the dateChanged method to reload the TableView and update the date text:

Available for download on Wrox.com

```
- (IBAction)dateChanged:(id)sender{
    //  Refresh the date display
    [tv reloadData];
}
```

EditDateController.m

Because there is only one cell in the TableView, implement the ViewTaskController screen and tableView:numberOfRowsInSection: to return 1:

Available for download on Wrox.com

```
- (NSInteger)numberOfSectionsInTableView:(UITableView *)tableView {
    return 1;
}

// Customize the number of rows in the table view.
- (NSInteger)tableView:(UITableView *)tableView
    numberOfRowsInSection:(NSInteger)section {

    return 1;
}
```

EditDateController.m

Implement tableView:cellForRowAtIndexPath: to show the date chosen in the DatePicker:

Available for download on Wrox.com

```
- (UITableViewCell *)tableView:(UITableView *)tableView
        cellForRowAtIndexPath:(NSIndexPath *)indexPath {

    static NSString *CellIdentifier = @"Cell";

    UITableViewCell *cell =
        [tableView dequeueReusableCellWithIdentifier:CellIdentifier];
    if (cell == nil) {
        cell =
            [[[UITableViewCell alloc]
                initWithStyle:UITableViewCellStyleDefault
                reuseIdentifier:CellIdentifier] autorelease];
    }

    // Set up the cell...
    if (indexPath.row == 0)
    {
```

```
        //  Create a date formatter to format the date from the picker
        NSDateFormatter* df = [[NSDateFormatter alloc] init];
        [df setDateStyle:NSDateFormatterLongStyle];
        cell.textLabel.text = [df stringFromDate:datePicker.date ];
        [df release];
    }

    return cell;
}
```

EditDateController.m

You can see that you are once again using an `NSDateFormatter` to convert the `NSDate` object into a string for display in the `TableViewCell`.

In the `dealloc` method, release the member variables that correspond to the class properties:

Available for
download on
Wrox.com

```
- (void)dealloc {
    [managedTaskObject release];
    [managedObjectContext release];
    [datePicker release];
    [tv release];
    [super dealloc];
}
```

EditDateController.m

Finishing Up the Editing Controllers

You have now finished implementing all of the edit controllers. The last thing that you need to do before you are ready to run the program is go back and add code to the `ViewTaskController.m` to use the new subcontrollers to edit the task data.

In `ViewTaskController.m`, add an import statement for each subcontroller:

Available for
download on
Wrox.com

```
#import "EditTextController.h"
#import "EditPriorityController.h"
#import "EditDateController.h"
#import "EditLocationController.h"
```

ViewTaskController.m

You will also need to add an import for the App delegate because you need to get a reference to the `managedObjectModel` in order to use your stored fetch request:

```
#import "TasksAppDelegate.h"
```

You can now implement the `didSelectRowAtIndexPath` method that you left out when you were implementing the `ViewTaskController` earlier in the chapter. This method runs when a user selects a row in the table. The method should display the correct edit View Controller based on which row the user selects.

The last two buttons in the table do not use edit View Controllers. The Hi-Pri Tasks button demonstrates how to use a fetched property to get a list of high-priority tasks. The "Tasks due sooner" button shows you how to use a stored fetch request.

The following is the code for `didSelectRowAtIndexPath`:

```objc
- (void)tableView:(UITableView *)tableView
    didSelectRowAtIndexPath:(NSIndexPath *)indexPath {

    // Deselect the currently selected row according to the HIG
    [tableView deselectRowAtIndexPath:indexPath animated:NO];

    // Based on the selected row, choose which controelr to push
    switch (indexPath.row) {
        case 0:
        {
            EditTextController* etc = [[EditTextController alloc]
                                        initWithStyle:UITableViewStyleGrouped];
            etc.managedObject = self.managedTaskObject;
            etc.keyString=@"text";
            etc.managedObjectContext = self.managedObjectContext;
            [self.navigationController pushViewController:etc animated:YES];
            [etc release];
            break;
        }
        case 1:
        {
            EditPriorityController* epc =
                [[EditPriorityController alloc]
                  initWithStyle:UITableViewStyleGrouped];
            epc.managedTaskObject = self.managedTaskObject;
            epc.managedObjectContext = self.managedObjectContext;

            [self.navigationController pushViewController:epc animated:YES];
            [epc release];
            break;
        }
        case 2:
        {
            EditDateController* edc = [[EditDateController alloc] init];

            edc.managedTaskObject = self.managedTaskObject;
            edc.managedObjectContext = self.managedObjectContext;

            [self.navigationController pushViewController:edc animated:YES];
            [edc release];
            break;
        }
        case 3:
        {
            EditLocationController* elc = [[EditLocationController alloc] init];
            elc.managedObjectContext = self.managedObjectContext;
            elc.managedTaskObject = self.managedTaskObject;
```

```objc
    [self.navigationController pushViewController:elc animated:YES];
    [elc release];
    break;
}

case 4:
{

    UIAlertView* alert =
        [[[UIAlertView alloc] initWithTitle:@"Hi-Pri Tasks"
                                    message:nil
                                   delegate:self
                          cancelButtonTitle:@"OK"
                          otherButtonTitles:nil  ] autorelease];

    // Use Fetched property to get a list of high-pri tasks
    NSArray* highPriTasks = managedTaskObject.highPriTasks;
    NSMutableString* alertMessage =
        [[[NSMutableString alloc] init] autorelease];

    // Loop through each hi-pri task to create the string for
    // the message
    for (Task * theTask in highPriTasks)
    {
        [alertMessage appendString:theTask.text];
        [alertMessage appendString:@"\n"];
    }

    alert.message = alertMessage;
    [alert show];

    break;
}
case 5:
{

    UIAlertView* alert =
        [[[UIAlertView alloc] initWithTitle:@"Tasks due sooner"
                                    message:nil
                                   delegate:self
                          cancelButtonTitle:@"OK"
                          otherButtonTitles:nil  ] autorelease];
    NSMutableString* alertMessage =
        [[[NSMutableString alloc] init] autorelease];

    // need to get a handle to the managedObjectModel to use the stored
    // fetch request
    TasksAppDelegate* appDelegate =
        [UIApplication sharedApplication].delegate;
    NSManagedObjectModel* model = appDelegate.managedObjectModel;

    // Get the stored fetch request
    NSDictionary* dict =
        [[NSDictionary alloc]
```

```
                    initWithObjectsAndKeys:managedTaskObject.dueDate,
                    @"DUE_DATE",nil];

            NSFetchRequest* request =
                [model fetchRequestFromTemplateWithName:@"tasksDueSooner"
                                    substitutionVariables:dict];

            [dict release];

            NSError* error;
            NSArray* results =
                [managedObjectContext executeFetchRequest:request error:&error];

            // Loop through eachtask to create the string for the message
            for (Task * theTask in results)
            {
                [alertMessage appendString:theTask.text];
                [alertMessage appendString:@"\n"];
            }

            alert.message = alertMessage;
            [alert show];

            break;
        }

    default:
        break;
    }
}
```

ViewTaskController.m

In the code for this method, cases 0 through 3 are very similar. Each creates an instance of the appropriate edit controller, populates the necessary properties, and then pushes the controller onto the navigation stack.

Case 4 implements the Hi-Pri Tasks feature, which uses the `highPriTasks` fetched property of the `Task` object that you defined in the previous chapter. If you don't remember, this property simply returns a list of all tasks that are marked as High Priority.

The interesting thing to notice about using the fetched property is that it returns an array of objects instead of a set. You can also see that using a fetched property is as simple as using a regular property. The code loops through each `Task` object returned from the fetched property and appends the `Task` name to a string. The code then displays the string using a `UIAlertView`.

Case 5 uses a stored fetch request to get a list of tasks that are due sooner than the current task. There are a couple of points of interest when using a stored fetch request. First, you need a reference to the managed object model because stored fetch requests reside in the model and not in your managed object class.

Next, if you specified substitution variables in the fetch request, you need to provide them to the fetch request in an `NSDictionary` that contains the objects and the keys. You can see that you are creating an `NSDictionary` using the `dueDate` property of the current `Task` object and the key text `DUE_DATE`. The key text is the same as the variable name that you specified in the previous chapter when defining the stored fetch request.

The code then creates an `NSFetchRequest`. It uses the `fetchRequestFromTemplateWithName:` method by supplying the name of the stored fetch request `tasksDueSooner` and the `NSDictionary` containing your substitution variables and keys.

The code then executes the fetch request against the context. Finally, the code iterates over the results, creating a string with the text from each returned `Task` object, and displays the string using a `UIAlertView`.

You are now ready to build and run the application. You should get a clean build with no errors or warnings. You should be able to add new tasks and edit all of the attributes of your tasks. You should also be able to create new locations and delete existing locations. Clicking the "hi-pri tasks" button in the task viewer will use the fetched property to display all of your high-priority tasks. The "Tasks due sooner" feature won't quite work yet because you have to implement date defaulting in the `Task` object. If you try to select "Tasks due sooner" and all of your tasks do not have due dates, you will get an error.

DISPLAYING RESULTS IN THE ROOTVIEWCONTROLLER

In this section, you are going to implement the filtering and sorting buttons on the `RootViewController`. The easiest way to implement this functionality is to modify the sort descriptor or predicate of the fetched results controller, and then execute the fetch.

Sorting Results with NSSortDescriptor

When the user taps the Asc or Dsc buttons, the `toolbarSortOrderChanged` method will run. In this method, you get a reference to the fetch request used by the fetched results controller and change the sort descriptor to match the sort order that the user selected. Then, you need to tell the `fetchedResultsController` to perform the fetch with the revised sort descriptor. Finally, you tell the `TableView` to reload its data. The following is the code for the `toolbarSortOrderChanged` method:

```
-(IBAction)toolbarSortOrderChanged:(id)sender;
{
    NSLog(@"toolbarSortOrderChanged");
    // Get the fetch request from the controller and change the sort descriptor
    NSFetchRequest* fetchRequest =  self.fetchedResultsController.fetchRequest;

    // Edit the sort key based on which button was pressed
    BOOL ascendingOrder = NO;
    UIBarButtonItem* button = (UIBarButtonItem*) sender;
    if ([button.title compare:@"Asc"]== NSOrderedSame)
        ascendingOrder=YES;
    else
        ascendingOrder=NO;
```

```
    NSSortDescriptor *sortDescriptor =
        [[NSSortDescriptor alloc] initWithKey:@"text" ascending:ascendingOrder];
    NSArray *sortDescriptors =
        [[NSArray alloc] initWithObjects:sortDescriptor, nil];
    [sortDescriptor release];

    [fetchRequest setSortDescriptors:sortDescriptors];
    [sortDescriptors release];

    NSError *error = nil;
    if (![[self fetchedResultsController] performFetch:&error]) {
        NSLog(@"Unresolved error %@, %@", error, [error userInfo]);
        abort();
    }

    [taskTableView reloadData];
}
```

RootViewController.m

You use the same method regardless of which sort button the user tapped. At runtime, the code checks the title of the button to determine if the user wants the data sorted in ascending or descending order. Then, you use the `compare` method of the `NSString` class to perform the sort.

You can also add additional sort descriptors to sort your data using multiple fields. Core Data applies the sort descriptors to the results in the order that you specify them in the array that you pass into the `setSortDescriptors` function. You will learn more about implementing sort descriptors in the next chapter.

Filtering Results with NSPredicate

When the user taps the Hi-Pri button, your code should filter the list of tasks to show only high-priority tasks. Conversely, when the user selects the All button, you need to clear the filter to show all of the tasks again. You can build these features as you did with the sorting functionality in the last section. However, instead of modifying the sort descriptor, you will be modifying the fetch request's predicate. You can use predicates to filter data in all sorts of data structures. Their use is not limited to Core Data. You learn more about predicates in the next chapter.

The `toolbarFilterHiPri` method needs to set the predicate used by the fetch request to return tasks with a priority of 3. Then, the method has to tell the `TableView` to reload its data. The following is the code for the `toolbarFilterHiPri` method:

```
-(IBAction)toolbarFilterHiPri:(id)sender{
    NSLog(@"toolbarFilterHiPri");

    // Change the fetch request to display only high pri tasks
    // Get the fetch request from the controller and change the predicate
    NSFetchRequest* fetchRequest =  self.fetchedResultsController.fetchRequest;

    NSPredicate *predicate = [NSPredicate predicateWithFormat:@"priority == 3"];
    [fetchRequest setPredicate:predicate];
```

```
          NSError *error = nil;
          if (![[self fetchedResultsController] performFetch:&error]) {
              NSLog(@"Unresolved error %@, %@", error, [error userInfo]);
              abort();
          }

          [taskTableView reloadData];

      }
```

RootViewController.m

The code gets a reference to the predicate used by the `fetchedResultsController`. Then, you create a new predicate with the criteria of `priority == 3`. Next, you set the predicate of the fetch request to your new predicate, perform the fetch, and tell the table to reload its data.

The `toolbarFilterAll` method simply removes the predicate from the fetch request. You do that by setting the predicate to `nil`, as follows:

```
-(IBAction)toolbarFilterAll:(id)sender
{
      NSLog(@"toolbarFilterAll");

      // Change the fetch request to display all tasks
      // Get the fetch request from the controller and change the predicate
      NSFetchRequest* fetchRequest =  self.fetchedResultsController.fetchRequest;

      // nil out the predicate to clear it and show all objects again
      [fetchRequest setPredicate:nil];

      NSError *error = nil;
      if (![[self fetchedResultsController] performFetch:&error]) {
          NSLog(@"Unresolved error %@, %@", error, [error userInfo]);
          abort();
      }

      [taskTableView reloadData];
}
```

RootViewController.m

This looks very similar to the `toolbarFilterHiPri` method except that here, you set the predicate to `nil` instead of creating a new predicate to apply to the `fetchRequest`. Removing the predicate effectively un-filters the data.

GENERATING GROUPED TABLES USING THE NSFETCHEDRESULTSCONTROLLER

In Chapter 3, you learned how to use the `UILocalizedIndexedCollation` class to create a `TableView` that organized data within sections. When you work with Core Data, you can use the `NSFetchedResultsController` to achieve the same results. In this section, you will build the

`LocationTasksViewController`. The application displays the `LocationTasksViewController` when the user selects the Location button on the `RootViewController`. The `LocationTasksViewController` displays all of the tasks grouped by location.

The first step is to create a new `UITableviewController` without XIB called `LocationTasksViewController`. Modify the header file by adding instance variables and properties for the context and a fetched results controller. Also, mark your class as implementing the `NSFetchedResultsControllerDelegate` protocol. The header should look like Listing 7-7.

LISTING 7-7: LocationTasksViewController.h

```
#import <UIKit/UIKit.h>

@interface LocationTasksViewController :
    UITableViewController<NSFetchedResultsControllerDelegate> {

    NSManagedObjectContext *managedObjectContext;
    NSFetchedResultsController *fetchedResultsController;
}

@property (nonatomic, retain) NSManagedObjectContext *managedObjectContext;
@property (nonatomic, retain)
    NSFetchedResultsController *fetchedResultsController;
@end
```

Moving into the implementation file, add `#import` directives for the `Location.h`, `Task.h`, and `ViewTaskController.h` headers:

```
#import "Location.h"
#import "Task.h"
#import "ViewTaskController.h"
```

LocationTasksViewController.m

Next, synthesize the properties that you declared in the header:

```
@synthesize managedObjectContext, fetchedResultsController;
```

Now, implement `viewDidLoad` to perform the fetch on the fetched results controller and set the title of the screen in the nav bar:

```
- (void)viewDidLoad {
    [super viewDidLoad];

    NSError* error;

    if (![[self fetchedResultsController] performFetch:&error]) {

        NSLog(@"Unresolved error %@, %@", error, [error userInfo]);
        abort();
```

```
    }

    // set the title to display in the nav bar
    self.title = @"Tasks by Location";
}
```

LocationTasksViewController.m

In `viewDidUnload`, set the properties that you declared in the header to `nil`:

```
- (void)viewDidUnload {
    self.managedObjectContext=nil;
    self.fetchedResultsController = nil;
    [super viewDidUnload];
}
```

LocationTasksViewController.m

Next, you will write the `fetchedResultsController` accessor method. You have implemented this method several times before. The difference in this case is that you will need to specify a `sectionNameKeyPath` when you initialize the `NSFetchedResultsController`.

The `sectionNameKeyPath` parameter allows you to specify a key path that the fetched results controller will use to generate the sections for your table. The fetched results controller will contain the entire set of `Task` objects. You want the tasks grouped by location. Remember that the `Task` object has a `location` property that refers to a related `Location` object. The `Location` object has a `name` property that contains the name of the `Location`. You really want the tasks grouped by the `name` property of the contents of the `location` property. Because you are holding a reference to a `Task` object, the key path to the `Location`'s name property is `location.name`. The following is the code for the `fetchedResultsController` accessor:

```
- (NSFetchedResultsController *)fetchedResultsController {

    if (fetchedResultsController != nil) {
        return fetchedResultsController;
    }

    /*
     Set up the fetched results controller.
     */
    // Create the fetch request for the entity.
    NSFetchRequest *fetchRequest = [[NSFetchRequest alloc] init];
    // Edit the entity name as appropriate.
    NSEntityDescription *entity =
        [NSEntityDescription entityForName:@"Task"
                    inManagedObjectContext:managedObjectContext];
    [fetchRequest setEntity:entity];

    // Edit the sort key as appropriate.
    NSSortDescriptor *sortDescriptor =
        [[NSSortDescriptor alloc] initWithKey:@"location.name"
                                    ascending:YES];
```

```
NSArray *sortDescriptors =
    [[NSArray alloc] initWithObjects:sortDescriptor, nil];

[fetchRequest setSortDescriptors:sortDescriptors];

// Edit the section name key path and cache name if appropriate.
// nil for section name key path means "no sections".
NSFetchedResultsController *aFetchedResultsController =
[[NSFetchedResultsController alloc]
    initWithFetchRequest:fetchRequest
    managedObjectContext:managedObjectContext
        sectionNameKeyPath:@"location.name" cacheName:@"Task"];

aFetchedResultsController.delegate = self;
self.fetchedResultsController = aFetchedResultsController;

[aFetchedResultsController release];
[fetchRequest release];
[sortDescriptor release];
[sortDescriptors release];

return fetchedResultsController;
}
```

LocationTasksViewController.m

If you look at the definition of the sort descriptor, you can see that you are also using the key path to the `Location` object's `name` property. In order for the fetched results controller to create the sections properly, you need to sort the result set using the same key that you use to generate the sections. As mentioned previously, the section key is set when initializing the `NSFetchedResultsController` in the `sectionNameKeyPath` parameter.

Next, you need to code the `controllerDidChangeContent` method to reload the data in the `TableView` when the contents of the fetched results controller changes:

```
- (void)controllerDidChangeContent:(NSFetchedResultsController *)controller {
    // In the simplest, most efficient, case, reload the table view.
    [self.tableView reloadData];
}
```

LocationTasksViewController.m

The next step is to implement the `TableView` methods. The `numberOfSectionsInTableView` method will look just like the corresponding method in the `RootViewController`. However, because you are using sections on this screen, the fetched results controller will not just return 1 for the number of sections. Instead, the fetched results controller will calculate the number of sections based on the number of different values in the `location.name` property.

The `tableView:numberOfRowsInSection:` method also uses the fetch results controller to populate the `TableView`. In this case, you get an `NSFetchedResultsSectionInfo` object from the fetched results controller that corresponds to the current section. The section info object has a `numberOfObjects` property that returns the number of objects in the section. This value is returned as the number of rows in the section.

Here are the implementations for the `numberOfSectionsInTableView` and `tableView:`
`numberOfRowsInSection:` methods:

```
- (NSInteger)numberOfSectionsInTableView:(UITableView *)tableView {
    return [[fetchedResultsController sections] count];
}

- (NSInteger)tableView:(UITableView *)tableView
    numberOfRowsInSection:(NSInteger)section {

    id <NSFetchedResultsSectionInfo> sectionInfo =
        [[fetchedResultsController sections] objectAtIndex:section];
    return [sectionInfo numberOfObjects];

}
```

LocationTasksViewController.m

The `tableView:cellForRowAtIndexPath:` and `tableView:didSelectRowAtIndexPath:` methods
are the same as in the `RootViewController`. You generate the cell text the same way and the
behavior when a user selects a row is the same. The following is the code for the `tableView:`
`cellForRowAtIndexPath:` and `tableView:didSelectRowAtIndexPath:` methods:

```
// Customize the appearance of table view cells.
- (UITableViewCell *)tableView:(UITableView *)tableView
        cellForRowAtIndexPath:(NSIndexPath *)indexPath {

    static NSString *CellIdentifier = @"Cell";

    UITableViewCell *cell =
        [tableView dequeueReusableCellWithIdentifier:CellIdentifier];
    if (cell == nil) {
        cell = [[[UITableViewCell alloc]
                initWithStyle:UITableViewCellStyleDefault
                reuseIdentifier:CellIdentifier] autorelease];
    }

    // Configure the cell.
    Task *managedTaskObject =
        [fetchedResultsController objectAtIndexPath:indexPath];
    cell.textLabel.text = managedTaskObject.text;

    // Change the text color if the task is overdue
    if (managedTaskObject.isOverdue==[NSNumber numberWithBool: YES])
    {
        cell.textLabel.textColor = [UIColor redColor];
    }
    else {
        cell.textLabel.textColor = [UIColor blackColor];

    }
    return cell;
}
```

```
- (void)tableView:(UITableView *)tableView
  didSelectRowAtIndexPath:(NSIndexPath *)indexPath {

    // Deselect the currently selected row according to the HIG
    [tableView deselectRowAtIndexPath:indexPath animated:NO];

    // Navigation logic may go here -- for example, create and push
    // another view controller.
    Task *managedObject =
        [fetchedResultsController objectAtIndexPath:indexPath];

    ViewTaskController* taskController =
        [[ViewTaskController alloc]
          initWithStyle:UITableViewStyleGrouped];

    taskController.managedTaskObject=managedObject;
    taskController.managedObjectContext = self.managedObjectContext;

    [self.navigationController pushViewController:taskController animated:YES];

    [taskController release];

}
```

LocationTasksViewController.m

There is one additional method that you need to implement `tableView:`
`titleForHeaderInSection:`. This method generates the titles for the sections of the table. Again,
you will use an `NSFetchedResultsController` to get these titles. The fetched results controller
maintains a `sections` array that contains the list of sections in the result set. You simply need to
get the item out of the array that corresponds to the section that the `TableView` is asking for.
Here is the code:

```
- (NSString *)tableView:(UITableView *)tableView
    titleForHeaderInSection:(NSInteger)section
{
    id <NSFetchedResultsSectionInfo> sectionInfo =
        [[fetchedResultsController sections] objectAtIndex:section];
    return [sectionInfo name];
}
```

LocationTasksViewController.m

Finally, modify the `dealloc` method to release your instance variables:

```
- (void)dealloc {
    [fetchedResultsController release];
    [managedObjectContext release];
    [super dealloc];
}
```

LocationTasksViewController.m

Now that you have built the `LocationTasksViewController`, you need to modify the `RootViewController` to call your new location controller when the user taps the Location button. In the `RootViewController.m` implementation file, add a `#import` directive to import the new controller:

```
#import "LocationTasksViewController.h"
```

Modify the code in the `locationButtonPressed` method to create an instance of your new controller and push it on to the navigation stack:

Available for
download on
Wrox.com

```
-(IBAction)locationButtonPressed:(id)sender
{
    NSLog(@"locationButtonPressed");

    LocationTasksViewController* ltvc =
        [[LocationTasksViewController alloc]
            initWithStyle:UITableViewStylePlain];
    ltvc.managedObjectContext = self.managedObjectContext;
    [self.navigationController pushViewController:ltvc animated:YES];
    [ltvc release];
}
```

RootViewController.m

You are now ready to build and run the application. You should be able to use all of the buttons at the bottom of the `RootViewController` to filter the data, sort the data, and bring up the tasks grouped by location screen.

IMPLEMENTING CUSTOM MANAGED OBJECTS

Up until this point, you haven't used any of the features of an `NSManagedObject` subclass. You could have written all of the Core Data code that you have seen so far in this chapter using key-value coding and generic `NSManagedObjects`.

In this section, you learn about the additional features that you can implement by using custom subclasses of `NSManagedObject`. These features include dynamically calculating property values at runtime, defaulting data at runtime, and single and multiple field validation.

Coding a Dynamic Property

You can use dynamic properties to implement properties that you need to calculate at runtime. In the data modeler, you should mark dynamic properties as Transient because you will compute their value at runtime and will not save this value in the data store.

In this example, you will code an `isOverdue` property for the `Task` object. This property should return YES if a task is overdue and NO if it is not. You may notice that when you declare a Boolean property in the data modeler, Xcode translates the property into an `NSNumber` in the generated code. This is not a problem because there is a class method in the `NSNumber` class that returns an `NSNumber` representation of a BOOL.

The following is the code for the isOverdue accessor method:

```
- (NSNumber*) isOverdue
{
    BOOL isTaskOverdue = NO;

    NSDate* today = [NSDate date];

    if (self.dueDate != nil) {
        if ([self.dueDate compare:today] == NSOrderedAscending)
            isTaskOverdue=YES;
    }

    return [NSNumber numberWithBool:isTaskOverdue];
}
```

Task.m

This code simply compares the dueDate in the current Task object against the current system date. If the dueDate is earlier than today, the code sets the isTaskOverdue variable to YES. The code then uses the numberWithBool method to return an NSNumber that corresponds to the Boolean result.

If you run the application now, any tasks that occurred in the past should turn red in the RootViewController.

Defaulting Data at Runtime

Just as you can dynamically generate property values at runtime, you can also generate default values at runtime. There is a method called awakeFromInsert that the Core Data framework calls the first time that you insert an object into the managed object context.

Subclasses of NSManagedObject can implement awakeFromInsert to set default values for properties. It is critical that you call the superclass implementation of awakeFromInsert before doing any of your own implementation.

Another consideration is that you should always use primitive accessor methods to modify property values while you are in the awakeFromInsert method. Primitive accessor methods are methods of the Managed Objects that are used to set property values but that do not notify other classes observing your class using key-value observing. This is important because if you modify a property and your class sends out a notification that results in another class modifying the same property, your code could get into in an endless loop.

You can set primitive values in your code using key value coding and the setPrimitiveValue: forKey: method. A better way is to define custom primitive accessors for any properties that you need to access in this way. In this case, you will be modifying the dueDate property in awakeFromInsert so you need to define a primitive accessor for the dueDate. Fortunately, Core Data defines these properties for you automatically at runtime. All that you need to do is declare the property in the Task header:

```
@property (nonatomic, retain) NSDate * primitiveDueDate;
```

Then, add an @dynamic directive in the implementation file to indicate that Core Data will dynamically generate this property at runtime:

```
@dynamic primitiveDueDate;
```

Now, you can set the dueDate property in the awakeFromInsert method without fear of any side effects that may occur because of the possibility that other classes are observing the Task for changes.

Implement the awakeFromInsert method to create an NSDate object three days from the current date and use the primitive property to set the default date. The following is the code for the awakeFromInsert method:

```
- (void)awakeFromInsert
{
    // Core Data  calls this function the first time the receiver
    // is inserted into a context.
    [super awakeFromInsert];

    // Set the due date to 3 days from now (in seconds)
    NSDate* defualtDate = [[NSDate alloc]
                            initWithTimeIntervalSinceNow:60*60*24*3];

    // Use custom primitive accessor to set dueDate field
    self.primitiveDueDate = defualtDate ;

    [defualtDate release];
}
```

Task.m

Before you build and run the application, delete the old app from the simulator first because you may have tasks that do not have due dates. Now you can run the application. New tasks that you create will now have a default due date set three days into the future. You should be able to use the "Tasks due sooner than this one" button on the task detail screen now because all tasks will have defaulted due dates.

Validating a Single Field

Single-field validation in a custom class is straightforward. Core Data will automatically call a method called validate*Xxxx* if you have implemented the method. The *Xxxx* is the name of your property with the first letter capitalized. The method signature for the validate method for the dueDate field looks like this:

```
-(BOOL)validateDueDate:(id *)ioValue error:(NSError **)outError{
```

A single field validation method should return YES if the validation is successful and NO if it failed. The method accepts an id*, which is the value that you are testing for validity and an NSError** that you should use to return an NSError object if the validation fails.

Because this method receives an `id*`, you *could* modify the object that is passed into the validation function, but you should never do this. Users of a class would not expect validation to modify the object that was submitted for validation. Modifying the object that was passed in would create an unexpected side effect. Creating side effects is usually a poor design choice which you should avoid. You should treat the object passed in for validation as read only.

In the validation of the `dueDate` of the `Task` object, you are going to enforce a rule that assigning due dates that have occurred in the past is invalid. Here is the implementation of the `dueDate` validation function:

```
-(BOOL)validateDueDate:(id *)ioValue error:(NSError **)outError{

    // Due dates in the past are not valid.
    // enforce that a due date has to be >= today's date
    if ([*ioValue compare:[NSDate date]] == NSOrderedAscending) {

        if (outError != NULL) {
            NSString *errorStr = [[[NSString alloc] initWithString:
                                        @"Due date must be today or later"]
                                        autorelease];
            NSDictionary *userInfoDictionary =
                [NSDictionary dictionaryWithObject:errorStr
                                            forKey:@"ErrorString"];
            NSError *error =
                [[[NSError alloc] initWithDomain:TASKS_ERROR_DOMAIN
                                  code:DUEDATE_VALIDATION_ERROR_CODE
                                  userInfo:userInfoDictionary] autorelease];
            *outError = error;
        }
        return NO;
    }
    else {
        return YES;
    }
}
```

Task.m

The first thing that you do is check the date that you receive as an input parameter and compare it to the current system date. If the comparison fails, you create an error string that you will return to the caller in the `NSError` object. Next, you add the error string to an `NSDictionary` object that you pass back to the class user as the `userInfo` in the `NSError` object. Then, you allocate and initialize an `NSError` object with an error domain and error code. The domain and code are custom values used to identify your error and can be any values that you like. For this sample, I have defined them in the `Task.h` header file like this:

```
#define TASKS_ERROR_DOMAIN              @"com.Wrox.Tasks"
#define DUEDATE_VALIDATION_ERROR_CODE   1001
```

Task.h

You pass the userInfo dictionary that you created to hold the error string to the initializer of the NSError object. Users of your Task class can interrogate the userInfo dictionary that they receive in the NSError to get details about the problem and act accordingly. Finally, you return NO to indicate that validation has failed.

If the validation succeeds, the code simply returns YES.

Run the application now and try to set the due date for a task to a date in the past. You should get an error indicating that this is invalid.

Multi-Field Validation

Multi-field validation is slightly more complicated than single-field validation. Core Data will call two methods automatically if they exist: validateForInsert and validateForUpdate. Core Data calls validateForInsert when you insert an object into the context for the first time. When you update an existing object, Core Data calls validateForUpdate.

If you want to implement a validation rule that runs both when an object is inserted or updated, I recommend writing a new validation function and then calling that new function from both the validateForInsert and validateForUpdate methods. The example follows this approach.

In this sample, you will be enforcing a multi-field validation rule that says that high-priority tasks must have a due date within the next three days. Any due date farther in the future should cause an error. You cannot accomplish this within a single field validation rule because you need to validate both that the task is high priority and that the due date is within a certain range. In the Task.h header file, add a new method declaration for the function that you will call to validate the data:

```
- (BOOL)validateAllData:(NSError **)error;
```

Here is the function that enforces the rule:

Available for
download on
Wrox.com

```
- (BOOL)validateAllData:(NSError **)outError
{
    NSDate* compareDate =
        [[[NSDate alloc] initWithTimeIntervalSinceNow:60*60*24*3] autorelease];
    // Due dates for hi-pri tasks must be today, tomorrow, or the next day.
    if ([self.dueDate compare:compareDate] == NSOrderedDescending &&
        [self.priority intValue]==3) {

        if (outError != NULL) {
            NSString *errorStr = [[[NSString alloc] initWithString:
                @"Hi-pri tasks must have a due date within two days of today"]
                                    autorelease];
            NSDictionary *userInfoDictionary =
                [NSDictionary dictionaryWithObject:errorStr
                                            forKey:@"ErrorString"];
            NSError *error =
                [[[NSError alloc] initWithDomain:TASKS_ERROR_DOMAIN
                                    code:PRIORITY_DUEDATE_VALIDATION_ERROR_CODE
                                    userInfo:userInfoDictionary] autorelease];
            *outError = error;
        }
```

```
        return NO;
    }
    else {
        return YES;
    }
}
```

Task.m

The code first generates a date to which to compare the selected dueDate. Then, the code checks to see if the dueDate chosen is greater than this compare date and that the priority of the task is high. If the data meets both of these criteria, it is invalid and you generate an NSError object just like in the last section. A new error code is used and should be added to the Task.h header:

```
#define PRIORITY_DUEDATE_VALIDATION_ERROR_CODE   1002
```

The code then returns NO to indicate that the validation has failed. If the validation is successful, the method returns YES.

Now, you have to add the two validation methods that Core Data calls and code them to call your validateAllData method:

```
- (BOOL)validateForInsert:(NSError **)outError
{
    // Call the superclass validateForInsert first
    if ([super validateForInsert:outError]==NO)
    {
        return NO;
    }

    // Call out validation function
    if ([self validateAllData:outError] == NO)
    {
        return NO;
    }
    else {
        return YES;
    }
}

- (BOOL)validateForUpdate:(NSError **)outError
{
    // Call the superclass validateForUpdate first
    if ([super validateForUpdate:outError]==NO)
    {
        return NO;
    }

    // Call out validation function
    if ([self validateAllData:outError] == NO)
    {
        return NO;
```

```
    }
    else {
        return YES;
    }
}
```

First, both of these methods call their superclass counterpart method. You have to call the superclass method because that method handles validation rules implemented in the model and calls the single-field validation methods. If the superclass validation routine is successful, the methods go on to call your `validateAllData` method.

Build and run the application. If you try to set the due date for a high-priority task to more than two days in the future, or if you try to set the priority of a task to high that has a due date more than two days in the future, you will get an error.

MOVING FORWARD

This chapter covered a lot of material. You learned how to implement the Core Data concepts that you learned about in the last chapter.

Now you have a fully functioning Core Data–based application that demonstrates many of the features of Core Data. You can use this application like a sandbox to play with these features or implement new functionality in the Tasks application on your own.

Now that you have built an entire application, I hope that you have confidence in your ability to implement an application using the Core Data framework. You should now be able to use Core Data effectively in your own applications.

In the next chapter, you will learn more about some features of Cocoa Touch that you often use with Core Data. You will explore key value coding and key value observing. You will also learn more about `NSPredicates` and how to implement sort descriptors using your own custom classes. Finally, you will learn how to migrate your existing data from one Core Data model version to another.

Core Data–Related Cocoa Features

WHAT'S IN THIS CHAPTER?

➤   Setting and getting data using key-value coding

➤   Implementing a loosely coupled application architecture with messaging and key-value observing

➤   Creating predicates in several ways and using them to filter data

➤   Building sort descriptors to order your data structures

In the last three chapters, you learned about the fundamentals of the Core Data architecture — how to model your data and how to build a complete data-centric application using the Core Data framework. This chapter provides a more detailed look at some of the Cocoa functionality that you used with Core Data. In addition to their application in Core Data, you can use these features in other interesting ways.

In this chapter, you learn more about some important Cocoa technologies: key-value coding, key-value observing, predicates, and sort descriptors.

While you have seen these features used with Core Data, they are an integral part of the Cocoa framework. You can use these concepts and their associated classes in ways that reach far beyond Core Data. For example, you can use predicates and the NSPredicate class to filter and query regular Cocoa data structures such as arrays and dictionaries. You can develop loosely coupled, message-based application architectures using the concepts of key-value coding and key-value observing. Adding a deeper knowledge of these Cocoa features will broaden your knowledge of the development platform and provide you with more tools for your developer toolbox.

KEY-VALUE CODING

You have already seen key-value coding, also referred to as KVC, in previous chapters. When you used Core Data with an NSManagedObject directly, instead of using an NSManagedObject custom subclass, you used KVC to set and get the attribute values stored in the NSManagedObject. KVC allowed you to get and set the attributes of the managed object by name instead of using properties and accessor methods.

The term "key-value coding" refers to the NSKeyValueCoding protocol. This informal protocol specifies a way to access an object's properties using a name or key rather than by calling the accessor method directly. This capability is useful when you are trying to write generic code that needs to operate on different properties of different objects. For example, in Chapter 7, you designed the EditTextController as a generic controller that you can use to provide a text-editing capability. If you recall, you used this controller class to edit text attributes with different names in two different objects. The EditTextController used KVC to specify the appropriate text field name for the object that you wanted to edit.

Keys and Keypaths

Keys are the strings that you use to reference the properties of an object. The key is generally also the name of the accessor method used to access the property.

Properties and accessor methods are closely related. When you type @property NSString* name, you are telling the Cocoa framework to create accessor methods for the name property for you. The @synthesize directive that you use in your implementation file causes Cocoa to actually create the methods. The framework automatically creates the -(NSString*)name getter method and the -(void) setName:(NSString*)newName setter method. You can choose to override one or both of these methods if the default implementation does not meet your needs. It is a general standard that property names start with a lowercase letter.

To get a specific value from an object using KVC, you call the -(id)valueForKey:(NSString *)key method. This method returns the value in the object for the specified key. The valueForKey method returns the generic id type. This means that it can return any Objective-C object type, which makes KVC ideal for writing generic code. The method is unaware of the type of object that it will return and can therefore return any type.

If an accessor method or instance variable with the key does not exist, the receiver calls the valueForUndefinedKey: method on itself. By default, this method throws an NSUndefinedKeyException, but you can change this behavior in subclasses.

Instead of passing a simple key, there are alternate methods that allow you to use keypaths to traverse a set of nested objects using a dot-separated string. In the example in the previous chapter, you used keypaths to access a Task's Location's name property. When addressing a Task object, you used the keypath location.name to get to the name property from the location attribute of the Task object (see Figure 8-1).

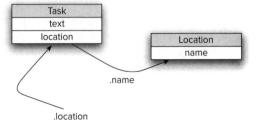

FIGURE 8-1: Accessing a value with a keypath

The first key in the keypath refers to a field in the receiver of the call. You use subsequent keys to drill down into the object returned by the first key. Therefore, when used with a `Task` object, the keypath `location.name` gets that `Task`'s `location` property and then asks that object for its `name` property. As long as keys in the keypath return references to objects, you can drill down as deeply into an object hierarchy as you wish.

You can use key-value coding to retrieve values from an object using a keypath instead of a simple string key by calling the `-(id)valueForKeyPath:(NSString *)keyPath` method. This works like `valueForKey` in that it returns the value at the given keypath. If anywhere along the keypath a specified key does not exist, the receiver calls the `valueForUndefinedKey:` method on itself. Again, this method throws an `NSUndefinedKeyException`, and you can change this behavior in subclasses.

Finally, the `-(NSDictionary *)dictionaryWithValuesForKeys:(NSArray *)keys` method can be used for bulk retrieval of values using KVC. This method accepts an `NSArray` of keys and returns an `NSDictionary` with the keys as the keys in the dictionary and the values returned from the object as the values.

Setting Values Using Keys

Just as you can retrieve values from an object using KVC, you can set values using KVC. You call the `-(void)setValue:(id)value forKey:(NSString *)key` method to set the value for a specified key. If an accessor method or instance variable with the key does not exist, the receiver calls the `setValue:forUndefinedKey:` method on itself. By default, this method throws an `NSUndefinedKeyException`, but you can change this behavior in subclasses.

You can also use a keypath to set a value in a target object using the `-(void)setValue:(id)value forKeyPath:(NSString *)keypath` method. If any value in the keypath returns a `nil` key, the receiver calls the `setValue:forUndefinedKey:` method on itself. Again, this method throws an `NSUndefinedKeyException`, but you can change this behavior in subclasses.

You can set a group of values in an object using KVC by calling the `-(void)setValuesForKeysWithDictionary:(NSDictionary *)keyedValues` method. This method sets all of the values on all of the key objects given in the dictionary. Behind the scenes, this method simply calls `setValue:forKey:` for each item in the dictionary.

Collection Operators

If your object contains an array or set property, it is possible to perform some functions on the list. You can include a function in the key path in a call to `valueForKeyPath`. These functions are called *collection operators*. You call collection operators using the form `pathToArray.@function.pathToProperty`.

The functions that you can use in a collection operator are:

➤ `@avg`: Loops over each item in the collection, converts its value to a `double` and returns an `NSNumber` representing the average

➤ `@count`: Returns the number of objects in the collection

➤ `@distinctUnionOfArrays`: Returns an array containing the unique items from the arrays referenced by the keypath

➤ `@distinctUnionOfObjects`: Returns the unique objects contained in the property

➤ `@max` and `@min`: Return the maximum and minimum values respectively of the specified property

➤ `@sum`: Loops over each item in the collection, converts its value to a `double`, and returns an `NSNumber` representing the sum

➤ `@unionOfArrays`, `@unionOfObjects`, and `@unionOfSets`: Function just like their distinct counterparts except they return all items in the collection, not just unique items

For further information on using these functions, see Apple's Key-Value Coding Programming Guide, which is included as part of the Xcode documentation set.

Additional Considerations When Using KVC

It makes no difference if you access the properties of a class by using the dot syntax, calling the accessor method, or by using KVC. You can see this illustrated in Figure 8-2. You are calling the receiver's accessor method either way. You should be aware, however, that because there is an added level of indirection when using KVC, there is a slight performance hit. The performance penalty is very small, so you should not let this deter you from using KVC when it helps the flexibility of your design.

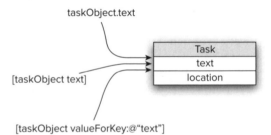

FIGURE 8-2: Accessing a value using different semantics

When building your own classes, you should pay attention to the naming conventions used by the Cocoa framework. Doing so helps to ensure that your classes will be key-value coding–compliant. For example, the correct format for accessor methods is `-var` for the getter and `-setVar` for the setter. Defining properties in your classes ensures that the accessor methods generated by the framework will be KVC-compliant.

There are additional rules for ensuring KVC compliance when your classes contain To-One or To-Many relationships. You should consult the Key Value Coding Programming Guide in the Apple docs for more detail on ensuring KVC compliance.

The `valueForKey:` and `setValue:forKey:` methods automatically wrap scalar and struct data types in `NSNumber` or `NSValue` classes. So, there is no need for you to manually convert scalar types (such as `int` or `long`) into Objective-C class types (such as `NSNumber`); the framework will do it for you automatically.

KEY-VALUE OBSERVING

In addition to obtaining property values using strings, you can take advantage of the `NSKeyValueCoding` protocol to implement another very powerful feature in Cocoa, *key-value observing* (or KVO). Key-value observing provides a way for objects to register to receive notifications when properties in other objects change. A key architectural feature of this functionality is that there is no central repository or server that sends out change notifications. When implementing KVO, you link observers directly to the objects that they are observing without going through an intermediary server. If you need to implement a centrally stored publish/subscribe capability, the NSNotification class provides this capability.

The base class for most Objective-C objects, NSObject, provides the basic functionality of KVO. You should generally not have to override the base class implementation in your own implementations. Using KVO, you can observe changes to properties, To-One relationships and To-Many relationships. By inheriting from NSObject, the base class implements KVO automatically on your objects. However, it is possible to disable automatic notifications or build your own manual notifications.

Observing Changes to an Object

To receive notifications for changes to an object, you must register as an observer of the object. You register your class as an observer by calling the addObserver:forKeyPath:options:context: method on the object that you want to observe.

The Observer parameter specifies the object that the framework should notify when the observed property changes. The KeyPath parameter specifies the property that you want to observe. Changes to this property will cause the framework to generate a notification. The options parameter specifies if you want to receive the original property value (NSKeyValueObservingOptionOld) or the new property value (NSKeyValueObservingOptionNew). You can receive both if you pass in both NSKeyValueObservingOptionOld and NSKeyValueObservingOptionNew using the bitwise OR operator. The context parameter is a pointer that the observed object passes back to the observer when a change occurs.

When the property that you are observing changes, the observer will receive a notification. Notifications come back to the observer through calls to the observer's observeValueForKeyPath: ofObject:change:context: method. The observed object calls this method on the observer when an observed property changes. Therefore, all observers must implement observeValueForKeyPath: ofObject:change:context: to receive KVO callbacks. You can see the relationship between the two objects along with the methods used to set up the relationship in Figure 8-3.

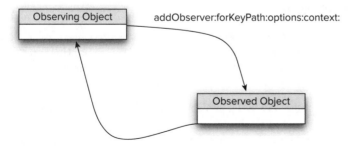

FIGURE 8-3: The KVO relationship

When the observed object calls `observeValueForKeyPath:ofObject:change:context:`, the observer receives a reference to the object that changed. Also sent to the receiver are the keypath to the property that changed, a dictionary that contains the changes, and the context pointer that you passed in the call that set up the relationship.

The `NSDictionary` that you receive in the callback contains information about the changes to the observed object. Depending on the options that you specified in the call to set up the observer, the dictionary will contain different keys. If you specified `NSKeyValueObservingOptionNew`, the dictionary will have an entry corresponding with the `NSKeyValueChangeNewKey` key that contains the new value for the observed property. If you specified `NSKeyValueObservingOptionOld`, the dictionary will have an entry for the `NSKeyValueChangeOldKey` key that contains the original value of the observed property. If you specified both options using a bitwise OR, both keys will be available in the dictionary. The dictionary will also contain an entry for the `NSKeyValueChangeKindKey` that gives you more information describing what kind of change has occurred.

When you are no longer interested in observing changes on an object, you need to unregister your observer. You accomplish this by calling the `removeObserver:forKeyPath:` method on the observed object. You pass the observer and the keypath to the property that the observer was observing. After you make this call, the observer will no longer receive change notifications from the observed object.

Automatic and Manual Implementations of KVO

The `NSObject` base class provides an automatic key-value observing implementation for all classes that are key-value coding compliant. You can disable automatic support for KVO for specific keys by calling the class method `automaticallyNotifiesObserversForKey:`. In order to disable keys, you need to implement this method to return `NO` for the specific keys that you do not want the framework to automatically support.

You can implement manual KVO notifications for finer control of when notifications go out. This is useful when you have properties that could change very often or when you want to batch many notifications into one. First, you have to override the `automaticallyNotifiesObserversForKey:` method to return `NO` for keys that you want to implement manually. Then, in the accessor for the property that you want to manually control, you have to call `willChangeValueForKey:` before you modify the value, and `didChangeValueForKey:` afterwards.

Key-Value Observing Example

Now that you are familiar with the concepts behind key-value coding and key-value observing, let's work through a simple example. The example will help to demonstrate how to use this functionality in practice. In this example, you will implement an iPhone version of a baseball umpire's count indicator. Umpires use this device to keep track of balls, strikes, and outs.

The sample application will use KVC and KVO to decouple the data object (`Counter`) from the interface (`UmpireViewController`). Even though this example is simplified, it will demonstrate how to use KVC and KVO to decouple your data objects from your interface. Keep in mind that this example is somewhat contrived in order to demonstrate using the principals of KVO and KVC in an application. You could easily implement this solution in many other, simpler ways, without using KVO and KVC. The `UmpireViewController` will use KVC to set the values for balls, strikes, and outs in the `Counter` object. The `UmpireViewController` will also observe changes for these fields and use the observation method to update the user interface.

Building the User Interface

The first task is to create the user interface in Interface Builder. Start a new project using the View-based Application template. Call your new application Umpire.

You should lay the interface out as shown in Figure 8-4. Open the `UmpireViewController.xib` interface file. Add three `UIButton` objects to the interface and change their titles to "balls," "strikes," and "outs." Add three `UILabel` objects, one above each button. Change the text in each one to the number 0.

Next, you need to modify the `UmpireViewController.h` header file to add outlets for the UI controls and an action method that will handle the action when the user taps on one of the buttons.

Open the `UmpireViewController.h` header file. Add an instance variable for each `UILabel` inside the `@interface` declaration:

```
UILabel* ballLabel;
UILabel* strikeLabel;
UILabel* outLabel;
```

FIGURE 8-4: Umpire application user interface

UmpireViewController.h

Next, add properties for the three labels:

```
@property (nonatomic, retain) IBOutlet UILabel* ballLabel;
@property (nonatomic, retain) IBOutlet UILabel* strikeLabel;
@property (nonatomic, retain) IBOutlet UILabel* outLabel;
```

UmpireViewController.h

Finally, add an action method that you will call when a user taps one of the buttons:

```
-(IBAction)buttonTapped:(id)sender;
```

Now you need to open the `UmpireViewController.m` implementation file. At the top, synthesize the properties that you just declared in the header file:

```
@synthesize ballLabel,strikeLabel, outLabel;
```

Add a stub method for `buttonTapped`:

```
-(IBAction)buttonTapped:(id)sender {
    NSLog(@"buttonTapped");
}
```

Now you need to go back into Interface Builder and connect your outlets and actions. Open the `UmpireViewController.xib` interface file. Connect the `ballLabel`, `strikeLabel`, and `outLabel` outlets of the File's Owner to the appropriate label in the view. Next, wire up each button in the interface to the `buttonTapped` action of File's Owner. Your user interface is complete. Save the file and close Interface Builder.

Build and run the application. It should build successfully with no errors or warnings. In the iPhone simulator, tap each button and verify that when you tap each button, you see the "buttonTapped" message in the console log.

The Counter Data Object

Now that your user interface is set up and working correctly, you will build a data object to hold the umpire data. Create a new class that is a subclass of `NSObject` and call it `Counter`.

Open the `Counter.h` header file. Add three `NSNumber` instance variables, one each for `balls`, `strikes`, and `outs`:

```
NSNumber* balls;
NSNumber* strikes;
NSNumber* outs;
```

Counter.h

Add property declarations for each of the instance variables:

```
@property (nonatomic, retain) IBOutlet NSNumber* balls;
@property (nonatomic, retain) IBOutlet NSNumber* strikes;
@property (nonatomic, retain) IBOutlet NSNumber* outs;
```

Counter.h

In the implementation file `Counter.m`, synthesize the properties:

```
@synthesize balls,strikes,outs;
```

You will be using this object in the `UmpireViewController` so you need to add a reference to the `Counter.h` header file in the `UmpireViewController.h` header. Open the `UmpireViewController.h` header file and add an `import` statement to import the `Counter.h` header:

```
#import "Counter.h"
```

Also in the `UmpireViewController.h` header file, add a `Counter` instance variable:

```
Counter* umpireCounter;
```

Next, add a property called `umpireCounter`:

```objc
@property (nonatomic, retain) Counter* umpireCounter;
```

The `umpireCounter` variable will hold the instance of the `Counter` that you will use to keep track of the ball and strike count.

Finally, in the `UmpireViewController.m` implementation file, synthesize the new `umpireCounter` property:

```objc
@synthesize umpireCounter;
```

Implementing Key-Value Observing

With the data object in place, you can now connect your View Controller to the data object using key-value observing. Open the `UmpireViewController.m` implementation file.

You need to initialize the `umpireCounter` variable and set up the KVO observation in the `viewDidLoad` method. Here is `viewDidLoad`:

Available for download on Wrox.com

```objc
- (void)viewDidLoad {
    [super viewDidLoad];
    Counter *theCounter = [[Counter alloc] init];

    self.umpireCounter = theCounter;

    // Set up KVO for the umpire counter
    [self.umpireCounter addObserver:self
                         forKeyPath:@"balls"
                            options:NSKeyValueObservingOptionNew
                            context:nil];
    [self.umpireCounter addObserver:self
                         forKeyPath:@"strikes"
                            options:NSKeyValueObservingOptionNew
                            context:nil];
    [self.umpireCounter addObserver:self
                         forKeyPath:@"outs"
                            options:NSKeyValueObservingOptionNew
                            context:nil];

    [theCounter release];

}
```

UmpireViewController.m

First, as usual, you call the superclass implementation of `viewDidLoad` to ensure that the object is set up properly and ready for use. Next, you create an instance of a `Counter` object and assign it to the `umpireCounter` property.

The next section sets up the KVO observation for each of the `balls`, `strikes`, and `outs` properties of the `Counter` object. Let's take a closer look at the call to set up the observer for the `balls` property:

```
[self.umpireCounter addObserver:self
                     forKeyPath:@"balls"
                        options:NSKeyValueObservingOptionNew
                        context:nil];
```

Remember that `Counter` inherits the `addObserver:forKeyPath:options:context:` method from `NSObject`. You are calling this method to configure the `UmpireViewController` as an observer of the `umpireCounter` object. Therefore, you pass `self` in as the object that will be the observer. This particular observer will be observing the `balls` property of the `umpireCounter`, so you pass the string "balls" in for the keypath. You don't really care what the old value of `balls` is; you are only interested in the new value when the value changes so you pass the `NSKeyValueObservingOptionNew` option in the method call. Finally, you set the context to `nil` because you do not need context data.

Finally, in the `viewDidLoad` method, you release the local variable `theCounter` because you incremented its retain count when you assigned it to the `umpireCounter` property.

Now that you've set up your code to become an observer, you need to implement the `observeValueForKeyPath:ofObject:change:context:` method that the observed object calls when observed properties change. Here is the method:

```
- (void)observeValueForKeyPath:(NSString *)keyPath
                      ofObject:(id)object
                        change:(NSDictionary *)change
                       context:(void *)context {

    // change gives back an NSDictionary of changes
    NSNumber *newValue = [change valueForKey:NSKeyValueChangeNewKey];

    // update the appropriate label
    if (keyPath == @"balls") {
        self.ballLabel.text = [newValue stringValue];
    }
    else if (keyPath == @"strikes") {
        self.strikeLabel.text = [newValue stringValue];
    }
    else if (keyPath == @"outs") {
        self.outLabel.text = [newValue stringValue];
    }
}
```

UmpireViewController.m

Remember that every time any observed property in the `umpireCounter` changes, the `umpireCounter` will call this method. The first line retrieves the new value from the change dictionary for the property that changed. Next, you examine the keypath that the `umpireCounter` passes in to determine which property has changed. Then, you use that knowledge to set the text of the appropriate label.

In the `viewDidUnload` method, you need to remove the KVO observers. You also set the properties of the class to `nil`. Here is the code for `viewDidUnload`:

```objc
- (void)viewDidUnload {
    // Release any retained subviews of the main view.
    // Tear down KVO for the umpire counter
    [self.umpireCounter removeObserver:self
                            forKeyPath:@"balls"];

    [self.umpireCounter removeObserver:self
                            forKeyPath:@"strikes" ];

    [self.umpireCounter removeObserver:self
                            forKeyPath:@"outs" ];

    self.ballLabel = nil;
    self.strikeLabel = nil;
    self.outLabel = nil;
    self.umpireCounter = nil;

    [super viewDidUnload];
}
```

UmpireViewController.m

Once again, you make a call to the `umpireCounter` object. This time, you call the `removeObserver: forKeyPath:` method to remove your class as an observer of the `umpireCounter`. You call this method once for each property that you are observing, passing `self` as the observer each time.

Then, you set each property to `nil` and call the superclass implementation of `viewDidUnload`.

While you are writing cleanup code, implement the `dealloc` method to release all of your instance variables and call the superclass `dealloc` method:

```objc
- (void)dealloc {
    [ballLabel release];
    [strikeLabel release];
    [outLabel release];
    [umpireCounter release];

    [super dealloc];
}
```

UmpireViewController.m

Updating Values with Key-Value Coding

The last thing that you need to do is implement the `buttonTapped` method that executes each time the user taps one of the buttons in the interface. Instead of specifically setting the property values of the `umpireCounter` using dot notation, you will use KVC in conjunction with the title of the button that was pressed to set the appropriate value. You also need to implement some business logic to limit the ball counter to a maximum of 3 and the strike and out counters to a maximum of 2. Here is the code for the `buttonTapped` method:

```
-(IBAction)buttonTapped:(id)sender {

    UIButton *theButton = sender;
    NSNumber *value = [self.umpireCounter valueForKey:theButton.currentTitle];

    NSNumber* newValue;

    // Depending on the button and the value, set the new value accordingly
    if ([theButton.currentTitle compare:@"balls"] == NSOrderedSame &&
        [value intValue] == 3) {

        newValue = [NSNumber numberWithInt:0];
    }
    else if (([theButton.currentTitle compare:@"strikes"] == NSOrderedSame ||
            [theButton.currentTitle compare:@"outs"] == NSOrderedSame )&&
            [value intValue] == 2) {

        newValue = [NSNumber numberWithInt:0];
    }
    else
    {
        newValue = [NSNumber numberWithInt:[value intValue]+1];
    }

    [self.umpireCounter setValue:newValue forKey:theButton.currentTitle];
}
```

UmpireViewController.m

First, you get a reference to the button that the user pressed to trigger the call to `buttonTapped`. Next, you use the title of that button as the key in a call to `valueForKey` to get the current value of that attribute from the `umpireCounter`. For example, if the user tapped the "balls" button, you are passing the string `balls` into the `valueForKey` method. This method will then retrieve the `balls` property of the `umpireCounter`. This method will work as long as the titles in the buttons match the property names in the data object.

The next line declares a new `NSNumber` that you will use to hold the value that you want to send back to the `umpireCounter`.

Next, you apply some business logic depending on which button the user pressed. If he pressed the "balls" button, you check to see if the old value was 3, and if it was, you set the new value back to 0. It does not make any sense for the balls counter to go higher than 3 because in baseball, 4 balls constitute a walk and the next batter will come up, erasing the old count.

The next line does a similar comparison for the strikes and outs counters, but you compare these values to 2. Again, values greater than 2 make no sense for each of these properties.

If you do not need to reset the particular counter back to zero, you simply increment the value and store the new value in the local `newValue` variable.

Finally, you use KVC to set the new value on the `umpireCounter` using the `currentTitle` of the button that the user pressed as the key.

The application is now complete. You should be able to successfully build and run. When you tap one of the buttons, the application should set the properties of the counter object using KVC. It should then fire the KVO callback method and update the count labels on the interface using KVO. Notice how you never explicitly retrieved values from the `umpireCounter` using properties or `valueForKey`.

USING NSPREDICATE

In the previous chapter, you learned how you could use predicates with Core Data to specify the criteria for a fetch. In general, you can use predicates to filter data from any class, as long as the class is key-value coding compliant.

Creating Predicates

You can create a predicate from a string by calling the `NSPredicate` class method `predicateWithFormat:`. You can include variables for substitution at runtime just as you would with any other string formatter. One issue to be aware of when creating predicates using strings is that you will not see errors caused by an incorrect format string until runtime.

When creating a predicate by calling the `predicateWithFormat` method, you must quote string constants in the expression. For example, you see that you have to quote the string literal URGENT in this method call:

```
[NSPredicate predicateWithFormat:"text BEGINSWITH 'URGENT'"]
```

However, if you use a format string with variable substitution (%@), there is no need for you to quote the variable string. Therefore, you could create the previous predicate using this format string:

```
[NSPredicate predicateWithFormat:"text BEGINSWITH %@", @"URGENT"]
```

You can also use variable substitution to pass in variable values at runtime like this:

```
[NSPredicate predicateWithFormat:"text BEGINSWITH %@", object.valueToFilter]
```

If you try to specify a dynamic property name using a format string and %@, it will fail because the property name will be quoted. You need to use the %K (Key) substitution character in the format string to omit the quotes.

Say, for example, that you wanted to create a predicate at runtime but wanted the field that you are filtering on to be dynamic, along with the value that you want to filter. If you tried this code, it would be incorrect because the property that you are trying to filter on would be incorrectly quoted by using the %@ substitution character:

```
[NSPredicate predicateWithFormat:"%@ == %@", object.property, object.valueToFilter]
```

The correct syntax for this predicate is as follows:

```
[NSPredicate predicateWithFormat:"%K == %@", object.property, object.valueToFilter]
```

You are not limited to creating predicates with keys. You can also create a predicate using a keypath. With respect to a Task object, the predicate location.name == "Home" is perfectly legal.

In addition to using the predicateWithFormat method, you can create predicates directly using instances of the NSExpression object and NSPredicate subclasses. This predicate creation method makes you write a lot of code, but it is less prone to syntax errors because you get compile-time checking of the objects that you create. You may also get some runtime performance increase because there is no string parsing with this method as there is with the predicateWithFormat: method.

To create the predicate text BEGINSWITH 'URGENT' using NSExpressions and NSPredicate subclasses, you code it like this:

```
NSExpression *lhs = [NSExpression expressionForKeyPath:@"text"];
NSExpression *rhs = [NSExpression expressionForConstantValue:@"URGENT"];
NSPredicate *beginsWithPredicate =
    [NSComparisonPredicate predicateWithLeftExpression:lhs
                            rightExpression:rhs
                            modifier:NSDirectPredicateModifier
                            type:NSBeginsWithPredicateOperatorType
                            options:0];
```

As you can see, this is quite a bit more than the simple one line of code shown previously. However, when using this method you do get the benefit of compile-time type checking.

The final method for creating predicates is to use predicate templates with variable expressions. You saw this technique in the previous chapter when you used a predefined fetch request from your data model. With this method, you create your predicate template using either of the previously mentioned methods but with $VAR as variables in the predicate. When you are ready to use the predicate, you call the predicateWithSubstitutionVariables: method on the predicate passing in a dictionary that contains the key-value pairs of the substitution variables and their values.

Using Predicates

You can evaluate any object that is KVC-compliant against a predicate using the evaluateWithObject method of the predicate. YES is returned if the object passed in meets the criteria specified in the predicate.

For example, suppose that you build a predicate called thePredicate with the criteria text BEGINSWITH 'URGENT' as described previously. If you had a reference to a Task object called theTask that had a text attribute, you could call the function [thePredicate evaluateWithObject: theTask]. If the Task's text attribute started with the string URGENT the call to evaluateWithObject would return YES. You can see that this functionality has nothing to do with Core Data. Again, you can use predicates with any object that is KVC-compliant.

The NSArray class has a method called filteredArrayUsingPredicate: that returns a new filtered array using the supplied predicate. NSMutableArray has a filterUsingPredicate: method that filters an existing mutable array and removes items that don't match the predicate. You can also use filteredArrayUsingPredicate: with the mutable array to return a new, filtered NSArray.

SORT DESCRIPTORS

Like predicates, the use of sort descriptors is not limited to Core Data. You can use sort descriptors to sort other data structures such as arrays, as long as the values contained within the array are KVC compliant. As you may recall from the previous chapter, you use sort descriptors to specify how to sort a list of objects.

Sort descriptors specify the property to use when sorting a set of objects. By default, sorting using a sort descriptor calls the compare: method of each object under consideration. However, you can specify a custom method to use instead of the default compare: method.

Keep in mind that the descriptor doesn't do the sorting. The sort descriptor just tells the data structure how to sort. This is similar to how an NSPredicate doesn't actually do the filtering; it simply specifies how to filter.

The first step in using a sort descriptor is to initialize a sort descriptor with the key that you want to sort on. You also need to specify if you want to sort the resulting data in ascending or descending order. You initialize a sort descriptor by using the initWithKey:ascending: method.

Next, you create an array of descriptors by calling the NSArray arrayWithObjects: method and passing in one or more descriptors. You need to create an array because this allows you to sort on more than one field at a time. The framework applies the sort descriptors in the order that you specify them in the array.

For example, if you had an array of Task objects called theTaskArray, you could sort the array first on dueDate and then on text by creating an array containing two sort descriptors and calling the sortedArrayUsingDescriptors method:

```
// Create the sort descriptors
NSSortDescriptor *dueDateDescriptor =
    [[NSSortDescriptor alloc] initWithKey:@"dueDate" ascending:NO];
NSSortDescriptor *textDescriptor =
    [[NSSortDescriptor alloc] initWithKey:@"text" ascending:YES];

// Build an array of sort descriptors
NSArray *descriptorArray =
    [NSArray alloc arrayWithObjects: dueDateDescriptor, textDescriptor, nil];

// Sort the array using the sort descriptors
NSArray *sortedArray =
    [theTaskArray sortedArrayUsingDescriptors:descriptorArray];
```

The `sortedArrayUsingDescriptors` method works by calling the `compare:` method on the type that you are sorting. If the compare method is not appropriate for your application, you can specify a different method to use when sorting by creating your sort descriptors with the `initWithKey: ascending:selector:` method.

Specifically, when comparing strings, Apple's String Programming Guide for Cocoa recommends that you use a localized string comparison. So instead of `compare:`, you should generally specify that the sort descriptor use the `localizedCompare:` or `localizedCaseInsensitiveCompare:` method using the `@selector (localizedCaseInsensitiveCompare:)` syntax.

Therefore, when sorting your `Task` objects based on the text field, which is a string, you should use a sort descriptor defined like this:

```
NSSortDescriptor *textDescriptor =
        [[NSSortDescriptor alloc]
            initWithKey:@"text"
            ascending:YES
            selector:@selector(localizedCaseInsensitiveCompare:)];
```

The `localizedCaseInsensitiveCompare:` method of the `NSString` class uses an appropriate localized sorting algorithm based on the localization settings of the device.

MOVING FORWARD

In this chapter, you learned how you can use some of the features of the Cocoa framework that you learned about in the context of Core Data, outside of Core Data.

You used key-value coding and key-value observing to build an application that has its user interface loosely coupled to its data model. Architecturally, loose coupling of application data and the user interface is generally a good thing.

Then you learned how to create predicates and use them to filter data in arrays. You also learned how you could use predicates to do an ad hoc comparison of an object to some specific criteria.

Finally, you learned how to create and apply sort descriptors to sort arrays.

You should now feel comfortable with using these features inside your Core Data–based applications. You should also be able to apply the same concepts and technologies to work with other data structures as well.

In the next chapter, you finish the exploration of the Core Data framework with a look at optimizing Core Data performance. You will also look at versioning your database and migrating existing applications from one database version to another.

Core Data Migration and Performance

WHAT'S IN THIS CHAPTER?

➤ Managing database schema changes with versioning and migration

➤ Implementing a threaded Core Data application

➤ Understanding and optimizing Core Data performance and memory usage

➤ Analyzing Core Data performance with the Instruments tool

In the preceding chapters, you learned about the Core Data framework and how to use it to provide the data storage capability in your applications. In this chapter, you will take a closer look at some advanced topics related to Core Data, including migration from one database schema to another and optimizing the performance of your Core Data–based application.

In this chapter, you learn how to handle change in your application data model using model versioning and migration. You also learn how to effectively manage memory when building a Core Data–based solution, safely implement a threaded Core Data application, and troubleshoot and analyze your Core Data application using the Instruments tool.

MODEL VERSIONING AND SCHEMA MIGRATION

It is very rare that a finished application turns out the way that you imagined when you started. In fact, many applications are never truly finished. If your customers like your application, you will almost certainly want to enhance it and build upon its existing feature set. Often, you will get feature requests from customers and clients, which can be a continuing source of revenue for you, the developer.

When you first sat down to design your application, you reviewed the requirements and designed the database that would store your data. As the application development process moves forward, things change, and you may need to modify your data store by adding entities and attributes, changing data types, or modifying relationships between your entities. This is a normal part of the development cycle. Although you may occasionally get a nasty error message from Core Data about using an incompatible data store, this is not a big deal. While you're developing, you can simply blow away your old application and its data, and your application will create a new data store that works with the current schema. This is not an option once you have shipped your application.

In general, users will not be very happy if they try to open an updated version of your application and it crashes because the data store schema does not match the schema of the data file. They will be even less happy if they contact you for support and you tell them that they have to delete the old application and all of their data to be able to run with the update. They will most likely not use your application, or any other applications that you build, ever again.

You are probably wondering how you can continue to extend your product while not losing all of your customer's existing work when he or she upgrades to the newest version of your application. Fortunately, Apple has provided a solution with Core Data Versioning.

Core Data implements a feature called *model versioning*, which allows you to specify and label different versions of your data model in your Xcode project. You can have many versions of the data model in your project. You need only specify which schema is the current model that your application should use.

Another tool provided by the framework is the *mapping model*. The mapping model lets you map the translation of data from one model into another. Finally, *data migration* is used with versioning and mapping to migrate a back-end data store from one schema version to another. I've illustrated this process in Figure 9-1.

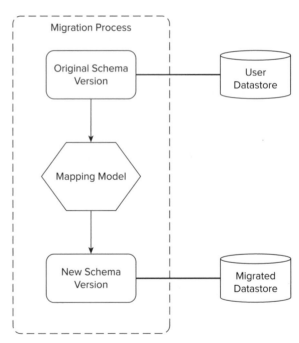

FIGURE 9-1: The data migration process

The Core Data framework thus solves your application update problem. You can create a new version of your schema to support your application enhancements, and then use schema migration to migrate the existing data store on your customer's device to the new schema.

Model Versioning

To Core Data, two models are compatible if there are no changes to the model that will affect a change in the back-end data store. For instance, you can add a transient property while maintaining compatibility between the existing and the new data store. Remember, that transient properties are not stored in the data store, so a change to a transient property will not break compatibility with the original data store.

If you make a change that alters how your data is stored in the data store, however, you are breaking compatibility with the existing data store. Actions such as adding new attributes or entities, changing attribute types, and renaming entities or attributes will all change the structure of the data store and will break compatibility.

There are some rules that you can use to determine if two models will be compatible. For an entity, Core Data compares the `name`, `parent`, and `isAbstract` flags. Core Data does not care about `className`, `userInfo`, and validation predicates because these are not stored in the data store. These items are only available to the developer at runtime.

For every property, Core Data examines the `name`, `isOptional`, `isTransient`, and `isReadOnly` elements. For attributes, Core Data also looks at the `attributeType`, and for relationships, Core Data examines the `destinationEntity`, `minCount`, `maxCount`, `deleteRule`, and `inverseRelationship`. Core Data does not compare the `userInfo` and validation predicates.

If any of these attributes of a model differ for any entity or any property of any entity, the models are incompatible.

In Xcode, you can create and specify different versions of your application data model. You will look at this functionality now using the Tasks project. Although you will not be adding any additional functionality, you will be modifying the database to purposely break compatibility with the existing data store to illustrate versioning and migration.

Find your existing Tasks application and copy it into a new folder. Open up the new Tasks project in Xcode. Next, open the data model Tasks.xcdatamodel. To create a new version of the model, choose Design ⇨ Data Model ⇨ Add Model Version from the menu bar.

If you look in the Resources folder in Xcode, you will notice that the Tasks.xcdatamodel file is gone. Xcode has replaced this file with a new file called Tasks.xcdatamodeld. Tasks.xcdatamodeld is actually a bundle and not a file at all. If you click on the disclosure indicator to open the bundle, you will see two data model files, Tasks .xcdatamodel and Tasks 2.xcdatamodel, as shown in Figure 9-2. At this point, the two files are identical. You may also notice that the Tasks.xcdatamodel file has a little green checkmark on the file icon. The checkmark indicates that this file is the Current Version. This is the version of the model that Core Data will use at runtime.

FIGURE 9-2: Two versions of the Tasks model

You will be making some changes to the new version of the model, version 2. You will want to use the new version of the model in your application, so you have to set it as the current version. Select

Tasks 2.xcdatamodel and choose Design ➪ Data Model ➪ Set Current Version from the menu bar. You should see the green checkmark move from the original model to the new version 2 model.

Now you will make a change to the model that will break compatibility with your existing Tasks data store. In the Tasks 2.xcdatamodel file, open the Location entity and add an address property of String type. Save the model. Make sure that you have the Tasks 2.xcdatamodel file selected as the current version. Clean your project by selecting Build ➪ Clean All Targets. Then build and run the application.

Because you have made a change to the model that breaks compatibility with the old data store, the application should raise an error and abort. In the console, you should see an error that looks like this:

```
2010-08-03 12:52:23.277 Tasks[6100:207] Unresolved error Error Domain=NSCocoaErrorDomain
Code=134100 "The operation couldn't be completed. (Cocoa error 134100.)"
UserInfo=0x5b298a0 {metadata=<CFBasicHash 0x5b2e1b0 [0x26db380]>{type = immutable dict,
count = 6,
entries =>
    0 : <CFString 0x5b2e1e0 [0x26db380]>{contents = "NSStoreModelVersionIdentifiers"} =
<CFArray 0x5b2e5e0 [0x26db380]>{type = immutable, count = 0, values = ()}
    2 : <CFString 0x5b2e550 [0x26db380]>{contents = "NSStoreModelVersionHashesVersion"}=
<CFNumber 0x5b1a8a0 [0x26db380]>{value = +3, type = kCFNumberSInt32Type}
    3 : <CFString 0x23dd324 [0x26db380]>{contents = "NSStoreType"} = <CFString 0x23dd2e4
[0x26db380]>{contents = "SQLite"}
    4 : <CFString 0x5b2e580 [0x26db380]>{contents = "NSPersistenceFrameworkVersion"} =
<CFNumber 0x5b2e230 [0x26db380]>{value = +320, type = kCFNumberSInt64Type}
    5 : <CFString 0x5b2e5b0 [0x26db380]>{contents = "NSStoreModelVersionHashes"} =
<CFBasicHash 0x5b2e6d0 [0x26db380]>{type = immutable dict, count = 2,
entries =>
    1 : <CFString 0x5b2e600 [0x26db380]>{contents = "Task"} = <CFData 0x5b2e630
[0x26db380]>{length = 32, capacity = 32, bytes = 0x4041451778c0bd9f84e09e2a91478c44 ...
abb9be2796761c30}
    2 : <CFString 0x5b2e610 [0x26db380]>{contents = "Location"} = <CFData 0x5b2e680
[0x26db380]>{length = 32, capacity = 32, bytes = 0xfa099c17c3432901bbaf6eb31dddc734 ...
97ebad533e2e5363}
}

    6 : <CFString 0x23dd464 [0x26db380]>{contents = "NSStoreUUID"} = <CFString 0x5b2e3a0
[0x26db380]>{contents = "6B5E801A-9B00-4F17-858D-726679EE28C3"}
}
, reason=The model used to open the store is incompatible with the one used to create
the store}, {
    metadata =     {
        NSPersistenceFrameworkVersion = 320;
        NSStoreModelVersionHashes =         {
            Location = <fa099c17 c3432901 bbaf6eb3 1dddc734 a9ac14d2 36b913ed 97ebad53
3e2e5363>;
            Task = <40414517 78c0bd9f 84e09e2a 91478c44 d85394f8 e9bb7e5a abb9be27
96761c30>;
        };
```

```
            NSStoreModelVersionHashesVersion = 3;
            NSStoreModelVersionIdentifiers =           (
            );
            NSStoreType = SQLite;
            NSStoreUUID = "6B5E801A-9B00-4F17-858D-726679EE28C3";
        };
        reason = "The model used to open the store is incompatible with the one used to
    create the store";
    }
```

You'll fix this error in the next section.

Lightweight Migration

In order to make your existing data work with your new data model, you need to migrate the schema to a new data store. If the changes that you have made are not too drastic, you can easily accomplish this using a process called *lightweight migration*.

Lightweight migration is a feature of Core Data that helps you to automatically migrate a data store from one model version to another. In the previous section, I briefly mentioned the mapping model. Core Data uses the mapping model to determine how to map data from one schema model into another. Lightweight migration allows Core Data to infer the mapping model based on the changes that you made to the model from one version to another.

Lightweight migration is particularly handy during development because you won't have to regenerate your test data every time you make a change to your model. It is also fast to implement because you don't have to go through the trouble of creating your own mapping model to map your data from one version to another.

For lightweight migration to work, the changes to your model have to be simple. Generally, if you add an attribute, make a required attribute optional, or make an optional attribute required and add a default value, lightweight migration will work for you. If you change the name of an entity or attribute, you need to set the renaming identifier for the renamed attribute in the user info pane to the old name of the attribute in the source model.

In the Tasks example, the model has changed, but you are still trying to use a data store that works with the old model. In this instance, you can use lightweight migration because you have only added a new field to the data store.

To use lightweight migration, you need to make a couple of changes to your application source code. If you recall from Chapter 5, "Introducing Core Data," the Persistent Store Coordinator is a Core Data object that associates a managed object model to a back-end data store. You can see this relationship in Figure 9-3. In your code, when you add a persistent store to the coordinator, you can specify an `NSDictionary` of options in the `addPersistentStoreWithType:configuration:URL:options:error:` method call. You will modify the code in the `TasksAppDelegate.m` file to specify the options to initiate a lightweight migration.

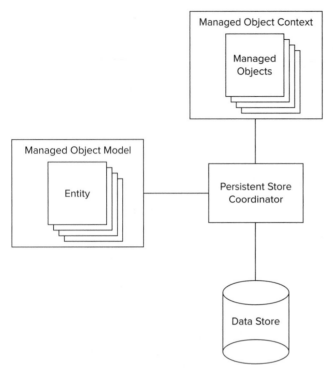

FIGURE 9-3: Core Data objects

Open the Tasks project and navigate to the `TasksAppDelegate.m` file. You will be adding code
to the `persistentStoreCoordinator` accessor method. The first thing that you need to do
is create an `NSDictionary` that contains the keys that you want to pass into the coordinator.
The two keys that you will set are `NSMigratePersistentStoresAutomaticallyOption` and
`NSInferMappingModelAutomaticallyOption`.

`NSMigratePersistentStoresAutomaticallyOption` tells the coordinator to automatically migrate
the persistent store to a new model if the store is not compatible with the current model. Core Data
will search the application bundle for a model that is capable of opening the existing data store and
then it will search for a mapping model that maps from the model that can open the data store to
the current model. Because you haven't created a mapping model, you have to add another option to
your options dictionary.

You use the `NSInferMappingModelAutomaticallyOption` option key to tell Core Data to try to
infer the mapping model from the differences between the model that can open the data store and
the current model.

In the `persistentStoreCoordinator` method, after the line that allocates and initializes
the `NSPersistentStoreCoordinator`, add the following code to initialize your options
dictionary:

```
NSDictionary *options = [NSDictionary dictionaryWithObjectsAndKeys:
                            [NSNumber numberWithBool:YES],
                            NSMigratePersistentStoresAutomaticallyOption,
                            [NSNumber numberWithBool:YES],
                            NSInferMappingModelAutomaticallyOption, nil];
```

TasksAppDelegate.m

This code creates a new `NSDictionary` and populates it with the keys as discussed previously.

Next, you have to change the call to `addPersistentStoreWithType:configuration:URL:options:error:` to use the new options dictionary that you have created. Change the line to look like this:

```
if (![persistentStoreCoordinator
        addPersistentStoreWithType:NSSQLiteStoreType
        configuration:nil URL:storeUrl options:options error:&error])
```

TasksAppDelegate.m

The complete method should look like this:

```
- (NSPersistentStoreCoordinator *)persistentStoreCoordinator {

    if (persistentStoreCoordinator != nil) {
        return persistentStoreCoordinator;
    }

    NSURL *storeUrl =
        [NSURL fileURLWithPath: [[self applicationDocumentsDirectory]
            stringByAppendingPathComponent: @"Tasks.sqlite"]];

    NSError *error = nil;
    persistentStoreCoordinator =
        [[NSPersistentStoreCoordinator alloc]
         initWithManagedObjectModel:[self managedObjectModel]];

    NSDictionary *options = [NSDictionary dictionaryWithObjectsAndKeys:
                                [NSNumber numberWithBool:YES],
                                NSMigratePersistentStoresAutomaticallyOption,
                                [NSNumber numberWithBool:YES],
                                NSInferMappingModelAutomaticallyOption, nil];

    if (![persistentStoreCoordinator
            addPersistentStoreWithType:NSSQLiteStoreType
            configuration:nil URL:storeUrl options:options error:&error]) {

        NSLog(@"Unresolved error %@, %@", error, [error userInfo]);
        abort();
    }

    return persistentStoreCoordinator;
}
```

TasksAppDelegate.m

Build and run your application. The migration should now succeed and the application should run just as it did before. Your error is gone, you've added a new field to the data store to support some new functionality, and your customer's data is intact.

 Make sure that you have a few tasks in your data store because you will be transforming the existing data in the next section. If you have no data, you will not see any results when you apply the transformation.

You can check in advance if the lightweight migration will work by calling the `inferredMappingModelForSourceModel:destinationModel:error:` method. If the mapping will work and the migration will succeed, you will get back a reference to the new model, if not, the method returns `nil`.

Generating a Mapping Model

If your model changes are too extensive or otherwise don't meet the criteria supported for performing a lightweight migration, you will have to generate a mapping model. Remember that you use the mapping model to tell Core Data how to migrate your data from one store to another. You can also use the mapping model to perform data transformations as you move the data from one data store to another.

Because of the relationship between the mapping model and the data model, the classes used to build a mapping model correspond with the classes used to build a data model. `NSMappingModel` is like the data model, `NSEntityMapping` is like an entity, and `NSPropertyMapping` is like a property or attribute.

The `NSEntityMapping` class tells the migration process how to handle mapping a source entity in the destination data store. The mapping type determines what to do with the specific entity in the destination data store. The mapping types are: add, remove, copy, and transform. The add mapping means that this is a new entity in the destination and should be added to the destination data store. Remove means that the entity does not exist in the destination and exists only in the source. Copy indicates that the mapping should copy the source object identically to the destination. Transform means that the entity exists in the source and the destination and the mapping should transform the source in some way to get from the source to the destination. You will see an example of how to transform data as it is being migrated from one model to another later in this chapter.

The `NSPropertyMapping` class tells the migration process how to map source properties to destination properties. You can provide a value expression to transform values while moving the data from the source data store to the destination data store. You can specify a value expression in the mapping model editor in Xcode.

In some cases, you may want to do a custom migration where you will use these classes, so it is good to have at least a cursory understanding of which classes are involved in performing a migration. More often, you will not work with the mapping classes in code because Xcode includes a graphical tool that you can use to create and edit your mapping model. You will create a mapping model to migrate your data store back to the original version of the data model. You will also transform some of the data in the data store along the way to demonstrate the transformation capabilities of executing the migration process using a mapping model.

In Xcode, select the `Tasks.xcdatamodel` file and make it the current model by selecting Design ⇨ Data Model ⇨ Set Current Model from the menu bar. To create the mapping model, select the Resources folder in Xcode and add a new file. In the New File dialog, under iPhone OS, select Resource. In the right-hand pane of the New File dialog, you should see an option for Mapping Model. Select the Mapping Model and click Next. On the next screen, enter the name for your new mapping model as "Map", and click Next.

You should now see the New Mapping Model File dialog. You will use this dialog to tell the mapping model which data model is the source and which is the destination. Open the Resources folder and the `Tasks.xcdatamodeld` bundle. Select the Tasks 2 model and click the Set Source Model button. Remember that you have a data store that is compatible with the Tasks 2 model and you want to migrate it to be compatible with the Tasks model. Finally, select the Tasks model and click the Set Destination model. Click the Finish button to have Xcode create your mapping model.

You should now see the mapping model tool. If you do not, make sure that you have selected the `Map.xcmappingmodel` file in the Resources folder in Xcode. You can see the mapping model tool in Figure 9-4.

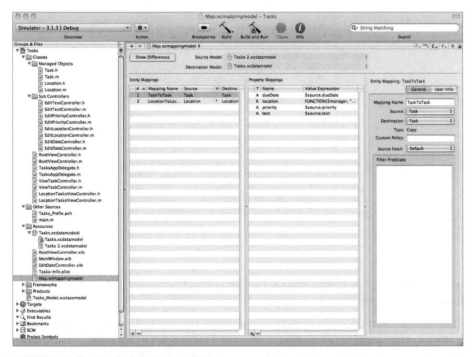

FIGURE 9-4: The Tasks mapping model

At the top of the screen, the tool lists the source and destination models. Below that is a three-column view. The left column displays the entity mappings, which the framework uses to migrate entities between datastores. The middle column displays the property mappings for the currently selected entity. The right column shows the details of the currently selected item.

In the top-left corner of the window is a valuable tool, the Show Differences button. Click this button to open a window that graphically shows all of the differences in the two data models, as shown in Figure 9-5. You can use this display to help plan the mapping model and to verify the changes that you made between the two models. You can see in Figure 9-5 that the address attribute that existed in the Location entity in the source model is missing in the destination model.

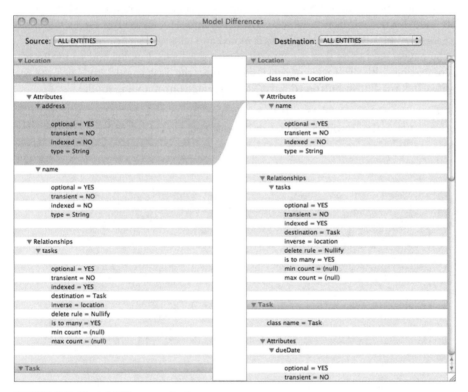

FIGURE 9-5: Model Differences tool

The Mapping Model tool has created the default entity and property mappings for you. You can successfully run with the default mapping model. However, you will apply some transformations using value expressions to demonstrate how you can transform data while performing a migration.

In the mapping model, you will notice two entity mappings — one for Tasks and one for Locations. Select the TaskToTask entity mapping. This mapping maps Task entities in the source data store to Task entities in the destination. As you can probably guess, the LocationToLocation entity mapping maps Location entities in the source data store to Location entities in the destination.

Now you will create a few value expressions to learn how to transform your data during a migration. Value expressions are instances of the NSExpression class. If you recall from the last chapter, this is the same class, with its subclasses, that you use as the right-hand side of a predicate.

First, you will modify the priority value expression to set the priority of every task to Medium (priority 2). Select the TaskToTask mapping in the Entity Mappings pane. In the Property Mappings pane, select the priority attribute. You will notice that the right-hand pane is context-sensitive: Its contents will change depending on the item that you have selected in the left or middle pane. When you have an Entity Mapping selected, the right-hand pane will display the mapping attributes that pertain to an Entity Mapping. When you select the priority attribute, the pane changes to display the fields that pertain to an Attribute Mapping.

The default value expression for the priority attribute is $source.priority. This expression directly migrates the priority from the source to the destination. The special variable $source is used to indicate that the value for this field in the destination should be taken from the corresponding source object. In the case of priority, the expression $source.priority gets the priority field from the source entity. However, instead of taking the value from the source, you want to change the priority for every task to 2. So, in the Value Expression field in the right-hand pane, change the value expression to the number 2.

Next, select the text attribute in the Property Mappings pane. The default value expression for the text property migrates the text from the source $source to the destination. You want to change the text of each task to NEW TASK so that you can see the effects of executing a transformation when the Tasks application opens. In the text property mapping, change the value expression field in the right hand pane to NEW TASK. This will change the text of every task to NEW TASK.

Next, let's change the dueDate of all of your tasks to today. Select the dueDate attribute in the Property Mappings pane. The default value expression for the dueDate property migrates the dueDate from the source to the destination. You want to set the new dueDate to today's date. You don't want to hard code a date because you do not know when the user will run the migration on his or her data store. It would be better if you could specify the date using a function.

You can call arbitrary functions in a value expression using function expressions by using the FUNCTION keyword. The syntax is FUNCTION(receiver, selectorName, arguments,...). In this case, you want the receiver to be NSDate and the selector that you want to call is the date method, which returns the current system date.

This is not as straightforward to implement as you might imagine. Passing the string, NSDate to the FUNCTION expression will evaluate NSDate as a string literal and not the class NSDate. In effect, you would be executing a call that looks like this: [@"NSDate" date] which is not what you want to do. You need to convert the receiver into a class object, not a string.

There is another function expression that you can use called CAST that accepts two strings and has the form CAST('string', 'type'). Therefore, you can call the function CAST("NSDate","Class") to get the class NSDate and not the string NSDate. Your final value expression for the dueDate mapping should be FUNCTION (CAST("NSDate","Class"), 'date').

This will call the method [NSDate date], which is what you want. Update the value expression and save the mapping file.

You are finished with the mapping model. You now need to go back into the TasksAppDelegate.m file and make a code change. Because you have created a mapping model, you no longer need Core Data to infer the mapping model from the data model changes. In fact, if you have Core Data infer the changes, the framework will not execute your transformations.

Change the options dictionary entry for NSInferMappingModelAutomaticallyOption to nil. This will cause Core Data to search the application bundle for a mapping model instead of determining the mappings automatically. Again, you must do this to execute your data transformations and direct Core Data to use your mapping model. The options dictionary creation code should now look like this:

```
NSDictionary *options = [NSDictionary dictionaryWithObjectsAndKeys:
                [NSNumber numberWithBool:YES],
                NSMigratePersistentStoresAutomaticallyOption,
                [NSNumber numberWithBool:NO],
                NSInferMappingModelAutomaticallyOption, nil];
```

TasksAppDelegate.m

You are ready to build the application and run it. You should see the text of all of the tasks change to NEW TASK and if you click any task, it should have a priority of Medium and the due date should be set to today's date.

SAFELY THREADING WITH CORE DATA

As you work through designing and developing your iPhone and iPad applications, you may begin to run into performance barriers that are difficult to overcome. For example, you may encounter situations where your user interface is unresponsive while waiting for a time-consuming operation to finish. Traditionally, moving these expensive operations off to their own thread is a technique that you could use to solve this and other performance issues. The iPhone and iPad are no exception.

Writing threaded code has typically been a difficult task. However, the iOS includes a framework that simplifies the task of creating threads and using these threads to execute your code. You will look at the classes that you can use in the iOS to implement concurrency in your application. Then, you will build a sample application that executes a time-consuming process. First you will run this process on the main thread; then you will move that process off to its own thread where you will see a significant improvement in the responsiveness of your application.

Designing for Threading

You should carefully consider the threading model for your application as early on in the design process as possible. It is somewhat difficult to retrofit threading into an application after you have completed the coding. If you can predict the operations that will be the most time consuming, or operations that are self-contained that you can run atomically in a concurrent fashion, you can design threading into your software from the beginning. While it is possible to implement threading in your application after you encounter a performance problem, your design will be better and your application code cleaner and more maintainable if you consider threading from the start.

As a designer, you should begin your consideration of threading once you have a thorough understanding of your application requirements. Based on these requirements, you should be able to determine the work that your application needs to perform. Once you understand this work, you should look to see if you could divide this work into atomic, self-contained operations. If you can easily break a task down to one or more atomic operations, it may be a good candidate for concurrency, particularly if the task is independent of other tasks.

A particularly useful case for implementing concurrency is to keep the main thread free to increase the responsiveness of your user interface. If you execute a long-running operation on the main application thread, the user will experience a frozen interface as the operation executes. This is potentially frustrating for users, as they cannot continue to work with your application while it is in this state.

In the example in this section, I will graphically illustrate this point. First, you will write an application that generates five random numbers and pauses for 1 second between each number. Because this operation will run on the main thread, you will be able to see that your user interface freezes while you are generating these numbers. I have illustrated this scenario on the left in Figure 9-6. Then, you will take the random number generation and move it to its own thread. After you do this, you will notice that the user interface is responsive as you generate the random numbers. You can see this expressed on the right in Figure 9-6.

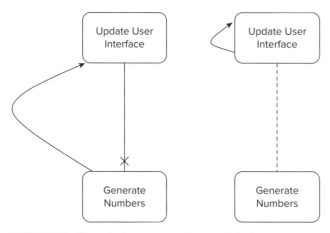

FIGURE 9-6: Threaded versus non-threaded design

Threading and Core Data

As you could probably guess, you will be using Core Data to store the data in your sample. The problem is that Core Data is not inherently thread-safe, mostly because the managed object context is not thread-safe. If you modify a managed object in a thread that is different from the thread on which you created the context, the context will not know about the changes to the managed object. This could cause your application to contain stale data. It is also possible to introduce data inconsistencies if you attempt to modify the same managed object on different threads. For these reasons, you should absolutely avoid passing Managed Objects across thread boundaries.

One approach to threading with Core Data is to create a separate managed object context on each thread. You can easily achieve this by passing (or obtaining) a reference to the Persistent Store Coordinator and manually creating a context in the thread. While the Persistent Store Coordinator is not thread-safe, the context knows how to lock the coordinator to enable concurrency using this method. You will follow this approach in the sample application. If you need to perform many operations on the context, you should create a new Persistent Store Coordinator on the thread as well. You will not be doing this in your sample.

While you never want to pass Managed Objects between threads, you can achieve a similar result by passing `objectID`s. The `objectID` uniquely identifies a managed object. You can obtain a managed object from the `objectID` by calling the `objectWithID:` method on the thread's context.

Threading with NSOperation

The concurrency model implemented in iOS does not require that you create individual threads directly. Rather, the developer creates operations designed to run concurrently and then hands them off to the system. The system then configures the optimal number of threads to use to run the specified concurrent tasks. It is possible to create threads yourself. However, if you create threads yourself, you are responsible for determining the optimum number of threads to create based on workload and the number of available processor cores. This is a difficult determination to make in real time. By using the concurrency classes provided in the iOS, the system takes care of this complexity by creating and scheduling the threads for you.

When you decide that you need to move a particular block of code off the main thread and on to its own thread, look no further than the `NSOperation` class. `NSOperation` is an abstract base class that you subclass to define and implement atomic operations that you want to dispatch to a separate thread.

When deciding to implement an operation, you have a couple of architectural choices. If you have an existing method in a class that you would like to execute asynchronously, you can use the `NSInvocationOperation` class. `NSInvocationOperation` is a concrete subclass of `NSOperation` that allows you to create an operation out of a class method and queue it for execution on a separate thread. If you are introducing threading into an existing application, `NSInvocationOperation` may be your best bet because you probably already have methods that perform the work that you would like to thread. It is also useful when you want to choose the method to execute dynamically at runtime because it accepts a selector as the method to run.

If you are building your threading model from scratch, you should implement threading by creating discrete subclasses of `NSOperation`. This will give you the freedom to implement your operations as you wish and alter the way that the operation reports status if your application calls for it.

In order to implement a subclass of NSOperation, at a minimum, you need to implement a custom initializer method that you use to configure your object for use and a main method that will perform the task. You can also implement any other custom methods that you need such as accessor methods to get at the operation's data or dealloc to free memory allocated by the operation.

Once you have created your operation classes, you need to tell the system to execute them. You accomplish this by creating an instance of NSOperationQueue and adding your NSOperation subclasses to the queue. The system uses operation queues to schedule and execute your operations. The system manages the queues, which handle the details of scheduling and executing your threads for you. It is possible to configure dependencies between operations when adding operations to an operation queue. You can also prioritize operations when you add them to a queue.

Core Data Threading Example

As I mentioned, this example application will generate five random numbers and pause for 1 second between each number to simulate a time consuming synchronous operation. This code will block the main thread causing the user interface to become unresponsive while you are generating the random numbers. Then, you will take the random number generation and move it on to its own thread. Once you do this, you will see that the user interface remains responsive while you generate the random numbers.

> *In this example, you will be inserting data into the Core Data context on an off thread. This is generally not recommended; however I am doing it in this example to demonstrate the mechanics of threading with Core Data. In production applications, you should generally only use threads to perform time consuming reads and queries from Core Data and not to perform inserts or updates.*

To get started, open Xcode and start a new Navigation-based application. Make sure that "Use Core Data for storage" is checked. Call your new application RandomNumbers.

The first thing that you will do is update the default data model to hold your random numbers. Open the data model file RandomNumbers.xcdatamodel. In the Event entity, change the name of the timeStamp attribute to randomNumber. Change the type of the randomNumber attribute to Integer16.

Next, you need to make some changes to the RootViewController implementation file. In the configureCell:atIndexPath: method, change the reference to the old timeStamp attribute to randomNumber. The configureCell method should look like this:

```
- (void)configureCell:(UITableViewCell *)cell
        atIndexPath:(NSIndexPath *)indexPath {

    NSManagedObject *managedObject =
        [fetchedResultsController objectAtIndexPath:indexPath];
```

```
        cell.textLabel.text =
            [[managedObject valueForKey:@"randomNumber"] description];
    }
```

You will also need to make this change in the `fetchedResultsController` accessor method:

```
- (NSFetchedResultsController *)fetchedResultsController {

    if (fetchedResultsController != nil) {
        return fetchedResultsController;
    }

    /*
     Set up the fetched results controller.
     */
    // Create the fetch request for the entity.
    NSFetchRequest *fetchRequest = [[NSFetchRequest alloc] init];
    // Edit the entity name as appropriate.
    NSEntityDescription *entity = [NSEntityDescription entityForName:@"Event"
        inManagedObjectContext:managedObjectContext];
    [fetchRequest setEntity:entity];

    // Set the batch size to a suitable number.
    [fetchRequest setFetchBatchSize:20];

    // Edit the sort key as appropriate.
    NSSortDescriptor *sortDescriptor = [[NSSortDescriptor alloc]
        initWithKey:@"randomNumber" ascending:NO];
    NSArray *sortDescriptors = [[NSArray alloc]
                                initWithObjects:sortDescriptor, nil];

    [fetchRequest setSortDescriptors:sortDescriptors];

    // Edit the section name key path and cache name if appropriate.
    // nil for section name key path means "no sections".
    NSFetchedResultsController *aFetchedResultsController =
        [[NSFetchedResultsController alloc]
        initWithFetchRequest:fetchRequest
        managedObjectContext:managedObjectContext
        sectionNameKeyPath:nil cacheName:@"Root"];

    aFetchedResultsController.delegate = self;
    self.fetchedResultsController = aFetchedResultsController;

    [aFetchedResultsController release];
    [fetchRequest release];
```

```
    [sortDescriptor release];
    [sortDescriptors release];

    return fetchedResultsController;
}
```

Blocking the Main Thread

Now you are ready to generate your random numbers and populate the Core Data database. You will implement the insertNewObject method, which runs when the user taps the plus button in the top-right corner of the application. Delete the existing implementation and add the following:

```
- (void)insertNewObject {

    // Create a new instance of the entity managed by the fetched results
    // controller.
    NSManagedObjectContext *context =
        [fetchedResultsController managedObjectContext];
    NSEntityDescription *entity =
        [[fetchedResultsController fetchRequest] entity];


    // Generate 5 random numbers waiting 1 second between them.
    for (int i=0; i<5; i++){
        NSManagedObject *newManagedObject =
            [NSEntityDescription insertNewObjectForEntityForName:[entity name]
                                      inManagedObjectContext:context];

        [newManagedObject
            setValue:[NSNumber numberWithInt:1 + arc4random() % 10000]
            forKey:@"randomNumber"];

        //  Simulate long synchronous blocking call
        sleep(1);

    }

    // Save the context.
    NSError *error = nil;
    if (![context save:&error]) {
        NSLog(@"Unresolved error %@, %@", error, [error userInfo]);
        abort();
    }
}
```

The method first obtains a reference to the context, and then creates an entity description based on the entity that the fetched results controller manages. In the `for` loop, you create a new managed object to hold your random number. Then, you generate a random number and assign it to the `randomNumber` attribute of your new managed object. Then you call the `sleep` function to sleep the thread for 1 second. Sleep is a blocking call, so you use it here to simulate some code that takes a significant amount of time to execute. Finally, you save the context.

Build and run the application. When the application starts, tap the plus sign in the top-right corner of the interface to invoke the `insertNewObject` method and generate some random numbers. Try to scroll the `TableView` while you generate the random numbers. Notice how the user interface becomes unresponsive while you are generating the random numbers. The synchronous call to `sleep` is blocking the main thread, which controls the UI. In about 5 seconds, you will see the random numbers appear in the interface and control will return to the user.

Moving the Blocking Call

Clearly, this is not a good situation for your application. Your users will be confused when the application doesn't respond when they try to scroll the list while the application is generating random numbers. You solve this problem by creating an `NSOperation` subclass and then moving the code to generate the random numbers onto a new thread.

Create a new Objective-C class that is a subclass of `NSObject` and call it `RandomOperation`. In the header file `RandomOperation.h`, change the base class from `NSObject` to `NSOperation`.

Remember that Core Data is inherently not thread-safe. When you use Core Data with threads, the key is to create a separate context on each thread. You create a context against a Persistent Store Coordinator. You need to write an initializer for your operation that accepts a Persistent Store Coordinator. You then use that coordinator to create a new context into which you will add your random numbers.

In the header file, add an instance variable and property for the coordinator. You should note that you do not need to retain the coordinator because you will only hold a pointer to the shared coordinator. Finally, add an `init` method called `initWithPersistentStoreCoordinator` that accepts `NSPersistentStoreCoordinator` as an input parameter. Here is the `RandomOperation` header:

```
#import <Foundation/Foundation.h>

@interface RandomOperation: NSOperation  {
    NSPersistentStoreCoordinator *coordinator;
}

-(id) initWithPersistentStoreCoordinator:(NSPersistentStoreCoordinator*)coord;

@property (nonatomic,assign) NSPersistentStoreCoordinator *coordinator;

@end
```

RandomOperation.h

Let's move on to the `RandomOperation` implementation file. In the implementation, synthesize the property and implement the `initWithPersistentStoreCoordinator` method like this:

```
@synthesize coordinator;

-(id) initWithPersistentStoreCoordinator:(NSPersistentStoreCoordinator*)coord
{
    if (self == [super init]) {
        self.coordinator = coord;
    }

    return self;

}
```

RandomOperation.m

All you are doing in this method is calling the superclass `init` method and then storing the `NSPersistentStoreCoordinator` input parameter in the class `coordinator` property.

Next, implement the `dealloc` method to call `dealloc` on the superclass:

```
-(void) dealloc {
    [super dealloc];
}
```

RandomOperation.m

Now, you need to implement the `main` method to actually do the work:

```
-(void) main {

    // Create a context using the persistent store coordinator
    NSManagedObjectContext *managedObjectContext;

    if (self.coordinator != nil) {
        managedObjectContext = [[NSManagedObjectContext alloc] init];
        [managedObjectContext setPersistentStoreCoordinator: self.coordinator];
    }
    else {
        return;
    }

    // Generate 5 random numbers waiting 1 second between them.
    for (int i=0; i<5; i++){
        NSManagedObject *newManagedObject =
        [NSEntityDescription insertNewObjectForEntityForName:@"Event"
                             inManagedObjectContext:managedObjectContext];

        [newManagedObject
         setValue:[NSNumber numberWithInt:1 + arc4random() % 10000]
```

```
        forKey:@"randomNumber"];

        //  Simulate long synchronous blocking call
        sleep(1);
    }

    // Save the context.
    NSError *error = nil;
    if (![managedObjectContext save:&error]) {
        NSLog(@"Unresolved error %@, %@", error, [error userInfo]);
        abort();
    }

    // Clean up
    [managedObjectContext release];
}
```

RandomOperation.m

Most of this method is the same as the `insertNewObject` method from the `RootViewController`. The major difference is that in the first part of the method, you use the class pointer to the Persistent Store Coordinator to create a new managed object context. There is some added safety code here to return from the method if you do not have a pointer to a valid coordinator. You then proceed to create Managed Objects containing the random numbers just as you did in `insertNewObject`. Finally, you call `save` on the context and release the local context. You are finished with the `RandomOperation` class.

Back in the `RootViewController`, you need to change the `insertNewObject` method to use your operation. At the top of the implementation file, add `#include` for the `RandomOperation` header and another `#include` to include the app delegate:

```
#import "RandomOperation.h"
#import "RandomNumbersAppDelegate.h"
```

RootViewController.m

You will get a reference to the coordinator from the app delegate and pass it into your `RandomOperation` in the initializer.

Delete all of the existing code from the `insertNewObject` method because you have moved this code into your `RandomOperation` class. You do, however, need to implement the `insertNewObject` method to use your `RandomOperation` class. The following is the implementation of `insertNewObject`:

```
- (void)insertNewObject {
    // Create an instance of NSOperationQueue
    NSOperationQueue* operationQueue = [[NSOperationQueue alloc] init];

    // Get a reference to the app delegate to get the coordinator
```

```
        RandomNumbersAppDelegate* appDelegate =
            [UIApplication sharedApplication].delegate;

        // Create an instance of the operation
        RandomOperation* ourOperation =
            [[RandomOperation alloc]
                initWithPersistentStoreCoordinator:
                    appDelegate.persistentStoreCoordinator];

        // Add the operation to the operation queue
        [operationQueue addOperation:ourOperation];

        // Clean up
        [ourOperation release];
        [operationQueue release];

    }
```

RootViewController.m

First, you create an instance of the NSOperationQueue that you will use to hold and execute your operation. Next, you get a reference to the App Delegate that you will use to get a reference to the Persistent Store Coordinator. Then, you create an instance of your RandomOperation class and pass it a reference to the Persistent Store Coordinator. Finally, you call the addOperation method on the operation queue to add your operation to the queue and instruct the queue to execute your operation. Last, you release the variables that you allocated in the method.

Before you run the application, you need to modify the App Delegate to expose the Persistent Store Coordinator property. In the RandomNumbersAppDelegate, move the interface declaration for the Core Data Stack properties out of the implementation file and into the header. Remove the @interface and @end beginning and ending tags. You need the coordinator to be public so that you can retrieve it when you go to create your operation. The app delegate header file should look like this:

```
#import <UIKit/UIKit.h>
#import <CoreData/CoreData.h>

@interface RandomNumbersAppDelegate : NSObject <UIApplicationDelegate> {

    NSManagedObjectModel *managedObjectModel;
    NSManagedObjectContext *managedObjectContext;
    NSPersistentStoreCoordinator *persistentStoreCoordinator;

    UIWindow *window;
    UINavigationController *navigationController;
}

@property (nonatomic, retain) IBOutlet UIWindow *window;
@property (nonatomic, retain) IBOutlet UINavigationController
    *navigationController;

@property (nonatomic, retain, readonly) NSManagedObjectModel
    *managedObjectModel;
```

```
@property (nonatomic, retain, readonly) NSManagedObjectContext
    *managedObjectContext;
@property (nonatomic, retain, readonly) NSPersistentStoreCoordinator
    *persistentStoreCoordinator;

- (NSString *)applicationDocumentsDirectory;

@end
```

RandomNumbersAppDelegate.h

Delete your old version of the application from the simulator to delete the old Core Data database. Now run the program and click the plus button to add some new random numbers. You will notice that the interface is now responsive while you are generating the random numbers. However, there is one problem: the numbers never appear. If you wait a few seconds, quit the application, and then restart it, you will see five new numbers in the TableView. The problem is that the context in the RootViewController is unaware that you have added records to the Core Data database on another thread, so the FetchedResultsController has not updated the TableView.

Fortunately, there is a way to handle this. Whenever a context performs a save, the context sends out an NSManagedObjectContextDidSaveNotification notification. The NSManagedObjectContext class has a method - (void)mergeChangesFromContextDidSaveNotification:(NSNotification *)notification that accepts a notification and merges the changes contained in the notification into the context. Therefore, you need to write some code to listen for and handle the notification. When you receive the notification, you need to call mergeChangesFromContextDidSaveNotification: to merge the changes into the context on the main thread.

In the viewDidLoad method in the RootViewController, you need to get a reference to the default notification center and add self as an observer for the NSManagedObjectContextDidSaveNotification message. You do this at the end of viewDidLoad. The following is the revised viewDidLoad method:

```
- (void)viewDidLoad {
    [super viewDidLoad];

    // Set up the edit and add buttons.
    self.navigationItem.leftBarButtonItem = self.editButtonItem;

    UIBarButtonItem *addButton = [[UIBarButtonItem alloc]
        initWithBarButtonSystemItem:UIBarButtonSystemItemAdd
                          target:self
                          action:@selector(insertNewObject)];
    self.navigationItem.rightBarButtonItem = addButton;
    [addButton release];

    NSError *error = nil;
    if (![[self fetchedResultsController] performFetch:&error]) {
        NSLog(@"Unresolved error %@, %@", error, [error userInfo]);
        abort();
    }

    // Add an observer for the NSManagedObjectContextDidSaveNotification message
```

```
        NSNotificationCenter* notificationCenter =
            [NSNotificationCenter defaultCenter];

    [notificationCenter addObserver:self
                          selector:@selector(contextSaved:)
                              name:NSManagedObjectContextDidSaveNotification
                            object:nil ];
    }
```

RootViewController.m

Any time that the `save` method is called on any context, Core Data generates an
`NSManagedObjectContextDidSaveNotification` message. You are now listening for this message,
and when you receive it, you will execute the `contextSaved` method in the `RootViewController`.
Now, all you have to do is implement the `contextSaved` method to take the notification and call
`mergeChangesFromContextDidSaveNotification`:

```
-(void) contextSaved:(NSNotification*)notification
{
    [self.managedObjectContext
        mergeChangesFromContextDidSaveNotification:notification];
}
```

RootViewController.m

The last thing that you need to do is implement `dealloc` to remove `self` as an observer on the
notification center:

```
- (void)dealloc {
    [fetchedResultsController release];
    [managedObjectContext release];
    [[NSNotificationCenter defaultCenter] removeObserver:self];
    [super dealloc];
}
```

RootViewController.m

Delete your old version of the application from the simulator to delete the old Core Data database.
Build and run the application. Click the plus button. Notice how the UI is still responsive. In a few
moments, the save occurs, the notification is sent, `contextSaved` is called, the changes are merged
into the context, and the `FetchedResultsController` updates the table with the new random
numbers. You have successfully moved a time-consuming blocking call off the main thread and on
to another thread.

CORE DATA PERFORMANCE

When designing and building an application, one of your primary concerns should be performance.
In the context of data-driven applications, let's look at a few specific aspects of overall application
performance.

The first aspect to consider is *perceived performance*. Perceived performance can be defined as how quickly your application appears to complete a task. The key word in this definition is *appears*.

The threading program that you built in the last section is a perfect example of perceived performance. In the first phase of the example, when your user interface was frozen, you probably felt that the performance of the application was poor because it locked up for 5 seconds as it generated the random numbers. After you moved the random number generation to another thread, the application probably felt much snappier, even though the length of time from when you tapped the plus button to the time when the random numbers appeared in the TableView was exactly the same. The difference was that the interface was responsive so you perceived the application to be working more quickly.

You have already learned how to use threading as a tool for increasing the responsiveness and therefore the perceived performance of your application. In this section, I will focus on another aspect of iOS programming that has a great impact on performance — memory management. On embedded devices such as the iPhone and iPad, you need to be particularly concerned about memory as the iOS does not currently support virtual memory or paging. If your application runs low on memory, the OS will tell certain parts of your application to unload. This will cause a time-consuming re-initialization to occur when the user needs to use these parts of your application again. Additionally, it is possible that your application can run out of memory, causing the OS to terminate your application.

After you look at some memory management items, you will look at a few ways that you can increase the actual speed of your applications.

Faulting

Core Data uses a technique called *faulting* to reduce the memory footprint of your application by keeping unused data out of memory. Faulted objects are instances of `NSManagedObject` or your `NSManagedObject` subclass that are retrieved in a fetch request, but not all of the properties of the object are immediately loaded into memory. Core Data can conserve memory by loading only the parts of an object or a relationship that you need.

Core Data does not populate a faulted object's properties until you access them. This process, called *fault realization*, happens automatically. You do not have to execute a fetch to realize a fault, but behind the scenes, Core Data may need to execute additional fetches to realize faults.

Faulting most often occurs when objects are associated with relationships. If you recall the sample from Chapter 6, "Modeling Data in Xcode," you had two entities, Task and Location, as illustrated in Figure 9-7. On the All Tasks screen, you queried Core Data for a list of all Tasks. Because the Task entity has a relationship entity, you would think that Core Data would load the related Location object into memory as well. However, it does not. The Location entity in this instance is faulted. Core Data has no reason to load a related Location object into memory unless the code asks for it.

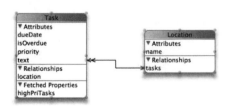

FIGURE 9-7: Tasks application data model

Core Data does not bring relationships to a faulted object into memory until you access them. This behavior allows Core Data to conserve memory by keeping unused objects out of memory until you need them.

In this example, Core Data is preventing only one object, the Location, from being loaded. You may be thinking that this doesn't save too much memory. That is true, but imagine if the location object were also related to a series of other objects, each with its own relations, and so on. In large object hierarchies, the memory conserved by faulting can be considerable.

Data Store Types

When using Core Data, you can specify the type of data store that Core Data uses to persist your data. Your options are SQLite, binary, and in-memory. Although you will usually use the SQLite store type, you will take a brief look at all of the types.

The in-memory store does not actually persist your data at all. As the name says, the data store is in memory. When your application quits, your data is gone. This could be useful in situations where you want to use Core Data to manage your application data when that data does not need to be persisted from session to session. This is typically not very useful in iOS applications as your application session could end at any time, particularly if the user of an iPhone gets a call.

The binary store type uses a proprietary binary format to store your data. The primary drawback of using the binary format is that all of the data stored in the data store is loaded into memory when the data store is loaded. There is no provision to leave parts of the data on disk. In contrast, an SQLite database remains largely left on disk and Core Data only brings the parts that you specifically query for into memory.

Although there is no "disk" on the iPhone or iPad, there is a difference between application memory and storage memory. When I say "on disk," I am referring to the space on the device that is used for data storage. The iPhone or iPad cannot use this storage space to execute applications, so there is a distinction between the application memory available for use by your application's execution and disk space, which is available for data storage.

Storing Binary Data

You may be tempted to store binary data such as images or sound clips in your Managed Objects using Core Data. In general, this is not a good idea. You are generally better off storing the binary data on disk and storing the path to the data in Core Data as you did in the catalog example earlier in the book because you may store a large chunk of data in an object and not realize that you are bringing all of that data into memory when Core Data loads the object. For example, if you stored the images for each of your catalog items in the database, but did not display them on the main catalog screen, these potentially large images would still be loaded into memory.

If you do store binary data in Core Data, do not store the data in frequently accessed rows. For example, you should not store an image in the same managed object that you use to display items in a table if you are not also displaying the image because the image will be loaded into memory regardless of whether you display the image or not.

Entity Inheritance

You may remember from Chapter 6 that you can implement an entity hierarchy in Core Data using inheritance and the parent field of an entity in the entity detail pane. I have illustrated a hypothetical entity hierarchy in Figure 9-8.

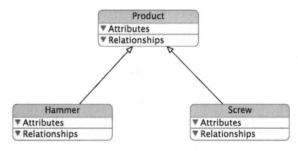

FIGURE 9-8: Entity inheritance hierarchy

Although this is a feature of Core Data, you need to be aware of how the implementation uses memory in the back-end SQLite data store. An entity hierarchy is not the same as the equivalent object hierarchy in an object-oriented design. In the entity hierarchy, all of the attributes of all of the entities in the hierarchy are stored in the same database table. This can lead to inefficiency in how the data is stored on disk, causing excessive memory usage.

To illustrate this, imagine that in the hierarchy illustrated in Figure 9-8, the Product entity has attributes P1 and P2, the Hammer has attributes H1 and H2, and the Screw has attributes S1 and S2. In the current implementation of Core Data, Core Data stores the data for all three of these entities in a single table, as illustrated in Figure 9-9. You can see that the Hammer entities have unused space in the table for the Screw-related fields and vice versa for Screw objects. Although this is a simple example, it illustrates the storage issue. The problem gets worse as your inheritance hierarchy gets larger and deeper.

Record	Product		Hammer		Screw	
	P1	P2	H1	H2	S1	S2
Hammer 1	value	value	value	value		
Hammer 2	value	value	value	value		
Hammer 3	value	value	value	value		
Screw 1	value	value			value	value
Screw 2	value	value			value	value
Screw 3	value	value			value	value

FIGURE 9-9: Core Data storage for entity inheritance

Runtime Performance

This chapter covered improving perceived performance with threading and being conscious of how Core Data is using memory. In this section, I will just lay out a few general tips that you can look to in an attempt to increase the runtime performance of your application.

First, when designing your model, avoid over-normalization of your data. Remember that you are not designing a relational database but an object persistence mechanism. Feel free to de-normalize your data if it makes building the displays for the application easier. You should try to find a balance between normalization and speeding up your queries for rapid display. Accessing data through a relationship is more expensive than retrieving an attribute. Consider this before normalizing your data. In addition, querying across relationships is expensive. Determine if you really need to do it, or de-normalize the data if it makes sense. For example, if you have an application that stores names and addresses, it may make sense from a UI perspective to keep the state name in the same table as the rest of the address as opposed to normalizing it out into its own table. You may not want to take the overhead penalty for following a relationship to a state table every time that you need to look up an address if you will always be showing the address and state together.

I know that it may seem obvious, but you should try to fetch only the data that you need when you need it. This tip ties in with the "Faulting" section from earlier in the chapter. Core Data will generally not bring in data that you are not going to use. Therefore, you should be careful to avoid building your queries in a way that forces Core Data to bring data into memory that you may not need.

Another thing that you can do to increase your application performance is take advantage of Core Data caching. The Persistent Store Coordinator holds fetched results in its caches. This is particularly useful when you can set up a background thread to fetch data while the foreground remains responsive. Then, the foreground thread can read the data from the persistent coordinator's cache when necessary, avoiding another trip to the data store.

The final tip has to do with the order of the items in your search predicate. Search order in predicates is important. Put likely-to-fail criteria first so the comparison can end quickly. The engine evaluates predicates in order, and if one part of the predicate fails, the engine will move on to the next record. You can potentially reduce query times by placing likely-to-fail criteria at the beginning of a predicate if it makes sense.

Managing Changes with the Fetched Results Controller

In this section, you will look at how you can use NSFetchedResultsController to update your TableView based on changes to a result set.

When the data managed by NSFetchedResultsController changes, the fetched results controller calls several delegate methods. You have the option to either use these delegate methods to update the associated TableView based on each individual change, or simply handle one delegate method and tell the TableView to reload its data.

Implementing the delegate methods to handle individual updates can yield better performance because you are not reloading all of the table data each time there is an update. There is a tradeoff, however, because if there are many simultaneous changes to the data, it may be cheaper to just reload all of the data because presenting many individual changes can be time consuming.

To keep the Tasks application simple, I took the latter approach. In the RootViewController, you implemented the controllerDidChangeContent delegate method to reload the data for the TableView. Here is the implementation:

Available for download on Wrox.com

```
- (void)controllerDidChangeContent:(NSFetchedResultsController *)controller {
    [self.taskTableView reloadData];
}
```

RootViewController.m

Compare how you just reloaded all of the data for the table in the Tasks application to how you handle individual cell updates in the random numbers application. In the random numbers project, you handled each update individually by accepting the template code for the RootViewControllers. The delegate methods that the NSFetchedResultsController calls are `controllerWillChangeContent:`, `controller:didChangeSection:atIndex:forChangeType`, `controller:didChangeObject:atIndexPath:forChangeType:newIndexPath:`, and `controllerDidChangeContent:`.

The `FetchedResultsController` calls the `controllerWillChangeContent:` and `controllerDidChangeContent:` methods to bracket the changes that are being made to the result set. You implement these methods to tell the table that changes will begin and end respectively. You can think of these methods as beginning and committing a transaction to the table. Here is the implementation in the RandomNumbers example:

```
- (void)controllerWillChangeContent:(NSFetchedResultsController *)controller {
    [self.tableView beginUpdates];
}

- (void)controllerDidChangeContent:(NSFetchedResultsController *)controller {
    [self.tableView endUpdates];
}
```

RootViewController.m

This code simply tells the TableView that updates are coming and that updates are finished. The `endUpdates` call triggers the TableView to display and optionally animate the changes to the data.

The `FetchedResultsController` calls the `controller:didChangeSection:atIndex:forChangeType` method when the sections of the TableView should change. The two types of changes that you will receive in this method are `NSFetchedResultsChangeInsert` and `NSFetchedResultsChangeDelete`. Your code will be able to determine if the changes to the data have added or removed a section from the TableView. Typically, you will implement a `switch` statement to handle these two cases, as shown in the RandomNumbers sample:

```
- (void)controller:(NSFetchedResultsController *)controller
      didChangeSection:(id <NSFetchedResultsSectionInfo>)sectionInfo
             atIndex:(NSUInteger)sectionIndex
        forChangeType:(NSFetchedResultsChangeType)type {

    switch(type) {
        case NSFetchedResultsChangeInsert:
            [self.tableView insertSections:
             [NSIndexSet indexSetWithIndex:sectionIndex]
                        withRowAnimation:UITableViewRowAnimationFade];
            break;

        case NSFetchedResultsChangeDelete:
            [self.tableView deleteSections:
             [NSIndexSet indexSetWithIndex:sectionIndex]
                        withRowAnimation:UITableViewRowAnimationFade];
            break;
    }
}
```

RootViewController.m

This code simply inserts or deletes the section that it receives in the method call.

Finally, the FetchedResultsController calls the controller:didChangeObject:atIndexPath:
forChangeType:newIndexPath: method when objects in the data store change. In this
method, your code needs to handle these four operations: NSFetchedResultsChangeInsert,
NSFetchedResultsChangeDelete, NSFetchedResultsChangeMove, and
NSFetchedResultsChangeUpdate. Again, you will usually handle calls to this method in
a switch statement and make the appropriate changes to your TableView as you did in the
RandomNumbers example:

```objc
- (void)controller:(NSFetchedResultsController *)controller didChangeObject:(id)anObject
       atIndexPath:(NSIndexPath *)indexPath
       forChangeType:(NSFetchedResultsChangeType)type
     newIndexPath:(NSIndexPath *)newIndexPath {

    UITableView *tableView = self.tableView;

    switch(type) {

        case NSFetchedResultsChangeInsert:
            [tableView insertRowsAtIndexPaths:
             [NSArray arrayWithObject:newIndexPath]
                         withRowAnimation:UITableViewRowAnimationFade];
            break;

        case NSFetchedResultsChangeDelete:
            [tableView deleteRowsAtIndexPaths:
             [NSArray arrayWithObject:indexPath]
                         withRowAnimation:UITableViewRowAnimationFade];
            break;

        case NSFetchedResultsChangeUpdate:
            [self configureCell:[tableView
                                 cellForRowAtIndexPath:indexPath]
                    atIndexPath:indexPath];
            break;

        case NSFetchedResultsChangeMove:
            [tableView deleteRowsAtIndexPaths:
             [NSArray arrayWithObject:indexPath]
                         withRowAnimation:UITableViewRowAnimationFade];
            [tableView insertRowsAtIndexPaths:
             [NSArray arrayWithObject:newIndexPath]
                         withRowAnimation:UITableViewRowAnimationFade];
            break;
    }
}
```

RootViewController.m

PERFORMANCE ANALYSIS USING INSTRUMENTS

When confronted with a performance issue in your application, the first place that you should turn is Instruments. Instruments is a GUI-based tool that you can use to profile your application in myriad ways. Instruments features a plug-in architecture that allows you to pick and choose from a library of recording instruments to use in profiling your application, as shown in Figure 9-10. Additionally, you can create custom instruments that use DTrace to examine the execution of your application.

Once you have selected the recording instruments that you would like to use, you can use Instruments to run your application, either in the iPhone Simulator or on the actual device, and gather the data that you

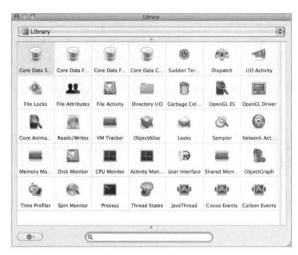

FIGURE 9-10: Instruments tool library

need to optimize your application. After you start your application, Instruments will profile the application in the background as the application runs. As your application is running, you will see the graphs in Instruments react to operations that you perform in the application.

The main feature of the tool's interface is the timeline. The premise is that you are recording the operation of your application in real-time and can later go back and look at the state of your application at any time during your test run. This is an incredibly powerful tool to use when trying to find problems in your application.

Once you narrow down a particular problem to a specific time on the timeline, you can drill down into the application stack. The stack provides information on the code that was executing at the time that Instruments took the sample. You can select your code segments in the stack to view the source code.

Typically, the biggest problems that you will find in your application are issues with memory management and leaks. Instruments has a couple of tools, ObjectAlloc and Leaks, that can be extremely helpful in detecting and crushing these often-illusive bugs. You will take a closer look at using these tools in Appendix A.

Instruments is an incredibly powerful tool and I cannot recommend it enough. If you have never used Instruments, you owe it to yourself to take a closer look at the tool. In this section, I walk you through the use of Instruments to profile your Core Data application using the Core Data–related tools.

Starting Instruments

In general, you can either start the Instruments tool by simply launching the application that is located, by default, in /YourDriveName/Developer/Applications or by selecting Run ➪ Run With Performance Tool from the menu bar in Xcode. Unfortunately, Apple does not support the

Core Data instruments for use with the iPhone or iPad. However, there is a workaround that you can use because Core Data notifications are broadcast system-wide and the iPhone simulator is not sandboxed from the rest of the Mac OS X operating system.

Even though Core Data is grayed out as an option in the "Run with Performance Tool" menu item, you can use the Core Data instruments with the Instruments tool. You first need to get Instruments to recognize your application as an instrument target. Open the RandomNumbers project in Xcode. The easiest way to get your project into instruments is to use the Run with Performance Tool ➪ CPU sampler menu item in Xcode. This will find your project binary and start it in Instruments while running the CPU sampler.

Because you want to use the Core Data tools and not the CPU sampler, you need to stop the Instruments session and add the Core Data tools to the instrumentation. Press the red button to stop recording. Now, Instruments knows where to find the RandomNumbers application.

Close the current window and discard the results of the CPU sampler run. From the Instruments menu bar, select File ➪ New to create a new instrument session. The new dialog displays a set of templates that you can use to create your Trace Document. Select All under Mac OS X in the left pane and select Core Data in the right pane. Finally, click Choose to create your new document. You should see a new Instruments window with three Core Data Instruments in the left-hand Instruments pane.

You now have to tell Instruments which program you want to execute. Open the Default Target pull down at the top of the window. Select Launch Executable ➪ RandomNumbers as shown in Figure 9-11.

FIGURE 9-11: Setting the Default Target

You are now ready to begin your test run. Click the red Record button in the top left of the application to start your recording. You will see the RandomNumbers application start up in the simulator. Once the application starts, you should see the timeline begin to move indicating that Instruments is profiling your application. You should also notice a spike in the top instrument, Core Data Fetches. This indicates that a fetch has occurred in the application. Tap the plus button in the simulator to generate some random numbers. In 5 seconds, you should see a spike in the Core Data Saves instrument indicating that a save has occurred. Stop the recording by clicking the red button.

The Instruments Interface

Now that you have finished your test run, you will want to analyze your data. To do this, you should understand how to use the Instruments interface. You can see the interface as it should look having completed your test run in Figure 9-12.

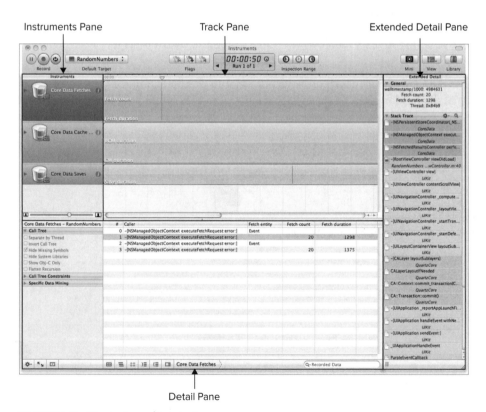

FIGURE 9-12: The Instruments interface

The Instruments pane shows all of the instruments that are active for the current test run.

The Track pane shows a graph representing different things for different instruments. For the Core Data Fetches instrument, the Track pane shows the count of items fetched and the duration of the fetch. The Track pane displays the time that an event occurred during the test run. You can adjust the time scale using the slider below the Instruments pane. You can also scroll the Track pane using the scrollbar at the bottom of the pane.

Below the Track pane is the Detail pane. Like the Track pane, the Detail pane shows different details based on the tool that you have selected in the Instruments pane. For the Core Data Fetches instrument, the Detail pane displays a sequence number, the caller of the fetch method, the fetched entity, the count of the number of items returned in the fetch, and the duration of the fetch in microseconds.

You can select an item in the Detail pane to view more detail about the item in the Extended Detail pane. The Extended Detail pane is particularly useful because it shows a stack trace for the method call that you have selected in the Detail pane. Select a fetch in the Detail pane to view its stack trace.

I find it useful to display the file icons in the Extended Detail pane because doing this makes the calls in the stack that originated in your code obvious. You can enable the file icons by clicking on the gear icon in the Extended Details pane. In Figure 9-12, you can see that the fetch selected in the Detail pane is initiated in the code in the `RootViewController viewDidLoad` method. If you double-click on an item in the call stack that corresponds to one of your source code files, in this case the call to the `RootViewController viewDidLoad` method, Instruments will display the source code in the Detail pane, showing you the exact line of code that made the fetch request. Click the Event List View button at the bottom left of the Detail pane to get back from the source code to the list of events.

The Core Data Instruments

Four instruments are available for use with Core Data: Core Data Saves, Fetches, Faults, and Cache Misses.

Core Data Saves reports the methods that invoke the Core Data save operation. It also reports the duration of the operation in microseconds. Opening the extended detail view shows the stack trace for the call and the time at which the call occurred.

You can use this tool to discover how often you are saving data and find a balance between saving too much and not saving enough. Each save operation causes a disk write, which can hurt performance, but not saving often enough results in using excess memory to hold the data in memory.

Core Data Fetches reports all fetches made against Core Data. The tool reports the name of the fetched entity, the caller, the number of records returned, and the duration of the fetch in microseconds. Opening the extended detail view shows the stack trace for the call and the time at which the call occurred.

Fetch operations are costly as they read from disk. You can use this tool to help optimize your search predicates to limit the number of rows returned by a fetch request.

Core Data Faults reports fault events that occur as the result of needing to realize object references in to-many relationships. The tool reports the method causing the fault, the object that was faulted, the execution duration in microseconds, the relationship fault source, the name of the relationship, and the relationship fault duration in microseconds. You can open the extended detail view to see the stack trace for the call and the time at which the call occurred.

As discussed earlier in this chapter, faulting is a memory-saving technique that comes at the expense of time when Core Data realizes the fault. If you find that Core Data is spending an excessive amount of time resolving faults, but your memory consumption is low, you could consider pre-fetching related objects instead of having them realized through a fault.

The Cache Misses tool reports fault events that result in cache misses. This is a subset of the information provided by the Faults instrument. The tool displays the method that caused the cache miss, the duration of execution for the fault handler in microseconds, the relationship cache miss source, the name of the relationship, and the relationship cache miss duration. Opening the extended detail view shows the stack trace for the call and the time at which the call occurred.

Similar to the remedy for extensive faulting, you can mitigate cache misses by pre-fetching data. If data is not in the cache, it leads to an expensive read from disk operation.

MOVING FORWARD

In this chapter, you learned how to version your data models and migrate between versions to help you add new features to your database and application. I also covered how to safely use Core Data in a threaded application with NSOperation to increase performance. You looked at some Core Data performance considerations and tips. Finally, you learned how to use the Instruments tool to observe your application's performance when using Core Data.

This ends the section of the book on Core Data. You should now feel confident that you are able to implement a data-driven application using this exciting and useful technology. You should also have all of the tools in your arsenal to be able to debug and troubleshoot problems that may arise while you are using Core Data.

In the next section of the book, you learn how to use XML and Web Services in your applications to communicate with other applications over the Internet.

PART III
Application Integration Using Web Services

10

Working with XML on the iPhone

WHAT'S IN THIS CHAPTER?

- ➤ Creating HTTP requests and receiving responses
- ➤ Understanding XML and how to use it in your applications
- ➤ Parsing XML to obtain the data that you need
- ➤ Using an external C library with your iPhone SDK applications
- ➤ Generating XML using the libxml library

In the first Part of the book, you learned how to get data out of an enterprise database and store it on the iPhone with SQLite. You also learned how to display data on the iPhone using the UITableView and customized UITableViewCell objects. In the second Part, you learned how to create and manage data on the iPhone using Core Data. In this section, you will learn how you can get your data off the device and into another system using XML and web services.

This chapter lays the groundwork for working with web services by showing you how to send data over the Web using the HTTP protocol and how to deal with the returned data in XML format.

You will learn how to communicate with external servers over the Web and how to deal with the response from a web server. I will cover the Cocoa classes that you will use in the following chapter for working with web services.

IPHONE SDK AND THE WEB

This section provides a quick refresh of the architecture of a Web-based application. Then you explore the classes in the iPhone SDK and the Cocoa framework that support network communication over the Web using the HTTP protocol. You finish this section by starting the chapter example, which will get data from the RSS feed for a web site and parse the returned XML.

Web Application Architecture

The majority of content on the Web, including web services, use HTTP (Hypertext Transfer Protocol) to communicate. HTTP is a standardized communication protocol that runs on top of the TCP/IP protocol that connects computers together. HTTP implements a request-response design like that typically used in client-server applications. The web server that deals out web pages is the server, and the web browser or application is the typical client.

In a request-response design, the client makes a request to the web server. Then, the web server processes the request and returns a response to the client, as illustrated in Figure 10-1.

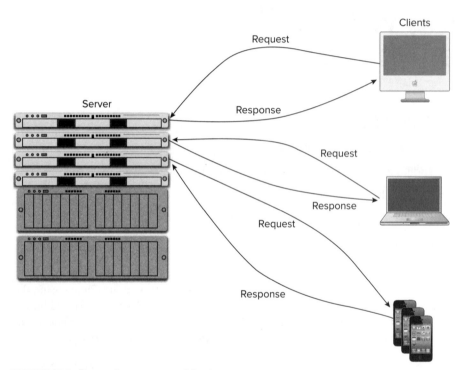

FIGURE 10-1: Request-response architecture

In order to initiate communication with a web site, you need a couple of basic elements. First, you need to know the address or the URL of the server to which you would like to connect. A URL, or Uniform Resource Locator, is a text representation of the numeric address of a web site. A name server then converts this text representation into a numbered IP address.

You can use a URL to create a request to ask a server for data. Then, you need to make a connection to the server and submit your request. If everything goes according to plan, the server will reply with a response that contains the data that you requested.

Synchronous Data Retrieval

The Cocoa framework provides helper methods on common classes to assist you in quickly and easily retrieving data from a web page. For instance, the NSString class has a class method called stringWithContentsOfURL:encoding:error: that you can use to create a string with the contents of a URL. Similarly, NSData supports the dataWithContentsOfURL: method, which you can use to retrieve arbitrary data from the Web.

As tempting as it may be to retrieve your web data with a single line of code, there are some serious drawbacks that you need to be aware of when considering this approach. First and foremost is that these operations are synchronous. If you call one of these helper methods on the main thread, your application will block until the call finishes. This may not seem like a huge limitation when running your iPhone sample code on your computer with a fast Internet connection. However, on a slow Internet connection such as 3G, or if you attempt to retrieve a large amount of data, the main thread could be tied up for a significant amount of time. Remember that your UI runs on this thread and that any long running operations on the main thread will cause your interface to become unresponsive.

Another issue is that these methods do not give you a lot of detail when a problem occurs with the call. Error handling is very important when working with Web-based services and networked calls in general. When writing networked code, you should code as defensively as possible. Network connections are notoriously unreliable. Your code should be able to handle cases where the connection may drop at any time. You should also code with the expectation that the service that you are calling may not be available or that it may return data that you are not expecting.

The stringWithContentsOfURL:encoding:error: helper call on NSString returns a reference to an NSError object that you can interrogate for details about the error. However, the NSData method simply returns nil if it cannot retrieve the desired data. This is not very good if you want to take different actions based on the type of error that occurs.

While the aforementioned class methods may be appropriate for simply retrieving data from a web site, you cannot use them to post data back to the site. Because the focus of this section of the book is on interacting with web services and exchanging data between the client and server, you won't be looking into these methods in any more detail. You should be aware that this functionality is available if you need or want to grab a little bit of data from the Web in a quick and dirty manner. However, I would not recommend using these methods in a production application for the reasons just discussed.

The URL Loading System

Apple calls the set of Cocoa classes included in the iPhone SDK for supporting communication using URLs and HTTP the *URL Loading System*. These classes support the request-response–based architecture described in the beginning of this section. You will take a brief look at the classes that make up this system and then move on to an example where you use this framework to connect to a web site and retrieve some data.

You use the NSURL and NSURLRequest classes to create the request that you will send to the server.

NSURL provides an object model that represents the address of a resource. You can use NSURL to reference local objects on the file system of a device as well as to find resources on a local network or the Internet.

The NSURLRequest class represents all of the data required to make a request to a web server, including its address as a URL. NSURLRequest objects are typically initialized by passing in an NSURL object. Additionally, the request can contain other data specific to the protocol, such as the HTTP method to use when submitting the request and HTTP header fields. If you need to modify these properties before submitting your request, you will need to use the NSMutableURLRequest type. You will see this in the next chapter when you look at sending POST requests to a web server.

Next, you will use the NSURLConnection class to make a connection to the server and submit your request. Once you submit your request via the connection, the framework calls the delegate methods of the NSURLConnection class based on the response received from the server.

Once enough data has come back from the server, the framework creates an NSURLResponse object and calls the delegate method connection:didReceiveResponse:. You can examine the response object to determine some information about the data that you will receive from the server including the expected content length and the encoding type of the incoming data.

Finally, you will implement the connection:didReceiveData: delegate method to accept the data returned by the server. This connection object will call this method multiple times, as data flows to your application from the web server. When the server is finished sending the response, the connection object calls the connectionDidFinishLoading: delegate method, at which point you can release the connection to the server and go about processing the data that you received. I have illustrated this process in Figure 10-2.

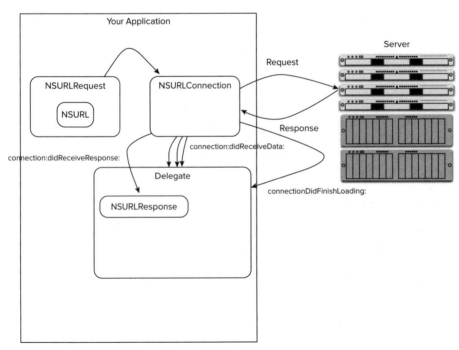

FIGURE 10-2: Request response process

In addition to the basic set of classes that you will typically use to handle URL requests and responses, the URL Loading System provides additional classes that you can use to support caching, authentication to secure sites and services, and cookies.

Web Access Sample

You should now have an understanding of the architecture behind making calls to a server over the Web and the classes that Apple provides to support this architecture. In this section, you will build an application that goes out over the Web and grabs the headlines from the RSS feed for CNN.com.

RSS stands for Really Simple Syndication. RSS is a well-defined schema for XML used to publish information to the Web. Newsreaders are applications that can consume RSS feeds and present the feed data to users. Apple's Safari browser has basic newsreader functionality, as does Mail.app.

The only thing that you typically need to access an RSS feed is the URL for the feed. After creating and sending a request for the feed's URL, the server processes the request and returns the XML data corresponding to the feed that you requested.

The first part of the example will use the URL Loading System classes that I described in the previous section to make a request for the top stories from CNN.com. You will simply dump the response to the console log in this example. After I cover parsing XML in the next section, you will add code to the sample to parse the data returned from the feed and display the title of each story in your interface. This may not be the most groundbreaking newsreader application, but it will introduce you to all of the technologies that you need to be able to use web services in the next chapter.

Starting the Application

Open Xcode and create a new View-based Application project. Call the new application RSSSample.

You will need a data object to hold the data that the server returns after calling it with your request. You also will need an action method to call when the user taps on a button in the application to start retrieving the feed data.

Open the `RSSSampleViewController.h` header file. Add an instance variable called `responseData` and the associated property for an `NSMutableData` object. This object will hold the data returned from the server in response to your web request.

You may not be familiar with the `NSData` class and its mutable subclass `NSMutableData`. `NSData` is a Cocoa wrapper for a byte buffer. Any time that you expect to handle a series of bytes, you will probably want to use `NSData`. If you need to modify that buffer, as you will in this example, you will need to use `NSMutableData`. In this example, you will be receiving the response data from the server in chunks. Each time you get a chunk, you will append it to your `receivedData` object. This is why you need to use `NSMutableData`.

Next, add an `IBAction` method called `buttonTapped`. You will hook this method up to a button in Interface Builder that will call this method. You will call this method when a user taps on the Send Request button that you add in Interface Builder in the next section.

The following is the header for the RSSSampleViewController:

```
#import <UIKit/UIKit.h>

@interface RSSSampleViewController : UIViewController {
    NSMutableData *responseData;
}

- (IBAction)buttonTapped:(id)sender;

@property (nonatomic,retain) NSMutableData *responseData;

@end
```

RSSSampleViewController.h

Now let's move on to the RSSSampleViewController implementation file. In the
RSSSampleViewController.m implementation file, synthesize the responseData property:

```
@synthesize responseData;
```

If you recall from previous chapters, I like to add a stub method for any UI-based action methods.
This way, you can run the application after you build the user interface and verify that you have all
of the actions and outlets properly connected. Add a stub method for the buttonTapped IBAction
method that logs the name of the method:

```
- (IBAction)buttonTapped:(id)sender {
    NSLog(@"buttonTapped");
}
```

Building the Interface

The next step in building the sample application is to build the user
interface. For the first part of the example, the user interface is very simple,
consisting of only a single button, as you can see from Figure 10-3.

To build the interface, you will need to open the
RSSSampleViewController.xib file in Interface Builder. Add a
UIButton to the view, resize the button as shown in Figure 10-3, and
change the text of the button to Send Request. Hook the Touch Up Inside
event of the button to the File's Owner buttonTapped method.

At this point in the example, that's all there is to the interface. You can
quit Interface Builder. To keep things simple, you will send the response
from the web server to the console log so that you can examine the
output. When you get to the XML parsing section, you will add a new
interface element to display the headlines retrieved from the RSS feed.

You are now ready to build and run the application. Once the application
comes up in the simulator, tap the button that you added in Interface
Builder. Make sure that you see the NSLog statement in the console log to
ensure that you have correctly hooked up the button to the code.

FIGURE 10-3: RSS sample
application interface

Requesting Data from the Server

When someone taps the Send Request button in the application interface, you want to make a request to CNN.com and get the contents of the RSS feed. In this section, you will use the classes in the URL Loading System framework to make a request to the server and handle the response.

Creating the Request

To make a request to a web server, you have to create an NSURLRequest object. There is a convenience method on the NSURLRequest that you can use to create the request with an NSURL object. Remember that you use the NSURL class to represent URLs. You can create an NSURL object using an NSString.

You will implement the buttonTapped method to create and submit the request to the CNN.com web server like this:

Available for download on Wrox.com

```
- (IBAction)buttonTapped:(id)sender {
    NSLog(@"buttonTapped");

    // Create the Request.
    NSURLRequest *request = [NSURLRequest requestWithURL:
        [NSURL URLWithString:@"http://rss.cnn.com/rss/cnn_topstories.rss"]
                cachePolicy:NSURLRequestUseProtocolCachePolicy
            timeoutInterval: 30.0];

    // Create the connection and send the request
    NSURLConnection *connection =
        [[NSURLConnection alloc] initWithRequest:request delegate:self];

    // Make sure that the connection is good
    if (connection) {
        // Instantiate the responseData data structure to store to response
        self.responseData = [NSMutableData data];
    }
    else {
        NSLog (@"The connection failed");
    }

}
```

RSSSampleViewController.m

The first thing that this code does is create an instance of an NSURLRequest object using the requestWithURL:cachePolicy:timeoutInterval: class method. You initialize the request by passing it an NSURL that you create from a string that points to the URL that you are interested in retrieving.

The cachePolicy parameter specifies how you want to handle obtaining the data for the request. You can either send the request directly to the server or attempt to retrieve the results from the cache. In this case, you specify the default caching policy specified by the protocol that you are using, in this case, HTTP.

You can pass another value in for this parameter to give you more fine-grained control of where the data for the request comes from:

➤ If you pass NSURLRequestReloadIgnoringLocalCacheData, the NSURLRequest object will ignore locally cached data and it will send the request to the server regardless of the data contained in the local cache.

➤ Passing NSURLRequestReloadIgnoringLocalAndRemoteCacheData has the same effect as passing NSURLRequestReloadIgnoringLocalCacheData, but it also instructs the object to ignore intermediary caches, such as those provided by proxy servers.

➤ NSURLRequestReturnCacheDataElseLoad instructs the request to always return data from the cache if it is available, and if it is not available to load the data from the server.

➤ Using NSURLRequestReturnCacheDataDontLoad instructs the request to use only cached data and to not attempt to get the data from the server if the data is not available in the cache. You could use this value to implement an Offline mode in your application.

➤ Passing NSURLRequestReloadRevalidatingCacheData allows the use of the cached data if the server validates that the cached data is current.

The final parameter in the requestWithURL:cachePolicy:timeoutInterval: method is the timeout interval. You use this to specify how long you want to wait for a response before failing with a timeout.

After creating the request, the code goes on to create a connection to the server by creating an instance of an NSURLConnection object. In the initializer, you pass in the request that you just created and declare the delegate for the connection to be self. Initializing the connection in this manner causes the NSURLConnection object to immediately send the request that you created to the server.

Finally, test that the connection is valid and then instantiate your responseData property that you will use to handle the data that the server returns to your application.

NSURLConnection Delegate Methods

Once you send your request to the server, the connection object will begin to call the delegate methods to inform you of the status of the request and response. You need to implement the delegate methods to handle the messages that the NSURLConnection is sending to you.

The first method that you will implement is connection:willSendRequest:redirectResponse:. The connection object calls this method when a redirect will occur based on the request made to the server. When making a request to a URL, the server will sometimes redirect your call to another server. Implementing this method handles that case. To proceed normally, simply return the request that the NSURLConnection object passed into the method. This is the proposed URL to which you will be redirected. You can return nil to prevent redirects from occurring. You should be prepared to receive this message multiple times if the web server performs multiple redirects. Here is the implementation:

Available for
download on
Wrox.com

```
// Called when a redirect will cause the URL of the request to change
- (NSURLRequest *)connection:(NSURLConnection *)connection
            willSendRequest:(NSURLRequest *)request
           redirectResponse:(NSURLResponse *)redirectResponse
```

```
{
    NSLog (@"connection:willSendRequest:redirectResponse:");
    return request;
}
```

The next delegate method is `connection:didReceiveAuthenticationChallenge:`. You will receive this message if the web server that you are calling requires authentication to complete the request. Because I am trying to keep this example simple to show the basics of using the URL Loading System, the example will not use any authentication. However, in a production application, you will often be required to authenticate to retrieve data from a URL.

When the `connection:didReceiveAuthenticationChallenge:` method is called, you can respond in one of three ways:

➤ Provide the necessary credentials by creating an `NSURLCredential` object and populating it with the data that the server expects. You can determine what the server expects by interrogating the `NSURLAuthenticationChallenge` object that you receive as a parameter to the `didReceiveAuthenticationChallenge:` method.

➤ Attempt to continue without passing credentials. You can do this by calling the `continueWithoutCredentialsForAuthenticationChallenge:` method on the sender of the challenge. Doing this will typically cause the request to fail, but it may allow the user to retrieve a URL that does not require authentication.

➤ Cancel the request by calling the `cancelAuthenticationChallenge` method on the sender of the challenge. Doing this will send the `connection:didCancelAuthenticationChallenge:` message to your delegate.

You can find more information about authentication in the "URL Loading System Programming Guide" in the Xcode help and on the Apple developer web site.

In this implementation, you will just log that the `NSURLconnection` object invoked this method:

```
// Called when the server requires authentication
- (void)connection:(NSURLConnection *)connection
    didReceiveAuthenticationChallenge:(NSURLAuthenticationChallenge *)challenge
{
    NSLog (@"connection:didReceiveAuthenticationChallenge:");
}
```

If you cancel the authentication challenge on the connection, the connection object calls the next delegate method, `connection:didCancelAuthenticationChallenge:`. Again, you implement this method by simply logging the call:

```
// Called when the authentication challenge is cancelled on the connection
- (void)connection:(NSURLConnection *)connection
    didCancelAuthenticationChallenge:(NSURLAuthenticationChallenge *)challenge
```

```
{
    NSLog (@"connection:didCancelAuthenticationChallenge:");
}
```

The next delegate method, `connection:didReceiveResponse:`, provides some useful information about the response received from the server. The connection object calls this method when the connection has enough data to create an `NSURLResponse` object. You can interrogate the response for some useful information such as encoding type and expected length:

Available for download on Wrox.com

```
// Called when the connection has enough data to create an NSURLResponse
- (void)connection:(NSURLConnection *)connection
    didReceiveResponse:(NSURLResponse *)response {
    NSLog (@"connection:didReceiveResponse:");
    NSLog(@"expectedContentLength: %qi", [response expectedContentLength] );
    NSLog(@"textEncodingName: %@", [response textEncodingName]);

    [self.responseData setLength:0];

}
```

It is possible to receive this method more than once, so to be safe, you discard the data in your received buffer when you receive a call to this method by setting the length of the `responseData` buffer to 0.

The next delegate method that you will implement is `connection:didReceiveData:`. The connection object calls this method each time the connection receives a chunk of data. You will receive calls to this method multiple times, as you receive data from the server. In the implementation, you append the data received in this method to the `responseData NSMutableData` instance. Remember that you need to use the mutable version of `NSData` because you will be appending data to the object each time this method runs. Here is the implementation:

Available for download on Wrox.com

```
// Called each time the connection receives a chunk of data
- (void)connection:(NSURLConnection *)connection didReceiveData:(NSData *)data
{
    NSLog (@"connection:didReceiveData:");

    // Append the received data to our responseData property
    [self.responseData appendData:data];

}
```

You will receive the `connection:willCacheResponse:` message before the connection caches the response. This method gives you a chance to change the cached response. There is a `userInfo` property that you can use to add information to the cached response before the connection object caches the response. You can implement this method to return `nil` if you do not want to cache the response. In the example, you will simply pass along the cached response:

```
// Called before the response is cached
- (NSCachedURLResponse *)connection:(NSURLConnection *)connection
                   willCacheResponse:(NSCachedURLResponse *)cachedResponse
{
    NSLog (@"connection:willCacheResponse:");
    // Simply return the response to cache
    return cachedResponse;
}
```

RSSSampleViewController.m

The last call that you receive will be either `connectionDidFinishLoading:` or `connection:didFailWithError:`. In the case of `connectionDidFinishLoading:`, the connection object calls this method when the connection has successfully received the complete response. The implementation takes the response data and converts it to a string for display in the console:

```
// Called when the connection has successfully received the complete response
- (void)connectionDidFinishLoading:(NSURLConnection *)connection
{
    NSLog (@"connectionDidFinishLoading:");

    // Convert the data to a string and log the response string
    NSString *responseString = [[NSString alloc]
                               initWithData:self.responseData
                               encoding:NSUTF8StringEncoding];
    NSLog(@"Response String: \n%@", responseString);

    [responseString release];
    // Free the connection
    [connection release];

}
```

RSSSampleViewController.m

The connection object calls the `connection:didFailWithError:` method when there is an error in receiving the response. This method simply dumps the error description to the log. In a production application, you will probably want to handle the error a little more robustly by possibly allowing the user to retry the operation, or at least providing some feedback as to why the operation failed. Here is the implementation:

```
// Called when an error occurs in loading the response
- (void)connection:(NSURLConnection *)connection
  didFailWithError:(NSError *)error
{
    NSLog (@"connection:didFailWithError:");
```

```
        NSLog (@"%@",[error localizedDescription]);

        // Free the connection
        [connection release];

    }
```

RSSSampleViewController.m

Finishing Up

You are just about ready to build and run your application. First, however, you need to implement `viewDidUnload` and `dealloc` to do some memory cleanup:

Available for download on Wrox.com

```
    - (void)viewDidUnload {
        // Release any retained subviews of the main view.
        // e.g. self.myOutlet = nil;
        self.responseData = nil;
    }

    - (void)dealloc {
        [responseData release];
        [super dealloc];
    }
```

RSSSampleViewController.m

Build and run the application. When the application starts, tap the Send Request button. Make sure that you have the console displayed by selecting Run ⇨ Console from the menu bar or by typing Command+Shift+R. If you have an active Internet connection, you should see a log entry in the console log for each delegate method as it runs. When the connection has finished downloading the data from the server, you should see the XML document that you retrieved from the CNN.com RSS feed.

 You need to have an active Internet connection for this code to work correctly.

XML AND THE IPHONE SDK

In this section, you learn about XML and how to integrate XML content into your application. You will extend the sample project to parse the XML contained in the response from the CNN.com web server using the `NSXMLParser` class.

Brief Overview of XML

XML (the eXtensible Markup Language) defines rules for the electronic transmission and storage of data. The W3C web standards body defines the XML 1.0 specification. You can find the entire specification at `http://www.w3.org/TR/REC-xml/`.

The goal of XML is to provide software engineers with a tool that they could use and extend to define arbitrary data. XML is extensible in that, unlike HTML or other markup languages, the designer can introduce and include arbitrary tags that make sense for his or her application. In conjunction with an arbitrary schema, the developer can provide a formal definition of the schema via XSD (XML Schema Definition) or DTD (Document Type Definition) files. Users of the XML data can then use these schema definitions to validate the XML document and ensure that it conforms to the defined schema.

There are many standardized schemas currently in use, including RSS (which you used in the chapter example), SOAP, Atom, and XHTML. Additionally, software vendors such as Apple and Microsoft use XML as the file storage format for many of their document-based software packages.

XML files are plain text and human readable, which helps make them easy for developers to deal with. XML files typically define data in a tree structure, as shown in Figure 10-4. Because the tree is a common software paradigm, programmers typically have little problem parsing and using the data contained in an XML file with this structure. The fact that the designer can make up his own tags makes XML extremely flexible to use while you are designing the structure of your data and messages.

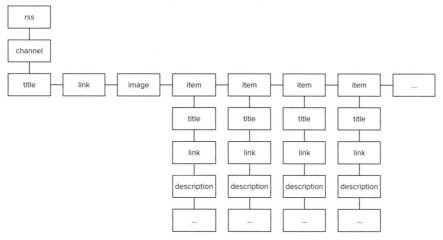

FIGURE 10-4: CNN.com RSS feed XML tree

You can use XML to store data locally. However, it is equally if not more common to use XML as a way to transfer data over the Internet. Many data transfer schemas, such as RSS and SOAP, rely on XML to exchange data. In the sample in the previous section, you received an XML response from the server in response to your request. In this section, you will learn how to parse that response to obtain the headlines contained in the feed.

Parsing XML with NSXML Parser

After you make a call to a web service or, in our case, an RSS feed, you often need to parse the XML response to get the data that you need for your application. There are a couple of different programming models when it comes to parsing XML, specifically, DOM and SAX.

DOM stands for Document Object Model. The DOM programming model represents the tree structure of XML as a tree of objects that you can access in your code. The objects in the DOM model represent Nodes, Attributes, Comments, and other XML elements. In your code, you can recursively navigate the tree or perform queries to return all nodes with a particular name, attribute, and so on.

When you use a DOM parser, the entire XML document that you are parsing is loaded into memory at one time. For large XML documents, a DOM model can consume quite a bit of memory. Because memory is such a scarce resource on mobile devices such as the iPhone and iPad, Apple chose not to provide a DOM parser with the SDK. However, if you need the functionality provided by a DOM parser, you can use the C library `libxml2`. I cover the use of `libxml2` later in this chapter in the section "Generating XML with libxml." Before you settle on using DOM, make sure that you consider the performance and memory implications of loading the entire XML document into memory.

The parser provided by Apple in the iPhone SDK is a SAX-based parser. SAX stands for Serial Access Parser. SAX implements an event-driven parser that calls delegate methods as the parser moves through an XML document. The parser navigates the XML document sequentially and calls methods in a defined order when it finds things like tags, attributes, and text characters. Apple has provided an event-driven SAX parser with the `NSXMLParser` class. While implementing the delegate methods to use a SAX parser can be cumbersome, it is far less resource intensive in terms of memory usage than using a DOM parser.

When you want to parse XML, you will typically follow a few specific steps. First, you need to locate the XML that you want to parse. You can obtain the XML from the Web through a URL, from a text file on a network or on the device, or from somewhere else and stored in an `NSData` object.

Once you have located your XML, you will create an instance of the `NSXMLParser` class. When you initialize your instance, you will pass in the XML data that you want to parse.

Once you have this code in place, you will need to code the delegate methods that the `NSXMLParser` calls as it encounters certain elements in the XML file.

The parser calls the `parserDidStartDocument` and `parserDidEndDocument` methods when it begins and finishes parsing the document respectively. You can add code to `parserDidStartDocument` to set up any variables that you intend to use during parsing. Likewise, you will want to clean up any of these variables in the `parserDidEndDocument` method.

When the parser encounters a start element or tag, it will call the `parser:didStartElement:namespaceURI:qualifiedName:attributes:` method. In this method, you will typically check to see which element was started and prepare to process the data within the element accordingly. The parser passes element attributes as a dictionary with the name of the attribute as the key in the dictionary and the value of the attribute as the value. The corresponding method that the parser calls when an element ends is `parser:didEndElement:namespaceURI:qualifiedName:`. In this method, you will typically take some action when an element that you are interested in has ended.

When the parser finds characters contained within an element, it calls the `parser:foundCharacters:` method. The parser may call this method multiple times for a single element, so you should append any characters sent to this method to a mutable string until you receive a `didEndElement` call. This is similar to the way that you handled the `connection:didReceiveData:` delegate method call from the `NSURLConnection` object earlier in this chapter.

If the parser encounters an error, it will call the `parser:parseErrorOccurred:` method. You should handle this method and provide some information to the user about the error that occurred.

Extending the Example, Parsing the XML

In this section, you will extend the example code that you developed in the first part of this chapter to get the CNN.com RSS feed from the Internet. You will take the XML document that you retrieve from the call to the web site, parse it, and display the titles of the headline stories.

Starting Out

Before you begin, you need to know what you are looking for in the XML that you retrieve from the server. Figure 10-5 shows a representative sample of the XML that you retrieve when you call the CNN.com RSS feed web site. You can download the complete XML file from this book's web site.

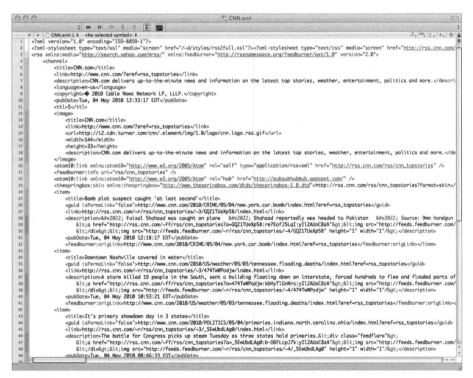

FIGURE 10-5: CNN.com RSS feed XML

You are interested in the `item` entities that encapsulate the information about a particular story item. Within the `item`, you only really want to grab the text inside the `title` element because your application will only display the title of each story. If you were building a more intricate application, you could create an item class with title, link, publication date, and description properties as well. However, for simplicity, you will only capture and display the title of the article.

Setting Up to Parse

If you do not have the RSSSample project open, open it now. You need to add an instance variable to the RSSSampleViewController to hold the characters captured from the XML for the title. In the RSSSampleViewController.h header, add an instance variable:

```
NSMutableString *capturedCharacters;
```

Notice that you use an object of type NSMutableString. You must use a mutable string because you will be appending to the current string each time you get a delegate method call to the parser: foundCharacters: method. Keep in mind that the NSString class is immutable, meaning that you cannot change it after its initial creation.

Next, you will add a Boolean flag variable so that you will know when you are inside an item element. You need to know this because the title element occurs in multiple places, but you are only interested in extracting the characters if you find a title element inside of an item element. Here is the declaration:

```
BOOL inItemElement;
```

While you are in the header, you need to add a method that will start parsing the XML. You will call this method once you are finished loading the URL from the web site. Call the new method parseXML:

```
- (void) parseXML;
```

Instead of just logging the results, you can show the output of your parsing in your application. To keep this example simple, just add a UITextView outlet to the interface so that you can access the property in Interface Builder. You will then stuff all of the headlines in that TextView. Add an instance variable for a UITextView to the header:

```
IBOutlet UITextView *textView;
```

Next, add a property for the UITextView:

```
@property (nonatomic, retain) UITextView *textView;
```

The following is the completed header file for the RSSSampleViewController class:

```
#import <UIKit/UIKit.h>

@interface RSSSampleViewController : UIViewController {
    NSMutableData *responseData;
    NSMutableString *capturedCharacters;
    BOOL inItemElement;
    IBOutlet UITextView *textView;
}

- (IBAction)buttonTapped:(id)sender;

- (void) parseXML;

@property (nonatomic,retain) NSMutableData *responseData;
```

```
@property (nonatomic, retain) UITextView *textView;

@end
```

Now let's move on to the implementation file. In RSSSampleViewController.m, synthesize the textView property:

```
@synthesize responseData,textView;
```

Add code to the viewDidUnload and dealloc methods to clean up the UITextView:

```
- (void)viewDidUnload {
    // Release any retained subviews of the main view.
    // e.g. self.myOutlet = nil;
    self.responseData = nil;
    self.textView = nil;
}

- (void)dealloc {
    [responseData release];
    [textView release];
    [super dealloc];
}
```

Next, modify the connectionDidFinishLoading delegate method to call the new parseXML method. When you finish loading all of the data from the URL, you want to parse and display it. Here is the connectionDidFinishLoading delegate method:

```
// Called when the connection has successfully received the complete response
- (void)connectionDidFinishLoading:(NSURLConnection *)connection
{
    NSLog (@"connectionDidFinishLoading:");

    // Convert the data to a string and log the response string
    NSString *responseString = [[NSString alloc]
                                initWithData:self.responseData
                                encoding:NSUTF8StringEncoding];
    NSLog(@"Response String: \n%@", responseString);

    [responseString release];
    [connection release];

    [self parseXML];
}
```

The next step is to implement the `parseXML` method to instantiate the parser, set the delegate, and begin parsing the XML:

```
- (void) parseXML {
    NSLog (@"parseXML");

    // Initialize the parser with our NSData from the RSS feed
    NSXMLParser *xmlParser = [[NSXMLParser alloc]
                                initWithData:self.responseData];

    // Set the delegate to self
    [xmlParser setDelegate:self];

    // Start the parser
    if (![xmlParser parse])
    {
        NSLog (@"An error occurred in the parsing");
    }

    // Release the parser because we are done with it
    [xmlParser release];

}
```

RSSSampleViewController.m

Modifying the Interface

You need to add a TextView to the user interface using Interface Builder. You will use this TextView to display the headlines that you retrieve from the RSS feed. Open Interface Builder and add a `UITextView` to the interface, as shown in Figure 10-6. Clear the default text from the TextView and move the Send Request button to the top of the screen. Finally, hook the `UITextView` up to the File's Owner `textView` property.

Implementing the Parser Delegate Methods

As the `NSXMLParser` works its way through the XML document, it calls a series of delegate methods. You need to implement these methods to get the information that you need from the XML document.

First, you implement the start and end document methods:

```
// Called when the parser begins parsing the document
- (void)parserDidStartDocument:(NSXMLParser *)parser {
    NSLog (@"parserDidStartDocument");
    inItemElement = NO;
}
```

FIGURE 10-6: RSSSample user interface

```
// Called when the parser finishes parsing the document
- (void)parserDidEndDocument:(NSXMLParser *)parser {
    NSLog (@"parserDidEndDocument");
}
```

The code is relatively straightforward. First, for illustrative purposes, you log the name of the method that you are executing. This will prove instructive when you look at the console log. Examining the order in which the parser calls the delegate methods will help you to better understand how the parser works. Additionally, it is useful for debugging purposes should you encounter an error in your parsing logic.

In the `parserDidStartDocument:` method, you also initialize the `inItemElement` flag to NO because you are not currently in an item element. In the `parserDidEndDocument` method, you log that you have reached the end of the document.

Next, you implement the start and end element functions. Here is the `parser:didStartElement:namespaceURI:qualifiedName:attributes:` method implementation:

```
// Called when the parser encounters a start element
- (void) parser:(NSXMLParser *)parser
didStartElement:(NSString *)elementName
   namespaceURI:(NSString *)namespaceURI
  qualifiedName:(NSString *)qualifiedName
     attributes:(NSDictionary *)attributeDict {
    NSLog (@"didStartElement");

    // Check to see which element we have found
    if ([elementName isEqualToString:@"item"]) {
        // We are in an item element
        inItemElement = YES;
    }

    // If we are in an item and found a title
    if (inItemElement && [elementName isEqualToString:@"title"]) {
        // Initialize the capturedCharacters instance variable
        capturedCharacters = [[NSMutableString alloc] initWithCapacity:100];
    }
}
```

This method receives the name of the element that has started as a parameter. You check the name of the element and set the `inItemElement` flag if you have started an `item` element. Next, check to see if you have started a `title` element. You may be wondering why you are checking to see if you have started a `title` element when you already know that you have started an `item` element. Remember that the parser calls this method each time an element begins. Because XML is typically organized as a tree data structure, you will almost certainly have elements nested within other elements. Therefore, each time that the parser calls this method, you could be starting a new element without having ended another element.

Notice that when you check for starting a `title` element, you also verify that you are in an `item` element. If you encounter a `title` element and you are not in an `item`, you don't need to do anything. If, however, you hit a `title` element and you are already in an `item` element, you initialize the `capturedCharacters` instance variable. You will use this `NSMutableString` to aggregate the characters from the `title` element in the call to `parser:foundCharacters:`.

You will do some similar processing in the `didEndElement` method:

```
// Called when the parser encounters an end element
- (void)parser:(NSXMLParser *)parser didEndElement:(NSString *)elementName
    namespaceURI:(NSString *)namespaceURI qualifiedName:(NSString *)qName {

    NSLog (@"didEndElement");

    // Check to see which element we have ended

    // If we are in an item and ended a title
    if (inItemElement && [elementName isEqualToString:@"title"]) {
        NSLog (@"capturedCharacters: %@" , capturedCharacters);

        self.textView.text = [self.textView.text
            stringByAppendingFormat:@"%@\n\n",capturedCharacters];

        // Release the capturedCharacters instance variable
        [capturedCharacters release];
        capturedCharacters = nil;
    }


    if ([elementName isEqualToString:@"item"]) {
        // We are no longer in an item element
        inItemElement = NO;
    }

}
```

RSSSampleViewController.m

First, check to see if you are in an `item` element and are ending a `title` element. If so, log the characters that you captured, append them to the `textView`, and release the `capturedCharacters` instance variable because you are finished with it for now. Next, check to see if the parser called this element because you are ending an `item` element. If that is the case, you set the `inItemElement` flag to NO. Remember that the parser will call this method each time an element ends. It is up to the developer to determine what element has ended and to act accordingly.

The last delegate method that you will implement is `parser:foundCharacters:`. In this method, you simply check to make sure that the `capturedCharacters` variable is not `nil`, and then append the characters passed into the method to the `capturedCharacters` mutable string. Keep in mind that the parser may call this method multiple times for the text inside of a single element. That is why you are using a mutable string and appending the characters to it each time that the parser calls this method. Here is the implementation:

```
// Called when the parser finds characters contained within an element
- (void)parser:(NSXMLParser *)parser foundCharacters:(NSString *)string {
    if (capturedCharacters != nil) {
        [capturedCharacters appendString:string];
    }
}
```

RSSSampleViewController.m

You are now ready to build and run the application. As long as you have an active Internet connection, the application should download and parse the RSS feed and display the top headlines from CNN.com in the text view.

Generating XML with libxml

Sometimes when you are building a connected application, you will need to generate XML from scratch. Thus far, you have only explored consuming XML. In this section, you learn how to build XML dynamically at runtime.

There are a several ways to build XML in your application. You should choose an appropriate method based on the needs of your application.

If you need to send a specific XML message with only limited dynamic data, your best bet is to build a format string using the XML and placeholders for your variables. For instance, if you were implementing an online address book, a message that you send to the server to add an entry may look something like this:

```
<address>
    <name>John Smith</name>
    <street>1 Ocean Blvd</street>
    <city>Isle Of Palms</city>
    <state>SC</state>
    <zip>29451</zip>
</address>
```

In this case, there is no need to build the XML document structure at runtime because you already know the structure of the message at compile time. Simply use a format string like this:

```
NSString *s = [[NSString alloc] initWithFormat:
                    "<address>"
                    "<name>%@</name>"
                    "<street>%@</street>"
```

```
"<city>%@</city>"
"<state>%@</state>"
"<zip>%@</zip>"
"</address>",name,street,city,state,zip];
```

On the other hand, if you are building an order entry system where the number of items in an order could change based on conditions in the application at runtime, you probably will need to generate the entire XML tree dynamically. While generating XML with the `NSXMLParser` is possible as outlined in Apple's "Event-Driven XML Programming Guide for Cocoa," it is difficult and not intuitive.

It is far easier to build an XML document using the DOM model for XML parsing. Apple does not provide a DOM parser on the iPhone, but there is a C XML library called libxml installed on the iPhone that you can use for DOM processing. It is free and available under the MIT license, which you can find at `http://www.opensource.org/licenses/mit-license.html`.

While generating XML dynamically at runtime, using libxml2 is far easier than using `NSXMLParser`. Unfortunately, the library is in C, so it is a little more difficult to work with than an Objective-C library. If you think that you will be building dynamic XML often, you may want to consider wrapping libxml in your own Objective-C wrappers. Additionally, there are several open source wrappers for libxml; however, you will not be looking at them. You will better understand how to use libxml by using the library directly in your code.

Using libxml in your project is as simple as adding the `libxml2.dylib` to your project and editing your header search paths so that the compiler can find the headers. Then you only need to include the headers that you plan to use in your source code and you are ready to go.

You may also want to use libxml if your application needs the capabilities of a DOM parser as opposed to the Apple provided SAX parser. The libxml library also supports XPath. XPath is a query language that you can use to search your XML. Additionally, libxml also supports validating XML files against a DTD (Document Type Definition). You can think of a DTD as the specification for the XML used in a document.

XML Generation Sample

In this section, you will build a very simple application that generates a simple XML document tree, as shown in Figure 10-7. The XML that you generate will look like this:

```
<?xml version="1.0"?>
<rootNode>
  <ChildNode1>Child Node Content</ChildNode1>
  <AttributedNode attribute1="First" attribute2="Second">
    <AttributedChild>Attributed Node Child Node</AttributedChild>
  </AttributedNode>
  <AttachedNode>Attached Node Text</AttachedNode>
  <!--This is an XML Comment-->
</rootNode>
```

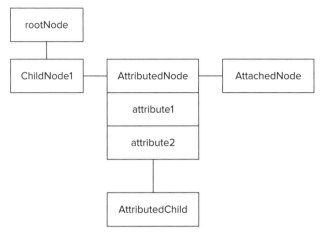

FIGURE 10-7: Tree representation of generated XML

Granted, this is not the most complex XML document, but the code will demonstrate everything that you will need to generate XML documents of limitless complexity.

Create a new View-based Application called MakeXML. The first thing that you have to do is tell Xcode that you will be using the libxml library. Right-click on the project in the left pane of Xcode and select Add New Group. Call the new group **C Libs**. Next, add a reference to the libxml2.dylib dynamic library. Right-click on the new group and select Add ➪ Existing Frameworks. In the dialog, select Dylibs from the dropdown and select libxml2.dylib. You should see libxml2.dylib appear in the C Libs group in Xcode.

You now have to alter the search path in Xcode so that Xcode can find the headers for libxml2 when you are ready to compile. Open the project build settings by selecting Project ➪ Edit Project Settings from the menu bar. In the Search Paths area, add the path /Developer/Platforms/ iPhoneOS.platform/Developer/SDKs/iPhoneOS3.1.3.sdk/usr/ include/libxml2 to the Header Search Paths item. Enable Xcode to search this directory and below by checking the recursive box. Note that you will have to change the SDK in the path based on which SDK you are compiling with. This example assumes that you are using the iPhone SDK version 3.1.3 and that you have installed the SDK in the default location.

FIGURE 10-8: MakeXML sample UI

Now you will build the UI for the application, as shown in Figure 10-8.

In the MakeXMLViewController.h header, add a UITextView instance variable and outlet. Add a method generateXML that you will call to generate the XML. Here is the complete MakeXMLViewController.h header:

```
#import <UIKit/UIKit.h>

@interface MakeXMLViewController : UIViewController {
```

```
        UITextView *textView;
}

@property (nonatomic, retain) IBOutlet UITextView *textView;

-(void) generateXML;

@end
```

MakeXMLViewController.h

In the `MakeXMLViewController.m` implementation file, synthesize the `textView` property:

```
@synthesize textView;
```

Next, implement `viewDidUnload` and `dealloc` to clean up the `textView` property and instance variable:

Available for download on Wrox.com

```
- (void)viewDidUnload {
    // Release any retained subviews of the main view.
    // e.g. self.myOutlet = nil;
    self.textView=nil;
}


- (void)dealloc {
    [textView dealloc];
    [super dealloc];
}
```

MakeXMLViewController.m

Open the `MakeXMLViewController.xib` file in Interface Builder and add a `UITextView` control. Resize the control to take up the whole screen. Connect the `UITextView` in Interface Builder to the `textView` property in File's Owner.

In the `MakeXMLViewController.m` implementation file, add the `import` statements for the `libxml` parser and `libxml` tree headers:

```
#import <libxml/parser.h>
#import <libxml/tree.h>
```

You will construct the XML in the `generateXML` method. I want to demonstrate a few different things in this method, so it's long. Let's walk through the method section by section, and then I will show the whole method in its entirety.

You first declare an `xmlDocPtr` object. `xmlDocPtr` is a `typedef` for a pointer to the `libxml` `xmlDoc` structure. This structure represents the entire XML document that you will be creating.

```
- (void) generateXML {
    xmlDocPtr doc;
```

Every XML document consists of a set of nodes. At the top of the tree of nodes is a special node called the *root* node. You need to declare the root node as an xmlNodePtr object. xmlNodePtr is a typedef to a pointer to an xmlNode struct. The library uses the xmlNode struct to represent all XML nodes. Here is the declaration of the root node:

```
xmlNodePtr rootNode;
```

Next, you call the xmlNewDoc library function to create a new document model. You assign the return to the doc object:

```
// Create a new xml document
doc = xmlNewDoc(BAD_CAST "1.0");
```

You may have noticed the frightening looking BAD_CAST parameter in the function call. BAD_CAST is simply a macro defined in the xmlstring.h header that you can use to cast a string to the xmlChar* type. You will likely use BAD_CAST anywhere that you use a string object with the library. Remember that libxml is a C library so you should omit the @ symbol that you use when defining NSString objects in Objective-C. In this case, you are using a C-style char* string.

The next step is to create the root node. You call the xmlNewNode function to create a new node. The method takes an xmlNsPtr and an xmlChar* as its parameters. You can use the xmlNsPtr parameter to specify a namespace for your node instance. You use namespaces to ensure that the XML elements defined in your document do not conflict with elements with the same name in other XML documents. You will not be using namespaces in this sample. The xmlChar* is the name of your new node. In this case, let's call the node rootNode:

```
// Create the root node
rootNode = xmlNewNode(NULL, BAD_CAST "rootNode");
```

Because the root element is the starting point for the document, you must explicitly set the root element. Call the xmlDocSetRootElement function and pass in a pointer to the document and the root node:

```
xmlDocSetRootElement(doc, rootNode);
```

Now you are ready to start adding additional nodes to the tree. The easiest way to add new nodes to your XML document tree is to use the xmlNewChild function. This function accepts a pointer to the parent node for the new node, a namespace pointer if you are using namespaces, the name of the new node, and the textual content of the node. You create ChildNode1 as follows:

```
// Create a new child off the root
    xmlNewChild(rootNode, NULL, BAD_CAST "ChildNode1",
             BAD_CAST "Child Node Content");
```

This statement creates a node called ChildNode1 that is a child of the rootNode and contains the string Child Node Content. Again, you can see that you use the BAD_CAST macro to pass string data into the library.

Next, you create a node that contains XML attributes. Attributes are another way to add data to an element node. Because you will append a child to this node, you declare an `xmlNodePtr` so that you can hold a reference to the new node. Then, you use the `xmlNewChild` function that you have already seen to create a new node. You will call the `xmlNewProp` function to add two attributes to the `attributedNode`, as follows:

```
// Add a node with attributes
    xmlNodePtr attributedNode;
    attributedNode = xmlNewChild (rootNode, NULL,
                                BAD_CAST "AttributedNode", NULL);
    xmlNewProp(attributedNode, BAD_CAST "attribute1", BAD_CAST "First");
    xmlNewProp(attributedNode, BAD_CAST "attribute2", BAD_CAST "Second");
```

MakeXMLViewController.m

So far, you have only added nodes as children of the root node. Part of the power of XML is the ability to express hierarchical data in a tree structure. To demonstrate this capability, let's add the next node as a child of the attributed node. You can accomplish this by passing the pointer to the attributed node into the call to `xmlNewChild`:

```
// Create a node as a child of the attributed node
    xmlNewChild (attributedNode, NULL, BAD_CAST "AttributedChild",
            BAD_CAST "Attributed Node Child Node");
```

MakeXMLViewController.m

Instead of appending the new `AttributedChild` node to the `rootNode`, this code appends the `AttributedChild` node to the `attributedNode`.

Sometimes it may be more convenient to build the node and its associated text separately. You can do this and then add the node to the tree after you have populated it with text or other subnodes. A new node and its text content are created in this snippet. Then, you add the text to the node and append the node to the root node, as follows:

```
// You can also build nodes and text separately then and add them
    // to the tree later
    xmlNodePtr attachNode = xmlNewNode(NULL, BAD_CAST "AttachedNode");
    xmlNodePtr nodeText = xmlNewText(BAD_CAST "Attached Node Text");
    // Add the text to the node
    xmlAddChild(attachNode, nodeText);
    // Add the node to the root
    xmlAddChild(rootNode, attachNode);
```

MakeXMLViewController.m

It is even possible to include XML comments using the `xmlNewComment` function:

```
// You can even include comments
   xmlNodePtr comment;
   comment = xmlNewComment(BAD_CAST "This is an XML Comment");
   xmlAddChild(rootNode, comment);
```

MakeXMLViewController.m

Now that you have built the complete tree for the document, you have to tell the library to output the contents so that you can put the document into an NSString. Because libxml is a C library, there is a function that outputs the document to a memory buffer. You need to declare a memory buffer of type xmlChar* and an int variable to hold the length of the buffer. Once you have these variables set up, you can call the xmlDocDumpFormatMemory function. This function outputs the XML document to the buffer that you pass in and returns the size of the buffer in a reference variable that you also pass in to the function. The last parameter to the xmlDocDumpFormatMemory function indicates that you would like space characters added to format the output. Here is the code:

```
// Write the doc
   xmlChar *outputBuffer;
   int bufferSize;

   // You are responsible for freeing the buffer using xmlFree
   // Dump the document to a buffer
   xmlDocDumpFormatMemory(doc, &outputBuffer, &bufferSize, 1);
```

MakeXMLViewController.m

Fortunately, because Objective-C is a superset of C, Apple has created plenty of helper functions for getting data from C types into Objective-C types. For instance, the NSString class has a method called initWithBytes:length:encoding: that accepts a C char* buffer, a length, and an encoding type, and initializes an NSString with that data. You use that function to create an NSString from your XML document dump:

```
// Create an NSString from the buffer
NSString *xmlString = [[NSString alloc] initWithBytes:outputBuffer
                                    length:bufferSize
                                encoding:NSUTF8StringEncoding];
```

Next, you log the XML document string to the console, put the string in the textView in the user interface, and release the NSString:

```
// Log the XML string that we created
NSLog (@"output: \n%@", xmlString);

// Display the text in the textview
[self.textView setText:xmlString];

// Free the xml string
[xmlString release];
```

MakeXMLViewController.m

Finally, you call some cleanup functions from libxml to free the memory that you allocated when creating your XML document. First, you free the output buffer that you just created with a call to xmlFree. Then, you free the memory used by the XML document with a call to xmlFreeDoc. You end with a call to xmlCleanupParser because you are completely finished with the XML parser:

```
// Clean up
// Free the output buffer
xmlFree(outputBuffer);

// Release all of the structures in the document including the tree
xmlFreeDoc(doc);
xmlCleanupParser();
```

MakeXMLViewController.m

You should be careful to ensure that you are not using the XML parser anywhere else in your code before calling xmlCleanupParser. This method cleans up any remaining memory that the XML parser allocated, including global memory. You should only call this function when your application is completely finished using libxml and all documents that you have created with the library.

Listing 10-1 shows the entire generateXML method call.

LISTING 10-1: The generateXML method

```
- (void) generateXML {
    xmlDocPtr doc;
    xmlNodePtr rootNode;

    // Create a new xml document
    doc = xmlNewDoc(BAD_CAST "1.0");

    // Create the root node
    rootNode = xmlNewNode(NULL, BAD_CAST "rootNode");

    // Set the root of the document
    xmlDocSetRootElement(doc, rootNode);

    // Create a new child off the root
    xmlNewChild(rootNode, NULL, BAD_CAST "ChildNode1",
                BAD_CAST "Child Node Content");

    // Add a node with attributes
    xmlNodePtr attributedNode;
    attributedNode = xmlNewChild (rootNode, NULL,
                                  BAD_CAST "AttributedNode", NULL);
    xmlNewProp(attributedNode, BAD_CAST "attribute1", BAD_CAST "First");
    xmlNewProp(attributedNode, BAD_CAST "attribute2", BAD_CAST "Second");
```

```
    // Create a node as a child of the attributed node
    xmlNewChild (attributedNode, NULL, BAD_CAST "AttributedChild",
                 BAD_CAST "Attributed Node Child Node");

    // You can also build nodes and text separately then and add them
    // to the tree later
    xmlNodePtr attachNode = xmlNewNode(NULL, BAD_CAST "AttachedNode");
    xmlNodePtr nodeText = xmlNewText(BAD_CAST "Attached Node Text");
    // Add the text to the node
    xmlAddChild(attachNode, nodeText);
    // Add the node to the root
    xmlAddChild(rootNode, attachNode);

    // You can even include comments
    xmlNodePtr comment;
    comment = xmlNewComment(BAD_CAST "This is an XML Comment");
    xmlAddChild(rootNode, comment);


    // Write the doc
    xmlChar *outputBuffer;
    int bufferSize;

    // You are responsible for freeing the buffer using xmlFree
    // Dump the document to a buffer
    xmlDocDumpFormatMemory(doc, &outputBuffer, &bufferSize, 1);

    // Create an NSString from the buffer
    NSString *xmlString = [[NSString alloc] initWithBytes:outputBuffer
                                            length:bufferSize
                                         encoding:NSUTF8StringEncoding];

    // Log the XML string that we created
    NSLog (@"output: \n%@", xmlString);

    // Display the text in the textview
    [self.textView setText:xmlString];

    // Free the xml string
    [xmlString release];

    // Clean up
    // Free the output buffer
    xmlFree(outputBuffer);

    // Release all of the structures in the document including the tree
    xmlFreeDoc(doc);
    xmlCleanupParser();

}
```

The last thing that you have to do before running the application is add a call to `generateXML` to `viewDidLoad`:

```
- (void)viewDidLoad {
    [super viewDidLoad];

    [self generateXML];
}
```

Now you are ready to build and run the application. You should see the XML generated in the console and displayed in the TextView in the iPhone simulator.

Many other features are supported by `libxml`. I strongly encourage you to visit the `libxml` web site at `http://xmlsoft.org/`.

MOVING FORWARD

In this chapter, you have learned how to communicate with remote servers over the Internet using the Cocoa URL Loading System. You implemented the `NSURLConnection` delegate methods to handle asynchronous loading of data from the Web. Then, you learned how to parse the XML that you receive as a response to a remote method call. Finally, you learned how to generate dynamic XML documents.

This chapter lays the foundation for integration with XML web services. The next chapter explores communication with XML web services; you build a sample project that queries a web service and then processes the response in an interesting way.

11

Integrating with Web Services

WHAT'S IN THIS CHAPTER?

➤ Learning what a web service is and its usefulness

➤ Understanding how to send data to an XML web service using the POST and GET methods

➤ Parsing the response messages from a web service and using the resulting data from within an iPhone SDK application

➤ Building location-based applications using the GPS functionality in the Core Location framework and the mapping capability of the MapKit framework

In the previous chapter, you learned how to ask for data from a web server by sending HTTP requests. You also learned about XML and how to parse the XML that you receive from web servers in response to your HTTP requests. In this section, you will take that knowledge a step further by integrating your application with Internet-based web services.

In this chapter, you will learn about web services and how to use them in your iPhone and iPad applications. You will also explore a couple of other interesting features of the iPhone SDK, including MapKit and Core Location.

This chapter builds on the knowledge that you gained from the last chapter to integrate iPhone SDK applications with web services. I will cover the use of the GET and POST HTTP methods to send data to a web service. You will then build a couple of sample applications that use web services as an integral part of the program.

NETWORK APPLICATION ARCHITECTURE

When you set out to start work on a new project, one of your first decisions involves designing the architecture of your application and determining how the parts of your system will work together. Most data-oriented applications will involve a database, and all iPhone applications will include a user interface. In order to get a better understanding of how to design applications where the iPhone and database need to communicate, you will take a brief look at a couple of typical network application architectures.

Two-Tier Architecture

The simplest network application architecture consists of a database and an interface. Architects refer to this design as two-tier or client-server architecture. You can see this design in Figure 11-1. In this design, the client application resides on the mobile device or computer, and implements the application interface. Additionally, the client software includes the implementation of the business rules that govern the functionality of the application. The server tier is generally an enterprise database such as Oracle, SQLServer, or MySQL, which can share its data with many connected clients.

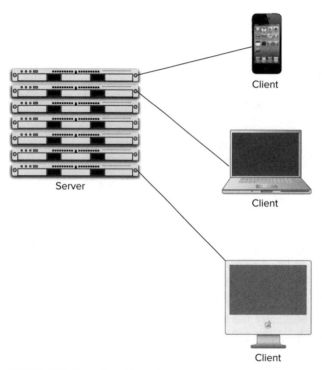

FIGURE 11-1: Two-tier architecture

You see this type of client-server architecture when you look at web servers, particularly web servers that serve simple HTML web pages. The client in this design is your web browser and the server is the web server. Many clients connect to the same web server to get data. The client web browser hosts the user interface and the logic to display the HTML data.

This architecture is most appropriate for simple applications. However, as the business rules for your application become more complex, you will likely outgrow this design. In order to maintain encapsulation of functionality, the client should be responsible for displaying data and the server for storing it. If there are minimal rules that govern the logic and data of the application, you could implement them either in the database or on the client.

As the number and complexity of the rules that define the functionality of your application increase, you will need to decide where you want to implement those rules. You could implement them on the client. If your client software were a "thick" desktop application, changing rules would mean re-deploying your application to your clients. If the client is a "thin" web-browser based client, you are constrained by the capabilities and performance of the browser and client-side languages such as JavaScript.

As the business rules of your application get more complex, you will often need to add a third tier to your application architecture. It is in this tier where the business rules reside. In this design, you can decouple your business rules from both the display logic of the client software and the storage system of the database.

Three-Tier Architecture (n-tier)

As you learned in the last section, you need to consider your application's ability to maintain a complex set of business rules in your design. As you design your system, you need to consider the complexity of the rules that govern your application and the likelihood that these rules could change. For instance, if you are building an order entry system, you need to consider the fact that customer discount percentages could change. You may not want to code these percentages into the user interface layer of your application because any changes to this data would require a redeployment of your software. In instances like this, it is common for the designer to pull these business rules out of the interface and place them in their own logical software layer. The client-server design then evolves into a three-tier (or n-tier if more than one business layer is necessary) architecture (see Figure 11-2).

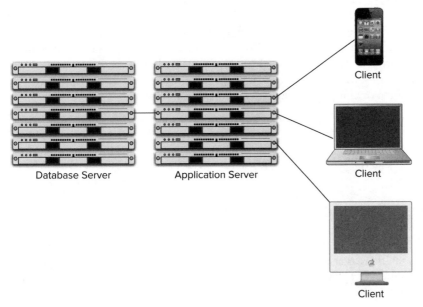

Database Server   Application Server   Client

Client

Client

FIGURE 11-2: Three-tier architecture

In a three-tier design, the application architect moves the business logic in to its own logical and perhaps physical process. You can therefore decouple the business rules from the user interface and the database. This gives the designer more flexibility when it comes to designing the database, the interface, and the business logic. It also effectively encapsulates each of these important features of a system. It is easier to manage the business logic of your system if you do not tightly couple this code to the database or the user interface. This simplifies making changes to any one of the layers of the design without affecting any of the other layers. In this design, all of the rules that govern what data can be added to the database and specific calculations that are performed on that data are moved out of the interface layer into their own tier. Many commercial application servers such as WebLogic, Apache Tomcat, and WebSphere perform this function.

Application Communication

Client applications need to be able to talk to the business tier or application server and the application server needs to be able to talk to the database.

Typically, the application server and database reside on the same local network, although this is not necessary. These two layers generally communicate through an interface layer that knows how to call functions in the database. A common interface API for database communication is Open Database Connectivity (ODBC). Most programming languages provide support APIs for connecting to databases as well. The Microsoft .NET platform provides an API called ADO.NET while the Java system provides JDBC.

For the client to business-tier communication, the designer can implement connectivity using a variety of methods depending on the languages and operating systems used in the implementation.

In the past, designers of Windows systems would have used DCOM or Distributed Component Object Model. This technology allowed components on different computers to talk to each other. In a Java-based system, the designer could choose a similar technology called Java Remote Method Invocation (RMI). In this system, objects running in one Java virtual machine can call methods on objects in another virtual machine. CORBA, or Common Object Request Broker Architecture, is another technology that enables remote machines to execute methods and share data with one another. The advantage of CORBA is that it is language independent. There are CORBA implementations for most major computer languages and operating systems.

A more current technology enables the designer to implement the functionality of the business tier as a web service. With this technology, the designer can expose the business logic of the application using a web server. Client software can then use well-known methods of the HTTP protocol to access the services exposed by the application server.

INTRODUCING WEB SERVICES

When you use a web browser to visit your favorite web site, you begin by sending a request to the site's server. If all goes well, the server accepts your request and returns a response. The response that you get is text in the form of HTML, which your browser renders into the page that you see on your screen.

Consumers of the HTML that a web server sends are generally people that view the HTML using a browser. Web services, on the other hand, respond to requests by sending back data that is intended for computers to consume.

Typically, most web services default to returning response data to you using XML. With some web services, however, you can request that your data be returned in other formats, such as JSON (JavaScript Object Notation). JSON is a text-based format, like XML. Unlike XML, however, JSON can be used directly in browser-based web applications that are backed by JavaScript code. Coverage of JavaScript is beyond the scope of this book, as is using JSON in browser-based applications. What you should know though is that there are parsers available to consume JSON response data for many languages, including Objective-C.

In the previous chapter, you looked at a snippet of XML that could be used to add an address entity to an address book application:

```
<address>
    <name>John Smith</name>
    <street>1 Ocean Blvd</street>
    <city>Isle Of Palms</city>
    <state>SC</state>
    <zip>29451</zip>
</address>
```

Here is the JSON representation of the same address:

```
{
    "name": "John Smith",
    "street": "1 Ocean Blvd",
    "city": "Isle Of Palms",
    "state": "SC",
    "zip": "29451"
}
```

Unlike XML, whose structure is defined by its users, JSON relies on data structures defined in JavaScript. Specifically, JSON can use one of two data structures: the `Object` or the `Array`. Because these data structures are common in almost all modern languages, it is easy to convert JSON messages into data structures that can be used in almost any language. The `Object` consists of a set of name-value pairs, and the `Array` is a list of values.

Application architects can design web services to act as the application server for their particular application. Third parties also build web services to provide specific services to their clients. In this chapter, you will develop two applications that use third-party web services from Yahoo! to implement some interesting functionality. The first service allows you to submit queries and returns the results based on proximity to the location of the search. The second service accepts a long string of text and returns a list of the most important words in the text.

In general, web services provide a way to expose some complex logic by using the simple and well-known interfaces of the Web.

For example, a designer can easily expose an external interface to a database by building a web service that allows clients to create records or query the data store. Consider the product catalog from Part I of this book. You could build a web service that exposes an interface that accepts orders and enters them directly into the back-end database. You could then build an iPhone order entry application that uses this web service to allow your sales force in the field to submit orders.

You can develop web services using many languages and frameworks such as Java, Microsoft.NET, and Ruby on Rails. Because of the variation in languages and platforms available, building a web service is beyond the scope of this book. This chapter teaches you how to integrate your application with existing web services.

SOAP Messaging

There are two predominant protocols used for exchanging data with web services: SOAP and REST. You will look at SOAP in this section and examine REST in the next.

Microsoft originally developed SOAP (Simple Object Access Protocol) in the late 90s and the W3C standards body has standardized the protocol. The designers built SOAP to be platform- and language-agnostic in order to replace technologies such as CORBA and DCOM. The designers chose XML as the format for the messages in an effort to avoid some of the problems associated with the binary-based messaging systems that SOAP would replace.

Unlike CORBA and DCOM, the designers of SOAP decided to send messages using the HTTP protocol, which makes network configuration easy. If users could see each other over the Web using a browser, they could send messages to each other using SOAP.

SOAP messages share a common element with other messaging formats such as HTML in that the message contains a header and a body. The header contains details about the type of message, format of the data, and so on. The body holds the "payload" or the data that the user intends to transmit.

One issue with using SOAP is the complexity of the messages. In order to transmit a little bit of data, users of SOAP often need to transmit long messages. For example, here is the SOAP request message that you would send to the eBay SOAP API to obtain the official eBay time (from eBay.com: using the eBay API to get the official eBay time):

```
<?xml version="1.0" encoding="utf-8"?>
<soapenv:Envelope xmlns:soapenv="http://schemas.xmlsoap.org/soap/envelope/"
    xmlns:xsd="http://www.w3.org/2001/XMLSchema"
  xmlns:xsi="http://www.w3.org/2001/XMLSchema-instance">
  <soapenv:Header>
    <RequesterCredentials soapenv:mustUnderstand="0"
       xmlns="urn:ebay:apis:eBLBaseComponents">
      <eBayAuthToken>ABC...123</eBayAuthToken>
      <ns:Credentials xmlns:ns="urn:ebay:apis:eBLBaseComponents">
       <ns:DevId>someDevId</ns:DevId>
       <ns:AppId>someAppId</ns:AppId>
       <ns:AuthCert>someAuthCert</ns:AuthCert>
      </ns:Credentials>
    </RequesterCredentials>
  </soapenv:Header>
  <soapenv:Body>
    <GeteBayOfficialTimeRequest xmlns="urn:ebay:apis:eBLBaseComponents">
```

```
            <ns1:Version xmlns:ns1="urn:ebay:apis:eBLBaseComponents">405</ns1:Version>
        </GetBayOfficialTimeRequest>
    </soapenv:Body>
</soapenv:Envelope>
```

This is quite a verbose message, especially considering that you are not even passing in any parameters. Although the API simply returns a timestamp that represents the current time, it is also quite verbose:

```
<?xml version="1.0" encoding="utf-8"?>
<soapenv:Envelope xmlns:soapenv="http://schemas.xmlsoap.org/soap/envelope/"
    xmlns:xsd="http://www.w3.org/2001/XMLSchema"
    xmlns:xsi="http://www.w3.org/2001/XMLSchema-instance">
    <soapenv:Body>
        <GetBayOfficialTimeResponse xmlns="urn:ebay:apis:eBLBaseComponents">
            <Timestamp>2005-05-02T00:07:22.895Z</Timestamp>
            <Ack>Success</Ack>
            <CorrelationID>
                00000000-00000000-00000000-00000000-00000000-00000000-0000000000
            </CorrelationID>
            <Version>405</Version>
            <Build>20050422132524</Build>
        </GetBayOfficialTimeResponse>
    </soapenv:Body>
</soapenv:Envelope>
```

While SOAP offers far more functionality than simple method calling, you can see why developers often mock the name "Simple" Object Access Protocol. Designers that simply needed to pass data between application layers or make basic method calls found that SOAP was overkill. This led to the development of a simpler messaging protocol called REST.

The REST Protocol

REST stands for REpresentational State Transfer. The designers of REST wanted to be able to call web service functions using the simple and well-known methods exposed by the HTTP protocol: GET and POST. The goal was to make it easy to invoke remote functions and provide response data in a more manageable format.

REST uses a simple URI scheme to communicate with web services. Developers who are comfortable using HTTP to make requests over the Web already know how to call REST services. Typically, a client application can simply issue an HTTP GET request to a URL to make a method call. The developer can pass parameters to the call using querystring parameters as if simply passing parameters to a regular web site.

Because REST is not standardized, it is possible that the client will receive response data from a REST-based service in an arbitrary format. However, XML is commonly used. Typically, REST-based web services can also return data using the JSON format instead of XML. This is preferable if you are developing Web-based applications.

In order to be able to easily determine the intent of a call, the HTTP GET method is used to query for data, and the HTTP POST method is used when you want to modify data such as in an INSERT or UPDATE to a database. This makes it easy to determine if the caller intends to simply query the service for data or make changes to the data managed by the service.

It is very easy to build simple web services using REST. If you already know how to implement server-side web scripts, REST implementations are typically straightforward. Both of the examples in this chapter will call web services based on the REST protocol. All of the concepts in this chapter are equally applicable if your application needs to call a SOAP-based service. The only real difference is the format of the message that you are sending and the format of the response message.

EXAMPLE 1: LOCATION-BASED SEARCH

One of the great features of the iPhone and iPad 3G is the GPS. Developers are able use GPS to determine the current location of the device and build applications that use this data to provide a wealth of information to users. This leads to some very creative applications.

In the first example in this chapter, you will take advantage of this capability of the device. You will use the Core Location framework to determine the current position of the device. Then, you will allow the user to input search terms into the application. You will then call a Yahoo! web service using the REST protocol and the HTTP GET method to obtain businesses that meet the search criteria and are close to the current location. Finally, you will use the MapKit framework to display the returned data on a map.

Don't worry if you don't have an iPhone. When you use Core Location with the iPhone simulator, the simulator conveniently returns the latitude and longitude of Apple headquarters in Cupertino, California.

The finished application will look like Figure 11-3.

Starting Out

Now that you have an idea of what the application will do and how it will look, let's get started. The first step, as always, is to open Xcode and create a new project. Because there will be only one view, you should create a new View-based application. Call the new application LocationSearch.

You will be using the Core Location and MapKit frameworks in this example. These frameworks are not included in iPhone projects by default, so you will have to add references to the frameworks to the project. Right-click on the Frameworks folder in the Groups & Files pane in Xcode. From the pop-up menu, select Add ⇨ Existing Frameworks. In the dialog that opens, select the CoreLocation.framework item and click the Add button. Repeat this procedure to add the MapKit .framework framework to your project as well.

FIGURE 11-3: Completed LocationSearch application

You will be using these frameworks in your `LocationSearchViewController` class. Therefore, you will need to import the headers for these frameworks in the `LocationSearchViewController.h` header. Add the following `import` statements to the `LocationSearchViewController.h` header file:

```
#import <MapKit/MapKit.h>
#import <CoreLocation/CoreLocation.h>
```

LocationSearchViewController.h

The user interface for the application consists of a search bar to accept the search criteria from the user and a map view that you will use to display the search results. Because you need access to both of these interface items in your code, you will need to add instance variables and outlets for these elements.

In the `LocationSearchViewController.h` header, add instance variables for an `MKMapView*` called `mapView` and a `UISearchBar*` called `searchBar` to the interface definition:

```
MKMapView* mapView;
UISearchBar *searchBar;
```

LocationSearchViewController.h

Now that you have declared your instance variables, declare `IBOutlet` properties for these UI elements so that you have access to them in Interface Builder:

```
@property (nonatomic, retain) IBOutlet MKMapView* mapView;
@property (nonatomic, retain) IBOutlet UISearchBar *searchBar;
```

LocationSearchViewController.h

Next, you will move into the implementation file `LocationSearchViewController.m`. You first need to synthesize your two new properties. Add a line to synthesize the `mapView` and `searchBar` properties to the implementation:

```
@synthesize mapView,searchBar;
```

Finally, any time that you use a property that retains its value, you need to clean up the memory used by the property in the `dealloc` and `viewDidUnload` methods. Add the code to set the outlet properties to `nil` in the `viewDidUnload` method:

```
- (void)viewDidUnload {
    // Release any retained subviews of the main view.
    // e.g. self.myOutlet = nil;
    self.mapView = nil;
    self.searchBar = nil;
}
```

LocationSearchViewController.m

Also, add the code to release the instance variables in the `dealloc` method:

```
- (void)dealloc {
    [mapView release];
    [searchBar release];
    [super dealloc];
}
```

LocationSearchViewController.m

Building the Interface

This application will have two elements in the interface, an `MKMapView` and a `UISearchBar`. Double-click on the `LocationSearchViewController.xib` file in the Resources folder of the Groups & Files pane in Xcode. This launches Interface Builder and opens the `LocationSearchViewController.xib` file.

In Interface Builder, make sure that you have the Library palette open. If you don't, you can open it from the menu bar by selecting Tools ➪ Library, or with the keyboard shortcut Command+-Shift+L. Locate the Search Bar item under the Library ➪ Cocoa Touch ➪ Windows, Views & Bars heading. Drag the search bar to the top of the view. Make sure that you choose the Search Bar from the Library window and not the Search Bar and Search Display Controller.

Next, locate the map view under Library ➪ Cocoa Touch ➪ Data Views in the Library window. Drag a map view into the view and place it below the search bar. Stretch the map view to take up the rest of the view window. Figure 11-4 shows what your interface should look like in Interface Builder.

Now that you have visually defined your user interface, you need to connect the user interface elements to the code. Hook up the `UISearchBar` to the `searchBar` outlet in File's Owner. Likewise, hook up the `MKMapView` to the `mapView` outlet in File's Owner.

That's all that you will need to do in Interface Builder so, you can close the `LocationSearchViewController.xib` file and quit Interface Builder.

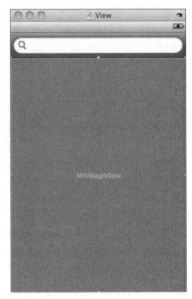

FIGURE 11-4: LocationSearchView Controller in Interface Builder

Core Location

The key ingredient in building a location-based application is getting the location of the user. Apple has built the Core Location framework to enable your applications to interface with the GPS hardware in the device. Using this framework, you can obtain the current location or heading of the device.

The Core Location Framework

Core Location is an asynchronous API that uses delegation to report location information for the device. To use this functionality, you first need to instantiate an instance of the CLLocationManager class. As the name implies, you use this class to manage the Core Location functionality. The class contains methods to start and stop location and heading updates as well as a property that returns the location of the device.

Once you have instantiated your CLLocationManager instance, you need to define a delegate. The delegate must conform to the CLLocationManagerDelegate protocol. This protocol defines methods that allow you to respond to location and heading change events as well as errors. You will typically write code in the locationManager:didUpdateToLocation:fromLocation: method to respond to changes in the device location.

In a production application, you should also implement the locationManager:didFailWithError: method. Core Location calls this method in case of error. Additionally, Core Location will automatically prompt the user to determine if he wants to allow your application to access their current location. If the user decides not to make this information available, Core Location will call this error method. Your application should be able to gracefully handle this situation.

After you have implemented the Core Location delegate methods and set the CLLocationManager's delegate, you will typically tell the manager to start updating the device's location. Core Location will return the location of the device as quickly as possible, often using a cached value if one is available. After the initial call, the device will continue to hone the position based on a value that you can set using the desiredAccuracy property. You can control the number of callbacks that you receive to the locationManager:didUpdateToLocation:fromLocation: method by setting the distanceFilter property. This property allows you to set the minimum distance that the device must move before the framework calls the method again.

Although the example will not use it, Core Location can also report heading information if the hardware of the device supports it. If you choose to enable heading data, your Core Location will call the locationManager:didUpdateHeading: method to report heading updates.

There are a few considerations to be aware of when developing software with Core Location. First, you should use the lowest level of accuracy that your application needs in order to implement its functionality. You can specify that the framework determine the device's location to the nearest three kilometers, one kilometer, one hundred meters, ten meters, or best possible accuracy. The default value is best possible accuracy. The GPS needs more power to determine the location of the device with higher precision. Power consumption on a mobile device is something that you should consider when building mobile applications. Therefore, you should always specify the least accuracy that you can accept while still providing the desired functionality in your application.

Another consideration is when to turn off Core Location. As I mentioned, using the GPS chip consumes a substantial amount of power. You should turn off location updates using the stopUpdatingLocation method as soon as is practical for your application. In the application, you only need to get the initial location of the device in order to perform your location search, so you will turn off location updates after you determine the device's location. Occasionally, you will need to obtain frequent location updates while your application is running — for example, when the application is providing turn-by-turn directions. Just keep in mind that using the GPS consumes a lot of power and that you should keep it enabled for the shortest possible length of time.

Using Core Location

Now that you have an idea of how to use Core Location, you will add Core Location functionality to your application. In the `LocationSearchViewController.h` header file, update the interface declaration to indicate that you will be implementing the `CLLocationManagerDelegate` protocol:

```
@interface LocationSearchViewController
: UIViewController <CLLocationManagerDelegate>
```

LocationSearchViewController.h

You will want to maintain a copy of the current location of the device. So, in the `LocationSearchViewController.h` header, add an instance variable for the current location:

```
CLLocation* currentLocation;
```

You will also add a property that references the current location:

```
@property (nonatomic, retain) CLLocation* currentLocation;
```

In the implementation file, synthesize the `currentLocation` property:

```
@synthesize mapView,searchBar, currentLocation;
```

Next, add code to clean up the instance variable and property in the `dealloc` and `viewDidUnload` methods:

```
- (void)viewDidUnload {
    // Release any retained subviews of the main view.
    // e.g. self.myOutlet = nil;
    self.mapView = nil;
    self.searchBar = nil;
    self.currentLocation=nil;
}


- (void)dealloc {
    [mapView release];
    [searchBar release];
    [currentLocation release];
    [super dealloc];
}
```

LocationSearchViewController.m

Now, you will add code to the `viewDidLoad` method to create the `CLLocationManager`:

```
- (void)viewDidLoad {
    [super viewDidLoad];

    // Create the Core Location CLLocationManager
    CLLocationManager *locationManager = [[CLLocationManager alloc] init];
    // Set the delegate to self
    [locationManager setDelegate:self];
    // Tell the location manager to start updating the location
    [locationManager startUpdatingLocation];

}
```

LocationSearchViewController.m

In this code, you first allocate and initialize a `CLLocationManager` object. The `CLLocationManager` object controls all communication with the GPS in the device. Next, you set the delegate for the location manager to `self`. You can do this because you have declared that your class will implement the `CLLocationManagerDelegate` protocol. Finally, the code tells the location manager to start updating the device location using the GPS.

The final step is to implement the Core Location delegate methods. For now, you will simply implement the `locationManager:didUpdateToLocation:fromLocation:` method to store the location of the device in the `currentLocation` property. Additionally, you will implement `locationManager:didFailWithError:` to log that you received an error. Here is the implementation:

```
// Called when the location manager determines that there is a new location
- (void)locationManager:(CLLocationManager *)manager
    didUpdateToLocation:(CLLocation *)newLocation
           fromLocation:(CLLocation *)oldLocation {
    self.currentLocation = newLocation;

}

// Called when an error occurs
- (void)locationManager:(CLLocationManager *)manager
       didFailWithError:(NSError *)error {
    NSLog (@"locationManager:didFailWithError");
}
```

LocationSearchViewController.m

The Local Search API

You will be using the Yahoo! local search service API to get your search results. This is a REST-based API. The URL for the web service is: `http://local.yahooapis.com/LocalSearchService/V3/localSearch`.

This service enables you to search for businesses near a given location. The results include the name of the business, latitude and longitude, and Yahoo! user ratings for the business.

The search API can accept many different parameters to help you narrow and filter your search. These include the radius from the base point to search for results, a route along which to search, or a specific category in which to search. To keep this sample simple, you will only pass in the latitude and longitude of the device as the location to search and the query search terms that you are looking for.

The XML that you get in response to a query request will look something like this:

```xml
<?xml version="1.0"?>
<ResultSet xmlns:xsi="http://www.w3.org/2001/XMLSchema-instance"
    xmlns="urn:yahoo:lcl"
    xsi:schemaLocation="urn:yahoo:lcl
    http://local.yahooapis.com/LocalSearchService/V3/LocalSearchResponse.xsd"
    totalResultsAvailable="2501" totalResultsReturned="10"
    firstResultPosition="1">
    <ResultSetMapUrl>
        http://maps.yahoo.com/broadband/?tt=pizza&amp;tp=1
    </ResultSetMapUrl>
    <Result id="21566059">
        <Title>Ciceros Pizza</Title>
        <Address>20010 Stevens Creek Blvd</Address>
        <City>Cupertino</City>
        <State>CA</State>
        <Phone>(408) 253-2226</Phone>
        <Latitude>37.322724</Latitude>
        <Longitude>-122.023665</Longitude>
        <Rating>
            <AverageRating>4.5</AverageRating>
            <TotalRatings>9</TotalRatings>
            <TotalReviews>5</TotalReviews>
            <LastReviewDate>1266107776</LastReviewDate>
            <LastReviewIntro>
                My favorite pizza in the world. I understand that everybody has
                personal preferences when it comes to pizza, but for me Cicero's
                is the best. I've had pizza in Italy, many places in Europe,
                New York and everywhere else I've traveled to. For me, the best
                pizza in the world is in Cupertino, Ca..
            </LastReviewIntro>
        </Rating>
        <Distance>0.73</Distance>
        <Url>http://local.yahoo.com/info-21566059-ciceros-pizza-cupertino</Url>
        <ClickUrl>
            http://local.yahoo.com/info-21566059-ciceros-pizza-cupertino
        </ClickUrl>
        <MapUrl>
            http://maps.yahoo.com/maps_result?q1=20010+Stevens+Creek+Blvd
            +Cupertino+CA&amp;gid1=21566059
        </MapUrl>
        <Categories>
            <Category id="96926234">Carry Out &amp; Take Out</Category>
            <Category id="96926236">Restaurants</Category>
            <Category id="96926243">Pizza</Category>
        </Categories>
    </Result>
</ResultSet>
```

In this instance, you sent a query for "pizza" with the latitude and longitude of Apple headquarters in Cupertino, CA. This XML represents the first result returned from the web service. You can see that the response includes relevant information such as the name and address of the business, the phone number, the latitude and longitude, and the distance from the origin of the query. The response also contains review information submitted to Yahoo! by users of their web search services. Finally, you can see that there are several URLs if you wanted to use this information to allow a user to click on a link in your application to bring up a map or to directly link to the site of the establishment.

If you look at the `ResultSet` element at the top of the XML, you will notice that it has a few attributes of interest: `totalResultsAvailable`, `totalResultsReturned`, and `firstResultPosition`. Because there may be a very large number of results for a query, the service returns the result set in batches. You can specify the batch size, up to 20 results at a time. You can also specify the start position of the results that you want to retrieve. In this particular case, there were 2,501 results, of which you received the first 10. Your application will only handle the first batch of results. However, in a production application, you will probably want to write some code to resend the query more than once, in order to retrieve more results. It is up to you to keep track of the result position and to send back the next starting position to the service. Keep in mind that web services are stateless. They typically do not maintain any state on the server regarding your last request. It is up to you to implement whatever paging functionality meets the requirements of your application.

You can find complete documentation of the API at `http://developer.yahoo.com/search/local/V3/localSearch.html`.

Using the Search Bar

This example added a `UISearchBar` control to your application. You will use this widget to get the search criteria from the user. Unlike the other user interface elements that you have used thus far, the search bar works using the delegation pattern. Therefore, you need to declare your class as the delegate for the search bar and implement the `UISearchBarDelegate` protocol. Then, when the search bar text changes or the user presses buttons, the search bar will call your code through the delegate methods.

In your `LocationSearchViewController.h` header file, you need to declare that you will implement the `UISearchBarDelegate` protocol. Change the interface declaration to include this protocol:

```
@interface LocationSearchViewController
  : UIViewController <CLLocationManagerDelegate,UISearchBarDelegate>
```

LocationSearchViewController.h

Now, you need to tell the `searchBar` property that you want the `LocationSearchViewController` to be its delegate. Add the following code to the `viewDidLoad` method:

```
// Set the delegate for the searchbar
   [self.searchBar setDelegate:self];
```

LocationSearchViewController.h

Next, you will write some code to handle the delegate events you are interested in. When a user taps the search button, you will take the text of the search bar and pass it to the location search web service. After submitting the request, you will receive callbacks from the NSURLConnection using its delegate methods. In order to hold on to the response data that you receive from the connection, you will set up an instance variable and property called responseData. Add an instance variable called responseData of type NSMutableData* to your LocationSearchViewController.h header file:

```
NSMutableData *responseData;
```

Now, add a corresponding property:

```
@property (nonatomic, retain) NSMutableData *responseData;
```

Synthesize the new property in the implementation file:

```
@synthesize mapView,searchBar, currentLocation,responseData;
```

You are now ready to implement your searchBar delegate methods. The search bar calls the first method, searchBarSearchButtonClicked:, when the user clicks the Search button. In this method, you will create a request using the text in the search bar and send it off to the web service for processing. Here is the code:

```
- (void)searchBarSearchButtonClicked:(UISearchBar *)localSearchBar {
    NSLog (@"searchBarSearchButtonClicked");

    // Construct the URL to call
    // Note that you have to add percent escapes to the string to pass it
    // via a URL
    NSString *urlString = [NSString
        stringWithFormat:
            @"http://local.yahooapis.com/LocalSearchService/V3/localSearch?"
             "appid=YOUR_ID_GOES_HERE&query=%@&latitude=%f&longitude=%f",
        [localSearchBar.text
         stringByAddingPercentEscapesUsingEncoding:NSASCIIStringEncoding],
        self.currentLocation.coordinate.latitude,
                        self.currentLocation.coordinate.longitude];

    // Log the string that we plan to send
    NSLog (@"sending: %@",urlString);

    NSURL *serviceURL = [NSURL
                        URLWithString:urlString];

    // Create the Request.
    NSURLRequest *request = [NSURLRequest
                        requestWithURL:serviceURL
                        cachePolicy:NSURLRequestUseProtocolCachePolicy
                        timeoutInterval: 30.0];

    // Create the connection and send the request
    NSURLConnection *connection =
```

```
    [[NSURLConnection alloc] initWithRequest:request delegate:self];

    // Make sure that the connection is good
    if (connection) {
        // Instantiate the responseData data structure to store to response
        self.responseData = [NSMutableData data];

    }
    else {
        NSLog (@"The connection failed");
    }

    [localSearchBar resignFirstResponder];
}
```

LocationSearchViewController.m

You are using the same technique to send a request and receive a response from a web server, as I introduced in the previous chapter. I will point out a few minor differences.

First, you create a string that represents the URL that you will be calling. You are using the `stringWithFormat` method because you will be plugging the search query text, latitude, and longitude in dynamically at runtime. Notice that you are using the standard HTTP method for passing parameters on the querystring. That is, you give the name of the URL (`http://local .yahooapis.com/LocalSearchService/V3/localSearch`) and append a question mark (?) to indicate that parameters follow. Parameters are then passed as name-value pairs using the format `parameterName=value`. You separate your parameter pairs using the ampersand (&) character.

You can see from your URL string that you are passing four parameters: `appid`, `query`, `latitude`, and `longitude`. The `latitude` and `longitude` are the coordinates around which you want to center your search. The `query` is the item for which you want to search. The `appid` is a token that you receive from Yahoo! when you sign up to be able to use their web service. You can obtain a token to use the Local Search Service by going to `https://developer.apps.yahoo.com/wsregapp/`. Make sure that you replace the text, `YOUR_ID_GOES_HERE` in the definition of the `urlString` variable in the preceding code with the `appid` that you receive from Yahoo!, or you will not be able to access the web service.

Another important thing to notice when examining your URL string is that you call the method `stringByAddingPercentEscapesUsingEncoding` on the text string that you obtain from the search bar. The HTTP protocol uses characters such as & and % in very specific ways. If your text contains those (and several other) characters, they need to be "URL encoded." Calling this method on your string ensures that you are properly formatting the string to be able to pass it as a querystring parameter.

The last part of constructing your string is to get the latitude and longitude from your `currentLocation` object and replace them in the URL.

The next line simply logs the string to the console so that you can verify that you are creating the request URL string properly.

Next, you go on to create the objects that you need to submit your query to the web service. You create an NSURL using the URL string that you built earlier. Then, you create an NSURLRequest with the NSURL and specify the cache policy and timeout that you want. Finally, you create your NSURLConnection with the request, setting the delegate of the connection object to self.

Once you validate that the connection object is good, you instantiate the responseData property. Finally, you send the resignFirstResponder message to the search bar. This tells the search bar to dismiss the associated keyboard.

The next bit of code you will write will implement the searchBar:textDidChange: delegate method. The search bar calls this method any time the text in the search bar changes. Later on, you will implement this function to remove the annotations from the MapView if the search is changing. For now, you will simply log a message indicating that someone called the method:

```
// Called when the searchbar text changes
- (void)searchBar:(UISearchBar *)searchBar textDidChange:(NSString *)searchText{
    NSLog (@"textDidChange");

}
```

LocationSearchViewController.m

Handling the Web Service Response

In this section, you will take a look at the code that you need to write to handle the response from the web service. First, you will implement the NSURLConnection delegate methods to deal with the raw data that you receive from the web service. Then, you will define a new Result class that will hold data about each result returned from the service. Next, you will parse the XML and generate an array of Result objects. Finally, you will use the MapKit API to plot the results on a map.

The NSURLConnection Delegate Methods

In the previous section, you wrote code to handle the user clicking the search bar. The code constructs the URL and uses the HTTP GET method to send the request to the web service. Now, you need to implement the NSURLConnection delegate methods to handle the response data that the web service returns from your request. This code is very similar to the code that you built in the last chapter. To simplify this sample and focus on the web service–related aspects, I have removed some of the delegate methods that you will not need to handle.

First, you will want to implement the connection:didReceiveResponse: method. The NSURLConnection calls this delegate method when there is enough data to create the response. The connection could call this method multiple times in cases where there are server redirects from address to address. Therefore, you need to reset your response data each time the connection calls this method. Here is the implementation:

```
- (void)connection:(NSURLConnection *)connection
didReceiveResponse:(NSURLResponse *)response {
```

```
        NSLog (@"connection:didReceiveResponse:");

        [self.responseData setLength:0];

}
```

Next, you will implement the `connection:didReceiveData:` method. The connection calls this method each time it receives a chunk of data so you simply append the received chunk to your `responseData` buffer:

```
- (void)connection:(NSURLConnection *)connection didReceiveData:(NSData *)data
{
        NSLog (@"connection:didReceiveData:");

        // Append the received data to our responseData property
        [self.responseData appendData:data];

}
```

Now, you need to implement `connectionDidFinishLoading`. This method runs when the connection has finished loading all of the requested data. Here, you convert the response data to a string, clean up the connection, and call the method that you will write to parse the XML:

```
- (void)connectionDidFinishLoading:(NSURLConnection *)connection
{
        NSLog (@"connectionDidFinishLoading:");

        // Convert the data to a string and log the response string
        NSString *responseString = [[NSString alloc]
                                initWithData:self.responseData
                                encoding:NSUTF8StringEncoding];
        NSLog(@"Response String: \n%@", responseString);

        [responseString release];

        [connection release];

        [self parseXML];
}
```

Finally, you will implement the `connection:didFailWithError:` method to log that an error occurred. Remember that you will want to provide some more robust error handling and reporting in a production application. You will also probably want to give the user some feedback as to why the error occurred. Here is the implementation:

```
- (void)connection:(NSURLConnection *)connection
  didFailWithError:(NSError *)error
{
    NSLog (@"connection:didFailWithError:");
    NSLog (@"%@",[error localizedDescription]);

    [connection release];

}
```

LocationSearchViewController.m

Note that you don't have to call a web service or a URL asynchronously, but it is certainly my recommendation that you do so. Alternatively, you could retrieve the XML from a URL directly by calling the `[[NSXMLParser alloc] initWithContentsOfURL]` method. However, using this method will cause a loss of responsiveness in your application, as the main thread will block while waiting for the response from the server. Using the URL loading framework as you've done in this example is asynchronous and will leave your interface responsive as the application downloads the XML response. Additionally, it gives you more control if you need to authenticate, or handle errors more responsively as I described in the previous chapter.

Defining the Result Class

The response XML that you receive from the web service contains a lot of information. Although you will not be using all of that information in the sample, you will parse it out and capture it. To hold this data, you will create a new class that represents an individual result. Then, when you parse the XML, you will create instances of this `Result` class, populate the data from the result of the web service call, and add the `Result` to an array. Here is the header for your `Result` class:

```
#import <Foundation/Foundation.h>
#import <MapKit/MapKit.h>

@interface Result : NSObject <MKAnnotation>{
    NSString *title;
    NSString *address;
    NSString *city;
    NSString *state;
    NSString *phone;
    double latitude;
    double longitude;
    float rating;
}

@property (nonatomic, retain) NSString *title;
@property (nonatomic, retain) NSString *address;
@property (nonatomic, retain) NSString *city;
@property (nonatomic, retain) NSString *state;
@property (nonatomic, retain) NSString *phone;
@property (nonatomic) double latitude;
```

```
@property (nonatomic) double longitude;
@property (nonatomic) float rating;

@end
```

Result.h

One thing to notice is that the `MapKit.h` header file is included. You need to do this because you will use this class to provide annotation data for your MapView. To accomplish this, you need to implement the `MKAnnotation` protocol. To implement this protocol, you must provide a `coordinate` property that returns a `CLLocationCoordinate2D` struct. This struct contains the coordinates of the point that you would like to annotate on the map. You will also include a `title` property that will display a title for the map annotation, and a `subtitle` property that you will use to build the subtitle. Here is the implementation for the `Result` class:

```
#import "Result.h"

@implementation Result
@synthesize title,address,city,state,phone,latitude,longitude,rating;

- (void)dealloc {
    [title release];
    [address release];
    [city release];
    [state release];
    [phone release];
    [super dealloc];
}

-(CLLocationCoordinate2D) coordinate
{
    CLLocationCoordinate2D retVal;
    retVal.latitude = self.latitude;
    retVal.longitude = self.longitude;

    return retVal;
}

- (NSString *)subtitle {
    NSString *retVal = [[NSString alloc] initWithFormat:@"%@",phone];

    [retVal autorelease];

    return retVal;

}

@end
```

Result.m

The `dealloc` method is straightforward. It simply releases the memory allocated by the properties maintained by the class.

The `coordinate` method implements the getter for the `coordinate` property that is required to implement the `MKAnnotation` protocol. You may have noticed that a property called `coordinate` was not declared, nor was a `coordinate` property synthesized. In Objective-C, properties are simply a convenience. Behind the scenes, using properties and the dot syntax simply calls the appropriate getter or setter methods. Therefore, instead of defining a property, you simply implement the getter method that the `MKAnnotation` protocol requires.

The implementation of the `coordinate` method is straightforward. You take the latitude and longitude that you received from the web service call and package it up into a `CLLocationCoordinate2D` struct as defined by the protocol. Then, you just return that struct.

You implement the `subtitle` property in the same way. Instead of defining it as a property, you simply implement the getter method. In this case, you want the subtitle to be the phone number of the business.

Parsing the Response XML

Now that you have defined your `Result` class, you can begin parsing the response XML and building your result set. Before you start, you need to make some additions to your `LocationSearchViewController.h` header file. Add an `import` statement for your new `Result` class:

```
#import "Result.h"
```

Add a new `parseXML` method declaration to the class interface:

```
- (void) parseXML;
```

Add instance variables to hold an individual result, an `NSMutableArray` that will hold the list of all of the results, and an `NSMutableString` that will hold the characters captured during the XML parsing:

```
Result *aResult;
NSMutableArray *results;
NSMutableString *capturedCharacters;
```

Finally, define a new property for the `results` array:

```
@property (nonatomic, retain) NSMutableArray *results;
```

Move into the `LocationSearchViewController.m` implementation file and synthesize the new `results` property:

```
@synthesize mapView,searchBar, currentLocation,responseData,results ;
```

Add code to `viewDidUnload` and `dealloc` to clean up the `results` property:

Available for
download on
Wrox.com

```
- (void)viewDidUnload {
    // Release any retained subviews of the main view.
    // e.g. self.myOutlet = nil;
    self.mapView = nil;
```

```
        self.searchBar = nil;
        self.results = nil;
        self.currentLocation=nil;
    }


    - (void)dealloc {
        [mapView release];
        [searchBar release];
        [currentLocation release];
        [results release];
        [super dealloc];
    }
```

LocationSearchViewController.m

Now you are ready to implement the parseXML method. You call this method from the connectionDidFinishLoading NSURLConnection delegate method when you finish receiving the XML response from the web service. Here is the implementation:

**Available for
download on
Wrox.com**

```
    - (void) parseXML {
        NSLog (@"parseXML");

        // Initialize the parser with our NSData from the RSS feed
        NSXMLParser *xmlParser = [[NSXMLParser alloc]
                                  initWithData:self.responseData];

        // Set the delegate to self
        [xmlParser setDelegate:self];

        // Start the parser
        if (![xmlParser parse])
        {
            NSLog (@"An error occurred in the parsing");
        }

        // Clean up the parser
        [xmlParser release];


    }
```

LocationSearchViewController.m

In this method, you first declare an instance of an NSXMLParser and initialize it with the response data that you received from the web service. Next, you set the parser's delegate to self. Then, you tell the parser to start parsing the XML. Finally, you release the parser.

Remember that the NSXMLParser is a SAX parser, which is event driven. Therefore, you need to implement the delegate methods that the parser calls as parsing events occur.

First, you will implement the `didStartElement` method. The parser calls this method each time a begin-element tag, such as `<Title>`, is found:

```objc
- (void) parser:(NSXMLParser *)parser
didStartElement:(NSString *)elementName
  namespaceURI:(NSString *)namespaceURI
 qualifiedName:(NSString *)qualifiedName
    attributes:(NSDictionary *)attributeDict {
  NSLog (@"didStartElement");

  // Check to see which element we have found
  if ([elementName isEqualToString:@"Result"]) {
      // Create a new Result object
      aResult = [[Result alloc] init];


  }
  else if ([elementName isEqualToString:@"Title"]||
           [elementName isEqualToString:@"Address"]||
           [elementName isEqualToString:@"City"]||
           [elementName isEqualToString:@"State"]||
           [elementName isEqualToString:@"Phone"]||
           [elementName isEqualToString:@"Latitude"]||
           [elementName isEqualToString:@"Longitude"]||
           [elementName isEqualToString:@"AverageRating"])

  {
      // Initialize the capturedCharacters instance variable
      capturedCharacters = [[NSMutableString alloc] initWithCapacity:100];
  }
}
```

LocationSearchViewController.m

In this code, you check the name of the element that you are currently processing. If the element is a `Result`, you create a new instance of your `Result` class to hold the result. If the name is another field that you are interested in, you allocate and initialize the `capturedCharacters` instance variable in preparation for the characters to come.

Next, you will implement the `foundCharacters` method. The parser calls this method any time that it encounters characters inside an element. You implement the `foundCharacters` method to append the characters to the `capturedCharacters` instance variable, if the variable is not `nil`. If `capturedCharacters` is `nil`, you are not interested in the characters so you do nothing. Here is the code:

```objc
- (void)parser:(NSXMLParser *)parser foundCharacters:(NSString *)string {
    if (capturedCharacters != nil) {
        [capturedCharacters appendString:string];
    }
}
```

LocationSearchViewController.m

Now, you need to implement the didEndElement method. The parser calls this method when an element ends. This method is a bit verbose, but its functionality is straightforward. When you use a SAX parser, you will often find yourself writing a function like this that has a giant if/else if block. This is the nature of working with a SAX parser because you need to code one method to handle ending any element. Without further ado, here is the code:

Available for download on Wrox.com

```
- (void)parser:(NSXMLParser *)parser didEndElement:(NSString *)elementName
  namespaceURI:(NSString *)namespaceURI qualifiedName:(NSString *)qName {

    NSLog (@"didEndElement");

    // Check to see which element we have ended
    if ([elementName isEqualToString:@"Result"]) {

        // Add the result to the array
        [results addObject:aResult];

        // release the Result object
        [aResult release];
        aResult=nil;
    }
    else if ([elementName isEqualToString:@"Title"] && aResult!=nil) {
        // Set the appropriate property
        aResult.title = capturedCharacters;

    }
    else if ([elementName isEqualToString:@"Address"] && aResult!=nil) {
        // Set the appropriate property
        aResult.address = capturedCharacters;

    }
    else if ([elementName isEqualToString:@"City"] && aResult!=nil) {
        // Set the appropriate property
        aResult.city = capturedCharacters;

    }
    else if ([elementName isEqualToString:@"State"] && aResult!=nil) {
        // Set the appropriate property
        aResult.state = capturedCharacters;

    }
    else if ([elementName isEqualToString:@"Phone"] && aResult!=nil) {
        // Set the appropriate property
        aResult.phone = capturedCharacters;

    }
    else if ([elementName isEqualToString:@"Latitude"] && aResult!=nil) {
        // Set the appropriate property
        aResult.latitude = [capturedCharacters doubleValue];

    }
    else if ([elementName isEqualToString:@"Longitude"] && aResult!=nil) {
        // Set the appropriate property
```

```
        aResult.longitude = [capturedCharacters doubleValue];
    }
    else if ([elementName isEqualToString:@"AverageRating"] && aResult!=nil) {
        // Set the appropriate property
        aResult.rating = [capturedCharacters floatValue];
    }


    // So we don't have to release capturedCharacters in every else if block
    if ([elementName isEqualToString:@"Title"] ||
        [elementName isEqualToString:@"Address"] ||
        [elementName isEqualToString:@"City"] ||
        [elementName isEqualToString:@"State"] ||
        [elementName isEqualToString:@"Phone"] ||
        [elementName isEqualToString:@"Latitude"] ||
        [elementName isEqualToString:@"Longitude"] ||
        [elementName isEqualToString:@"AverageRating"])
    {
        // Release the capturedCharacters instance variable
        [capturedCharacters release];
        capturedCharacters = nil;
    }

}
```

LocationSearchViewController.m

As I said, it's verbose. However, it is actually simple. The first part of the `if` statement checks
to see if you are ending a `Result` element. If so, you add the `aResult` object to the `results`
array, release `aResult`, and set it to nil. Every other `else if` clause of that `if`/`else if` block
simply sets the appropriate property of your `Result` object. The last piece of the code releases the
`capturedCharacters` instance variable and sets it to `nil`.

The last delegate method that you will implement is `parserDidEndDocument`. The parser calls this
method when it has finished parsing the document. In this method, you will call a method of your
class, `plotResults`, which will plot your results on the map:

Available for
download on
Wrox.com

```
- (void)parserDidEndDocument:(NSXMLParser *)parser {
    NSLog (@"parserDidEndDocument");

    // Plot the results on the map
    [self plotResults];
}
```

LocationSearchViewController.m

You are now finished with the XML parser delegate methods. Next, you will take a brief look at
MapKit and then implement the `plotResults` method.

Using MapKit

The MapKit framework enables you to display maps within your application. You can programmatically add annotations to the map as you are doing in this example. The major feature of the framework is the MKMapView user interface control that you add to your views to make maps available in your application.

You are not limited to the basic annotation styles provided by the framework. You can build your own annotation view classes and use them as annotations on the map. For the sake of simplicity, this example does not do that.

Finally, the framework provides functionality to determine the user's current location and display it on the map. You will implement this feature in the viewDidLoad method. You will also implement the MKMapViewDelegate protocol to use colored pins for your annotations.

To get started, you will have to modify the LocationSearchViewController.h header file. You need to declare that you are implementing the MKMapViewDelegate protocol:

```
@interface LocationSearchViewController
: UIViewController <CLLocationManagerDelegate,UISearchBarDelegate,
    MKMapViewDelegate>
```

LocationSearchViewController.h

Next, you will add the plotResults method to the interface:

```
- (void) plotResults;
```

You are now completely finished with the LocationSearchViewController.h header file. Here is the complete header so that you can verify that your code is coordinated with the example:

```
#import <UIKit/UIKit.h>
#import <MapKit/MapKit.h>
#import <CoreLocation/CoreLocation.h>
#import "Result.h"

@interface LocationSearchViewController
: UIViewController <CLLocationManagerDelegate,UISearchBarDelegate,
    MKMapViewDelegate> {

    MKMapView* mapView;
    UISearchBar *searchBar;
    CLLocation* currentLocation;
    NSMutableData *responseData;
    NSMutableString *capturedCharacters;
    Result *aResult;
    NSMutableArray *results;
}

@property (nonatomic, retain) IBOutlet MKMapView* mapView;
@property (nonatomic, retain) IBOutlet UISearchBar *searchBar;
@property (nonatomic, retain) CLLocation* currentLocation;
```

```
@property (nonatomic, retain) NSMutableData *responseData;
@property (nonatomic, retain) NSMutableArray *results;


- (void) parseXML;
- (void) plotResults;


@end
```

LocationSearchViewController.h

Now you need to move into the implementation file. The first thing that you want to do is center the map on the current location of the device. To do this, you will implement the Core Location delegate method `locationManager:didUpdateToLocation:fromLocation:`. If you recall from the section entitled "Core Location," the location manager calls this method when it determines that the device has moved. Here is the complete implementation:

Available for
download on
Wrox.com

```
- (void)locationManager:(CLLocationManager *)manager
      didUpdateToLocation:(CLLocation *)newLocation
            fromLocation:(CLLocation *)oldLocation {
   self.currentLocation = newLocation;

   // Create a mapkit region based on the location
   // Span defines the area covered by the map in degrees
   MKCoordinateSpan span;
   span.latitudeDelta = 0.05;
   span.longitudeDelta = 0.05;

   // Region struct defines the map to show based on center coordinate and span
   MKCoordinateRegion region;
   region.center = newLocation.coordinate;
   region.span = span;

   // Update the map to display the current location
   [mapView setRegion:region animated:YES];

   // Stop core location services to conserve battery
   [manager stopUpdatingLocation];

}
```

LocationSearchViewController.m

First, you will set the `currentLocation` property to the current location of the device. Then, you create an `MKCoordinateSpan` struct. This struct defines the area that you want to display on the map. You are declaring that you would like the map to display 0.05 degrees of latitude and longitude. The span determines how far in you want to zoom the map. A larger span results in a larger area displayed on the map, thus a lower zoom factor. A small span zooms in on a small area therefore producing a high zoom factor.

Next, you define an `MKCoordinateRegion` struct. You will pass this struct to the `mapView` to define the region that you want to display. An `MKCoordinateRegion` consists of a span and a center point. You will center the map on the coordinate that you receive from Core Location.

Next, you tell the `mapView` to set the region displayed on the map and to animate the transition to your new region. Finally, you tell the Core Location manager to stop getting location updates from the GPS. Because your application does not need extremely accurate resolution, nor do you need constant updates from the GPS, you can conserve power by turning the GPS off.

For the next step, you need to make a couple of additions to the `viewDidLoad` method. Because you will be customizing the pin colors for your annotations, you need to set the `mapView` delegate to `self`. In addition, for illustrative purposes, you will display the user's location on the map by setting the map view's `showsUserLocation` property to `YES`. When using the `showsUserLocation` property, you need to be aware that this will cause the map view to use Core Location to retrieve and maintain the user's location on the map. This forces the GPS receiver to remain on, consuming valuable battery power. You should carefully consider if your application needs this functionality or not before using it. This example uses this feature to demonstrate a capability of the map view to display the user's current location. Here is the complete implementation of `viewDidLoad`:

Available for
download on
Wrox.com

```
- (void)viewDidLoad {
    [super viewDidLoad];


    // Create the results array
    self.results = [[NSMutableArray alloc] init];


    // Create the Core Location CLLocationManager
    CLLocationManager *locationManager = [[CLLocationManager alloc] init];
    // Set the delegate to self
    [locationManager setDelegate:self];
    // Tell the location manager to start updating the location
    [locationManager startUpdatingLocation];

    // Set the delegate for the searchbar
    [self.searchBar setDelegate:self];

    // Set the delegate for the mapView
    [self.mapView setDelegate:self];

    // Use Core Location to find the user's location and display it on the map
    // Be careful when using this because it causes the mapview to continue to
    // use Core Location to keep the user's position on the map up to date
    self.mapView.showsUserLocation = YES;

}
```

LocationSearchViewController.m

When the user clears the text from the search bar, you want to clear the old annotations from the map. You can do this by implementing the `searchBar:textDidChange:` delegate method like this:

```
// Called when the searchbar text changes
- (void)searchBar:(UISearchBar *)searchBar textDidChange:(NSString *)searchText{
    NSLog (@"textDidChange");

    // If the text was cleared, clear the map annotations
    if ([searchText isEqualToString:@""])
    {
        // Clear the annotations
        [self.mapView removeAnnotations:self.mapView.annotations];

        // Clear the results array
        [self.results removeAllObjects];
    }

}
```

LocationSearchViewController.m

You implement this code to check to see if the user has cleared the search string. If he has, you remove the annotations from the map and clear your `results` array.

In the last bit of code, you will implement the `mapView:viewForAnnotation:` delegate method. The map view will call this method when the map needs the view for an annotation. If you wanted to implement a custom view for your annotations, you would do it in this method. Instead of implementing a custom view, you will use the `MKPinAnnotationView`; however, you could easily replace this with your own view. You will change the color of the pin based on the user rating of the business that you are plotting on the map. Here is the code:

```
- (MKAnnotationView *)mapView:(MKMapView *)mapView
            viewForAnnotation:(id <MKAnnotation>)annotation
{
    // If we are displaying the user's location, return nil
    //  to use the default view
    if ([annotation isKindOfClass:[MKUserLocation class]]) {
        return nil;
    }

    // Try to dequeue an existing pin
    MKPinAnnotationView *pinAnnotationView =
        (MKPinAnnotationView *)
        [self.mapView dequeueReusableAnnotationViewWithIdentifier:@"location"];

    if (!pinAnnotationView) {
        // We could not get a pin from the queue
        pinAnnotationView=[[[MKPinAnnotationView alloc]
                        initWithAnnotation:annotation
```

```
                         reuseIdentifier:@"location"] autorelease];

        pinAnnotationView.animatesDrop=TRUE;
        pinAnnotationView.canShowCallout = YES;

    }

    // We need to get the rating from the annotation object
    //  to color the pin based on rating
    Result *resultAnnotation = (Result*) annotation;

    if (resultAnnotation.rating > 4.5) {
        pinAnnotationView.pinColor = MKPinAnnotationColorGreen;
    }
    else if (resultAnnotation.rating > 3.5) {
        pinAnnotationView.pinColor = MKPinAnnotationColorPurple;
    }
    else {
        pinAnnotationView.pinColor = MKPinAnnotationColorRed;
    }


    return pinAnnotationView;

}
```

LocationSearchViewController.m

The first line of the method checks to see if the annotation is for the user location view. If it is, you simply return `nil` to tell the map to use the default annotation.

Next, you will see the attempt to dequeue an existing annotation view. The MapView works very much like the TableView in this respect. It doesn't make sense to keep invisible map annotations in memory. Therefore, the MapView creates and releases annotations as they become visible or disappear from the map respectively. Instead of creating new annotation instances every time, the MapView maintains an internal queue of annotation objects that it can reuse. Therefore, you first try to dequeue an annotation. If you cannot, you create a new pin annotation view with the correct reuse identifier. Then, you set the attributes of this view.

Next, you cast the annotation that the MapView is asking for to a `Result` object. Then, you use the `rating` property of the `Result` to set the color of the pin. Finally, you return the `pinAnnotationView`.

Finishing Up

The code is now complete. You should be able to successfully build and run the application. If you attempt to run the application in the simulator, you will see that the device thinks that it is at Apple headquarters, regardless of where you are actually located. This is by design. Enter a search term in the search bar and watch the pins drop to show you the results. You can view the XML returned by the web service in the console.

EXAMPLE 2: TERM EXTRACTION

When making calls to a web service, you will often use the HTTP GET method to send parameters to the service. When dealing with REST-based web services, you use GET to indicate that you are performing a query for some data from the server. There are occasions where you will need to POST data to the server. Many SOAP-based web services use POST to send data. REST uses the POST method to indicate that you are sending data to the server and intend to modify the database.

Sending a POST request is very similar to sending a GET request with some minor exceptions, as you will see in the example code.

In this example, you will make a call to the Yahoo! Term Extraction service. This service returns a list of what it deems to be the significant words and phrases in the text passage that you submit. There is no definition of what Yahoo! determines to be "significant," nor is their algorithm to determine significance public. Because of the length of the string that you can submit to the service, it is not practical to use the GET method; therefore, the service requires that you use POST to send your string into the web service. You can apply the same principles that you use here to any web service that requires you to submit data using the POST method. The completed example will look like Figure 11-5.

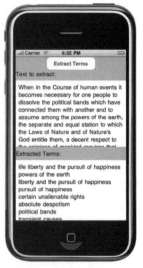

FIGURE 11-5: Complete term extraction application

Getting Started

To get started, open Xcode and create a new View-based application called TermExtract. In the `TermExtractViewController.h` header file, add instance variables for two `UITextView` variables:

```
UITextView *textToExtractTextView;
UITextView *extractedTermsTextView;
```

Next, add properties for these `UITextView`s:

```
@property (nonatomic, retain) IBOutlet UITextView *textToExtractTextView;
@property (nonatomic, retain) IBOutlet UITextView *extractedTermsTextView;
```

Also, add instance variables for the response data that you will receive from the server in response to your request, and the characters that you will capture during XML parsing:

```
NSMutableData *responseData;
NSMutableString *capturedCharacters;
```

Now, add a property for the `responseData`:

```
@property (nonatomic, retain) NSMutableData *responseData;
```

Next, add an IBAction method called extractTerms that you will call after the user enters the text to send to the service. Finally, add an instance method called parseXML that you will invoke to start the XML processing:

```
- (IBAction) extractTerms:(id)sender;
- (void) parseXML;
```

The complete header should look like this:

```
#import <UIKit/UIKit.h>

@interface TermExtractViewController : UIViewController {
    UITextView *textToExtractTextView;
    UITextView *extractedTermsTextView;
    NSMutableData *responseData;
    NSMutableString *capturedCharacters;

}

@property (nonatomic, retain) IBOutlet UITextView *textToExtractTextView;
@property (nonatomic, retain) IBOutlet UITextView *extractedTermsTextView;
@property (nonatomic, retain) NSMutableData *responseData;

- (IBAction) extractTerms:(id)sender;
- (void) parseXML;

@end
```

TermExtractViewController.h

In the implementation file, synthesize the textToExtractTextView, extractedTermsTextView, responseData properties:

```
@synthesize textToExtractTextView,extractedTermsTextView,responseData;
```

Then, add the code to clean up the properties in the viewDidUnload method:

```
- (void)viewDidUnload {
    // Release any retained subviews of the main view.
    // e.g. self.myOutlet = nil;
    self.textToExtractTextView=nil;
    self.extractedTermsTextView=nil;
    self.responseData=nil;
}
```

TermExtractViewController.m

Finally, release your instance variables and call the superclass's `dealloc` method in `dealloc`:

```
- (void)dealloc {
    [textToExtractTextView release];
    [extractedTermsTextView release];
    [responseData release];

    [super dealloc];
}
```

TermExtractViewController.m

Building the User Interface

You will now build the user interface for the application using Interface Builder. Double-click on the `TermExtractViewController.xib` file in Xcode to open the file in Interface Builder. Once the interface view is open, add two `UITextViews`, two `UILabels`, and a `UIButton`, as shown in Figure 11-6.

Change the `title` attribute of the `UIButton` to read "Extract Terms." Change the text of the top `UILabel` to read "Text to extract:" and the bottom `UILabel` to "Extracted Terms:".

As default text in the "Text to extract:" TextView, I set the text to the Declaration of Independence. I have included a text file containing the declaration, or you could use your own text or just provide text at runtime. Delete the default text from the extracted terms TextView.

Next, you need to hook up the TextViews to the proper outlets in Interface Builder. Hook up the Extract Terms button to the `IBAction extractTerms` in File's Owner. In the `TermExtractViewController.m` implementation file, implement

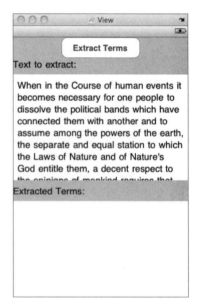

FIGURE 11-6: Term extract user interface

a stub `extractTerms` method to log when someone calls the method. You will use this to verify that you have correctly wired up the button in Interface Builder. Here is the stub code:

```
- (IBAction) extractTerms:(id)sender
{
    NSLog (@"extractTerms");
}
```

Build and run the application. Click the `extractTerms` button and verify that you see the log message in the console. This shows that you have correctly wired the button to the method. If you do not see the message in the console, make sure that you have properly wired the button to the message in Interface Builder.

You are finished with the user interface, so you can close Interface Builder.

Implementing the POST Call

You will implement the `extractTerms` method to POST the request to the web service.

The first thing that you do in this method is to dismiss the keyboard by calling the `resignFirstResponder` method on the TextView. Next, you clear the list of extracted terms to eliminate old results:

```
- (IBAction) extractTerms:(id)sender
{
    NSLog (@"extractTerms");

    // Hide the keyboard
    [self.textToExtractTextView resignFirstResponder];

    // Clear the old extracted terms
    self.extractedTermsTextView.text = @"";
```

TermExtractViewController.m

Now, you create a string to hold the URL that you plan to call. This is the address of the Yahoo! Term Extraction web service. Next, you create an NSURL object with this string:

```
    // Create a string for the URL
    NSString *urlString =
        @"http://search.yahooapis.com/ContentAnalysisService/V1/termExtraction";

    // Create the NSURL
    NSURL *url = [NSURL URLWithString:urlString];
```

TermExtractViewController.m

The next line is where using the POST method differs from using GET. If you recall, when using the GET method, you simply set the URL string, set the parameter values inline, and sent the request off through the NSURLConnection. When using the POST method, you need to do things a little differently. After you create the NSURLRequest, you will need to modify some of its properties. Therefore, you must use an NSMutableURLRequest instead:

```
    // Create a mutable request because we will append data to it.
    NSMutableURLRequest *request = [NSMutableURLRequest requestWithURL:url
        cachePolicy:NSURLRequestUseProtocolCachePolicy
        timeoutInterval: 30.0];
```

TermExtractViewController.m

The first change that you will make to the request is to set the HTTP method that you plan to use. Remember that you are using the POST method. The default method is GET, so you have to change this in the request to POST using the setHTTPMethod method:

```
// Set the HTTP method of the request to POST
    [request setHTTPMethod:@"POST"];
```

TermExtractViewController.m

Next, you will build a string to hold your parameters. In this example, there is only one parameter, but many parameters can optionally be passed using the POST method. You should note that parameters must be passed using the HTML parameter passing syntax name=value just like when using the GET method. In your implementation, make sure that you replace the appid with the actual appid that you receive from Yahoo! after you register your application. Here is your parameter string:

```
// Build a string for the parameters
    NSString *parameters = [[NSString alloc] initWithFormat:
        @"appid=YOUR_ID_GOES_HERE&context=%@",
        self.textToExtractTextView.text];
```

TermExtractViewController.m

When you use the GET method to call a web service, you pass the parameters in the query string of the HTTP request. However, when you use POST, you pass those parameters in the body of the HTTP message. Therefore, you have to set the HTTP body using the setHTTPBody method:

```
// Set the body of the request
    [request setHTTPBody:[parameters dataUsingEncoding:NSUTF8StringEncoding]];
```

TermExtractViewController.m

The rest of the code for the method is the same as you have seen before. First, you create the NSURLConnection:

```
NSURLConnection *connection =
    [[NSURLConnection alloc] initWithRequest:request delegate:self];
```

TermExtractViewController.m

Next, you instantiate your responseData property:

```
// Make sure that the connection is good
    if (connection) {
        // Instantiate the responseData data structure to store to response
        self.responseData = [NSMutableData data];

    }
```

```
else {
    NSLog (@"The connection failed");
}
```

Finally, you need to clean up your local variables:

```
// Clean up our local variables
[urlString release];
[parameters release];
```

Here is the complete method implementation:

```
- (IBAction) extractTerms:(id)sender
{
    NSLog (@"extractTerms");

    // Hide the keyboard
    [self.textToExtractTextView resignFirstResponder];

    // Clear the old extracted terms
    self.extractedTermsTextView.text = @"";

    // Create a string for the URL
    NSString *urlString =
        @"http://search.yahooapis.com/ContentAnalysisService/V1/termExtraction";

    // Create the NSURL
    NSURL *url = [NSURL URLWithString:urlString];


    // Create a mutable request because we will append data to it.
    NSMutableURLRequest *request = [NSMutableURLRequest requestWithURL:url
        cachePolicy:NSURLRequestUseProtocolCachePolicy
        timeoutInterval: 30.0];


    // Set the HTTP method of the request to POST
    [request setHTTPMethod:@"POST"];

    // Build a string for the parameters
    NSString *parameters = [[NSString alloc] initWithFormat:
        @"appid=YOUR_ID_GOES_HERE&context=%@",
        self.textToExtractTextView.text];

    // Set the body of the request
    [request setHTTPBody:[parameters dataUsingEncoding:NSUTF8StringEncoding]];

    // Create the connection and send the request
```

```
        NSURLConnection *connection =
        [[NSURLConnection alloc] initWithRequest:request delegate:self];

        // Make sure that the connection is good
        if (connection) {
            // Instantiate the responseData data structure to store to response
            self.responseData = [NSMutableData data];

        }
        else {
            NSLog (@"The connection failed");
        }

        // Clean up our local variables
        [urlString release];
        [parameters release];
    }
```

TermExtractViewController.m

Receiving the XML Response

In order to receive the response from the web service, you need to implement the NSURLConnection delegate methods as you did in the previous example.

First, you will implement the connection:didReceiveResponse: method. This delegate method is called when the NSURLConnection creates the response. The connection could call this method multiple times, so you need to reset your response data by setting its length to zero each time this method runs. Here is the implementation:

Available for
download on
Wrox.com

```
// Called when the connection has enough data to create an NSURLResponse
- (void)connection:(NSURLConnection *)connection
didReceiveResponse:(NSURLResponse *)response {
    NSLog (@"connection:didReceiveResponse:");
    NSLog (@"expectedContentLength: %qi", [response expectedContentLength] );
    NSLog (@"textEncodingName: %@", [response textEncodingName]);

    [self.responseData setLength:0];

}
```

TermExtractViewController.m

Next, you need to implement the connection:didReceiveData: delegate method. The connection calls this method each time it receives data so you need to append the received data to your responseData buffer:

Available for
download on
Wrox.com

```
// Called each time the connection receives a chunk of data
- (void)connection:(NSURLConnection *)connection didReceiveData:(NSData *)data
{
```

```
NSLog (@"connection:didReceiveData:");

// Append the received data to our responseData property
[self.responseData appendData:data];

}
```

Now you need to implement `connectionDidFinishLoading`. The delegate calls this method when the connection has completed loading the requested data. In this method, you convert the response data to a string, clean up the connection, and call the method to parse the XML:

Available for
download on
Wrox.com

```
// Called when the connection has successfully received the complete response
- (void)connectionDidFinishLoading:(NSURLConnection *)connection
{
    NSLog (@"connectionDidFinishLoading:");

    // Convert the data to a string and log the response string
    NSString *responseString = [[NSString alloc]
                                initWithData:self.responseData
                                encoding:NSUTF8StringEncoding];
    NSLog(@"Response String: \n%@", responseString);

    [responseString release];
    [connection release];

    [self parseXML];
}
```

Finally, you should implement the `connection:didFailWithError:` method. Here you will log that an error occurred. In a production application, you would want to provide more robust error handling. Here is the implementation:

Available for
download on
Wrox.com

```
// Called when an error occurs in loading the response
- (void)connection:(NSURLConnection *)connection
    didFailWithError:(NSError *)error
{
    NSLog (@"connection:didFailWithError:");
    NSLog (@"%@",[error localizedDescription]);

    [connection release];

}
```

Parsing the Response XML

After you submit your request, you will receive an XML response from the web service. The response will contain the most relevant words and phrases from the text that you sent into the service, in order of relevance. The response that I received when I sent the declaration to the web service looked like this:

```
<?xml version="1.0"?>
<ResultSet xmlns:xsi="http://www.w3.org/2001/XMLSchema-instance"
 xmlns="urn:yahoo:cate" xsi:schemaLocation="urn:yahoo:cate
 http://search.yahooapis.com/ContentAnalysisService/V1/
 TermExtractionResponse.xsd">
    <Result>life liberty and the pursuit of happiness</Result>
    <Result>powers of the earth</Result>
    <Result>liberty and the pursuit of happiness</Result>
    <Result>pursuit of happiness</Result>
    <Result>certain unalienable rights</Result>
    <Result>absolute despotism</Result>
    <Result>political bands</Result>
    <Result>transient causes</Result>
    <Result>decent respect</Result>
    <Result>long train</Result>
    <Result>direct object</Result>
    <Result>usurpations</Result>
    <Result>sufferance</Result>
    <Result>laws of nature</Result>
    <Result>one people</Result>
    <Result>form of government</Result>
    <Result>when in the course of human events</Result>
    <Result>evils</Result>
    <Result>prudence</Result>
    <Result>mankind</Result>
</ResultSet>
```

You need to implement the parseXML function, just as you did in the previous example, to parse this response XML:

```
- (void) parseXML {
    NSLog (@"parseXML");

    // Initialize the parser with our NSData from the RSS feed
    NSXMLParser *xmlParser = [[NSXMLParser alloc]
                               initWithData:self.responseData];

    // Set the delegate to self
    [xmlParser setDelegate:self];

    // Start the parser
    if (![xmlParser parse])
    {
        NSLog (@"An error occurred in the parsing");
    }
```

```
        // Release the parser because we are done with it
        [xmlParser release];
    }
```

TermExtractViewController.m

In this method, you first declare an instance of an NSXMLParser and initialize it with the response data that you received from the web service. Next, you set the parser's delegate to self. Then, you tell the parser to start parsing the XML. Finally, you release the parser.

Finally, you will implement your NSXMLParser delegate methods:

Available for
download on
Wrox.com

```
// Called when the parser encounters a start element
- (void) parser:(NSXMLParser *)parser
didStartElement:(NSString *)elementName
   namespaceURI:(NSString *)namespaceURI
  qualifiedName:(NSString *)qualifiedName
     attributes:(NSDictionary *)attributeDict {

    // Check to see which element we have found
    if ([elementName isEqualToString:@"Result"]) {
        // Initialize the capturedCharacters instance variable
        capturedCharacters = [[NSMutableString alloc] initWithCapacity:100];
    }
}

// Called when the parser encounters an end element
- (void)parser:(NSXMLParser *)parser didEndElement:(NSString *)elementName
  namespaceURI:(NSString *)namespaceURI qualifiedName:(NSString *)qName {

    NSLog (@"didEndElement");

    // Check to see which element we have ended

    // We ended a Result element
    if ([elementName isEqualToString:@"Result"]) {
        NSLog (@"capturedCharacters: %@" , capturedCharacters);

        self.extractedTermsTextView.text = [self.extractedTermsTextView.text
            stringByAppendingFormat:@"%@\n",capturedCharacters];

        // Release the capturedCharacters instance variable
        [capturedCharacters release];
        capturedCharacters = nil;
    }



}

// Called when the parser finds characters contained within an element
```

```
- (void)parser:(NSXMLParser *)parser foundCharacters:(NSString *)string {
    if (capturedCharacters != nil) {
        [capturedCharacters appendString:string];
    }
}
```

TermExtractViewController.m

Because you are only interested in Result elements, this code is straightforward. If you encounter the start of a Result element, you initialize your `capturedCharacters` instance variable in the `didStartElement` method. In `didEndElement`, you check to see that you ended a Result element. Then, you append the `capturedCharacters` string to the `extractedTermsTextView`.

Finishing Up

The application is now complete. You should be able to successfully build and run the program. When you tap the Extract Terms button, you will send the query to the web service. If you have an active Internet connection, and you have properly configured your own `appid`, you should receive an XML result set back that contains the extracted terms. You can verify this in the console log. The code will take the text contained in each Result element, parse it, and append it to the `extractedTermsTextView` in the user interface. Feel free to paste in any block of text that you find interesting to see what the Yahoo! service feels are the most significant words or phrases in the document.

MOVING FORWARD

In this chapter, you learned about the basics of XML web services. Then you learned how to call XML web services using both the HTTP GET and POST methods. This will enable you to call any web service available on the Internet.

You also learned how to use the Core Location framework to access the GPS functionality and determine a device's location. Then, you learned how to use the MapKit framework to display and annotate maps.

Over the course of this entire book, you have explored the full spectrum of dealing with data on the iPhone and iPad. You learned how to display data on the device, extract data from enterprise systems and store it on the device, use Core Data to generate and manage data on the device, and use web services to communicate from your application to other services.

You now have all of the tools necessary to build robust, data-driven applications. I hope that you find the exploration of the frameworks and functionality available in the iPhone SDK helpful in your daily work. I hope that you take this knowledge, go out, and build amazing applications, because the iPhone and iPad are amazing platforms for your software. We are still only at the beginning for these devices. As these technologies evolve, the capabilities of the devices will only get better, allowing you to build applications that are even more amazing!

Tools for Troubleshooting
Your Applications

In this book, I have covered various topics related to building data-centric iPhone and iPad applications. Because most readers are already familiar with iOS software development, this book does not include in-depth coverage of the tools that experienced developers may already know about such as Instruments and the Static Analyzer.

This appendix covers these tools, which can be invaluable when troubleshooting your applications. The techniques that you learn in this appendix are general. You should be able to use these techniques as-is with the current version of Instruments, and apply the same principles to future versions of the tool. If you already know about these tools, perhaps you will learn a new tip or trick. If you have never used these tools, you will learn how to use them to effectively track down problems in your code.

INSTRUMENTS

Instruments is a graphical tool that helps you to gather information about your application at runtime. You can then use this information to help track down difficult bugs such as memory leaks. Instruments is also valuable in profiling the performance of your application and helping you to track down and fix bottlenecks. Many different tools are available in the Instruments application to help you to troubleshoot a variety of application problems.

The Instruments application consists of a set of instruments that you use to collect data about your application as it runs. You can see all of the instruments that are available for use in Figure A-1. The instruments generally display their results graphically. You can have many instruments running concurrently with their resulting graphs displayed together in the application interface. This can help you analyze the relationships between the data collected by different instruments.

You can also create custom instruments that use DTrace to examine the execution of your application. DTrace is a dynamic scripting tool that Sun created and Apple ported to OS X.

You cannot use DTrace custom instruments on the iPhone OS directly, but you can use them in conjunction with the simulator

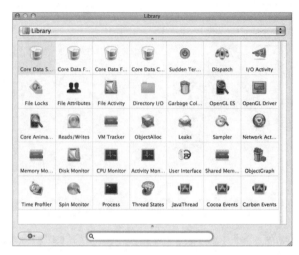

FIGURE A-1: Available instruments

when running your application on your development machine. While this reduces the usefulness of custom instruments because you cannot use them for performance profiling on the device, you can still build instruments to help you to debug your applications in the simulator.

Because DTrace instruments are of limited usefulness to iPhone developers, I will not cover them in detail. You can refer to the Instruments user guide located at `http://developer.apple.com/iphone/library/documentation/DeveloperTools/Conceptual/InstrumentsUserGuide` for more details on creating custom instruments using DTrace.

Starting Instruments

You can start the Instruments tool by launching the application, which is located, by default, in `/YourDriveName/Developer/Applications` or by selecting Run ➪ Run With Performance Tool from the menu bar in Xcode.

If you start the application directly, you will see a list of templates for the trace document that you are about to start. The trace document holds the set of all of your individual trace runs. You can save your trace documents so that you can review all of the data collected from your traces at any time. If you start Instruments from within Xcode, you are effectively selecting the template that you will use when you choose an option under Instruments in the menu bar.

The templates consist of default sets of instruments designed to assist you with specific tasks. For instance, you would select the Leaks template if you were interested in troubleshooting memory leaks in your application. After you select the Leaks template, the Instruments application appears with both the Leaks and ObjectAlloc instruments loaded into the trace document. If you examine the definitions of each tool, you will see that you often want to use the ObjectAlloc instrument in conjunction with the Leaks instrument because ObjectAlloc can give you insight into the history of an object that the Leaks tool reports as a leak.

The Trace Document

The trace document is the group of tools that you are using, along with any test runs. You can see an example of a trace document in Figure A-2.

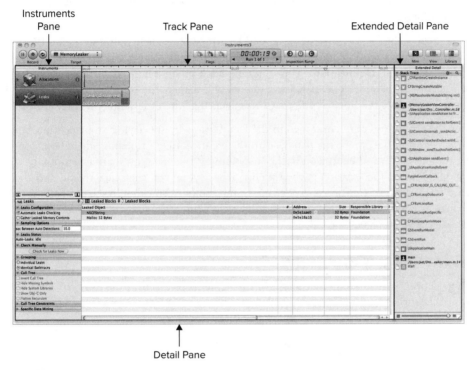

FIGURE A-2: The trace document

The Instruments pane shows the list of instruments that you are using for the current trace. Clicking the info button for an instrument displays that instrument's configuration options. You can add instruments to the Instruments pane by dragging them from the instruments library (displayed with Command+L) and dropping them into the Instruments pane.

The Track pane displays the graphical output of the instrument in a timeline. Each instrument records its data into its own track. The Track pane shows the time that an event occurred during the test run. You can adjust the time scale using the slider at the bottom of the Instruments pane. You can scroll the Track pane using the scrollbar at the bottom of the pane.

The small triangle that appears at the top of the Track pane is the *playhead*. The playhead indicates the current time of the test run. You can move the playhead to review the state of your application at any given time during its execution. You can add a flag at the current location of the playhead by clicking the flag icon with the plus sign next to it in the toolbar. You can navigate forward to the next flag or back to the previous flag by clicking the flag icons to the right or the left of the add flag icon respectively.

The Detail pane shows the details of the currently selected tool. The Detail pane shows different details based on the tool that you have selected in the Instruments pane. You can select an item in the Detail pane to view more detail about the item in the Extended Detail pane. The Extended Detail pane is particularly useful because it shows a stack trace for the method call that you have selected in the Detail pane.

I find it useful to display the file icons in the Extended Detail pane because doing so makes the calls in the stack that originated in your code obvious. You can enable the file icons by clicking on the gear icon in the Extended Details pane. If you double-click on an item in the call stack that corresponds to one of your source code files, Instruments will display the source code in the Detail pane. Instruments highlights the line of code that was executing when the sample was taken.

You can narrow the amount of data contained in the Detail pane by specifying an inspection range. To specify an inspection range, move the playhead to the location in the timeline where you want the range to begin and click on the left icon in the Inspection Range icon group in the toolbar. Next, move the playhead to the location in the timeline where you want the range to end and click on the right icon in the Inspection Range icon group in the toolbar. You should see the data in the Detail pane reduce down to include only the data collected during the time window specified by the inspection range that you have created.

Objective-C Memory Management

In the upcoming section, you will explore the use of Instruments to discover the cause of a memory leak. First, let's take a brief detour to make sure that you understand how memory management works in Objective-C.

Although garbage collection is a nice feature available to developers on the Mac platform, there is currently no garbage-collected version of the Objective-C runtime available for the iPhone or iPad. Therefore, you are responsible for managing the memory consumed by the objects that you create in your applications. If you fail to properly free the memory that you allocate, the total amount of memory consumed by your application will grow as the application runs. This failure to clean up unused memory results in a memory leak. Eventually, if your program consumes too much memory, the OS will terminate your application.

All Objective-C classes that inherit from NSObject have a *retain count*. When an object is allocated using alloc or new, its retain count is set to 1. The retain count is a counter that indicates the number of bits of code that are interested in the object. When you need to hold on to a reference to an object, you increment the retain count by calling the retain method on the object. When you are finished with an object, you call release to decrement the retain count. The retain count determines when the object should be de-allocated and its dealloc method called.

You need to be careful to balance calls to new, alloc, or retain with calls to release. If you have too few calls to release, the retain count for the object will never drop to 0 and the object will never be released, resulting in a memory leak. If you call release too many times, you will over-release the object, causing a segmentation fault and an application crash.

In general, adding an object to a collection such as `NSMutableArray` increments the retain count. Likewise, removing an object from a collection decrements the retain count. Simply obtaining an object from a collection typically returns an autoreleased object. If you need to hold on to the reference to an autoreleased object, you need to call `retain` on it.

You can also send the message `autorelease` to an object. This indicates that the runtime should release the object at a point in the future, but not right away. You use autorelease pools to keep track of all autoreleased objects. There is an application-wide autorelease pool that the project template creates automatically when you begin your application. You can create local pools yourself as well.

Autorelease is particularly useful for returning objects from methods. You can allocate the object that you plan to return from the method, configure it, and then autorelease it. It is then the caller's responsibility to retain the object to ensure that it has the proper retain count. The Objective-C runtime will send an autoreleased object to the `release` message one time for every time you call `autorelease` on it when the autorelease pool is drained or de-allocated.

When you create an object with a helper method that has `alloc`, `new`, or `copy` in its name, it is your responsibility to release it. Objects created in this way, by convention, have a retain count of 1. If you use a method that returns an object such as `stringWithString` to get an instance of an object, you should assume that the object is autoreleased.

If you need to hold on to a reference to an autoreleased object, it is your responsibility to call `retain`. The default autorelease pool will de-allocate autoreleased objects each time through the application's run loop. So, if you get an autoreleased object in a function, use it right away, and don't need it after the method call is complete, you do not need to worry about retaining it. However, if you plan to put an autoreleased object into an instance variable for access at a later time, you have to call `retain` on it or else it will be de-allocated at the end of the run loop and your application will crash with a segmentation fault when you try to send a message to the de-allocated object.

You should use `release` instead of `autorelease` whenever possible as there is less overhead in calling `release`. If you are going to be creating and autoreleasing many objects, in a loop perhaps, you should wrap the loop in its own autorelease pool.

You can send the `retainCount` message to any `NSObject` to obtain the current retain count of that object. You generally won't use this method in a production application, but it can be helpful to log the retain count of an object as you are trying to debug memory problems.

The rules of memory management are simple. To summarize:

➤ If you create an object with `alloc`, `new`, or `copy`, the object will have a retain count of 1 and you are responsible calling `release`.

➤ If you get a reference to an object in any other way, you can assume that it has a retain count of 1 and has been autoreleased. If you need to hold on to a reference to the object, `retain` it.

➤ If you call `retain` on an object, you have to balance the call to `retain` with a call to `release`.

A memory leak occurs when you lose the reference to a pointer for an object that you have not deleted from the heap, or if you do not match the number of calls to `retain`, `alloc`, `new`, or `copy` to the number of calls to `release`. This is called over-retaining an object. Over-retaining will result in the object's retain count never reaching 0 at which time the runtime frees the memory consumed by the object. Because the object is not freed, you have leaked the memory consumed by the object for the remainder of the life of the program.

Sample Memory Leak Application

Now that you have an understanding of memory management and Objective-C, you will build an application with a memory leak and then use Instruments to find and fix that leak. The application will be very simple with only a single button for the user interface, as you can see in Figure A-3. When you tap the Go button, a routine with a memory leak will run and log to the console.

Start a new View-based Application project for iPhone called MemoryLeaker. Open the `MemoryLeakerViewController.h` header file and add an action for the Go button as follows:

FIGURE A-3:
MemoryLeaker application

```
#import <UIKit/UIKit.h>

@interface MemoryLeakerViewController : UIViewController {

}

-(IBAction) goPressed:(id) sender;


@end
```

Now, you need to build the interface in Interface Builder. Open the `MemoryLeakerViewController` `.xib` file in Interface Builder. Add a `UIButton` to the View and wire the `TouchUpInside` event to File's Owner `goPressed` method. Save the XIB file and close Interface Builder.

Next, you are going to implement the `goPressed` method in the `MemoryLeakerViewController.m` implementation file. Remember that this code has a memory leak so don't use it in any of your applications. Here is the implementation of the `goPressed` method:

```
-(IBAction) goPressed:(id) sender
{

    NSMutableString *theString = [[NSMutableString alloc] init];

    [theString appendString:@"This"] ;
    [theString appendString:@" is"] ;
    [theString appendString:@" a"] ;
    [theString appendString:@" string"] ;

    NSLog(@"theString is: %@", theString);

}
```

This method simply creates an `NSMutableString` object, appends four strings to it, and logs the string to the console. Take a second and see if you can discover the memory leak on your own. The leak occurs because you allocated the `NSMutableString` object `theString` using a call to `alloc`, but you never released this object. After this method ends, the pointer to the string object will be gone. This memory is now unrecoverable, resulting in a memory leak.

Build and run the application. When the simulator comes up, click on the Go button. You should see this text in the console: `theString is: This is a string`.

Analyzing a Memory Leak in Instruments

Now that you have the sample application coded and ready to go, it's time to find the memory leak in the application using Instruments. In Xcode, select Run ⇨ Run with Performance Tool ⇨ Leaks from the menu bar. Once the application starts in the simulator, you will see a dark gray triangle at the top of the Track pane start to move from left to right. This indicates that Instruments is recording data from the running application.

The Leaks instrument is configured to auto-detect leaks in your application every ten seconds. You can force manual detection of leaks at any time by clicking on the Check for Leaks Now button that appears in the left side of the Detail pane when you have the Leaks instrument selected in the Instruments pane. After the application starts and Instruments is running, click the Go button in the iPhone simulator. In a few moments, when the leak check occurs, you will see a red bar in the top part of the Leaks tool in the Track pane and a purple repeating bar below, as you can see in Figure A-4. You have now collected the data that you need, so stop Instruments from collecting data by clicking the Stop button in the top-left corner of the application.

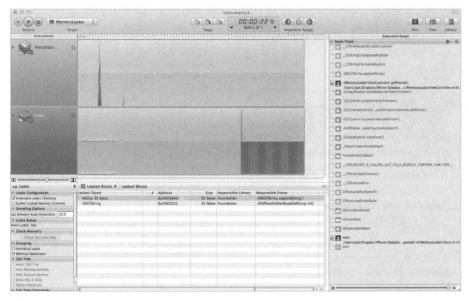

FIGURE A-4: Memory leak in Instruments

The red bar indicates that a leak was found, and in fact, shows the number of leaks. The purple bar shows the total number of bytes leaked. For the sake of clarity, I have stopped Instruments on this run after triggering the memory leak one time. If you repeatedly tap on the Go button in the application, you will see a stair step pattern in the Leaks instrument, as memory is lost each time the button is pressed.

Make sure that you have the Leaks instrument selected by clicking Leaks in the Instruments pane. If you examine the Detail pane, you will see that there are two line items. Each line item in the Detail pane shows you a leaked block of memory. In this case, there were two leaked blocks. The first block is the NSCFString that holds your NSMutableString. The mutable string allocated the second block behind the scenes to hold the new contents of the string after you append data to your mutable string. If you had coded the application to release the NSMutableString, as you will in a moment, you would not see either of these blocks in the Detail pane.

Now, let's see how Instruments can help pin down where the leak has occurred. Make sure that you have the Extended Detail pane open. Then, click on the NSCFString line item in the Detail pane. The Extended Detail pane should show a stack trace that indicates the state of your application at the time that the leak occurred. Notice that the fourth line down in the stack trace is in your code, specifically, in the MemoryLeakerViewController goPressed method. Double-click on the line item in the Extended Detail pane and the source code for the MemoryLeakerViewController goPressed method will replace the leaked blocks in the Detail pane, as you can see in Figure A-5.

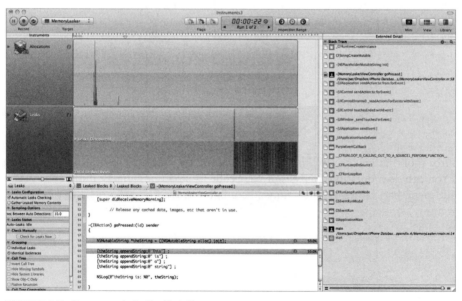

FIGURE A-5: Source code in the Detail pane

If you examine the Detail pane, you will see the code fragment that Instruments is reporting as a leak. In this case, the Leaks instrument has flagged the line where you allocated theString as being responsible for 50.0% of the memory leak and the first call to the appendString as responsible for the other 50.0%. Instruments is telling you that you have allocated theString on the indicated line and then the object leaked. It is up to you to draw your own conclusion from there, but using the Leaks instrument has given you the exact location of the origin of the leaked object. Now, you just need to clean it up.

To fix the memory leak, you need to release the NSMutableString object when you are finished with it. So, change the code in the goPressed method as follows:

```
-(IBAction) goPressed:(id) sender
{

    NSMutableString *theString = [[NSMutableString alloc] init];

    [theString appendString:@"This"] ;
    [theString appendString:@" is"] ;
    [theString appendString:@" a"] ;
    [theString appendString:@" string"] ;

    NSLog(@"theString is: %@", theString);

    [theString release];

}
```

Now, re-run the application with Instruments. No matter how many times you press the Go button in the application, you should not see a memory leak. Congratulations, you just learned how to use the Instruments tool to track down and fix a memory leak, one of the most difficult types of bugs to locate!

THE STATIC ANALYZER

In the most recent versions of the Xcode tool set, Apple has included the Clang static analyzer. Clang is an open source tool that you can use to analyze your code for problems before you even attempt to execute it. You can do a one-time analysis of your code by selecting Build ⇨ Build and Analyze from the Xcode menu bar. However, I recommend configuring your Xcode project to run the analyzer each time that you build. You can do this by selecting Project ⇨ Edit Project Settings from the menu bar. Under Build Options, select Run Static Analyzer.

Now, you will see the static analyzer in action. Go back into the MemoryLeaker project and the goPressed method and remove the line that releases the NSMutableString variable theString. You have now reintroduced the memory leak into your application. Select Build and Analyze from the Build menu. You should see an icon in the left-hand margin at the end of the goPressed method. This indicates that the static analyzer has found an issue. On the right margin of the same line, you will notice that the analyzer has noted that there is a potential leak of an object. Click on this notification and you should see something like Figure A-6.

FIGURE A-6: Using the static analyzer

Sometimes a picture is worth a thousand words and that is definitely the case with the static analyzer. The lines and arrows tell the story. The arrow on line 58 shows that you have created an NSMutableString. The line going from line 58 to the end of the method shows that you have not released the string at the end of the method.

The comments that the static analyzer adds to the right margin explain the problem in detail. The comment associated with line 58 tells you that the `alloc` method returns an Objective-C object with a +1 retain count. This is also called the *owning reference*. On line 67, at the end of the method, the analyzer is reporting that the object allocated on line 58 is no longer referenced after this point, yet it still has a retain count of 1. Therefore, you have leaked the object.

Once again, add the line of code to release `theString` after the `NSLog` statement. Re-run the analyzer by selecting Build ➪ Build and Analyze from the Xcode menu bar. You should see the analyzer messages disappear as you have corrected the memory leak.

The static analyzer can find many other problems, too. For instance, it will flag a dead store in which you write to a variable but never read the value back. To see this, change the `goPressed` method as follows:

```
-(IBAction) goPressed:(id) sender
{

    NSMutableString *theString = [[NSMutableString alloc] init];
```

```
int i=0;
i=5;

[theString appendString:@"This"] ;
[theString appendString:@" is"] ;
[theString appendString:@" a"] ;
[theString appendString:@" string"] ;

NSLog(@"theString is: %@", theString);

[theString release];

}
```

You can see that you are declaring the variable i, setting it to 5, and then never reading it again. If you run the static analyzer now, you will get an error indicating that the value stored in i is never read. Dead stores can often be a sign of a logic problem in your application.

Another logic error is using an uninitialized variable as the left-hand operand in an equality operation. Change the goPressed method as follows:

```
-(IBAction) goPressed:(id) sender
{

    NSMutableString *theString = [[NSMutableString alloc] init];

    int i;

    if (i==5)
    {
        [theString appendString:@"This"] ;
        [theString appendString:@" is"] ;
        [theString appendString:@" a"] ;
        [theString appendString:@" string"] ;
    }
    NSLog(@"theString is: %@", theString);

    [theString release];

}
```

In this case, you have declared the variable i, but you are using it in an equality test without assigning a value to it. Run the analyzer on this code and you will get a flag on the line where you declared the variable i saying that it has been declared without an initial value. Then, on the next line, the analyzer informs you that the left operand of the == operator is a garbage value.

There are many more problems that you can find even before you run your code using the static analyzer. Although it slows down your build slightly, you should definitely enable the analyzer to run during each build. It will save you many hours of debugging in the end.

INDEX

? (question marks), 48, 317